THE DAY FREEDOM DIED

THE DAY FREEDOM DIED

THE COLFAX MASSACRE, THE SUPREME COURT, AND THE BETRAYAL OF RECONSTRUCTION

CHARLES LANE

HENRY HOLT AND COMPANY

NEW YORK

Henry Holt and Company, LLC
Publishers since 1866
175 Fifth Avenue
New York, New York 10010
www.henryholt.com

Henry Holt ® and ® are registered trademarks of
Henry Holt and Company, LLC.

Library of Congress Cataloging-in-Publication Data
Lane, Charles, 1961–
  The day freedom died: the Colfax massacre, the Supreme Court, and the betrayal of
Reconstruction / Charles Lane.—1st ed.
       p.   cm.
  Includes bibliographical references and index.
  ISBN-13: 978-0-8050-8342-2
  ISBN-10: 0-8050-8342-1
  1. Colfax (La.)—Race relations—History—19th century.   2. African Americans—Crimes
against—Louisiana—Colfax—History—19th century.   3. Massacres—Louisiana—Colfax—
History—19th Century.   4. Violence—Louisiana—Colfax—History—19th century.
5. Racism—Louisiana—Colfax—History—19th century.   6. Reconstruction (U.S. history,
1865–1877)—Louisiana.   7. Beckwith, James, 1832–1912.   8. Lawyers—Louisiana—
Biography.   9. Trials (Murder)—United States—Case studies.   10. United States. Supreme
Court—History—19th century.   I. Title.
  F379.C59L36 2008
  976.3'67—dc22   2007037514

Henry Holt books are available for special promotions and
premiums. For details contact: Director, Special Markets.

First Edition 2008

Maps by Laris Karklis
Designed by Kelly S. Too

Printed in the United States of America
1   3   5   7   9   10   8   6   4   2

For My Family:

Cati, David, Nina, and Johanna

In law, what plea so tainted and corrupt
But being season'd with a gracious voice
Obscures the show of evil?

WILLIAM SHAKESPEARE

The law cannot be enforced when everyone is an offender.

CHINESE PROVERB

· CONTENTS ·

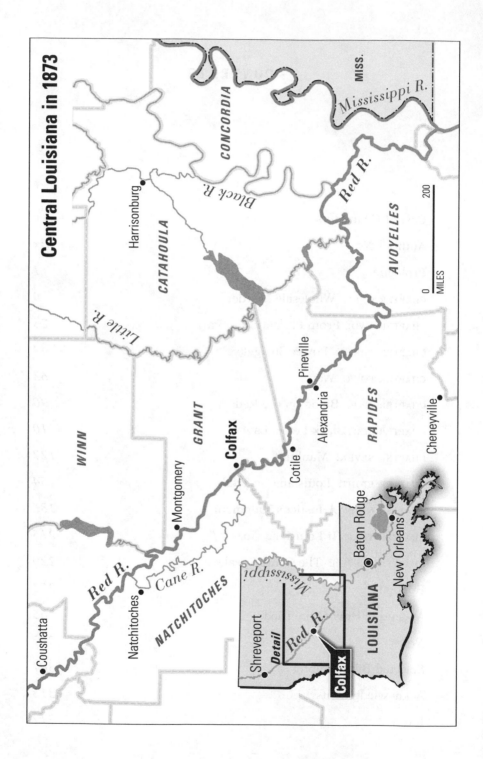

Central Louisiana in 1873

MISS.

CONCORDIA

Mississippi R.

Red R.

Black R.

Harrisonburg

CATAHOULA

AVOYELLES

200

Little R.

Pineville

MILES

0

GRANT

Colfax

Alexandria

Cheneyville

RAPIDES

WINN

Cotile

Montgomery

Baton Rouge

Red R.

Cane R.

New Orleans

Coushatta

Natchitoches

NATCHITOCHES

Mississippi

Shreveport

Detail

Red R.

LOUISIANA

Colfax

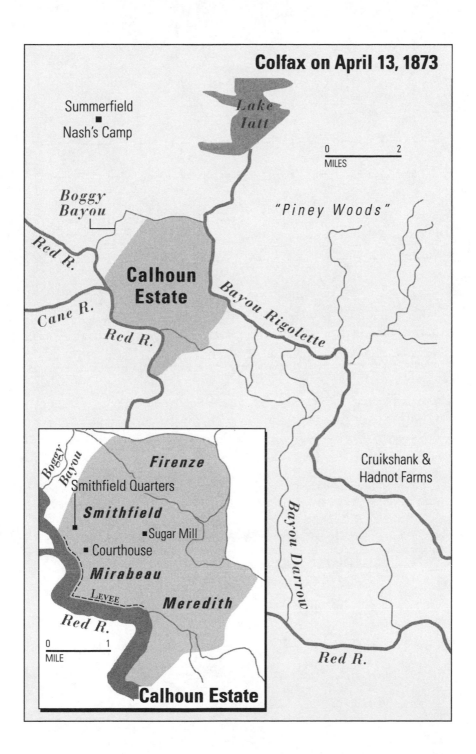

Colfax on April 13, 1873

Summerfield

Nash's Camp

Lake Iatt

0   2
MILES

Boggy Bayou

"Piney Woods"

Red R.

Cane R.

Calhoun Estate

Red R.

Bayou Rigolette

Cruikshank & Hadnot Farms

Bayou Darrow

Boggy Bayou

Firenze

Smithfield Quarters

Smithfield

■ Sugar Mill

■ Courthouse

Mirabeau

Meredith

LEVEE

Red R.

0   1
MILE

Red R.

Calhoun Estate

· CAST OF CHARACTERS ·

COLFAX: THE REPUBLICANS

William Smith Calhoun: Heir to Meredith Calhoun's gigantic Red River cotton and sugar operation; founder of Grant Parish.

Delos White: New York–born former Union officer and Freedmen's Bureau agent; first sheriff of Grant Parish. Murdered September 25, 1871.

William B. Phillips: Alabama-born white politician and first judge of Grant Parish.

William Ward: Black ex–U.S. cavalry trooper; cashiered Louisiana state militia leader; state representative for Grant Parish.

Eli H. Flowers: Black U.S. Army veteran from Pennsylvania; schoolteacher in Grant Parish and close friend of William Ward.

Alexander Tillman: Negro political activist. Exercised command over courthouse defenders on April 13, 1873.

Henry Kearson: Leader of Grant Parish black political faction opposed to William Ward.

Daniel Wesley Shaw: White sheriff of Grant Parish in 1873. Summoned posse to courthouse.

Levi Allen: Negro commander at the Colfax courthouse on April 13, 1873.

Jesse McKinney: Negro farmer in Colfax; his murder triggered a rush of refugees toward the courthouse.

Benjamin Brim: Negro farmer shot and critically wounded on April 13, 1873; key prosecution witness in 1874 trials.

Levi Nelson: Survivor of Colfax Massacre and key prosecution witness.

Pinckney Chambers: Freedman; ordered by whites to set fire to courthouse on April 13, 1873.

Robert C. Register: Delaware-born white politician active in Grant Parish.

COLFAX: WHITE SUPREMACISTS

William J. "Bill" Cruikshank: Planter; former Grant Parish police juror; defendant in 1874 Colfax Massacre trials.

James W. Hadnot: Reputed leader of 1868 election violence against Negroes; would-be white supremacist state representative in 1873; killed April 13, 1873.

Christopher Columbus Nash: Ex–Confederate soldier, violent white supremacist and would-be sheriff of Grant Parish. Commanded white forces on April 13, 1873.

William R. Rutland: Kentucky-born lawyer who moved to Grant Parish and tried to secure local government for Fusionists in early 1873.

Wilson L. Richardson: Ex–Republican lawyer; helped Rutland's effort to install Fusionists in Grant Parish.

Johnnie Hadnot: Nephew of James W. Hadnot; Colfax Massacre defendant.

Jim and Jeff Yawn: Mississippi-born brothers accused of attacks on Negroes in Grant Parish in 1871.

Alfred C. Shelby: Sheriff of Grant Parish in 1871. Ignored pleas to arrest white terrorists and helped murder Republican leader Delos White.

THE POLITICIANS

Andrew Johnson: President of the United States, 1865–69.

Ulysses S. Grant: President of the United States, 1869–77.

Amos T. Akerman: Attorney General of the United States, 1870–72.

George H. Williams: Attorney General of the United States, 1872–75.

J. Madison Wells: Rapides Parish planter; white Unionist; Governor of Louisiana, 1866–67.

Henry Clay Warmoth: Republican governor of Louisiana, 1868–72; formed electoral alliance with white supremacists in 1872 election.

William Pitt Kellogg: Republican governor of Louisiana, 1873–77.

John D. McEnery: Fusionist claimant to governorship of Louisiana, 1872–73.

THE JUDGES

Morrison R. Waite: Chief Justice of the United States, 1874–88; author of *United States v. Cruikshank.*

Joseph P. Bradley: Associate Justice of the Supreme Court, 1870–92.

Samuel F. Miller: Associate Justice of the Supreme Court, 1862–90; author of *The Slaughterhouse Cases.*

William B. Woods: U.S. Circuit Judge for the Fifth Circuit, 1870–80; presided over 1874 Colfax Massacre trials; Associate Justice of the Supreme Court, 1881–87.

Hugh Lennox Bond: Maryland abolitionist; Republican judge; presided over the Ku Klux Klan trials of 1871–72.

THE LAWMEN

James R. Beckwith: U.S. Attorney in New Orleans, 1870–77. Investigated Colfax Massacre and prosecuted the suspects.

Stephen B. Packard: U.S. Marshal for Louisiana during Reconstruction; chief of the state's Republican Party, 1872–77.

John J. Hoffman: Secret Service operative; conducted undercover investigation of Colfax Massacre.

Theodore W. DeKlyne: Deputy U.S. Marshal in Louisiana; led manhunt for Colfax Massacre suspects.

THE LAWYERS

Robert H. Marr: New Orleans–based white supremacist strategist and lead attorney for the defendants in the 1874 Colfax Massacre trials.

E. John Ellis: Defense attorney in the Colfax Massacre trials; popular white supremacist politician.

William R. Whitaker: Northern-born defense lawyer in Colfax Massacre trials.

THE SOLDIERS

Philip H. Sheridan: Lieutenant General of the U.S. Army; cavalry hero of the Civil War; Reconstruction-era commander of U.S. forces in Deep South.

William H. Emory: Major General of the U.S. Army in command of troops in Louisiana 1872–75.

Jacob H. Smith and Arthur W. Allyn: Commanders of army company in Colfax after April 13, 1873.

Terms such as *Negro* and *colored,* as well as *mulatto*, are used throughout most of this book. I understand that these words are obsolete and that readers may find them repellent. No offense is intended; rather, I employed them because I could see no alternative. Practically all Americans—regardless of their race or their views about race—employed them during the period covered by this narrative. They pervaded the speech and writing of the times. I felt it would have been anachronistic and, in a sense, untrue to the story to use the preferable, modern term, *African-American.*

THE DAY FREEDOM DIED

PROLOGUE

At ten o'clock in the morning on March 4, 1873—Inauguration Day—the president and first lady emerged from the White House and headed for their carriage, a grand four-wheeled barouche pulled by four horses. Washington was draped in red-white-and-blue flags, pennants, and bunting; bold triumphal arches, fashioned out of intertwined flags from around the world, spanned the streets. Pennsylvania Avenue, swept clean, stretched like a bright ribbon to the Capitol, where, at noon, Ulysses Simpson Grant would take the oath of office for the second time.

A blue sky lifted spirits, but, as one reporter noted, "its sunny promise of Spring was contradicted by a fierce north wind that seemed the very breath of Winter." The gale roared at forty miles per hour, making four degrees above zero (the official temperature at dawn) feel like thirty below. Grant and his wife, Julia Dent Grant, pressed together on the leather bench of the open barouche as more than two hundred West Point cadets marched ahead of them in cloth dress gray uniforms. One of the shivering young men collapsed and had to be rushed indoors.

Thousands had journeyed to Washington from out of town; the hotels were sold out, even after filling their hallways and lobbies with extra beds. The visitors, not a few of whom employed whiskey against the cold, waited all along the avenue to salute the Civil War hero they had re-elected the previous November. No group cheered Grant more heartily than the Negro men and women who lined his route. These members of the audience could point with pride to the Lincoln Zouaves, a colored military unit from Baltimore, resplendent in their tasseled fezzes, baggy red pants, white leggings, and red-trimmed black jackets. Colored spectators sang along when musicians struck up "Marching Through Georgia," the Civil War ditty celebrating General William Tecumseh Sherman's drive from Atlanta to the sea. "Hurrah! Hurrah! The jubilee has come," they chorused. "We'll all join the Union and fight for Uncle Sam! Sherman's marching through Georgia."

Negro support for Grant was an expression of hope—the fervent belief that only Grant and his Republican Party, the party of Lincoln, could keep America's promise of equal rights for all men. Lincoln had been the first president to invite Negro participation in the inaugural pageant; Grant was the second. But for Grant, freedom and equal rights were matters of principle, not symbolism. More than even the most progressive-minded white Americans of his time, he rejected prejudice. "I don't know why a black skin may not cover a true heart as well as a white one," he said. He knew his soldiers had sacrificed not only to hold the nation together but also to make men free. He did not want those sacrifices to have been in vain.

The North might not have won the Civil War without Grant, and his contributions to the liberation of four million people of color had continued. But at first, Reconstruction was directed by Andrew Johnson, the Tennessee tailor who became vice president in March 1865, then succeeded Lincoln after his assassination a month later. Johnson had ceded control of Southern state legislatures to former Confederates, who in turn enacted Black Codes that all but reenslaved the freedmen. The codes contradicted the Thirteenth Amendment, which abolished slavery when ratified in December 1865, and Johnson faced growing resistance from a "Radical" Republican Congress—culminating in the Reconstruction Act adopted on March 2, 1867, over Johnson's veto. The legislation required Southern states to repeal the Black Codes and recognize the political equality of Negroes—both by granting them the vote and by ratifying the Fourteenth Amendment, which, for the first time, made Negroes citizens with the same rights as white people.

Grant, too, resisted Johnson's version of Reconstruction. As the U.S. Army's top-ranking officer, Grant had encouraged his generals in the South to enforce the Reconstruction Act strictly, especially its provisions on voter registration, which barred unrepentant ex-rebel officials from voting. He occasionally supplied troops to put down violence against the freedmen and authorized the military to make arrests for racial offenses where civilian law enforcement had broken down. In 1868, when Johnson provoked his impeachment and near conviction in the Senate by trying to fire the Radical Republican secretary of war, Edwin Stanton, Grant backed Stanton. After his own successful campaign for president in 1868, Grant lobbied hard for the Fifteenth Amendment, which required states to let all eligible voters cast a ballot, regardless of race. It was controversial not only in the South but also in the North, where many states still banned or restricted voting by colored men.

Negro voting rights were politically necessary for Grant and his party. Before the Civil War, the Republicans were exclusively a Northern party; but afterward, they would have to win elections in the South, state and federal, lest the Southern-based Democratic Party retake control of the federal government and reverse the Union victory. And the Republicans could not do that unless Negroes, their natural—and most numerous— constituency, were free to vote.

Grant's enthusiasm for the Fifteenth Amendment, though, went beyond expediency. When it won ratification, on February 3, 1870, he exulted that the people had completed the eradication of the notorious *Dred Scott* decision, handed down by the Supreme Court in 1857, which had decreed that neither slaves nor free men of color could be citizens of the United States. He called the amendment "a measure of grander importance than any other one act of the kind from the foundation of our free government to the present day."

And President Grant tackled the Ku Klux Klan.

SOUTHERN FREEDMEN LIVED IN POVERTY AFTER THE CIVIL WAR, BUT SO DID most of the region's whites, for whom economic misery was compounded by the shock and humiliation of defeat. Searching for companionship amid the devastation, some ex-Confederates formed clubs where they could drink, reminisce, and complain. One such group, founded in Pulaski, Tennessee, in late 1865, grew into a secret society with "dens" across the southeastern United States. By 1870, most white men in that part of the country either belonged to the organization or sympathized with it. "This is an institution of Chivalry, Humanity, Mercy and Patriotism, embodying in its genius and its principles all that is chivalric in conduct, noble in sentiment, generous in manhood and patriotic in purpose," the Ku Klux Klan declared. Its goals were to "protect the weak, innocent and defenseless," and "to protect and defend the constitution of the United States." Actually, the Klan aimed to terrorize all Negroes and the white Republicans who supported them.

In 1868, the Klan assassinated a Negro Republican congressman in Arkansas and three black Republican members of the South Carolina legislature—and in Camilla, Georgia, four hundred Klansmen, led by the sheriff, fired on a black election parade and hunted the countryside for those who fled, eventually killing or wounding more than twenty people. A Klan-led "nigger chase" in Laurens County, South Carolina, claimed thirteen lives in the fall of 1870. Thanks in part to Klan intimidation of Republican voters—white and black—Democrats had returned to power in Alabama, Virginia, Tennessee, North Carolina, and Georgia in the 1870 elections. This only seemed to encourage more Klan terror elsewhere. In January 1871, five hundred masked men attacked the Union County jail in South Carolina and lynched eight black prisoners. In March 1871, the Klan killed thirty Negroes in Meridian, Mississippi.

For Grant and the Republican Congress, tolerating the Klan was out of the question, but the Northern public was in no mood for a new war against it, either. The only alternative was to treat white terrorism as a crime—to investigate the Klan, identify its murderers, and try them in federal courts. The problem was that fighting crime had always been a state function; federal law enforcement was still an unfamiliar concept in mid-nineteenth-century America. Even many Republicans doubted its constitutionality.

Nevertheless, the Fourteenth Amendment said Congress had the power to enforce civil rights, and the Fifteenth Amendment said Congress had the power to protect qualified Negro voters from discrimination. On May 31, 1870, invoking the new amendments as authority, Congress passed the Enforcement Act, which made racist terrorism a federal offense. To help put it into effect, Grant and Congress created the Department of Justice, with authority over all federal civil and criminal cases. Its first leader, Attorney General Amos T. Akerman, was a Republican who had been born in New Hampshire but settled in Georgia before the war. He loathed the Klan. "These combinations amount to war," he said, "and cannot be effectually crushed under any other theory."

When Klan violence persisted, Grant had sought more authority from Congress, personally lobbying for amendments known as the Ku Klux Klan Act. Enacted on April 20, 1871, the legislation imposed heavy new penalties and branded the Klan an "insurrection" and a "rebellion" against the United States. For the remainder of his first term, the president would be empowered to suspend the writ of habeas corpus anywhere state and local authorities had fallen under the sway of Klan "insurgents." In such cases, the president could use the army to round up Klansmen and present them for trial in federal court.

In October 1871, Grant had declared a "state of lawlessness" in nine Klan-dominated counties of South Carolina, dispatching troops who helped arrest hundreds of Klansmen and drive another two thousand out of state. Rank-and-file Klansmen who confessed and quit the organization were let go, but 220 leaders were indicted, of whom 53 pled guilty and 5 were convicted at trial—before juries which included colored men. By July 1872, there were some 65 Klan leaders from across the South incarcerated in the federal prison at Albany, New York, serving sentences of up to five years. "Peace has come to many places as never before," the black abolitionist Frederick Douglass wrote. "The scourging and slaughter of our people have so far ceased."

YET GRANT'S ATTACK ON THE KLAN TRIGGERED A POLITICAL BACKLASH WHICH ultimately spread to the Republicans' own ranks. The reaction was strongest in the South, of course, but for many Northern whites, the struggle with the Klan simply underscored the fact that Reconstruction, for all its initial promise, had turned into a long, violent slog. As a postwar economic boom accelerated in the North and West, the press in those regions covered the South as if it were some troubled foreign land. Papers vividly described alleged corruption in Republican Southern state governments, which were reportedly controlled by Northern adventurers who owed their offices to the manipulated votes of illiterate Negroes. More and more white Northerners agreed with their Southern brethren that colored men were unfit for citizenship—and that, in some sense, they and not the Klan were to blame for the mess the South had become.

In the 1872 election, Grant's main opponent had been an apostate Republican: Horace Greeley, the publisher of the *New York Tribune*. Greeley's so-called Liberal Republicans, who included such prominent senators as Carl Schurz of Missouri and Charles Sumner of Massachusetts, walked out of their old party under the banner of "reform." Their main issue was corruption: namely, the shameless activities of railroad lobbyists and Grant's distribution of government favors to cronies and party hacks. Greeley's other campaign theme was the injustice of Grant's policy in the South. Once an ardent abolitionist, Greeley had soured on the freedmen. Their failure to prosper disappointed him. "They are an easy, worthless race, taking no thought for the morrow," he said. Backed by the Democrats, the party of the white South, Greeley ran on a platform that denounced Grant's Klan policy as "arbitrary measures" and called for "local self-government" in the ex-Confederacy.

Grant ultimately defeated Greeley easily. Thanks in part to the president's timely crackdown on the Klan, the November 1872 election was the most peaceful of Reconstruction, and a half-million Southern Negroes cast ballots printed with Grant's name. In Alabama, Republicans even took back the governorship and legislature. But the Liberal Republican challenge had heightened the contradictions within the Republican Party. It had forced Grant and his party to leaven their tough approach to the Klan with concessions. The Republican Congress shelved a civil rights bill, and, in May 1872, it enacted an amnesty law that restored full political rights to the vast majority of ex-Confederates who had been barred from office under a special provision of the Fourteenth Amendment. Only a few hundred top Confederate officials remained unpardoned. This act energized Southern white politics with a fresh injection of leadership. Perhaps more important, it betrayed a hint of irresolution in Washington.

GRANT FINISHED THE TRIP DOWN PENNSYLVANIA AVENUE, AND, AT THREE MINutes before noon, entered the Senate chamber. Awaiting him were the senators, fifty foreign diplomats in colorful dress uniforms, the Supreme Court justices in their black robes—and two thousand men and women prominent and lucky enough to have tickets. Impassive in his black suit, Grant sat through some speeches before following the Supreme Court out to the East Portico of the Capitol, where an inauguration platform had been erected and decorated with flags and evergreens. Julia Dent Grant emerged first, escorted by her brother, General Frederick Dent. On the president's arm was his daughter Nellie, seventeen years old. Grant sat briefly in the same mahogany chair George Washington had used at his first inaugural. Little puffs of condensed breath, swirling in the wind, floated among the assembled dignitaries.

Slowly, the chief justice of the United States, Salmon P. Chase, made his way toward the president. Pale and feeble, Chase, sixty-five years old, had coveted the presidency himself for many years, but now he was a dying man, clutching an open Bible supplied by the clerk of the Supreme Court. Grant rose, removed his hat, and placed his left hand on the pages. He raised his right hand and repeated the oath of office after Chase: "I do solemnly swear that I will faithfully execute the Office of President of the United States, and will to the best of my ability preserve, protect and defend the Constitution of the United States—so help me God."

Then, following a tradition that Washington had started, Grant leaned forward to kiss the words upon which his hand had lain. As Grant had requested, the Bible was open to Isaiah, chapter 11, "Christ's Peaceable Kingdom." The passage was a prophecy of wise government and a tribute to his father, Jesse Grant.

> And there shall come forth a rod out of the stem of Jesse
> And a branch shall grow out of his roots
> And the spirit of the Lord shall rest upon him

The spirit of wisdom and understanding
The spirit of counsel and might
The spirit of knowledge and of fear of the Lord
And shall make him of quick understanding in the fear of the Lord
And he shall not judge after the sight of his eyes
Neither reprove after the hearing of his ears
But with righteousness shall he judge the poor
And reprove with equity for the meek of the earth.

A roar went up from the crowd. The howitzer battery of the Naval School and the Army Light Artillery joined in a twenty-one-gun salute. Grant rose from Washington's chair and stood before the shivering multitude. He hated public speaking and dreaded it. Yet by his usual standard, Grant's second inaugural address was positively expansive. He began with a firm defense of his policy in the South: "The effects of the late civil strife have been to free the slave and make him a citizen. Yet he is not possessed of the civil rights which citizenship should carry with it. This is wrong, and should be corrected. To this correction I stand committed, so far as Executive influence can avail." Grant assured whites that "social equality is not a subject to be legislated upon." Yet, in issuing that disclaimer, he supported the freedmen. He would do nothing, he said, to "advance the social status of the colored man except to give him a fair chance to develop what there is good in him, give him access to the schools, and when he travels let him feel assured that his conduct will regulate the treatment and the fare he will receive."

As Grant knew, even this moderate agenda—an allusion to provisions of the civil rights bill which the Republicans had downplayed during the campaign—was anathema to Southern whites, and many Northern ones, too. Still, Grant claimed that the old Confederacy was coming around. Answering those who charged him with despotism for using the military against the Klan, he noted that "the States lately at war with the General Government are now happily rehabilitated, and no Executive control is exercised in any one of them that would not be exercised in any other state in like circumstances." In any case, Grant continued, the telegraph and steamboat were breaking down barriers to mutual understanding: "Our Great Maker is preparing the world, in His own good time, to become one nation, speaking one language, and when armies and navies will be no longer required," he declared.

Finally, he took a parting shot at his political enemies. "I did not ask for place or position" before the war "and was entirely without influence or the acquaintance of persons of influence," Grant said. All he had done since the firing on Fort Sumter was his duty. Yet, "throughout the war, and from my candidacy for the present office in 1868 to the close of the last campaign, I have been the subject of abuse and slander scarcely equaled in political history, which today I feel that I can afford to disregard in view of your verdict, which I gratefully accept as my vindication." Fortunately for Grant, given the rancor of this peroration, the wind shrieked so loudly that only people next to him could hear what he said.

As the president left the podium, he might have noticed the bright fezzes of the Lincoln Zouaves bobbing among the crowd. He surely spotted a group of Union veterans, standing beneath frayed flags emblazoned with the names of historic battles: Fredericksburg, Roanoke, Atlanta. The tattered banners flapped in the wind, emblems of Grant's glory days. That night, technicians illuminated the Capitol dome with the new technology known as electric light. Fireworks boomed and sparkled. The president and the first lady went off to the Inaugural Ball, which was being held near the Capitol in a hangarlike temporary pavilion made out of pine boards draped with muslin. Dignitaries gamely shuffled across the dance floor in their overcoats, as horn and tuba players squeaked out music through the frozen valves of their instruments. Dozens of birdcages dangled from the ceiling; the canaries inside were supposed to accompany the orchestra. But the cold was so intense that the birds shivered, tucked their beaks under their wings, and then began to drop dead.

The truth was that Grant had won a battle in November 1872—not a war. The victory he interpreted as personal vindication, and which gave his black supporters hope, kept Reconstruction alive. But it hardly extinguished all threats to the political rights of freedmen in the South or to the Republican-led national government that protected—and depended upon—the exercise of those rights. Rather, the conflicts with the Klan and the Liberal Republicans, though won by Grant, had exposed, and widened, the political and racial fissures menacing Reconstruction.

As of Inauguration Day 1873, only two of the eleven states that had once made up the Confederacy—black-majority South Carolina and Mississippi—remained under firm Republican control. Georgia, North Carolina, Tennessee, and Virginia had long since been "redeemed," thanks in part to Klan violence. Republicans governed Alabama, but Democrats had conceded the statehouse only under pressure from U.S. troops sent by Grant. In Texas and Florida, Democrats controlled all or part of the state legislatures and were harassing Republican governors. Arkansas's Republican Party had split in two.

And Louisiana was in chaos.

CHAPTER ONE

"WHOLESALE MURDER"

A cloudy evening was fading into darkness as the steamboat *Southwestern* approached the eastern bank of the Red River on April 13, 1873—Easter Sunday. The boat had reached a bend in the river where Captain Thornton Jacobs was certain he would find pine logs for his vessel's four hungry engines. The woodpile was about a mile north of Colfax, Louisiana.

The *Southwestern* carried its own gangplanks: a pair of long wooden walkways which jutted like alligator teeth from the vessel's bow. Jacobs's crew had just lowered them when a young man charged out of the gloom onto the boat. Heavily armed, he was obviously agitated. Jacobs's crew looked him over, preparing for a fight; in these lawless times, robberies and gunplay plagued river traffic. Yet this gunman was not out to empty the safe or hijack the cotton. He wanted Jacobs to take the boat straight to Colfax.

The *Southwestern* was a 180-foot packet steamer, three years old and valued for insurance purposes at the princely sum of ten thousand dollars. Usually stacked high with cotton and crowded with passengers, it ran the New Orleans–Shreveport route along the Mississippi and the Red, twice a week in high-water season. Captain Jacobs had a schedule to maintain, but the wise river hand, careful of both his customers and his cargo, granted the gunman's request. He maneuvered his 411-ton steamer away from shore as gritty clouds, smelling of resin, poured from its smokestacks. In the stern, a paddlewheel churned the water with a steady *slap-slap-slap*.

There had been a gun battle in Colfax, the new passenger claimed; two men lay seriously wounded and in need of the doctor in Alexandria, twenty-two miles downriver. Relaxing a bit, the man elaborated, even joked a little about all the killing. The fight had pitted white men against Negroes, he explained, and the latter had been soundly defeated. "If you ever wanted to see dead niggers," he mused, "this is your chance."

It was rare to see large numbers of people in Colfax; it was not a proper town but a scattering of buildings on flat "bottom land" sandwiched between the Red to the west and pine-clad hills in the east. Just a few white men—lawyers and merchants—actually lived within Colfax. Their little houses had extra rooms, grandly labeled *hotels*, which they rented to the odd traveler. In the country around the town lay cotton plantations, their tumbledown fences and skinny livestock showing the impact of the war and ensuing economic distress. The planters' houses were a bit grander than those in Colfax, but even their paint was peeling. In and around the cotton fields lived hundreds of Negroes, most still occupying the cypress-board cabins they had built before emancipation. They survived on modest wages from white employers—augmented by hogs, chicken, corn, and vegetables they raised, and small game they shot or trapped in the nearby woods.

Though Colfax epitomized Southern languor, it was the capital of Grant Parish, a new jurisdiction carved out of two older ones in 1869. A courthouse had been fashioned from the stable of a cotton plantation; parish court met here, as did the five-man legislature, known in Louisiana's distinctive parlance as the *police jury*. The sessions could be contentious, because there was a lot at stake: taxes, the control of stray animals, the fate of cattle thieves. Congress, the president, and the state government could affect how life in Grant Parish was lived, but generally locals were more concerned with what happened inside that stuffy old brick building, where the judge and the sheriff wielded power over life and death.

IT WAS RAINING WHEN THE *SOUTHWESTERN* PULLED INTO COLFAX AT ABOUT 8:00 p.m. The boat's passengers and crew went ashore over the gangplanks, moving gingerly through the dark and wet. In the damp grass, the men sensed something strange underfoot, as a lantern flickered and glowed, casting ghostly shadows. Gradually, they realized they were stumbling over dead Negroes, most facedown and shot almost to pieces. One of the men from the *Southwestern*, a Texan named R. G. Hill, counted eighteen. But the young gunman who had invited him and the others on this grisly tour boasted that was barely a quarter of the total.

Fewer than one hundred yards to the east, flames danced in the sky. The courthouse was on fire, and a terrible stench attacked the passengers' nostrils, making them ill. At least one of the dead, apparently, had been literally broiled in the courthouse. Hill could make out his charred remains. "Let's go back," someone cried.

But they did not go back. Somehow, they could not, and soon they came upon more dead. Smoke was still winding upward from one corpse's scorched clothing. A passenger commented that he looked alive, and, hearing this, one of the local whites cocked a six-shooter. "I'll finish the black dog," he promised—but Hill and others from the *Southwestern* restrained him. When somebody turned the body over, it was stiff, and there was no life left in it. A tall, muscular Negro, probably a veteran of many years of labor in the fields, lay on the grass, propped up on one elbow as if he had died in the middle of a rare afternoon's rest. The white man with the six-shooter angrily kicked the corpse. "Oh, he's dead as hell," he muttered.

A crowd of armed white men milled around on the bank. Walking their guests back to the boat, they confirmed the story of a battle between the races. Three weeks earlier, they said, armed Negroes, stirred up by white Radical Republicans, seized the courthouse, throwing out the rightful officeholders: the white judge and sheriff. Then the Negroes installed defeated Republican candidates and rampaged around the town, driving out white families and robbing homes. They dug military-style trenches around the courthouse and even built a couple of cannon out of old pipe. Openly proclaiming their intention to kill all the white men, they boasted they would use white women to breed a new race.

In self-defense, the whites continued, men from Grant Parish and surrounding parishes had organized a posse, which had offered the Negroes a chance to lay down their arms. But the blacks refused, leaving the posse no choice: at midday, about eight hours ago, the whites counterattacked. Fighting was fierce; one white man died. The blacks retreated into the courthouse. The only option was to smoke them out, and a Negro was bribed to set fire to the building's wooden roof. At that point, the Negroes waved a white flag. Whites approached, but the blacks fired again, seriously wounding the two men now in need of a doctor, one of whom was James W. Hadnot, the Grant Parish state representative. After that treachery, the whites resumed firing and kept shooting at the Negroes even as they ran from the flames. They did not stop until they had killed or captured every black man they could find.

AS HADNOT AND SIDNEY HARRIS, THE OTHER WOUNDED MAN, WERE TAKEN aboard the *Southwestern*, R. G. Hill glanced at the Negro prisoners, huddled together in a wooden storehouse. About eight wounded captives were lying on the porch, trying to stay dry as white guards, heavily armed, eyed every twitch they made. Hill asked one guard if he might speak with the Negroes. "No," came the brusque response.

Hill did not press. He understood that ex-slaves and their white Republican instigators were forcing decent whites to endure the unendurable all over the South. In Hill's own hometown of Marshall, Texas, not far from the Louisiana border, a Negro policeman had shot and killed a white schoolteacher. Last Hill heard, it appeared a judge would grant the black killer bail. Meanwhile, whites had to pay taxes for a Negro school.

The boat's engine groaned, then roared, a blast of pine smoke sweetening the foul atmosphere as the steamer returned to the river. On board, Hill wrote down everything he had observed. It was a "very sad occurrence," he noted; the bare facts were terrible. "Excited" townspeople had told him there might be one hundred Negroes dead, but he felt that the true toll "will probably amount to between twenty-five and thirty." More important were the lessons of it all: In Hill's view, it might "be productive of good results . . . for it will call the attention of the authorities in Washington to the fact that matters are becoming serious here, as well as in other places throughout the South." Once people up North heard about this outbreak of Negro violence, they would have to rethink their opinions of the situation in the South. "Hundreds of instances to illustrate the difficulties the Southern people are laboring under could be cited," Hill wrote, "and no observing Northern man can come here and not sympathize with them."

The *Southwestern* dropped off the wounded and continued to New Orleans, pulling in at about one o'clock in the afternoon of Tuesday, April 15. Hill took his news straight to the *New Orleans Times*, whose editors splashed it onto the next morning's front page, under a bold, black headline: WAR AT LAST!!

JAMES BECKWITH DID NOT KNOW QUITE WHAT TO MAKE OF THE ARTICLE. AS U.S. attorney for Louisiana, he (along with the U.S. marshal) was one of the state's top two federal law enforcement officials. Under the Enforcement Act, it was his job to prosecute political and racial violence. The events in Colfax, as recounted by Hill, riveted his attention. "You know workmen by the chips they leave," Beckwith liked to say. And that made him concerned; when dead Negroes lay thick on the ground in the post–Civil War South, it was usually the work of white terrorists.

According to Hill, though, the event had begun as a pitched battle between evenly matched armed groups. At least one white man was dead, and two others were badly hurt. The blacks might have brought on the worst killing by violating a flag of truce. Beckwith had never been to Colfax. He didn't know much about it except that it was once part of a huge plantation run by a wealthy former Republican state legislator. Most Negroes who lived there were the man's former slaves or their descendants. Beckwith had heard whites say that the Negroes in Colfax were especially insolent and mean. Just a few days earlier, a white lawyer from Colfax had visited, claiming that the Colfax Negroes had staged a riot and were threatening white families in Grant Parish. He demanded that the U.S. attorney issue warrants for their arrest. Beckwith asked the man to swear out a criminal complaint, but the visitor left and did not come back. After finding out what he could, Beckwith had concluded that it might be wise for the U.S. Army to help keep peace in Colfax. He was surprised to learn upon reading the *Times* that no troops had been sent.

LOUISIANA HAD BEEN SEETHING FOR MONTHS. THE DISCONTENT AND RUMBLING originated in a split in the state Republican Party similar to the division in the national party. Governor Henry Clay Warmoth, elected as a Republican in 1868, defected to the Liberal Republicans in 1872 and, like the national Liberal Republicans, joined forces with the Democrats before the November 1872 election. The resulting "Fusionist" coalition in Louisiana nominated John McEnery, an ex-Confederate battalion commander, to succeed Warmoth. Opposing him on the Republican ticket was Vermont-born William Pitt Kellogg, one of Louisiana's U.S. senators.

Voting on November 4, 1872, was peaceful enough, but the vote count lit the spark for all that followed. A Fusionist-dominated state "returning board," which had absolute power to include or exclude votes based on whether it thought they had been validly cast, declared McEnery and his slate elected. But the board split, with a pro-Kellogg faction declaring the Republican governor. On January 13, 1873, each side staged a separate inauguration ceremony. The state could not pick a U.S. senator, since that required a vote by the legislature—and in Louisiana, two bodies, one dominated by Fusionists, the other by Republicans, claimed to be the legislature.

Kellogg had taken his case to a Republican federal judge in New Orleans, who ordered both Kellogg and the Republican-majority legislature to be seated. This gave the Republicans an advantage, creating a legal basis for federal military intervention on their behalf. President Grant authorized U.S. Army troops based near New Orleans to enforce the court order and protect Kellogg's government. Grant was "extremely anxious to avoid any appearance of any undue interference in state affairs," as he put it in a February 25, 1873, message to Congress. But given the federal court's presumably valid order, and the lack of any alternative plan from Congress, Grant explained, he had no choice.

Congress adjourned March 4 without settling the crisis—whereupon the heavily armed Fusionists attempted to shoot their way into power. On March 5, about two hundred armed McEneryites marched on the Cabildo, an old Spanish colonial building on Jackson Square then serving as the state arsenal. But state police and militia loyal to Kellogg had been tipped off and used artillery to pin down the insurgents. U.S. Army troops then appeared under a white flag of truce and ordered the Fusionists to disperse. The next day Kellogg's militia arrested dozens of McEneryites, including the leaders of the Fusionist "legislature."

The victory gave Kellogg control over New Orleans, but the interior of the state remained tense. Both would-be governors had attempted to fill parish offices by issuing purported commissions to their respective parties' candidates for judge, sheriff, police jury, and other posts. Even after the pro-McEnery coup failed, Fusionist and Republican claimants to these offices, brandishing their documents, struggled for power in towns and villages across rural Louisiana. One of those towns was Colfax.

THE TELEGRAPH LINES DID NOT REACH COLFAX, SO BECKWITH AND OTHER OFFI-cials in New Orleans followed the events in Grant Parish through reports from arriving steamboat travelers. These witnesses gave their accounts either in person or to the local newspapers: the pro-Kellogg *New Orleans Republican* and the pro-Fusionist *Times, Bee,* and *Daily Picayune.* Information was correspondingly sketchy and biased; by the second week of April, the two sides were publishing threats against each other in the papers. But from what could be determined, the parish had been in an uproar since late March, when Republican office seekers occupied the courthouse, supplanting Fusionists who had previously purported to run the parish.

Finally, on April 12, a day before the massacre, Kellogg had dispatched two state militia colonels, Theodore W. DeKlyne and William Wright, who doubled as deputy U.S. marshals, to Colfax—a two-day journey from New Orleans. The two officers carried arrest warrants for fifty white men, presumed instigators of the trouble, as well as a set of commission papers for a new, compromise slate of parish officers. Kellogg apparently hoped that these threats and inducements would pacify the parish. Beckwith decided to wait for the Kellogg emissaries to come back before ringing the alarm in Washington. "Reports from Colfax are conflicting and uncertain," he telegraphed the Department of Justice on April 16. "A Deputy Marshal will arrive from there tonight with an authentic report. It is believed to have been a massacre of from twenty to thirty Negroes. I will report in detail as soon as I have reliable information."

THIS WAS THE SENSIBLE RESPONSE OF A GOOD YANKEE LAWYER, WHICH—despite the fact that he had spent most of his career in New Orleans—is what James Roswell Beckwith was. The oldest son of a prosperous farm couple, he was born in Cazenovia, New York, twenty miles south of Syracuse, on December 23, 1832. Cazenovia was part of upstate New York's "burned-over district," named for its successive evangelization by Mormons, Seventh Day Adventists, and spiritualists—and for the fiery feminism and abolitionism which flourished there. Madison County, which included Cazenovia, contained several stops on the Underground Railroad. Frederick Douglass spoke at Cazenovia's Free Church, as did antislavery politician Gerrit Smith and Quaker abolitionist Lucretia Mott. In late August 1850, as Congress debated the Fugitive Slave Law, which made it a federal offense to harbor escaped slaves, Douglass, Smith, and other abolitionist leaders assembled in a Cazenovia orchard. This "Cazenovia Convention" drew more than two thousand people—roughly half of Cazenovia's population. It is hard to imagine that James Beckwith, then seventeen years old, did not join the crowd, if only out of curiosity.

A few weeks after the Cazenovia Convention, Beckwith enrolled at the Methodist-run Oneida Conference Seminary, whose teachers drilled their students in antislavery doctrine. But after a year there, he asked his parents for permission to go to New York City and read law. He aspired to be a "real, thorough" lawyer—"the noblest work of science," as he put it. In 1854, he joined the New York bar. After finishing his legal training, Beckwith headed west, first to Michigan, where he served as a district attorney. Somewhere along the way, Beckwith found a kindred spirit in a young lady named Sarah Catherine Watrous, and, in 1860, they married. Catherine, as she liked to be called, came from Ashtabula County, Ohio, which was also antislavery territory. Of the twenty-one men who joined John Brown's ill-fated attempt to start a slave revolt by seizing the federal arsenal at Harpers Ferry, Virginia, in 1859, thirteen came from Ashtabula County. Catherine was a feminist novelist; her nom de plume, "Mrs. J. R. Beckwith," mocked the prevailing subordination of wives to husbands.

The Beckwiths moved to New Orleans, 1,400 miles from Cazenovia; it was exotic, and not altogether pleasantly so. In 1860, the tropical port was the sixth-largest city in America; but its 169,000 residents included a disproportionate number of gamblers, prostitutes, and petty criminals. Outside of magnificent, cobblestoned Canal Street, there were three paved roads; everywhere else, horse-drawn streetcars meandered down narrow, muddy tracks. The city's highest point was just fifteen feet above sea level, and some parts were actually below it. Human and animal waste accumulated in the gutters. People took their trash to the Mississippi and tossed it in, or left it lying on the crumbling levees. Dead mules, dogs, and cats were disposed of similarly. Owing to high humidity and legendarily sweltering heat, the refuse sent up a mélange of odors.

Yellow fever swept New Orleans thirty-six times between 1796 and 1869, including the 1853 epidemic which killed more than ten thousand people. Because of the foul water, there were also eleven cholera epidemics between 1832 and 1869. A public health expert described the city's record as "one long, disgusting story of stagnant drainage, foul sewerage, environing swamps, ill and unpaved streets, no sanitary regulations and filth, endless filth everywhere."

The Beckwiths braved the odors and the heat and the sickness. But they must have hated the slave markets, where human beings were herded into "showrooms" or displayed from balconies. When buyers came to inspect, the slaves would be lined up by height, in clean clothes and ordered to smile, lest they receive a whipping. If a buyer was interested, the merchandise would be taken behind closed doors and stripped. White men chose "fancy girls"—attractive, light-skinned women—to be auctioned off in front of French Quarter hotels.

For all that, the Crescent City was a logical destination for a lawyer. New Orleans was the point from which the Deep South's cotton and sugar flowed into the world market; textiles, farm implements, machinery, and immigrants flowed in. Commerce created work for bankers, insurance underwriters, cotton brokers—and lawyers. By 1855, there were seventy-five law firms in town. New Orleans was cosmopolitan; the soft cadences of French could be heard in its parlors, along with quick phrases of Spanish and guttural German—the latter spoken by central European immigrants, including Jews numerous enough to support several synagogues. New Orleans was home to roughly twenty thousand free people of color, the largest such community in the United States. These mixed-race New Orleanians were craftsmen, professionals, and businessmen who could sometimes be found shopping in the slave markets themselves. The native white Creole elite were as haughty as any Bostonians.

During 1860, the Beckwiths settled in the "American Sector," across Canal Street from the French Quarter. But on January 26, 1861, Louisiana seceded from the Union. The U.S. Navy blockaded ships from the South, and all northbound rail and river routes were cut. Still, of all

Southern towns for two young Northern Republicans to be stranded in, New Orleans was the least hopeless. Lincoln was determined to recapture the strategic port, and the rest of Louisiana, quickly.

UNION SYMPATHIZERS MOSTLY LAY LOW UNTIL MAY 1, 1862, WHEN FEDERAL LAND and naval forces took New Orleans and the "Florida Parishes" of southeastern Louisiana. The rebel state government fled north to Shreveport, and in 1864, after a period of military rule, the federals in New Orleans set up a "free state." The new regime gave the vote only to a limited number of colored men—those whom the legislature might later enfranchise by virtue of their Union military service, payment of taxes, or "intellectual fitness." This was essentially the policy Lincoln urged in his last public speech on April 11, 1865.

That was too much for John Wilkes Booth, who heard Lincoln and resolved to kill him. And it was too much for many white supremacists in Louisiana. Once the war was over, they reorganized the Democratic Party and announced in their 1865 platform, "We hold this to be a Government of white people, made and to be perpetuated for the exclusive benefit of the white race, and . . . that people of African descent cannot be considered as citizens of the United States, and that there can, in no event, nor under any circumstances, be any equality between white and other races."

In March 1865, J. Madison Wells, a Red River Valley planter with conservative racial attitudes who opposed Negro suffrage, became governor. Though a Unionist, he courted ex-Confederates and did not prevent white-dominated local governments from harshly restricting civil rights: In Opelousas, 150 miles west of New Orleans, Negroes could not live in the town or carry firearms. In December 1865, a newly elected Louisiana state legislature, dominated by ex-Confederates, decreed that Negro laborers must make contracts with plantation owners in the first ten days of January, after which they could not leave their places of work without a pass. Negroes who refused to work could be arrested and sent to labor on public works without pay. As Carl Schurz observed, such legislation was "a striking embodiment of the idea that, although the former owner has lost his individual right of property in the former slave, 'the blacks at large belong to the whites at large.'"

This was unacceptable even for Wells. He changed course, breaking with the "rebel" legislature and urging a "reconvocation" of the 1864 convention which had drafted the state's constitution. The meeting,

scheduled for July 30, 1866, in New Orleans, would call for Negro suffrage and disenfranchisement of ex-Confederates—assuming it was allowed to take place peacefully.

It was not. On the morning of July 30, city policemen, the vast majority of whom were ex-Confederate soldiers, mobbed the gun shops of
New Orleans, buying up pistols. Along with like-minded white civilians,
they gathered around the convention site: the Mechanics' Institute on
Baronne Street. As a parade of Negro Republicans led by colored Union
army veterans approached the fortresslike building, black marchers
and white onlookers exchanged a few pistol shots. When the parade
reached the Mechanics' Institute at about 12:30, white civilians pelted
the Negro marchers with bricks, the marchers fought back with shoves
and gunfire—and police commanders sounded the local fire bell, signal-
ing the cops to attack the Negroes.

As Negroes fled into the building, police fired wildly after them and
eventually battered down the doors. Negro men swinging chairs and
sticks tried to drive the police and white vigilantes back but were quickly
overcome. The police grabbed Anthony P. Dostie, a white Republican
dentist who had given an incendiary speech at a mostly Negro rally the
previous Friday, and shot him five times before running him through
with a sword. The killing spilled over into the streets, where Negroes
were chased and beaten to death or randomly dragged from streetcars
and shot. When it was over, thirty-eight people were dead, all but four of
them people of color; and 184 lay wounded.

James Beckwith witnessed the New Orleans Massacre, as it was
called. The awful spectacle, which Andrew Johnson blamed on Republican agitation, helped convince Northern voters that the president could
not be trusted to run Reconstruction. They elected an overwhelmingly
Republican Congress in November 1866, which then overturned Johnson's policies. By April 1868, thanks to new laws passed by Congress,
Louisiana had a Republican-drafted constitution and a newly elected Republican state government.

But soon Beckwith and the rest of the state saw even more devastating bloodshed in the countryside. In the second half of 1868, white terrorists tried to prevent the Republicans from winning the November
presidential election. Over three days in September, they killed some two
hundred freedmen in St. Landry Parish. Later that month, in Bossier
Parish, just across the Red River from Shreveport, a drunken trader
from Arkansas shot an elderly black Republican. When men of color organized a posse to capture the gunman, the "Negro revolt" electrified
whites, who killed and wounded several colored men. The Negroes fired

back and killed two whites. Hundreds of armed whites poured into Bossier Parish, scouring the countryside for armed Negroes—which soon turned into an all-out "nigger hunt," complete with bloodhounds. The killing lasted through October and the death toll reached 168.

Later, a congressional investigation counted 1,081 political murders in Louisiana between April and November of 1868. The vast majority of the victims were Negroes. Some 135 people were shot and wounded; 507 were whipped, clubbed, threatened, or otherwise "outraged." The terror was so intense that the Republican Party stopped campaigning in the final week of the race and all but conceded the presidential vote to the Democrats.

BY 1868, J. R. BECKWITH, AS HE WAS KNOWN PROFESSIONALLY, WAS AN ACCOM-plished member of the bar with a deep voice and distinctive looks: high forehead, strong cleft chin, and bristling walrus mustache. He was still only in his midthirties and might easily have left Louisiana; New Orleans was bankrupt, its steamboat-based economy sagging under the competi-tive pressure of rail transportation. But he loved the city and the chal-lenges of his work, which usually kept him up late. Though he disdained politics and the "tricksters" who used it "for themselves and their emolu-ments," something from Cazenovia still motivated him. His wife, Cather-ine, recognized it. In her novel, *The Winthrops*, she modeled the fictional lawyer Fred Houghton on her husband, depicting him as an "ardent champion for all the varieties of the oppressed, and [an] earnest rectifier of injustice."

That spirit appears to have prompted him to join Republican-led ef-forts to govern his adopted city and state. In 1870, Beckwith served as city attorney under Mayor Benjamin Franklin Flanders, a veteran Re-publican originally from New Hampshire. In late 1870, the U.S. attorney for Louisiana was found dead in his office, blood seeping from a gash in his throat. After some suspicions, the death was ruled a suicide. New Or-leans Republican leaders urged President Grant to replace him with Beckwith. Probably the most important endorsement came from James F. Casey, customs collector for the port of New Orleans—and the hus-band of the first lady's sister. He telegraphed Grant that Beckwith was "a good lawyer, perfectly honest, conversant with the business of the office, [a] good Republican and worthy of the appointment." The president nominated Beckwith in December 1870, and by January 1871, Beckwith was at work on the second floor of the U.S. Custom House on the "French" side of Canal Street. He had made sure to remove the carpet soaked with his predecessor's blood.

· · ·

AT 9:30 A.M. ON MONDAY, APRIL 14, 1873, THE STEAMBOAT CARRYING KELLOGG'S
two emissaries reached Pineville, which lay on the eastern side of the
Red River, directly opposite Alexandria. Theodore W. DeKlyne and
William Wright crossed over to Alexandria and rode north to Colfax, but
the many dangerous-looking armed white men unnerved them and they
stopped at Cotile, about fifteen miles south of Colfax, rather than risk arriving at the battleground after dark. The next morning, the two officers
and their party resumed their ride over the reddish brown earth. De-
Klyne had served briefly as a federal official helping Negroes in the Red
River Valley after the war; he knew the area and its people. He could tell
that something was not right: The Negroes' corn and sugarcane fields
along the river seemed neglected. Many cabins looked abandoned.

Still, after riding more than fourteen miles, the two colonels had seen
nothing to confirm R. G. Hill's report, or the even bloodier rumors that
they had heard since their arrival. Suddenly, about a third of a mile from
the courthouse, DeKlyne and Wright spotted Negroes pulling something
along the ground with a rope. Soon they could see that it was a board with
a colored man sprawled on top, dirty and smeared with blood. Unconscious, he was bleeding from several gunshot wounds, but breathing. Two
other black men lying nearby were not, however. After another two hundred yards, the officials came upon three more Negro bodies, shot in the
head. From that point on, the grass was littered with dead.

DeKlyne and Wright were ex-Union officers, and they had seen combat and its aftermath. But many of these dead men had been shot in the
backs of their heads or necks. Six men had been killed as they cowered
under a porch. Another corpse was in a kneeling position, hands still
clasped together, as if he had begged for his life. One lay dead with his
throat slashed. Another, stripped to the waist, was charred. One man's
head had been so badly beaten that no facial features were recognizable;
next to him lay the broken stock of a double-barreled shotgun. All that
remained of the courthouse were its singed brick walls, reeking of
smoke. In the ruins, the officials found a human skeleton.

The most awful to gaze upon was Alexander Tillman, a politically active freedman whom DeKlyne knew from Republican Party meetings.
His clothes were ripped off, and his body was punctured with deep stabs.
His throat had a gash in it big enough to put a man's fist through, and his
face was battered. Blood saturated the ground around him.

DeKlyne and Wright counted sixty bodies in all. Not one was white.
Searching for weapons, all they turned up were nine burned-up rifles

piled in the courthouse ash. Apparently, none of the freedmen had died armed. Amid the carnage, the Negro women of Colfax scoured the ground, searching for familiar swatches of clothing, perhaps, or pairs of shoes—anything that might help identify a loved one

Terrified, gasping out their story between sobs, they and several colored men told the two officials what had happened. In broad outline, the Negroes' version matched the whites' tale. Negro men, defending what they considered the Republican Party's rightful victory for local offices in the 1872 election, had gathered in the courthouse. When they saw groups of armed whites patrolling the area, they dug a semicircular trench around the courthouse. A large group of white men, mounted and armed with rifles, revolvers, and a small cannon, had arrived in Colfax Easter Sunday, demanding that the colored men surrender, stack their arms, and leave. When the Negroes refused, the whites attacked, setting the courthouse ablaze and gunning the colored men down like dogs.

In crucial particulars, however, the colored people's version of the story was new. There had been no riot and pillage by the Negroes, they said, but rather a fearful rush of families into Colfax when they heard that armed whites were approaching. That flow turned into a flood about a week before the battle, when word got out that whites had killed a Negro farmer, Jesse McKinney, in cold blood. The whites had not bribed a colored man to torch the courthouse; they had kidnapped one and forced him to do it. The colored witnesses denied that anyone had fired under a flag of truce. And at night, after the *Southwestern* had left, the whites had marched their Negro prisoners away in pairs—and then shot each of them in the head.

DeKlyne and Wright quickly realized there was no use for Kellogg's papers. They were too late to prevent a slaughter and too few to investigate or punish it. All they could do was report back to New Orleans, which they reached on April 17. Their descriptions were crisp and understated, but their disgust filtered through. "We are informed," they wrote, "that since the fight, parties of armed men have been scouring the countryside, taking the mules and other property of the colored people."

BECKWITH'S INITIAL SKEPTICISM TURNED TO OUTRAGE AS HE READ THE OFFICERS' words. *You know workmen by the chips they leave.* If the death toll was correct, Colfax had been worse than the New Orleans Massacre. In fact, in the entire bloody epoch of Reconstruction, there might never have been a bloodier one-day incident of white terror than this frenzied killing on Easter Sunday.

Beckwith sent an urgent telegram to Attorney General George H. Williams. "The details are horrible," Beckwith wrote.

THE DEMOCRATS (WHITE) OF GRANT PARISH ATTEMPTED TO OUST THE INCUMBENT PARISH OFFICERS BY FORCE AND FAILED, THE SHERIFF PROTECTING THE OFFICERS WITH A COLORED POSSE. SEVERAL DAYS AFTERWARD RECRUITS FROM OTHER PARISHES, TO THE NUMBER OF 300, CAME TO THE ASSISTANCE OF THE ASSAILANTS, WHEN THEY DEMANDED THE SURRENDER OF THE COLORED PEOPLE. THIS WAS REFUSED. AN ATTACK WAS MADE AND THE NEGROES WERE DRIVEN INTO THE COURTHOUSE. THE COURT-HOUSE WAS FIRED AND THE NEGROES SLAUGHTERED AS THEY LEFT THE BURNING BUILDING, AFTER RESISTANCE CEASED. SIXTY-FIVE NEGROES TERRIBLY MUTILATED WERE FOUND DEAD NEAR THE RUINS OF THE COURTHOUSE. THIRTY, KNOWN TO HAVE BEEN TAKEN PRISONERS, ARE SAID TO HAVE BEEN SHOT AFTER THE SURRENDER, AND THROWN IN THE RIVER. TWO OF THE ASSAILANTS WERE WOUNDED. THE SLAUGHTER IS GREATER THAN IN THE RIOT OF 1866 IN THIS CITY. WILL SEND REPORT BY MAIL.

THE BLOODBATH IN COLFAX MADE HEADLINES FROM BOSTON TO CHICAGO. R. G. Hill thought that the incident would arouse Northern sympathy for the South. But this was not the case. "Jealousy of race and hatred of their former servants can alone explain the outbreak," the *Cincinnati Gazette* declared. "The passions that inspired that hellish agency of murder and persecution, the Ku Klux, are still alive," the *Philadelphia Press* warned. The *New York Times* likened the Louisiana incident to Fort Pillow, the notorious 1864 massacre in which General Nathan Bedford Forrest's Confederate cavalry slaughtered hundreds of U.S. colored troops as they tried to flee or surrender. The *Times* demanded that President Grant act decisively to quell "that worst of human calamities, a war of races."

Attorney General Williams had previously considered the rumors of a massacre in Louisiana exaggerated. But after the report he scrambled to prove that this apparent resurgence of Klan-style terrorism would be stopped. He answered Beckwith swiftly, releasing his cable to the press: "You are instructed to make a thorough investigation of the affair in Grant Parish," Williams wrote, "and if you find that the laws of the United States have been violated, you will spare no pains or expense to cause the guilty parties to be arrested and punished." Brandishing the federal government's ultimate weapon, Williams also promised Beckwith U.S. Army troops if needed to help enforce the law. Untangling the truth about Col-fax, and bringing the perpetrators to justice, was now the U.S. government's official duty—and James Beckwith's personal mission.

CHAPTER TWO

FROM PLANTATION TO PARISH

Oscar Watson couldn't stop talking about the great gun battle in Colfax. A clerk in his father's Grant Parish country store, the twenty-two-year-old had been too young for the Civil War. April 13, 1873, was his day of glory; he had stood side by side with rebel veterans, who called him a hero. In late May 1873, when Watson recounted the story to a visitor, he proudly displayed his two six-shooters—explaining that the first gun was the one he had used to kill Negroes at Colfax, and the second was a prize his comrades had given him for his bravery.

The visitor, John J. Hoffman, listened attentively. He told Oscar Watson and others he met in Grant Parish that he was from Cincinnati, by way of New Orleans. What he didn't say was that he worked for the U.S. government. He was an undercover agent of the Treasury Department's Secret Service Division. James R. Beckwith had sent him to infiltrate the white community and identify the Colfax killers. As far as Hoffman was concerned, Oscar Watson could brag all day if he wanted.

Hoffman was ranging far from the mission assigned to the Secret Service when it was established in July 1865: investigating counterfeiters. But the division was so good at its original job that the government expanded its responsibilities.* Among these tasks was the infiltration of the Ku Klux Klan during the Grant administration's crackdown in 1871. Posing as traveling salesmen and itinerant laborers, Secret Service men penetrated the white terrorist movement from top to bottom. Their information led to hundreds of arrests and was one of the keys to Grant's success against the Klan in South Carolina.

As soon as he got the Colfax case, Beckwith decided to put the Secret Service's Klan-fighting experience to work for him. He cabled a request for a detective to Attorney General Williams in Washington, who relayed

---

*The Secret Service did not become a presidential bodyguard until after the assassination of President William McKinley in 1901.

it to Secret Service headquarters in New York. The Secret Service dispatched Hoffman—probably because he had visited the Red River Valley previously and had acquaintances there who did not know his real job.

After weeks of listening to the whites of Rapides and Grant parishes express their true thoughts and feelings about what had happened on Easter Sunday, the Secret Service man sent his report to Beckwith. It was a chilling document. Oscar Watson was hardly the only one who boasted of his deeds, Hoffman reported; whites throughout the region hated the federal government, and they were completely unapologetic about the massacre. Most, in fact, "uphold the doings of the mob," he noted.

The 1872 election had triggered the massacre, Hoffman explained, but its true origins went deeper. There was no way to comprehend the events of April 13, 1873, unless one first understood that both Colfax and the Negroes who lived there had formerly been the property of a single extraordinary white family. The Calhouns once used their economic and political power to uphold slavery. But after the Civil War, Hoffman wrote, a new Calhoun took over the estate; he "became a Republican . . . and was favorable to the Negroes."

And that was when the trouble started.

ON NOVEMBER 3, 1868, THE UNITED STATES HELD A PRESIDENTIAL ELECTION UNlike any before it. For the first time colored men in the American South could participate in choosing the nation's chief executive. In Louisiana, with its large population of free men of color, many Negroes and mulattoes reached this moment equipped with the literacy and property generally considered necessary for "intelligent" use of the franchise. But the vast majority of them were illiterate rural laborers. For them, to pick a president of the United States must have been both exhilarating and terrifying—not least because of the intimidation they faced.

As Election Day dawned in the Red River Valley, one community of freedmen gathered under the cypress trees to form a solid phalanx. Shoulder to shoulder, they strode over the same flat red soil they once had plowed for white masters, carrying a banner proclaiming support for the Republicans—and clutching paper tickets printed with the names of the party's candidates: Ulysses S. Grant for president, Schuyler Colfax for vice president, and Joseph P. Newsham, a twenty-nine-year-old lawyer and former Union army officer originally from Illinois, for Congress. They were on the way to enter the polls, announce themselves as registered voters, and put their tickets in the ballot box.

As astonishing as the Negro parade was the presence of a white man at its head: William Smith Calhoun, heir to fourteen thousand acres in the Red River Valley, by far the most extensive estate in the region and probably one of the most gigantic in the entire South. If you climbed the pine-covered ridges just east of the Red River's junction with the Cane River and looked back west toward the valley, most of the land you would see—along with just about every barn and outhouse—belonged to the Calhouns.

For all his wealth and power, though, Willie Calhoun had never quite fit in with his neighbors. His childhood was privileged, but strange and unhappy. Born in Paris on April 19, 1835, he returned to the United States with his parents and soon suffered a broken back in a carriage accident. As young Master Willie recuperated, he was cared for by a male Negro slave who never left his side. In 1842, his parents took him back to France, to the Orthopedic Institute in Passy, hoping that the doctors there could cure the weakness in his legs and the hump in his back. His treatment, which lasted several years, included walking around the hospital grounds wearing a metal apparatus that forcibly straightened his spine. Much of the time, though, he simply sat and played cards, as his mother and father continued their travels. The treatments left his back as misshapen and his legs as lame as they had been before. In 1848, Willie and his family returned to the United States.

As a young man in the 1850s, Willie Calhoun sympathized with the Union and condemned rebellion. In the 1860 election, he supported the anti-secession Northern Democrat Stephen A. Douglas. Calhoun invested two thousand dollars of his own money to buy half ownership of a newspaper and turn it into a pro-Douglas sheet. He had emerged from his painful upbringing possessed of a certain hauteur and a contrarian, sarcastic manner that his Louisiana neighbors generally found unpleasant. They mocked him during the war—for his Union sympathies and his disabilities. People called him a hunchback, though he spoke of "curvature of the spine." Confederate authorities made Calhoun travel to Shreveport to prove that he was physically unfit to serve in the rebel army, an indignity he never forgot or forgave.

Whether because of his exposure to the ideas of continental Europe, or because of his contempt for his neighbors, Willie Calhoun grew defiant of Southern society's conventions, including the most sacred one: absolute white supremacy. After the war, Calhoun joined the Republican Party—the party of Negro suffrage—a choice which, in the eyes of most whites, made him a contemptible "scalawag." More scandalous, Calhoun lived with Olivia Williams, a mulatto teenager who was not his wife; people whispered that she was a "fancy girl" from New Orleans. By Election Day 1868, Olivia had given birth to a boy, Eugene. The acerbic planter may have enjoyed the private joke of a mixed-race child whose name came from the Greek for "well-born." But no one publicly acknowledged the boy's paternity; when census takers arrived, Eugene was listed under his mother's last name.

WHEN CALHOUN AND THE NEGRO VOTERS ARRIVED AT THE POLLS ON THE MORN- ing of November 3, 1868, about a dozen white men were waiting for them, armed with clubs and revolvers. Leading the whites was the Democratic candidate for Congress, Michael Ryan. A lawyer and planter from nearby Alexandria, the capital of Rapides Parish, Ryan had op- posed secession before the war. He had even agreed to be Willie Cal- houn's partner in his newspaper venture. But the partnership—and their friendship—collapsed when Ryan backed out of the deal, probably be- cause he feared his neighbors' disapproval.

After the firing on Fort Sumter, Ryan embraced the rebel cause, send- ing local gray-uniformed troops off to war with a speech in which he called the Union army "Lincoln hirelings, Hessians and vandals." He do- nated five five-hundred-pound bales of his plantation's cotton to the rebel army and held officer's rank in a "Sunday company" of reservists. He was bitter after the war because the U.S. government refused to compensate him for his emancipated slaves.

To Ryan, the parade of freedmen approaching with Willie Calhoun portended more of the degradation that had been the lot of Louisiana's whites since the South's defeat. In Rapides Parish, Negroes outnum- bered whites almost three to two. Simple arithmetic showed that their enfranchisement would produce "Negro domination." Across central and northwestern Louisiana, all up and down the Red River, Ryan and other like-minded white men came together to suppress black voting. They agreed among themselves not to hire any freedman who voted Re- publican; they bought black votes for the white man's Democratic Party.

Bolder whites, those who were "wide awake" to the threat of Negro domination, had done even more. They had ridden out at night, whips and guns in hand, threatening freedmen, flogging them, and burning their cabins. On the night of Saturday, August 29, 1868, a mob of vigi- lantes had surrounded the home of Ryan's "carpetbagger" opponent, Joseph Newsham, shouting death threats. When his terrified wife ap- peared, they pointed their weapons at her and threw burning torches on the Newshams' porch. Then, having made their point, they left.

And some white men had killed. White vigilantes had murdered Republicans of both races in at least four of the ten parishes that made up the Fourth Congressional District, in which Ryan and Newsham were competing. The election-season body count reached 2 each in DeSoto and Winn parishes, 42 dead in Caddo Parish, and a sickening 168 in Bossier Parish, the scene of the October "nigger hunt."

One of the most notorious night riders in Rapides Parish was Ryan's companion at the polls on November 3, 1868: John G. P. "Paul" Hooe. An ex–Confederate soldier who had drifted down from Virginia, Hooe had told fifty freedmen that he would whip them if they voted Republican. He had openly threatened to "shoot the top of the head off the first radical son of a bitch who votes."

Ryan and Hooe had come to the polls because, as far as they were concerned, the voting was supposed to be at a store operated by Hooe on Ryan's land. But Calhoun had used his power as a local election commissioner to have the ballot box relocated to a spot where the freedmen would feel safer: a fellow white Republican's plantation store, on a property called Plaisance. Ryan found out just minutes before the polls opened, too late to prevent it.

When Calhoun limped up to the store, Ryan confronted him. The whole election was illegal, he shouted. Not only had Calhoun moved the polls without his approval, but the poll watchers had not been properly sworn in. Some voters had failed to countersign their registration papers. When Lewis Taylor, a Negro deputy sheriff, tried to quiet Ryan, the white lawyer threatened to have him arrested for assault and battery. Ryan was probably especially furious because he had offered Taylor a mule if he would vote for Ryan and campaign for him among other freedmen—and he thought Taylor had accepted. Then Ryan tried telling the Negro voters that he would be their ally if they voted for him. He lied and said he was a Republican. "Here is a boy named Finlay," Ryan said, pointing to one of the voters. "He was in jail and I took him out, and now he won't vote for me. Next time I will just let him stay there and rot." But the black men replied that Finlay's own bail money, not Ryan's lawyering, had secured his release. Finally, Ryan voiced the true source of his irritation: "This election should not be carried on here by Calhoun and his niggers!"

Ryan's protestations were "a Democratic trick," Willie Calhoun called out. "You see? The Democrats say they are your friends, but they don't want you to vote." With that, Lewis Taylor put an end to Ryan's complaints, ushering him out of the crowded room. Hooe tried an appeal to the black men's pride. "You are free," he told them. "You can vote for

whoever you choose. But don't let yourselves be led by a damned puppy."
His speech had no more effect than Ryan's. When all the votes in the Plaisance box were counted, there were 318 for the Republican ticket and
only 49 for the Democrats.

Ryan returned to Alexandria with his story of Calhoun's chicanery. On
November 4, the day after Election Day, a surly, heavily armed white
crowd, including Michael Ryan and Paul Hooe, greeted Lewis Taylor as
he rode into the parish seat to deliver the Plaisance ballot box. "Hang
him! Shoot the son of a bitch!" the people cried. "I am a-going to stand
by this box," Taylor insisted. But he was soon overwhelmed. Ryan ran
up, shaking his fist in the deputy sheriff's face. "You son of a bitch, I will
kill you!" Ryan screamed. Agreeing to leave the ballot box with the
whites, Taylor pleaded with them not to destroy it. "We'll throw it in the
river," someone said. Fearing for his life, Taylor fled.

Next, Ryan swore out a criminal complaint against Willie Calhoun for
allegedly holding an illegal election. On November 7, a deputy sheriff
from Alexandria came to arrest Calhoun at his home. Calhoun, thinking
his life unsafe, asked a friend to escort him to court in Alexandria—
where Ryan, accompanied by dozens of Democrats armed with six-
shooters, was waiting. Amid threats and insults, Calhoun was hauled in
front of a justice of the peace, who ruled that Ryan's charges warranted a
trial and ordered Calhoun released on a one-thousand-dollar bond,
pending a court date in May 1869.

Calhoun paid and went home, facing ostracism and the unraveling of
his political plans—or worse. His enemies were numerous, well armed,
and brazen. Speaking for its readership, the *Louisiana Democrat*, published in Alexandria, declared in a November 9 editorial that it would "as
ever and to the end, continue the war and war to the knife against the
thieves, adventurers, scalawags and carpet-baggers who infest Louisiana
and have made Rapides a hell on earth." If the Democrats didn't kill Calhoun, they would surely throw him in jail on the trumped-up election-
rigging charge. In case there was any doubt about that, the *Louisiana
Democrat* accompanied its threatening editorial with an article denouncing "Sweet Willie's" "cheat and fraud."

But it was not in Calhoun's nature to surrender.

HE CAME BY HIS PUGNACITY NATURALLY: WILLIE CALHOUN'S GREAT-GRANDFATHER
(and namesake), William Smith, was a South Carolinian who rose from
nothing to become a state judge, a member of Congress, a U.S. senator—
and a very wealthy landowner. Short in stature, Smith had thin black

hair and delicate features. His deadliest weapons in political combat were a prodigious memory and a stinging wit. "He was," a biographer wrote, "a bitter and vindictive enemy, witheringly sarcastic and never conciliatory, inclined to be opinionated and prejudiced."

Eventually, Smith made one political enemy too many in South Carolina. In March 1833, at the age of seventy-one, he took his principles and fled—first to New Orleans and then on to the Red River Valley, where he had quietly bought up several thousands of acres of copper-tinted cotton fields near a spot where the Red joined the smaller Cane River. Smith had sold all of his South Carolina real estate, but not his slaves. He had hundreds, from newborn infants to elderly women and men. And when he went west, they came too. Reports vary as to exactly how many Negroes Smith forced to migrate to the Louisiana frontier. But it was a massive, cruel expedition—a perverse caricature of the wagon trains that carried white settlers to freedom and opportunity in the West.

Harried and miserable though they were, the Smith slaves still must have gaped in wonder at the Red River Valley. The region was almost otherworldly. "It seemed to me a land of enchantment," wrote a midcentury white visitor from the North. "We had never known such luxuriance of vegetation." Wild osage-orange flowers and white roses grew fifteen feet high along old Indian trails. Alligators lazed in the bayous, emerging to snack upon abundant possums and raccoons. At sunset the sky flamed pink, purple, and red.

But the heat and humidity were oppressive, and disease was everpresent. The muddy Red was undrinkable; the slaves had to collect rainwater, when it came. Gradually, the relentless rhythm of cotton cultivation took over their lives. Lest they be whipped, slaves had to be up and in the fields before dawn. The entire labor force worked under no more than half a dozen white overseers, mounted and armed with revolvers, shotguns, and whips. A select handful of black men were given whips and the privilege of "driving" the others. True to its founder's predictions, the Smith estate proved productive, though Smith spent most of his time at another plantation in milder Huntsville, Alabama. In 1839, it shipped 1,175 bales of cotton, each of which weighed five hundred pounds, to New Orleans. At the time, it was the largest crop ever sent down the river on one boat.

As the years passed and Smith's Red River Valley property grew—reaching over seven thousand acres by 1838—his family also became larger. Smith and his wife, Margaret, had adopted their granddaughter, Mary Smith Taylor, after her mother—their daughter—died in childbirth. In May 1834, she wed Meredith Calhoun, a Philadelphia-born merchant,

at Natchez, Mississippi. Smith's new grandson-in-law was a capable, re-
fined young man who was educated in France and did business in the
port of Le Havre, and when William Smith passed away in 1840, followed
by Margaret in 1841, the Philadelphian took over management of the Red
River Valley estate.

What had been a prosperous plantation developed into an agro-
industrial complex. Meredith Calhoun set up a brick-making operation
where slaves pressed the alluvial soil into firm blocks. In turn, the bricks
became barns, a cotton gin, stables, and a shed stocked with plows, hoes,
wagons, picks, and shovels imported by steamboat via New Orleans.
There was a blacksmithing shop where skilled slaves shod horses and
mules, and repaired or fabricated tools. And on the edge of a bayou that
ran through the eastern portion of the estate, Meredith built one of the
largest and most productive sugar mills in Louisiana. It cost him over
$100,000.

By 1860, Meredith Calhoun was producing $167,000 worth of cotton
per year. He reigned over fourteen thousand acres, which, together with
other property—including some 709 slaves—was worth $1.1 million. His
land stretched seven miles along the eastern bank of the Red, and three
miles deep into the surrounding hills. He divided five thousand acres of
prime land near the river into four plantations, naming them to reflect his
European travels or family pride. At the northern end was Smithfield, for
cotton and corn; to the southeast of that was Firenze, locus of the sugar
operation; and then, farther to the south, came two cotton-growing plantations, Mirabeau and Meredith. There was a busy little boat landing near
the brick stable at the junction of the Red and the Cane. Calhoun established a country store there, emblazoning the wall facing the river with
his name in letters large enough to be seen from far away. Everyone in
central Louisiana knew Calhoun's Landing.

THE POPULATION OF MEREDITH CALHOUN'S ESTATE FLUCTUATED. DEATH FRE-
quently visited; in the summer of 1851, cholera killed ninety slaves and
an overseer. Babies were constantly being born, too, including many
whose skin was a light brown that favored their white overseer fathers.
In 1847, Calhoun illegally purchased a large group of slaves smuggled directly from Africa by a Spanish trader, in violation of the U.S. ban on the
transatlantic slave trade. Like the other Calhoun Negroes, they now inhabited the slave cabins, which were arranged in clusters of twelve on
each of the four plantations.

Calhoun firmly believed in the benevolence of his labor system. Providence had ordained that the Negro should labor as the white man's chattel, he thought. The proof, he said, was the disastrous condition of the British West Indies, where the Crown abolished slavery in 1833—or even the lamentable situation of free blacks in the North. Having visited Moscow, where he witnessed the beating of one serf by another, Calhoun was also quite convinced of slavery's moral and economic superiority to the Russian system. In America, he reasoned, no one would tolerate such abuse of his property. Calhoun thought that his slaves enjoyed a better life than the Northern white workingman, who, in his view, was "degraded, stupid, unable to take care of himself." The slaveholder, unlike the capitalist employer, had an incentive to take care of his laborers, Calhoun argued.

Though Calhoun was oblivious to injustice and to the true feelings of his slaves, both were perfectly plain to one white Northerner who visited the estate. In March 1853, Frederick Law Olmsted arrived at Calhoun's Landing. Within five years, Olmsted would begin work on New York's Central Park, the project which would establish him among the greatest American landscape architects. At this juncture, however, he was working for the *New York Times*, which had dispatched him to document the inner workings of the slave economy and render them intelligible for Northern readers.

There was no more pressing issue. In 1850, Congress had made a compromise on slavery. In exchange for the South's acceptance of California's admission as a free state and the abolition of the slave trade in Washington, D.C., Northern lawmakers had accepted the Fugitive Slave Law. Every Northerner became a potential slave catcher. The law created heated antislavery sentiment that fueled the market for vivid novels about slavery, such as Harriet Beecher Stowe's *Uncle Tom's Cabin*, and for vivid journalism of the kind Olmsted provided the *Times*.

Olmsted fervently believed that God's design called for free men to work the free soil of America. No other arrangement was consistent with the dignity and personal responsibility necessary to true productivity. To be sure, Olmsted duly noted Calhoun's "commodious and well-built cabins." He acknowledged that field hands "had plenty, and often some left, of bacon, eggs, corn bread and molasses." They were allowed to keep livestock, sell the products of their gardens, and trap game. (Hunting, which would have put firearms in Negro hands, was forbidden.) Slaves were "rarely separated" from their families, Olmsted noted. He interviewed Calhoun, recording his views on the relative merits of slavery and Northern industrial capitalism.

But there was no denying the harsh and violent realities of Calhoun's plantation. Calhoun's slaves constantly tried to run away. Overseers regularly had to threaten them with extra work on Sundays, or beatings, unless they stopped smuggling food to runaway friends and relatives in the woods and swamps. And, of course, once runaways returned, they were beaten. Olmsted watched as an overseer savagely flogged "Sal," an eighteen-year-old slave woman, on her naked back and thighs. She had tried to slip away from work earlier in the day and then lied about it when the overseer caught her hiding in some brush. "Oh, don't; Sir, oh, please stop, master; please, Sir, please, Sir! Oh that's enough, master," Sal screamed, as each blow landed with a sickening *thwack*. "Oh, Lord! Oh, master! Master!" Sal writhed on the ground, her cries becoming so heartrending that the New Yorker couldn't bear to listen. He spurred his horse and fled.

In the Red River Valley, the slaves' constant dream was of freedom; the whites, outnumbered by their slaves, were haunted by the same nightmare that unnerved the rest of the South: Negro rebellion. Indeed, in 1837, slaves in the vicinity of the Calhoun estate had plotted among themselves to flee en masse to the Texas republic, and thence to Mexico. A Negro named Lew Cheney put the word out that he was organizing a company strong enough to fight its way out. At a preselected spot in the swamps, he assembled a large number of runaways, together with stolen mules, corn, and bacon. They were about to leave when their hiding place was discovered. Cheney, having concluded that the project was doomed, had informed on his companions to save his own skin—adding the false claim that they intended to murder every white person in their path.

This claim, which grew in the telling as it traveled from one plantation to the next, filled the local whites with panic. Their fear of Negro revolt had come true. Soon whites were saying that the Negroes had planned not only to escape but also to raise a black army and march on New Orleans. This called for swift and certain punishment. Nine slaves and three free men of color were taken in chains to Alexandria and, on August 10 and 12, hanged in the public square. Whites continued hanging supposed conspirators until planters began to complain about the destruction of their property. They called in U.S. troops from the Texas border to tear down the gallows. Lew Cheney escaped. But the experience remained fixed in white memory. In 1860, the killing of an overseer north of Alexandria set off another wave of lynchings.

IN THE SPRING OF 1864, UNION TROOPS HAD ROARED INTO THE RED RIVER VALley, bent on capturing Shreveport, the rebel state capital. But the U.S.

Army could not defeat the rebels of northwestern Louisiana, tough-as-nails French and Scotch-Irish from the pine-covered hills beyond the alluvial plain. Skilled and committed, they knew every swamp and bayou. Meanwhile, Union ironclads floundered in unfamiliar channels of the Red, and the Union advance ended thirty miles south of Shreveport, where the rebels won a decisive battle on April 8, 1864. The Red River Campaign was the last major Southern victory of the Civil War. Only after General Robert E. Lee surrendered at Appomattox did Confederates in Louisiana reluctantly lay down their arms.

Lincoln's January 1, 1863, Emancipation Proclamation had not applied to the border states or to Union-held territory in Louisiana. It definitly applied to rebel strongholds like the Red River Valley—and the slaves knew it. As the Federals retreated south in the summer of 1864, thousands of blacks flocked to the Union camps, carrying their beds in bundles on their heads, along with frying pans, kettles, and other possessions—some of which had been looted from their masters. "Many of the soldiers formed an acquaintance with some one of these swarthy damsels and they marched along side by side in apparent entertaining conversation, thus beguiling the tedium of the march," a Union soldier wrote. Negro men joined the Union forces to do battle with the Confederate army. More than a third of military-age black males in Louisiana joined the Union army, a higher proportion than in any other Southern state.

The Calhoun slaves hailed the Union forces. On April 2, 1864, a clear and mild spring day, the Union warship *Jennie Rogers* steamed up the Red, right by Calhoun's Landing. Negroes thronged the banks to see the North's soldiers and sailors. Women donned bonnets and aprons, and waved their handkerchiefs with a "Hurrah!" for Lincoln. A half dozen sang "Welcome Brothers" as the Union boat approached and "Good-Bye Brothers" as it chugged away. They ran along the bank to accompany the federals for a quarter of a mile—and then dashed back to Calhoun's Landing to await the next boat.

When the Confederacy fell, the Red River Valley economy collapsed completely. The U.S. Army established a base at Alexandria. Formerly the hub of the region, the parish seat of Rapides Parish presented a tableau of poverty and near anarchy. Partly burned during the war, it consisted mostly of dirt streets lined by one-story cottages. Elizabeth Custer, whose husband, the Union cavalry officer George Armstrong Custer, had been placed in charge of Alexandria, wrote that the houses of Northern mechanics "had more conveniences and modern improvements." There was only one well. Every house had a cistern on top to catch rainwater. Cats prowled the edges of the rusty cisterns by day and yowled eerily at night. Along the river's bank, houses sat on high piles, with pigs frolicking underneath. Ex-rebel soldiers were a constant threat to order, and Custer dealt with them severely. "If there still be any who, blind to the events of the past four years, continue to indulge in seditious harangues," he declared, "all such disturbers of the peace will be arrested, and brought to these headquarters."

Local whites might be sullen, but blacks were making the most of their freedom. Refugees from the surrounding plantations flocked to the Union camp. Elderly ex-slaves, abandoned by their masters, presented a pathetic sight; but even a one-hundred-year-old Negro woman told Custer she was joyous at the feeling of freedom. Regular prayer meetings among the old folks celebrated "the day of jubilee." For younger freedmen, however, work was not a top priority. Elizabeth Custer wrote, "At the least intimation of a 'show' or a funeral—which is a festivity to them, on account of the crowds that congregate—off went the entire body of men, even if the crops were in danger of spoiling for want of harvesting."

This was understandable. But Custer's commander in chief, President Andrew Johnson, was in no mood to tolerate such indolence and made his views known to officials in Louisiana. Custer ordered blacks who were not directly employed by the army back to their old plantations for the 1865 harvest. He threatened violators with jail and even enforced a pass system that required Negroes to stay at their places of work unless they carried written permission from their masters.

In December 1865, the country ratified the Thirteenth Amendment. In a single majestic sentence, it enshrined in law what the Union army had accomplished on the bloody ground of Gettysburg, Shiloh, and Vicksburg: "Neither slavery nor involuntary servitude, except as a punishment for crime whereof the party shall have been duly convicted, shall exist within the United States, or any place subject to their jurisdiction." For freedmen and their white Republican supporters, its meaning was clear and expansive. It meant that they were free not merely from their masters; they were free to pursue their dreams: education, money, land.

For white planters, the Thirteenth Amendment merely eliminated one way of controlling the labor force. That was a far cry from letting Negroes do what they wanted, whenever they wanted to do it, much less making them citizens. Indeed, the last few months of chaos in Alexandria and the surrounding plantations had confirmed to whites what they had always believed: blacks would not work without compulsion, and a Black Code was necessary. At first, blacks in the Red River Valley balked at working under the code adopted in December 1865 because they still believed that the federal government was going to distribute the proverbial "forty acres and a mule." But by the start of 1866, blacks had signed up on the plantations, and planters were looking forward to the new year. As the *Louisiana Democrat* put it, the freedmen had "nearly all abandoned their idle and loafing ways and hired for the year on plantations."

THEN THE RAINS CAME. IN THE SPRING OF 1866, THE RED RIVER OVERFLOWED ITS banks, sending silt-thickened water sloshing across thousands of acres of freshly furrowed and seeded cotton land. Planters already distressed by the uncompensated loss of their slaves now faced ruin. What little crop they did make that year was sold to pay interest to their banks instead of wages to their laborers.

Meredith Calhoun, now sixty-five years old, had been in no mood to start over again after the war. Departing with Mary to Paris, he turned his cotton and sugar operations over to their son, Willie. Unlike other planters, however, Willie Calhoun did not try to balance his books on the backs of his workforce. He gave his parents' hogs and cattle to the former slaves. He rented eight hundred acres to tenant farmers. He permitted a school for black children; by May 1866, it had thirty-five students. In the fall of 1866, when the sheriff seized his crop to pay creditors, Calhoun went to court to get it back so he could finance his workers' wages. The money was tied up in litigation for a year, but the case showed that the new boss at Calhoun's Landing thought differently from his neighbors. A government report from mid-1866 declared that the freedmen on his place were "doing remarkably well, and quite beyond the expectations of their employer, whom they are well satisfied with."

Meanwhile, the freedmen were also gaining friends in Washington. On April 9, 1866, Congress adopted the Civil Rights Act, overriding Johnson's veto. A response to the Black Codes, the law provided that "all persons born in the United States . . . are hereby declared to be citizens of the United States," with the same right "to make and enforce contracts, to sue, be parties, and give evidence, to inherit, purchase, lease, sell, hold, and convey real and personal property and to full and equal benefit of all laws and proceedings for the security of person and property, as is enjoyed by white citizens, and shall be subject to like punishment, pains, and penalties, and to none other, any law, statute, ordinance, regulation, or custom, to the contrary notwithstanding."

On July 16, 1866, Congress, again acting over Johnson's veto, extended the life of the Freedmen's Bureau, established in June 1865, and gave it new authority, thereby strengthening the first federal agency dedicated to the welfare of men and women of color. Its agents, many of whom had served in the Union army, fanned out across the South, bargaining with planters to get the freedmen better wages and conditions, and distributing blankets, corn meal, and salt pork to black families. Black children— and quite a few adults, too—took their first lessons at Freedmen's Bureau schools. When whites beat blacks, whipped them, or killed them, the Freedmen's Bureau hauled offenders before military commissions for trial and punishment.

In the flooded Red River Valley, the bureau seized some planters' cotton in 1866 and cashed it out for the benefit of Negro workers who had not yet been paid. The next year, a young bureau agent named Delos W. White arrived in the region, establishing his office at Montgomery, a mostly white market town just twelve miles or so north of Calhoun's Landing. For White, born in Flushing, New York, in 1842, this was a return trip. As a lieutenant in the Second New York Veteran Cavalry—the "Empire Light Cavalry"—he had fought in the Red River Campaign.

White's predecessor, also a former Union army officer, had been murdered under murky circumstances. Undaunted, White showed that he would bring toughness as well as compassion to his new assignment. The former cavalryman linked up with U.S. troops to pursue his predecessor's killers. A brother of one fugitive threatened White's life; but the young bureau agent persisted, eventually forcing the suspects to flee to Texas, where one of them was shot dead by the army.

When Red River Valley crops failed again in 1867 because of flooding and pests, White ordered the planters to give freedmen corn so they wouldn't starve. He constantly battled planters' schemes to cheat colored laborers and insisted that white men accept IOUs from Negroes. "I claim that as a general thing the freedmen are a much more honest class of people than those who are trying to get their labor and not pay them for it," he wrote to a local justice of the peace. Most important, he used his power to punish whites for violence against Negroes. When a white man attacked a seventy-five-year-old black man with a stick and beat him nearly to death, claiming that the Negro owed him a dollar, White had the assailant arrested and sent to New Orleans for trial before a military commission.

WILLIE CALHOUN WELCOMED DELOS WHITE AND THE NEW ORDER HE REPRE-sented. He did not find it unthinkable that the Red River Valley's former slave labor force could develop into a citizenry—with guidance from enlightened whites such as himself, of course. Calhoun enlisted two Negroes, including one of his father's former slave drivers, as political organizers. With their help, he urged the former Calhoun slaves to vote Republican in the September 1867 election for a new state constitutional convention. And he threw his support behind a candidate, a twenty-six-year-old white man named William B. Phillips.

Phillips was born and raised in Franklin County, Alabama, upland territory where Union sympathy remained strong during the Civil War. But he served in an elite cavalry unit of the Confederate army, the Fifty-third Partisan Rangers, which fought at both Vicksburg and Chickamauga. He came to Rapides Parish in the fall of 1865, apparently with the idea of pursuing the legal studies that he had started prior to the war. During his first six months in Alexandria, he worked as the deputy clerk of the local court and read law in the office of Thomas C. Manning, a former justice of the prewar Louisiana Supreme Court and a leading local white supremacist. By the spring of 1867, however, Phillips was ready to launch his political career—as a Republican.

A talented public speaker, Phillips took to the stump in black-majority Rapides Parish, promising freedmen that, if elected, he would fight to get them new schools, land, horses, and farm equipment. His message frightened local whites, who reported to the Alexandria Freedman's Bureau that Phillips was instigating blacks to threaten to fight whites for these goods if the government didn't provide them. The local Bureau agent visited the plantations and found no evidence of this. But he told the freedmen anyway that Phillips was "misguiding" them. Then, on the instructions of his superiors, the agent warned Phillips to "confine his remarks to the truth," or else face "forcible measures."

This appeared to reflect a long-standing dispute between the agent and the young Republican orator. On May 23, Phillips sent a pseudonymous letter to the editor of the *New Orleans Republican*, accusing the agent of "truckling" to local "rebels," and listing attacks on freedmen that the local bureau had tolerated. Still, the young Alabaman moderated his message. In a June 30, 1867, speech to hundreds of freedmen, he warned them not to vote for the Democrats, the party responsible for "the cruelty and injustice" of slavery. But he also urged them to "forget and forgive the wrongs of the past," and "instead of paying twenty-five cents for a drink of whiskey, purchase a spelling-book, and go to work and . . . prove yourselves worthy citizens and deserving of a home among a good people."

Phillips did not win a seat in the constitutional convention. However, the election helped create a black-majority electorate in Louisiana. The voter-eligibility rules set forth in the Reconstruction Act were enforced in the state by General Philip H. Sheridan, the great Union cavalry commander who had ravaged Virginia's Shenandoah Valley. In 1867, Grant engineered Sheridan's appointment as commander of the military district of Texas and Louisiana. Based in New Orleans, Sheridan fired several state and city officials, including the mayor, for complicity in the 1866 New Orleans Massacre. His officers registered eighty-three thousand black voters and only forty-five thousand whites in the summer of 1867. This reflected his orders not to sign up any white male over twenty-one who refused to renounce his rebel past—about half the eligible white voters in the state.

As a result, the Republicans triumphed; indeed, fifty of the ninety-eight men elected to the Louisiana constitutional convention were black. When it convened in New Orleans in November 1867, it was the first governmental body in American history whose members were mostly nonwhite. The document the convention produced on March 2, 1868, was a Radical Republican's dream: it guaranteed equal political rights regardless of race, laid the basis for integrated public schools, and took the vote away from all ex-rebel civilian and military officers who refused to publicly disavow their former support for secession.

At a two-day election on April 17 and 18, 1868, Louisiana's new electorate overwhelmingly approved the new constitution. As governor, they chose Henry Clay Warmoth, a twenty-six-year-old Republican former Union army colonel, originally from Illinois, who promised to work with all races to improve the state. His lieutenant governor was Oscar J. Dunn, a forty-eight-year-old mulatto ex-slave from New Orleans. The Republicans held a 56–45 majority in the new state house of representatives and a 20–16 majority in the state senate. Given the wide spectrum of pigmentation among Louisiana's population, it was difficult to determine how many of the new legislators were black. But seven of the thirty-six senators were said to be colored; thirty-five members of the House appeared to be black, too. Among the day's white Republican winners was Willie Calhoun, the newly elected state representative from Rapides Parish.

IN ALL OF RURAL LOUISIANA ONLY 1,452 WHITES VOTED FOR THE 1868 CONSTITU-tion. The rest either voted against it or boycotted the election. For whites, the liberation of the slaves, and the prospect of having to live with them on terms of rough equality, stirred a powerful mix of feelings: outrage, disgust, humiliation, fear. Antipathy toward the Negro raged not only among former slaveowners but also among white yeoman who inhabited the "piney woods." The war had doubly devastated them: they sacrificed their sons, brothers, and husbands, and then were left scratching meager crops from the thin upland soil or cutting logs for sale to passing steamboats. Poverty in the piney woods shocked a Northern traveler, who wrote of "the vacant faces of the filthy children of poor white trash and negroes. Even the pigs were gaunt and famished." What pride these whites still had came from their memories of valor in battle against the Yankees—and their claim of racial superiority. "It follows," wrote a journalist who visited the region, "that they are to a man Democrats and to a man have a holy horror of the colored people."

Across Louisiana, white men of all social classes organized into secret terrorist organizations: some groups called themselves the Ku Klux Klan, some Wide Awake Clubs, and some Innocents Clubs. But the most common name was the Knights of the White Camellia. The first "lodge" of Knights began as a "White Man's" or "Caucasian" Club in Franklin, the seat of St. Mary's Parish, on May 23, 1867. By November 1868, half of white men in the southern portion of the state were believed to be members. A lodge formed near Calhoun's Landing and soon had roughly three hundred members.

As one leader put it, the Knights' purpose was "the better preservation of the white race, and to see that the white blood was handed down unmixed with the offensive globule of African blood." Membership was open only to "persons of the purest of white blood," who would swear an oath that they would never marry a Negro woman and never had done so before. Members must also swear that they would never vote for anyone who was not white—or even for anyone who supported permitting nonwhites to vote or hold office. One Knight could always recognize another by the secret sign: a quick flick of the left index finger across the left eye. New recruits to the Knights, known as *candidates*, would be brought, hooded, to safe houses, where sponsoring friends—*conductors*—would present them to local *commanders*. The conductor would knock twice at the door. "Who comes here?" the commander would ask from inside. "A son of your race," the conductor would answer. The prescribed dialogue would ensue.

What does he wish?
> Peace and order, the maintenance of the laws of God, and the maintenance of the laws and Constitution established by the patriots of 1775.

To obtain this, what must be done?
> The cause of our race must triumph.

And to make it triumph what must be done?
    We must be united as are united the flowers which grow on the same stem
    and in all circumstances band ourselves as brothers.
Are you opposed to allowing the political affairs of this country to go in whole or
in part in the hands of the Negro or African race and will you do everything in
your power to prevent this?
    Yes.

WHITE VIGILANTES HAD BEGUN HARASSING REPUBLICANS IN RAPIDES PARISH prior to the April 1868 vote. In early 1867, a group of fifteen men visited William B. Phillips's rented room in Alexandria and said they were there to "put him out of the way." He wasn't home. But for several nights thereafter, a mob picketed his abode, shouting that he was "a damned Yankee" and "a damned radical." On December 17, 1867, Phillips was attacked and beaten by nine men armed with six-shooters. They would have shot him, he later said, but another group of men, potential witnesses, happened along on horseback.

For the most part, though, the Knights and others kept their powder dry during the run-up to the April balloting, apparently waiting to see if other tactics might get Negroes to reject the new state constitution. These methods, surprisingly enough, included not only bribery and threats, but also stump speeches and barbecues. The Republican triumph in April 1868 proved the futility of this approach. "The election has gone against us," the *New Orleans Daily Picayune* lamented. "The new government is revolutionary in its origins, African on its basis, and tainted all over by fraud." Now it was time for violence: In October, white terrorists destroyed the Alexandria offices of the *Rapides Tribune*, a new Republican newspaper. Klansmen paraded through the town on horseback several nights a week. Menacing visits to Phillips's place resumed. Just a week after the April election, five men with pistols and double-barreled shotguns told him to get out of the parish. "Calhoun will never see the legislature," they barked. Phillips took the threat seriously and decamped for New Orleans, where Calhoun got him a staff job in the legislature. Phillips swore out federal criminal complaints against the men who had threatened his life. Deputy U.S. marshals duly arrested four Alexandria Knights, but they were later released on bond and the case went nowhere.

Governor Warmoth repeatedly asked the U.S. Army to help stop the Knights. But by the fall of 1868, Sheridan was no longer in charge of the military in Louisiana. Johnson had ordered Grant to replace him, and, after a tense White House meeting, the general had bowed. Johnson later installed a close friend, a former Democratic politician from Kentucky, who refused either to let Warmoth create a state militia or to deploy U.S. forces. White terrorism raged as 2,254 U.S. soldiers sat in their barracks. Johnson's general told Warmoth that the best way to protect his constituents would be to call off the Republican campaign and urge blacks not to vote. Warmoth reluctantly agreed.

The Republican vote practically vanished. In Caddo Parish, 1,242 people voted for Warmoth in April; in November, only one person voted the Grant-led Republican ticket. In Winn Parish, just north of Calhoun's Landing, the Republican vote shrank from 232 to 43; in Bossier, from 727 to 1; in Sabine, from 196 to 1. In DeSoto Parish, where 649 people voted Republican in April, not one person did so in November. Statewide, the Democrat Horatio Seymour trounced the Republican Grant, 88,225 to 34,859.

With the box full of Republican tickets cast by Willie Calhoun's ex-slaves now resting on the bottom of the Red River, the Democrat Michael Ryan claimed a landslide victory in the Fourth Congressional District.

Bloodshed and death crept closer to Calhoun's Landing.

HAL FRAZIER, A MAN OF COLOR WHO EMBODIED OPTIMISM AND SUCCESS, MADE his home just fifteen miles north of Calhoun's Landing. Before the war, he had been owned by John Frazier, a white man, but saved up to buy his freedom. After the war, he bought his former master's sawmill and two thousand acres of his land. His son, Brantley Frazier, taught school on the property. Hal Frazier served as an election commissioner in the Democratic stronghold of Montgomery during the 1868 elections. He and the other men in his family voted the Republican ticket.

On December 8, 1868, two white strangers visited Frazier's sawmill to inquire about buying a load of lumber. Not finding him there, they left. They came back at noon the next day. This time, Frazier was at his place of business. One of the visitors asked him to go around to the back of the mill, supposedly so that they could measure lumber for a house he wanted to build. Frazier kneeled on the ground. Using a stick, he sketched a plan of his customer's proposed house in the reddish dirt. Suddenly, the man pulled out his pistol and shot Frazier through the right eye. In the next moment, the second gunman shot and killed a Negro who worked for

Frazier at the mill. The murderers grabbed three hundred dollars in cash from Frazier's pockets, mounted their horses, and rode away.

DELOS WHITE HAD RESIGNED THE FREEDMEN'S BUREAU IN SEPTEMBER 1868. BUT he had become deeply attached to the colored people he met in the Red River Valley, and devoted to their cause. Before his resignation, he had told his superiors at the bureau in a letter that he would stay with the local freedmen "to the last." Thus he stayed on as a commissioner of elections in Winn Parish, despite death threats from whites angered by his efforts to register black voters. He did not quit when white terrorists broke up Freedmen's Bureau schools for black children. But he could not withstand the murder of Hal Frazier. Two days after the attack, White fled Montgomery, taking refuge on the Calhoun estate. In a letter to Phillips in New Orleans, Willie Calhoun reported that he, too, feared for his life, adding, "The fact is, Phillips, if you were here I would not give two bits for your hide." Calhoun was receiving so many threats that he no longer felt safe to travel in Rapides Parish.

The situation called for a solution that was both drastic and inventive. If Rapides Parish was incurably hostile to Calhoun and his Republican allies, white and colored alike, they would have to shift their political operations to a new parish where they would be safe. Calhoun decided to create such a parish, centered on his own vast estate. Calhoun was chairman of the state house of representatives committee on parish boundaries. His protégé, Phillips, was the committee clerk. They drafted a bill to combine part of Winn Parish, which lay north of Calhoun's Landing, with a portion of Rapides Parish lying to the south and east. The statute transferred Michael Ryan's illegal-election case against Calhoun from the Rapides Parish court to the new parish, where a court sympathetic to Calhoun would quickly dismiss it.

Willie Calhoun's new parish officially opened for business on March 4, 1869, the day that Ulysses S. Grant took the presidential oath for the first time—flanked by his new vice president, Schuyler Colfax. Calhoun leased the parish a brick stable his father's slaves had built at Calhoun's Landing; the dingy but sturdy structure would be the new courthouse. The population of the parish totaled about 4,500, of whom about 2,400 were Negroes living on the lowlands along the eastern bank of the Red. The white minority, other than a few white Republicans clustered around Calhoun's place, consisted of a handful of planters and a larger number of piney woods yeomen. Negroes also made up the majority of registered voters.

Local Democrats fumed. "The whole concern is simply a Radical bone to feed the loyal mendicants who long crowd Sweet Willie's domains and gotten up for no other purpose than to rob and pillage the State and the people taken in by the new parish," the *Louisiana Democrat* declared. "The seat of justice will of course be one of Sweet Willie's plantations, composing New Africa." But Calhoun's enemies could not stop him. At Calhoun's suggestion, Governor Warmoth appointed William B. Phillips as the first parish judge and Delos White as sheriff. Now, the band of white Republicans had a haven; in their new parish, *they* were the law.

Willie Calhoun had his revenge. All that remained was to savor it. The planter reached into his reserve of hereditary sarcasm and produced a name for the new parish that would enrage the Michael Ryans and Paul Hooes of the world. He called it Grant Parish, a tribute to the new Republican president. And he renamed Calhoun's Landing, the parish seat, in honor of Grant's vice president. Henceforth, it would be known as Colfax.

CHAPTER THREE

POWER STRUGGLE

As spring planting began in 1869, a superficial normality settled over Grant Parish. Up before dawn, families of Negroes made their way from their cabins to the fields, where the first task of the season was to divide the land into "beds" wide enough for four to six furrows, depending on the expected growth of the crop. Then a field hand using a small plow called a *scouter* would cut the furrows, followed by his wife and children, who dropped seeds into the moist earth. After the women and children came another field hand with a bent board called a *harrow*, covering the seeds up again with soil. Once the plants sprouted, the difficult tasks of trimming and weeding the cotton would begin—tedious, grueling work with hoes.

Life was familiar—but much had changed. The Negroes planting cotton this spring were doing so neither as slaves nor, in many cases, as wage laborers. Many rented land from Willie Calhoun, bought tools, seeds, and feed from Calhoun's new supply store, and pledged to pay him back out of the proceeds of their crops. As the impact of the previous years' floods faded, Negro families had a bit more cash to buy cornmeal and bacon. Quite a few of them acquired property: a mule, perhaps, or pots and pans. One colored man, a Union army veteran, opened a country store of his own, where people could buy staples such as cornmeal and animal feed—or a glass of whiskey. The Negroes pooled their money to finance a new school for their children. Eventually, they hired a teacher, a free man of color from Pennsylvania who had also come south with the U.S. Army. Encouraged by Willie Calhoun and other white Republicans, colored men formed political clubs and prepared to exercise their right to vote.

One of those white Republicans, the new sheriff, Delos White, had long believed that this was how Reconstruction should—and could—work. As a Freedmen's Bureau agent, he had written that the former Calhoun slaves were "sober and industrious" and of "superior moral character" to their white neighbors. "With any kind of favorable chance," he had argued, "they will most assuredly outstrip the whites in material prosperity." White belonged to the Knights of Pythias, a fraternal order which believed the country could be healed by friendships like that between the ancient Greeks Damon and Pythias. When Pythias was wrongly sentenced to death for treason, Damon agreed to serve as a hostage for Pythias, putting his life at risk while Pythias bid his wife and child good-bye. Then Pythias returned and set Damon free. Both men were pardoned. With secret passwords and initiation rites of their own, the Knights of Pythias were a benign mirror image of the Knights of the White Camellia. Some of White's dedication to his Republican friends in the Red River Valley—black and white—may have reflected his Pythian creed.

But to most white people in Grant Parish, the Republicans' little domain was a confused, sickening place, in which all the most sacred values of the South were being mocked and trampled. A white planter's daughter wrote of the white Republicans as villainous strangers who "sought the companionship of the blacks . . . ate with them, drank with them, lived with them on terms of perfect equality; embraced them also in the fullness of their confidence as their unsuspecting dupes." Negroes even took positions of official responsibility, albeit minor ones: parish surveyor, justice of the peace, a constable or two.

Whites blamed Delos White, but the man they hated was William B. Phillips, the new parish judge. Often, they framed their objections to him as complaints about his lack of qualifications for the two-thousand-dollar-a-year position he held: he was not even a full-fledged lawyer, yet Willie Calhoun and Henry Clay Warmoth had set him to rule over their court. On top of that, he was a know-it-all whose argumentative personality closely resembled that of Calhoun, his patron.

But to whites, the true essence of Phillips's corruption was racial. He lived with a seventeen-year-old mulatto mistress, who was pregnant with Phillips's child. He even installed her elderly mother in a home next door to his, with two men, one white and one colored, as boarders. When his baby came in August 1869, Phillips did not discreetly cover up his paternity, as Willie Calhoun had done with his mixed-race offspring. He gave the child the name Robert G. Phillips, as if it were perfectly natural for an unmarried man and an unmarried woman of different races to start a family. The *Louisiana Democrat* called him "the great Radical Miscegenator and Renegade."

The death threats began when Grant Parish was barely a month old. In the first week of April 1869, two white men, heavily armed, approached Delos White and ordered him to resign as sheriff. The former

New York cavalryman ignored them and went about his business. A few days later, another group accosted him and told him that he was trying their patience; it would no longer be enough for him simply to step down. They were giving him twenty-four hours to leave the parish—for good. Phillips got similar visits and similar warnings.

White and Phillips might have been alarmed, but they could not have been very surprised. The Knights of the White Camellia had ostensibly disbanded at the end of 1868. Yet the statewide network of white vigilantes was still in place. Some Knights even resumed their nocturnal assemblies, coining new passwords and renaming themselves, obscurely, "the 298s." The two Republican leaders must have known that the creation of the new parish would provoke a response from these forces.

But now, as the top law enforcement officers of a parish established in part for their protection, they felt they could defy the danger. The *New Orleans Republican*, which got much of its information about Grant Parish from Phillips, reported the threats, confidently predicting that they would amount to nothing. "We think the majesty of the law will be vindicated," the paper averred. Instead of fleeing, the two men dug in. White moved to Phillips's big new house, and they planted corn and cotton crops of their own.

IN NEW ORLEANS, GOVERNOR WARMOTH DID NOT LIKE WHAT HE WAS HEARING about the way the Republicans were running Grant Parish. During his 1868 election campaign, Warmoth had promised the freedmen "political equality" and "small farms." But he was against radical measures. Still in his twenties, Warmoth had his sights set on a long career in power, and he had his own ideas about how to ensure the Republican Party's survival in Louisiana's peculiar political environment.

Born in Illinois and raised in the border state of Missouri, Warmoth wanted to lift the state to Northern standards by cleaning New Orleans's filthy streets, repairing the levees, and, above all, building railroads. Warmoth saw jobs, contracts, and patronage as the cement that would bind a grand coalition of freedmen, Unionist whites, and pragmatic ex-Confederates. "Let our course, while resolute and manly, be also moderate and discreet," he announced in his June 1868 inaugural address. Only then, Warmoth said, could Louisiana "harmonize the two races" and "live together on the basis of equal civil and political rights."

As 1870 began, Warmoth focused on winning the fall elections. The Republicans would have to prevent a repeat of the disastrous violence of 1868, and so the governor and the Republican legislature instituted measures to cripple their opponents and protect their friends. One new election law gave the governor authority to appoint the officials who registered voters in every parish; another created a five-man "returning board" headed by Warmoth to count ballots and compile official returns. And, crucially, Warmoth succeeded in forming a state militia under his personal control, consisting of the paramilitary Metropolitan Police in New Orleans and a five-thousand-man force for the rest of the state.

But, ever mindful of the state's fragile racial and political balance, Warmoth made a great show of reassuring whites, including ex-Confederates. He asked the legislature for a constitutional amendment repealing the 1868 constitution's provision denying ex-rebels the vote. As militia commander, he appointed James A. Longstreet, a former general in Robert E. Lee's Army of Northern Virginia, who had moved to Louisiana and registered Republican. In the new militia, he created units made up of white Union veterans, black Union veterans, and white Confederate veterans. Warmoth went out of his way to offer patronage to conservative whites— "respectable" lawyers, merchants, small planters—and to recruit them as Republican candidates for local offices.

Warmoth was inclined to blame the unsatisfactory situation in Grant Parish on William B. Phillips and Delos White, not the white supremacists who had threatened to kill them. To Warmoth, it was axiomatic that the Republicans must co-opt as many whites as possible, but White and Phillips seemed bent on alienating them. In mid-March 1870, just a year after he had appointed the two men, Warmoth fired them. He replaced them with conservative Republicans. The new judge was a Kentucky-born lawyer and former Confederate officer; the new sheriff was a long-time resident of the Red River Valley who had been a lawman in Rapides Parish during slavery times.

WILLIE CALHOUN WAS IN NO POSITION TO PROTEST. HE WAS TOO BUSY TRYING TO save his family's estate from financial distress. Though the cotton crop of fall 1869 was better than that of each of the previous two or three years, it was still far short of what the Grant Parish area had produced before the Civil War. Compounding the crisis was the death of Meredith Calhoun on May 14, 1869. He had contracted huge debts in his own name during and after the war. But when he passed away, his wife, Mary, inherited his obligations. And that meant that the creditors could threaten to repossess the plantations, which were in her name. As 1870 began, the state seized part of her land for back taxes.

In early 1870, Calhoun, still representing Rapides Parish in the state legislature, proposed a new law to help protect the estate. The bill would transfer all lawsuits concerning his father's estate to the Grant Parish courts, where he believed he would have a better chance of keeping creditors at bay. The bill could not become law without Warmoth's signature, and the governor was not in the habit of giving something for nothing. Perhaps Calhoun's acquiescence in the ouster of Phillips and White was his price for approving Calhoun's bill. The timing suggests as much. Warmoth signed the bill on March 16, 1870, the same day that Warmoth replaced White as sheriff, and three days before he replaced Phillips as judge.

This turn of events undoubtedly infuriated Phillips and White, who had stood with Calhoun through almost three years of dangerous political battles. They decided to establish a Republican organization of their own, with the goal of recovering power in the November 1870 elections. Phillips and White recruited Calhoun's former Negro political lieutenants to their cause and nominated their own slate, with Phillips himself as the nominee for parish judge, and the martyred Hal Frazier's son Brantley as a candidate for one of the parish's seven justices of the peace.

Louisiana's 1870 election was the fairest and most peaceful of Reconstruction, and the Republicans won. In Grant Parish, in fact, Republicans were practically the only ones who participated. The Democratic state ticket received 256 votes out of 952 cast, a figure that suggested only about half of registered whites turned out. Phillips won election as parish judge, and two of his backers were elected justice of the peace and constable. But the parish's more conservative Republicans got Alfred C. Shelby, a hard-drinking, illiterate forty-nine-year-old farmer originally from Tennessee, elected sheriff.

For a while, Phillips and Shelby got along—until it became clear that they had incompatible ideas about how the law should be enforced. The system was supposed to be fairly simple. A victim of a crime would come to the judge and swear out a complaint against the alleged perpetrator. The judge would issue a warrant, and the sheriff would make an arrest, with the help of his own chosen deputies or, sometimes, a posse made up of citizens specially sworn in for the task.

But the system did not work when Phillips tried to enforce the law against Grant Parish's white vigilantes—especially the family, friends, and neighbors of forty-nine-year-old James W. Hadnot. Hadnot was an Alabama-born planter who had moved to Louisiana as a young man. During the Union's Red River Campaign in 1864, Hadnot's place, situated on the east bank of the Red twelve miles downriver from Colfax, became a battleground where thirty-three Union soldiers and twenty-five Confederates died. His war record was obscure; too old for regular Confederate service, he probably served in a local reserve unit. He had the accoutrements: a sword, a rosette badge, and a bright red sergeant's sash which he liked to wear around his waist.

Negroes in Colfax knew—and feared—Jim Hadnot as a leader of violent attacks during the 1868 presidential election. Since the founding of Grant Parish, two of Hadnot's associates, brothers from Mississippi named Jim and Jeff Yawn, had become notorious for riding out at night to beat and whip colored people. Colored men came to Phillips with harrowing reports of abuse at the hands of the Yawns, pleading with him to bring them to justice. The judge issued one arrest warrant after another. But, each time, nothing happened. Sheriff Shelby simply refused to do his job. Possibly, the sheriff was intimidated. More likely, Shelby, who boasted that he was a Confederate veteran like Jim Yawn, sympathized with the white vigilantes.

Sheriff Shelby had developed a strong dislike for his predecessor, Phillips's friend Delos White, with whom Shelby was rumored to have had an unfortunate quarrel over money. Grant Parish was not big enough to hold both him and White, Shelby declared—and he didn't seem to care who heard him say it. As for Phillips, Shelby called him a "grand scoundrel" within earshot of a Negro Republican. On yet another occasion, he called Phillips a "scamp" who would "steal the country if he could." By the second week of September 1871, the new sheriff was offering Negroes money to kill the parish judge. One colored man said the sheriff promised him one hundred dollars to do the job.

Strange and violent events multiplied in the humid summer nights. The body of a young white Confederate veteran, a boarder with Phillips and White, appeared near a place called Rock Island, brutally murdered. Given where he lived, he might have been the accidental victim of an assassination attempt intended for Phillips and White. But word spread that White himself was the culprit, and the victim's family agitated for Shelby to arrest him. He did, though White quickly made bail, thanks to Judge Phillips.

In late August, someone fired about twenty shots into a house near Hal Frazier's old mill. At the beginning of September, a fire broke out in the middle of the night at the home of a leading white supremacist about a mile north of Phillips and White's place. The man and his family rushed out in their pajamas as flames consumed their property. Though Phillips helped them escape, white supremacists blamed his party for the blaze; the Republicans blamed white vigilantes.

. . .

AT ONE IN THE MORNING OF SEPTEMBER 25, 1871, HORSEMEN MOVED STEALTHILY through woods outside the home of William B. Phillips and Delos W. White. There were about sixty men in all, armed with double-barreled shotguns and wearing white armbands, probably so that they could recognize one another in the moonlight. The Yawns were in the mob, at the head of which rode Sheriff Alfred C. Shelby.

A short distance from the house, they found a local Negro, out for a late-night walk, and seized him to keep him from revealing their presence. Behind the house, they crossed a bridge over the Bayou Grappe and slipped from their horses. Hitching the animals to some trees, they quickly surrounded the rectangular building, posting a dozen men each at the front and back, and four at each end. They doused the roof with "coal oil," as kerosene was then known, and touched it with a torch.

Inside, Phillips and White awoke amid heat and smoke. Wearing nothing but nightshirts, the two Civil War vets seized their revolvers and ran for the front door. White was the first to make it. Yanking the door open, he found himself staring straight at the inky black eyes of Christopher Columbus Nash.

White had seen those penetrating eyes, that black beard, and that Confederate slouch hat—with the brim pulled up to reveal a broad forehead—many times before. A barrel-chested man who stood about five feet eight inches tall, Nash lived in Colfax and ran a store not too far from the Phillips-White abode. As Alfred Shelby's deputy sheriff, he had helped arrest White on the phony murder charge just a few weeks earlier. White knew that Christopher Columbus Nash was a hard man and no stranger to violence.

Born in Mississippi on July 21, 1838, Nash grew up in Louisiana's Sabine Parish, hard by the Texas border. Nash's parents raised him on stories of his Southern ancestors' political and military exploits. His grandfather's Continental army officer's commission became a family heirloom that Nash would treasure until the day he died. And when the South's own war for independence came in 1861, Nash rushed to enlist in a Confederate volunteer company called the Sabine Rifles.

Nash traveled to Virginia and saw action in the South's victory at the First Battle of Bull Run, then went on to the Shenandoah Valley, Antietam, Winchester, and the greatest battle of all, Gettysburg. Late in the day on July 2, 1863, Nash's unit took part in a charge up Cemetery Hill. Letting out a rebel yell—the high-pitched, quavering whoop that had so frightened Union soldiers in earlier engagements—the Louisianans dashed up the grassy slope, shooting and clubbing Union defenders in the twilight. They took the objective—an artillery battery—but had to retreat because supporting units did not arrive in time to stave off the Union counterattack.

On November 7, 1863, Nash and his company found themselves back in Virginia, at a place called Rappahannock Station. That night, Union forces mounted a fierce bayonet charge against the rebels and took 1,600 prisoners, including Nash. The Yankees sent him to a prison for Confederate officers at Johnson's Island, Ohio, a dreary chip of land in Lake Erie where Nash and other men from the Deep South huddled together against the Great Lakes winter, surviving on a piece of bacon and hard bread each day—sometimes supplemented by the rodents they caught and ate in their barracks.

The Christopher Columbus Nash who swore allegiance to the United States and walked out of prison on June 13, 1865, was a different man from the fresh-faced twenty-two-year-old who had enlisted so enthusiastically four years earlier. He had known the pride and glory of fighting under great men like Robert E. Lee and Stonewall Jackson. But he had also tasted rat meat in a frigid prison a thousand miles from home. He had shot or stabbed his share of Yankees and heard them scream; he had witnessed the anguish of wounded friends, many of them young kids whom he, as their officer, had been bound to protect. And when he came home, he had found his erstwhile comrades in arms humiliated and disenfranchised, subject to the will of Yankee invaders and their Negro minions.

Possibly that was the final grievance which had propelled Nash to this confrontation with White, the former Union officer. But whatever the motive or motives that brought Nash to that time and place, his grim face, illuminated by fire, would be the last thing Delos White saw. Nash raised his gun, aimed it at the New Yorker, and squeezed the trigger twice, perhaps three times. The shots blew away the top of White's head, and his lifeless body crumpled to the ground. The fire raged higher. Burning pieces of wood dropped from the porch roof onto White's corpse.

Nash and the rest of Shelby's posse kept up a steady fire, pouring shot after shot into the blazing house. Seeing his comrade lying in the front doorway, Phillips turned and fled out the back. Once outside, he flung himself on the ground, pretending to be dead.

Satisfied that their mission had been accomplished, Shelby and Nash ordered their men to leave a calling card. They tied the torch to a twelve-foot pole, which they planted in the ground outside the house. About three feet from the top, they attached a copy of Phillips's June 1867 campaign speech—the one in which he had called upon freedmen to "forget the past," to "unite heads, hands and hearts" and "reconstruct the disorganized state."

A whistle-blast pierced the midnight air: the signal to pull out. Shelby, Nash, and the others ran to their horses, sprang into the saddles, and rode away into the blackness. In Montgomery the next day, white women cheered when they heard the news of Delos White's murder.

William B. Phillips dissolved into fury. The fire had consumed ten thousand dollars' worth of his property, everything he could claim as his own. What enraged him, though, was that the flames had destroyed Delos White's body. The courageous cavalryman, who had brushed aside death threats only to perish in a sneak attack, would not even get a proper burial. "Mr. White was burned up in the house," Phillips wrote ruefully to the *New Orleans Republican* two days later. "I could not get him out."

There was nothing to be done, but Phillips told friends that he would spend his last dollar to make sure that the killers "suffer[ed] the penalty of law"—death on the gallows. Phillips had a pretty good idea who the culprits were; he had probably recognized some of them himself in the fire's orange light. The question was how to make good on his vow.

DELOS WHITE'S MURDER CAME AMID THE CRACK-UP OF THE REPUBLICAN PARTY OF Louisiana. The rift pitted Warmoth and his supporters against Republican federal officials, most of them from the North, whose domination of the bureaucracy in the New Orleans Custom House gave them control over a huge stream of revenue and nearly six hundred federal jobs. The dispute was complicated, but personality and power were key to it. President Grant, the ultimate patron of the Custom House, despised Henry Clay Warmoth, and Warmoth reciprocated.

Their feud went back to the Civil War. In May 1863, Warmoth was wounded in Grant's first unsuccessful attack on Vicksburg, Mississippi. While recuperating, he voiced his low opinion of Grant's generalship to a Chicago newspaper. Grant fired him. But Warmoth went over Grant's head to Lincoln and won reinstatement. He went on to serve in Louisiana, settled in New Orleans during the Union occupation, and eventually edged out a wealthy free man of color for the Republican gubernatorial nomination.

As his 1873 inaugural address showed, Grant saw himself as a man who made it to the top through real achievements. He instinctively disliked Warmoth as a "political soldier" who rose thanks to powerful mentors. Grant famously showed up at Appomattox in a mud-stained private's coat, feeling abashed in Lee's magnificently attired presence. All through his rise to national prominence, he had battled political enemies and inner demons. The blue-eyed, verbally gifted Warmoth glided to the top, pausing only to squire a succession of attractive ladies including Mary Harlan, daughter of a U.S. senator and future wife of Abraham Lincoln's son Robert. Warmoth was, Grant wrote, "the shrewdest, boldest, ablest and most conscienceless young man I ever knew."

Grant's dislike for Warmoth was dutifully shared by his wife's sister's husband, James F. Casey, whom Grant had made customs collector of New Orleans in 1870. The appointment enabled Casey to keep an eye on Warmoth for Grant, and put the president's brother-in-law—not Warmoth—in charge of the Custom House's pot of federal patronage. Casey soon had his own reason to detest Warmoth; in 1871, the governor imposed his choice for U.S. senator from Louisiana, a job that Casey also coveted.

In late summer 1871, the Custom House faction took over the state Republican Party and hatched a plan to impeach Warmoth, so that he could be replaced by his lieutenant governor, Oscar J. Dunn, who had defected to the Custom House. The plot required the Custom House Republicans to seek the Democrats' support, since they did not have enough votes in the legislature to impeach and remove Warmoth on their own. The white man's party hated Warmoth but would be reluctant to support Dunn, a mulatto, for governor. The Custom House Republicans apparently thought they would nevertheless cooperate for the right price, and began negotiating.

On November 22, 1871, Dunn suddenly died of "brain congestion." (Rumors that he was poisoned have never been substantiated.) Warmoth, aware of the machinations against him, pounced on the opportunity to install a lieutenant governor who would be favorable to him and hostile to the Custom House faction. He picked P. B. S. Pinchback, the mulatto state senator from New Orleans who had been Dunn's chief rival among the Negro politicians of New Orleans.

But the Custom House Republicans did not give up. Throughout the rest of 1871, they maneuvered to oust both Warmoth *and* Pinchback. They would accomplish this by sending Custom House Republican and Democratic members of the state senate on a voyage aboard a federal revenue cutter, *The Wilderness*, thus depriving the upper house of a quorum. Then they would hold the impeachment vote in the house of representatives. Once impeached, Warmoth and Pinchback would be suspended until tried by the senate—which could not meet without a quorum. House Speaker George Carter, a Custom House ally, would be acting governor, and through him, the Custom House Republicans would rule the state.

The scheme was so convoluted it could probably only have germinated in the political hothouse of Reconstruction-era Louisiana.

FLEEING TO NEW ORLEANS SHORTLY AFTER THE ATTACK ON HIS HOUSE, WILLIAM B. Phillips hastened to the federal authorities and swore out a complaint against Shelby, Nash, and other local white vigilantes. The affidavit charged them with violating the Enforcement Act by conspiring to prevent him from living and voting in Grant Parish—through such overt acts as the murder of White and the burning of the two men's house. Soon, two deputy U.S. marshals were on their way to Colfax with arrest warrants.

The marshals would need muscle, but with no federal troops available, the only possible military support was Warmoth's state militia. A new company had just been formed in Colfax, under a U.S. Army veteran by the name of William Ward. And Ward was like no other military officer the Red River Valley had ever seen: he was black.

William Ward was born a slave in Charleston, South Carolina, in 1840. His master sold him as a teenager to a man from Richmond, Virginia, who employed Ward as a "body servant"—his personal valet. Ward learned to read and write, and acquired carpentry skills. In slavery's hierarchy, he ranked above the field hands, and that conferred a certain dignity. A fellow slave who met Ward at a Richmond hotel in 1859 recalled him as "quite a sporting man and proud fellow" who "liked to play cards."

As the Civil War raged across Virginia, Ward escaped to the Union's Fortress Monroe in Hampton, a hundred miles east of Richmond. On January 10, 1864, he enlisted in the First United States Colored Cavalry Regiment. Ward rose to the rank of sergeant and saw some action in Virginia. But for the most part his war service consisted of occupation duty in Portsmouth, where he served from August 1864 until a couple of months after Lee's surrender. The twenty-four-year-old cavalryman rode through the conquered town, five feet ten inches tall and striking in his blue uniform with yellow sergeant's chevron. Colored women noticed. But the girl who caught Ward's eye was a twelve-year-old, known simply as Sarah, who lived across the street from his camp. They met when he asked her to wash his uniform one day, and Ward kept young Sarah as his mistress until June 10, 1865, when the army sent his unit to Brazos Santiago, Texas, on a remote island near the mouth of the Rio Grande.

In February 1866, the army disbanded Ward's unit, and he went back to Virginia. One night in Portsmouth, Ward got into a barroom brawl, which ended when someone smashed him on the forehead with a brick.

He reeled over to Sarah's house for help but found her married to one of his friends—and nursing a three-month-old baby. The little girl was, in fact, Ward's child, but neither he nor Sarah could admit that. Sarah dressed Ward's wound, and he departed for Richmond.

There, he worked as a carpenter and met a mulatto woman, Mary Staves. Ward moved in with her, but the arrangement was fraught with potential embarrassment as long as Sarah and her baby were close at hand. In October 1867, Ward reenlisted as a private in the U.S. Army, which sent him to Ship Island, Mississippi, about sixty miles east of New Orleans in the Gulf of Mexico. Mary came with him.

At the remote fort, Ward contracted tuberculosis and began coughing up blood. TB didn't kill him, but it did get him a medical discharge from the army. On June 5, 1868, he hobbled out of the fort on crutches, accompanied by Mary. Going back to Virginia was not an option. They caught a steamer for New Orleans and stayed about a year; but in the summer of 1869, cholera and yellow fever were once again epidemic in the Crescent City. Ward was plagued by shortness of breath and joint pain, and a doctor told him to find somewhere more healthful to live. Other than Virginia, the only place he had any connections was Grant Parish, where the Negro parish surveyor, also an ex-soldier, was a friend of a friend.

By the time he got to Colfax, probably early in 1870, William Ward was about thirty years old. He had dark, chocolate brown skin, and his forehead was creased by a deep scar, three inches long—a souvenir of the brawl in Portsmouth. Despite his illness, he was imposing, with a powerful personality that impressed blacks and scared whites. "In his face he bears the indications of all the worst qualities of his race and none of the better," a white supremacist would later write. A Republican mixed-race member of the state legislature described Ward more objectively as "a man of a peculiar disposition, brave and determined, a good man."

By early 1871, Warmoth was once again fine-tuning the racial and ideological balance of the Grant Parish government. In January, he appointed Delos White to the vacant post of parish recorder, perhaps to mend fences with him and Phillips and their supporters, who had demonstrated strength at the polls in 1870. On April 29, 1871, Warmoth also removed two white conservatives from the police jury. He replaced one of them with a moderate white Republican who had previously served as sheriff. The other spot went to Ward, who probably came to Warmoth's attention through his friend the former Grant Parish surveyor.

Warmoth offset Ward on the police jury with one of Jim Hadnot's neighbors and friends, a planter by the name of William J. Cruikshank. Born in 1826 in Kent County, Maryland, Bill Cruikshank had been brought to the Red River Valley by his parents long before the Civil War. The family made a fortune in the rich alluvial soil. Bill Cruikshank's brother, forty-year-old Andrew, a druggist and planter in Alexandria, had owned dozens of slaves before the war, and though they were free now, his land was still worth fifteen thousand dollars. Bill also planted cotton, on a tract of land which, in Grant Parish, was second in size only to the Calhoun estate. Neither he nor Andrew fought in the war, probably because they were too old. But what Bill Cruikshank lacked in actual military experience he made up in attitude. A stout, bearded fellow, he liked to ride around on a white mare, armed with a shotgun.

Cruikshank and two other white supremacists on the police jury wasted no time in reacting. On July 3, 1871, they voted Ward and Warmoth's other appointee off the body, citing a provision of state law that required all police jurors to have been residents of the parish for at least two consecutive years. The remaining three white police jurors then elected Cruikshank president of the police jury.

But it was not so easy to outflank Henry Clay Warmoth. In mid-1871, he was ready to expand his fledgling state militia to the countryside, where it was arguably most needed as the state headed toward the 1872 election. The Warmoth administration chose Grant Parish as one of the first new recruitment points. In apparent retaliation for the ouster of Ward from the police jury, Warmoth installed him as the commanding officer of Company A, Sixth Infantry Regiment, Louisiana State Militia, headquartered in Colfax.

William Ward became Captain Ward. He recruited two lieutenants, eleven noncommissioned officers, and seventy-two privates. One lieutenant was a former political ally of Willie Calhoun; the other was one of Ward's army buddies from Ship Island. Every member of the unit was colored. Ward began parading and drilling his men.

WARMOTH KNEW THAT SENDING ARMED NEGROES AFTER DELOS WHITE'S KILLERS could inflame the white population. The U.S. marshals were part of the Custom House apparatus, and, by this point, any cooperation with the Custom House was distasteful to the governor. But given the gravity of the crime and the threat to order it represented, the governor had little choice but to lend the marshals Ward's company. In October 1871, Warmoth had his militia chief, James Longstreet, send Ward about ninety Enfield rifles—surplus weapons that had been supplied to Louisiana by the War Department. But Longstreet attached orders telling Ward that he was to keep them stored unless he had specific permission to take them out. For now, the only purpose for which Ward was authorized to use the guns was to help arrest the murderers of Delos White.

The marshals and Ward's freshly armed militia quickly snapped up Alfred Shelby and Christopher Columbus Nash, along with four coconspirators. Rushing to the arrested men's defense, Thomas C. Manning of Alexandria, the prewar Louisiana Supreme Court justice in whose law office William B. Phillips had once studied, came up with a legal strategy to nullify the arrests. He would take the case to a sympathetic local judge and get him to declare the federal warrants invalid.

On Monday morning, October 23, John W. Osborn, a conservative Republican state district judge whose jurisdiction encompassed Grant, Rapides, and Natchitoches parishes, gaveled court to order in the old Calhoun stable at Colfax. Ward, accompanied by Phillips, marched the prisoners in, their boots scuffling over the floorboards. Judge Osborn examined Manning's petition for a writ of habeas corpus and then squinted at the arrest warrants, which were presented to him by Phillips. Osborn called William Ward to testify. The militia captain brought a chair to the front of the room and slammed it down next to the judge, then sat with his arms folded across his chest. He answered Manning's questions testily, explaining that everything he had done was pursuant to an order from Longstreet, who was in turn acting under the instructions of the U.S. commissioner in New Orleans. That wasn't good enough for Osborn. As Manning had hoped, he claimed jurisdiction of the case and declared that he would deal with it right there in Colfax.

Manning rose to address the court, but at that very moment, the steamboat *Right Way* came into view, approaching the landing at Colfax en route to New Orleans. A deputy U.S. marshal rushed into the little courtroom, demanding custody of the prisoners so that he could take them on board. The judge refused to give them up—whereupon Ward called in his militia and took the six defendants away at bayonet point. "This is an outrage on the dignity of the court," Osborn spluttered. "Damn the court!" Ward replied. Soon, Shelby, Nash, and the others were behind bars in New Orleans.

Word of Ward's performance quickly spread, and Nash's white allies responded. The brother of one of the whites arrested by Ward began openly gathering men and guns, threatening to hijack the *Right Way* and liberate the prisoners. There was also talk of a frontal assault on Ward's militia, to crush it once and for all. Neither of those threats materialized. But the night riders busied themselves in other ways. On October 24, "the Grant Parish safety committee" left a note in the front yard of a prominent Northern-born Republican, Jules Lemeraux, who lived near

Montgomery. "You must leave this parish by November 1," it read. Lemeraux tried to remain. But each night after the deadline, he heard prowlers outside his doors. He fled to New Orleans on November 4, writing later, "[I feared] I would meet the fate of Captain White, or that I would wake some night with a blazing roof over my head."

Undaunted, Ward continued pursuing dozens of whites suspected of participating in the attack on the Phillips-White home in September. On the night of Saturday, November 25, Ward's men clashed with a group of whites wearing Ku Klux Klan regalia. After an exchange of fire, the militia killed one of the whites and captured another. When they removed the dead man's hood, they saw that he was Jeff Yawn. Their prisoner was John Bullock, Jim Yawn's old Mississippi cavalry comrade. Under interrogation, Bullock admitted that he had been a member of the mob that murdered Delos White. He fingered Nash as the triggerman in White's death and confirmed that whites in the area had organized a secret society, complete with passwords and signs, whose purpose was to kill or expel leading Republicans and prevent blacks from voting. This secret society, Bullock revealed, had 360 members—a figure which, if accurate, would represent more than half of all adult white men in Grant Parish.

To Grant Parish's whites, Ward's counterattack was a "reign of terror." White emissaries from Grant Parish and neighboring Rapides Parish, including Nash's defense lawyers, made sure that Warmoth and Longstreet knew that the state militia was out of control up in the Red River Valley, and demanded that they stop it.

On November 2, Warmoth ordered two white militia colonels to visit Colfax to "investigate and report the facts connected with outrages alleged to have been committed in burning the house of W. B. Phillips, Parish Judge, and at the same time killing Mr. D. W. White." Once they reached Grant Parish, however, Warmoth's investigators spent most of their time hearing about the alleged depredations of Ward and his militia, and duly conveyed the charges to New Orleans. "Reports have reached us," Longstreet later wrote, "that the men of [Ward's] company have been parading with their arms in a semi-military organization, committing deeds highly prejudicial to good order and to the general interests of the community at large."

For Warmoth, the aggressive actions of Ward's militia company—though assisted by federal officials and arguably authorized by the governor himself—threatened the precarious political and racial balance he was constantly trying to maintain. Moreover, this was probably a good time to do a favor for the Democrats, to help dissuade them from joining the Custom House plot against the governor.

Warmoth ordered Longstreet to rein in Ward. The militia commander sent an officer to Colfax in early December, apparently to get Ward to demobilize quietly. When Ward refused, Longstreet issued a "special order" on December 11, 1871, claiming the governor never authorized Ward's campaign and that Ward had "armed and paraded his company in violation of the laws of the state and the orders governing the State Militia." Still, it took time to bring Ward to heel. As of late December, his troops, aided by federal deputy marshals, were still making arrests in Grant Parish. Finally, Longstreet suspended Ward from the militia, placed him under arrest, and pledged to pursue criminal charges against him. The Negro militia's "reign of terror" was over.

AS U.S. ATTORNEY, JAMES BECKWITH HANDLED THE PROSECUTION OF SHELBY, Nash, and their friends. The first step was a hearing before a U.S. commissioner, who would decide if there was enough evidence to justify holding the men without bail. Then there would be a grand jury investigation and, if indictments were issued, a trial in New Orleans's federal court.

The bail hearing began November 10. William B. Phillips told of the "secret hostility" that Shelby harbored against him and White, and described the awful raid in the predawn hours of September 25, 1871, in which his friend was gunned down and their home put to the torch. Four colored witnesses, two of whom took the stand wearing the blue uniforms of Ward's militia company, backed up his story. A militiaman told of inhaling the odor of coal oil, and of seeing Delos White lying at the doorway of his house with "fire falling in on him." A worker on Phillips's cotton farm testified to Shelby's threats against Phillips; he told of hiding in the bushes near the scene of the crime, from where he saw Nash and Shelby in the crowd of armed men.

Witnesses for the defense, white and colored, contradicted them on every point. George Scarborough, who shared his house in Colfax with Nash, swore that Nash had been with him all night. A local woman made the same claim with regard to Sheriff Shelby. These obvious lies were not necessarily a problem for Beckwith; he well knew that the Knights of the White Camellia swore to protect one another, even to the point of committing perjury—and that Negroes could be bribed or intimidated to testify in favor of white supremacists.

More troubling was defense testimony by Henry Kearson, Grant Parish's black Republican member of the state house of representatives. A minister and ex–Calhoun slave, Kearson was born in 1816 on Willie

Calhoun's great-grandfather William Smith's South Carolina plantation. Kearson liked Willie Calhoun, who had at least tried to correct his family's past abuses. Nowadays, Kearson saw politics as a path to patronage, which, to him, seemed of greater tangible benefit to his race than William Phillips's grand talk of revolution.

As a Custom House loyalist, Kearson would have understood that it was his duty to help them curry favor with the Democrats, so as to thwart Warmoth. Possibly for that purpose, he told the court that race relations in Grant Parish were "peaceable," and that he "[did] not think there [was] any political meaning in this affair of the burning of Judge Phillips' house." This was crucial since an Enforcement Act case against the killers would hinge on showing that they interfered with constitutionally protected civil and political rights. To make sure there was no confusion, Kearson added, "I have heard the colored people in the parish complain of the Radical people and the militia that they will not leave them alone, trying to get them in trouble."

Beckwith was doing his best to stay out of political quarrels. The defendants were pretty plainly guilty, but they had managed to produce enough witnesses—truthful or not—to generate some reasonable doubt. Not only was Beckwith politically cautious; he was, above all, a scrupulous lawyer. He liked to say that he would prosecute his own brother if he thought his duty required it. By the same token, Beckwith regarded it as a matter of principle never to prosecute anyone if he didn't think he could convince a jury of the defendant's guilt beyond a reasonable doubt.

Beckwith implied his misgivings by declining to present rebuttal witnesses after the defense case, and by resting his case without making a closing argument. On November 15, 1871, the commissioner dismissed the charges against one defendant and granted three others bail. Only Alfred Shelby and Christopher Columbus Nash would remain in custody. There was enough evidence against these two alleged ringleaders to keep them locked up pending a full investigation by a grand jury.

THE CUSTOM HOUSE'S PLAN TO UNSEAT WARMOTH WENT SMOOTHLY AT FIRST. When the Louisiana Senate tried to meet on January 1, 1872, it had to adjourn for lack of a quorum because three Democratic senators and eleven anti-Warmoth Republicans were on *The Wilderness*. As for the Louisiana House, on January 2 it elected George Carter, the Custom House's man, as Speaker by a vote of 49–45. This presaged a similar margin in favor of impeachment when the house reassembled the next day.

At that point, however, Warmoth went to work twisting arms—and, undoubtedly, greasing palms. When the house returned the next day, it voted 49–46 to undo its vote for George Carter. Carter was able to keep the Speaker's chair only with the aid of armed thugs who appeared on the dais to defend him from a rush of Warmoth men.

Now the Custom House Republicans panicked, asking for U.S. Army troops to "preserve order." On January 4, as the local army commander weighed the request, the Custom House induced four state legislators, including the ubiquitous Henry Kearson, to swear out a criminal complaint against Warmoth, Pinchback, three pro-Warmoth state senators, and eighteen pro-Warmoth members of the house—all for supposedly conspiring to "deprive the representatives of the general assembly of the State of Louisiana . . . of their rights, privileges and immunities as such under the Constitutions both of the state of Louisiana and of the United States," in violation of the Enforcement Act. The idea was to get them sent to jail and, while they were there, have the remaining house members impeach Warmoth.

But the Custom House Republicans had not reckoned with Beckwith. He had too much respect for the true purposes of the Enforcement Act to let anyone abuse it for this one. He declined to oppose bail for Warmoth and his men, and by 1:30 p.m.—two hours after their arrest—Warmoth was back on the street, rallying the legislature and ordering the state militia to fend off Carter's armed backers. Warmoth took time to send a tart telegram to Washington, demanding to know where President Grant stood. Sheepishly, the president replied that the Custom House's behavior was "extraordinary" and would be "investigated."

Grant refused to help the Custom House plot with troops. And early on January 5, Amos Akerman, in one of his last acts as attorney general, cabled Beckwith, telling him to "keep the legal process of the United States from being abused for political purposes. Collision with the state government must be avoided, if possible." This gave the U.S. attorney authority—and political cover—to do what he thought was right anyway. Two more times, on January 5 and 6, the Custom House tried to have Warmoth and his supporters in the house of representatives arrested. Both times, Beckwith thwarted the plans. By the third week of January, it was clear Warmoth had weathered the crisis. On January 20, a quorum of the senate met and reaffirmed his appointment of Pinchback as lieutenant governor.

As calm returned, Beckwith was able to convene the grand jury proceedings against Alfred Shelby, Christopher Columbus Nash, and their fellow defendants. But both he and U.S. district judge Edward H. Durell, a New Hampshire–born Republican who was supervising the case, were mindful of Attorney General Akerman's instructions. Also fresh in their memories was the spectacle, so deeply embarrassing to the president of the United States, created by the Custom House's clumsy attempt to manipulate the Enforcement Act. In addition, Akerman had recently adopted a policy of selective prosecution toward white terrorism, because the Justice Department already had its hands full with the mass trial of Klansmen in South Carolina. Durell instructed the grand jury to treat the evidence against the defendants skeptically; on February 1, Beckwith consented to release Shelby and Nash on bail.

On February 5, 1872, Shelby and Nash faced Durell and pledged to return to face the charges if and when they were put on trial. At their side stood Jim Hadnot, who was there to post a $1,500 bond for each man. Soon, Shelby and Nash were on their way back to Grant Parish.

Given Akerman's instructions, the political crisis still swirling in the city, and his own objection to prosecuting less-than-ironclad cases, Beckwith probably considered the result a tolerable one. He would have abundant reason to regret it later.

WITH DELOS WHITE'S MURDERERS ONCE AGAIN FREE TO ROAM THEIR COMMU-nity, the Grant Parish Republicans grew fearful. They and Republicans from Rapides Parish sent a delegation to Longstreet in New Orleans, pleading for his help in getting U.S. Army troops sent to the Red River Valley. "Armed organizations, secret in their character and purposes," had simply grown too strong for them, the delegates explained. Longstreet conveyed their concerns, and the army saw enough merit in them to send twenty-one soldiers to Colfax. But after less than two weeks, during which the secret "armed organizations" kept a low profile, the troops withdrew. Their orders from New Orleans noted simply that they were "no longer required."

The final blow came on June 28, 1872, when the Louisiana state militia issued its decision in William Ward's case. There would be no criminal trial for the former captain of Company A. But Longstreet cashiered him. In fact, Longstreet dissolved the Grant Parish unit—albeit not without an official statement from the commander in chief, Governor Warmoth, who said he wanted to "thank them for the services which they have rendered to the state, and to commend them for the good discipline which they have always maintained, and the promptness and alacrity with which they have obeyed all orders."

William B. Phillips resigned as parish judge and fled once again to New Orleans. The remaining Republicans of Grant Parish, white and black, would have to fend for themselves.

CHAPTER FOUR

WAR

On the evening of January 5, 1872, Henry Clay Warmoth summoned James Beckwith to the Mechanics' Institute on Baronne Street, a block west of Canal. The thick-walled brick building, its exterior painted and stuccoed to look like granite, had been pressed into service as the Louisiana statehouse, despite the fact that the New Orleans Massacre had occurred there in 1866. Warmoth had an office on the first floor, while the state house of representatives met in a large assembly room on the second floor. When he arrived, Beckwith found the governor holed up with his legislative allies amid clouds of tobacco smoke and an equally thick ambience of intrigue. Warmoth was practically spitting with fury. He told Beckwith that the Custom House's warrants for his arrest were part of an assassination plot: the Custom House had actually been seeking an excuse to march him out of the building—and through a lynch mob. As proof, he thrust the previous day's *New Orleans Bee* at Beckwith, pointing to a front-page ad from a violent white supremacist group known as "76," calling on members to assemble a block north of the institute.

After this, there could be no reconciliation between Warmoth and his intraparty rivals. Once he had survived the crisis, politically and physically, Warmoth's thoughts turned instead to revenge, as he publicly voiced his contempt for the Custom House Republicans and their leader. "My friend Jim Casey is a clever fellow," Warmoth said. "He hasn't sense enough to be a bad fellow. A man to be a bad fellow must have some character—he hasn't any."

Horace Greeley's Liberal Republican movement would be the instrument of the Louisiana governor's vengeance. In May 1872, Warmoth led one hundred Louisianans to the Liberal Republican national convention in Cincinnati, which nominated Greeley for president. By September, he had struck a bargain with the very Democrats who had joined the Custom House Republicans to oust him a few months before. He agreed to stand aside as governor and use his power over the state electoral apparatus to ensure victory for the Democrat John McEnery, a forty-year-old lawyer and cotton planter from Monroe, who was known as one of Louisiana's fieriest Negro-baiters. In return, the Democrats would send Warmoth to Washington as a U.S. senator.

This "Fusionist" alliance was opposed by a coalition of the Custom House and the Negro followers of P. B. S. Pinchback, Warmoth's lieutenant governor. Pinchback, despite his admiration for Warmoth, simply could not support a deal with the likes of McEnery; that would be racial betrayal. With the backing of both the Custom House and Pinchback, U.S. senator William Pitt Kellogg became the Republican candidate for governor.

GRANT PARISH QUICKLY PRODUCED A LOCAL "FUSIONIST" TICKET PARALLEL TO THE statewide one. The Fusionists were counting on the support of all the ex-Confederates who were once again eligible to vote and hold office—thanks to the constitutional amendment Warmoth had sponsored while courting whites in 1870. In addition to hard-line white supremacists, the new movement attracted "respectable" conservative whites who had earlier answered Warmoth's call to join the Republican Party. William Ward scared such men. At the other end of the political spectrum, white supremacists demanded that moderates define themselves. "Conservative Republican is the new and long name, now in vogue, for a good Radical," the *Louisiana Democrat* announced on December 27, 1871. And with hundreds of white vigilantes operating around Grant Parish, it was not safe to be a Radical.

By the end of September, the Grant Parish Fusionists had their ticket. Jim Hadnot, the candidate for state representative, headed the list. Running for judge was lawyer Alphonse Cazabat, a former Republican who had been born in France in 1828, served briefly in the Confederate army as a lieutenant—and represented Christopher Columbus Nash before the federal authorities in New Orleans. Nash was the candidate for sheriff. Having rid the parish of the two men whites most detested, Delos White and William Phillips, he had become a hero to his race; the man with the black beard and slouch hat was tough, and, it seemed, untouchable.

William Ward was as much of a hero to many Negroes as Nash was to whites. With the help of his closest colored friend, a fellow former soldier from Ship Island named Eli H. Flowers, Ward now asserted himself within the Grant Parish Republican Club. The Republicans picked him to run as their candidate for the state house of representatives in the November 1872 election. Despite Ward's own radical reputation, however, his political group was hardly in favor of black power. Their official slogan was "Honesty, Justice and Equality to all men before the law, regardless of past differences of race or color." And though White and Phillips were gone, several white men played important roles in Ward's club, among them Thomas Montfort Wells, the son of former governor J. Madison Wells, and Willie Calhoun.

But whereas the Fusionists were fully united behind their ticket, the Republicans were divided, between those aligned with Ward and supporters of Henry Kearson, who had sided with Ward's enemies during the court case in New Orleans. Arguments grew bitter. On the Fourth of July, 1872, some colored men drew guns on Samuel E. Cuney, a black Colfax shopkeeper and postmaster who backed Kearson. Two days later, Ward's group tried to smooth over the differences, approving a statement condemning the incident as a "violation of the true spirit of Republicanism," but Kearson refused the olive branch. The dispute simmered until September 1872, when a delegation of state Republican leaders came to Colfax and essentially ordered the Grant Parish party to unite behind Ward.

The resulting Republican ticket was headed by Ward for state representative. But he was the only Negro nominee for a major office. The candidate for sheriff was the same moderate white Republican with whom Governor Warmoth had replaced Delos White in 1870. For judge, the Republicans nominated a sixty-five-year-old Georgia-born farmer who had lived in the valley for years. The candidate for clerk was a Delaware-born "carpetbagger" who was on good terms with many of the "respectable" whites who had defected to the Fusionists. All things considered, it was one of the most moderate tickets the Grant Parish Republicans had yet fielded.

THE 1872 CAMPAIGN PROCEEDED RELATIVELY PEACEFULLY ACROSS THE STATE. Maybe there was so little violence because the Fusionists were devoting their energy to rigging the vote. Working through parish registrars whom Warmoth had picked from the ranks of local Democratic organizations, the Fusionists made sure that the voter rolls included as many whites as possible and a minimum number of colored men. A favorite ploy was to change the registration site without notifying colored voters; some registrars demanded that elderly Negroes prove that they were over twenty-one years old, not easy for those who had no birth certificates because they were born in slavery. At Warmoth's instructions, his state election supervisors kept federal election monitors, appointed by the Custom House, away from the ballot boxes on Election Day.

In Grant Parish, a white plantation owner in the Montgomery area circulated among his colored labor force before the election, threatening to expel all Republican voters from the homes they rented on his land. Similar threats were reported elsewhere in the parish. On Election Day itself, the Fusionists tampered with the ballots. When Thomas Montfort Wells and Eli Flowers asked to inspect a suspicious-looking ballot box, white state officials snatched it away. A Fusionist kept it inside his house overnight. When the box emerged the next day, it had a hole in the side through which ballots had apparently been stuffed.

Grant Parish's Fusionists claimed a landslide victory. By their count, McEnery beat Kellogg in the parish 514 to 405, Hadnot beat Ward 522 to 338, Nash won the race for sheriff 489 to 359, and Cazabat was elected judge by a vote of precisely 523 to 404. These "returns" were almost certainly fabricated; to the extent they were accurate, they reflected illegal intimidation of Negro voters. Registered colored voters outnumbered whites 776 to 630 in Grant Parish. In the 1870 election, which no one challenged, the Republican ticket had captured 656 votes. How could the Republican vote suddenly have plunged by more than 250? The defections of conservative white Republicans accounted for a small fraction of the difference. Only fraud and intimidation could explain the rest.

Similar chicanery all over Louisiana led to the debacle of dueling Fusionist and Republican vote counts, followed by competing legislatures and governors, and, ultimately, the failed Fusionist coup in New Orleans on March 5. As part of that bizarre struggle, Warmoth's returning board declared Grant Parish's Fusionists elected on December 4, and Warmoth issued commissions to "Judge" Alphonse Cazabat and "Sheriff" Christopher Columbus Nash later the same day. On January 2, 1873, the Fusionists walked into the courthouse and took their oaths of office, without which their commissions would not be valid—then sent the documents to "Governor" McEnery in New Orleans.

William Pitt Kellogg countered. He, too, began filling parish offices around the state—including the offices in Grant Parish. On January 17 and 18, Kellogg named the entire Republican slate of candidates as the new local government for Grant Parish and issued them commissions. None of these officials took the oath of office, however, or even entered the courthouse. Nash had the keys—and refused to hand them over. The Republicans backed off, and Nash and Cazabat remained in control, holding court in the old stable right through the month of February.

WELL BEFORE THE FAILED MARCH 5 COUP, JIM HADNOT HAD FIGURED OUT THAT McEnery might well never be governor. This apparently prompted Hadnot to engage in some discreet conversations with Kellogg about the political future of Grant Parish. In early March, he returned from New Orleans, where he had been taking part in the Fusionist "legislature." He called a meeting of his political allies in a Colfax law office and revealed to them that Kellogg had promised to recognize the Grant Parish Fusionist slate. It was an extraordinary claim: after struggling for months against what he insisted was massive Fusionist election fraud, the Republican had offered to deliver at least some of the fruits of victory to his enemies.

Yet, given Kellogg's character, Hadnot's story was plausible. Born on December 8, 1830, in Orwell, Vermont, a sheep-raising community on Lake Champlain, William Pitt Kellogg had migrated to Illinois as a teenager with his family. He became a lawyer, an early adherent of the new Republican Party, and a close associate of Abraham Lincoln, who gave him a series of high-level federal appointments. The sweetest of these was customs collector in New Orleans, a post to which Lincoln named him on the day before his fateful visit to Ford's Theater. As collector, Kellogg faithfully carried out President Andrew Johnson's orders to staff the Custom House with Democrats and conservative Republicans. Meanwhile, Kellogg bought railroad stock and purchased fifteen prime lots on St. Charles Street for about thirty thousand dollars. He spent as little time as possible in New Orleans, escaping North during the malarial summers. In 1868, the new Republican-led state legislature sent him to Washington as a U.S. senator.

Kellogg was an able administrator who would eventually reduce both Louisiana's debt and its tax burden. But he utterly lacked Warmoth's charisma. He was a thin man with fine features, a bulbous forehead, and a peculiar pair of eyelids that always seemed just about to drop shut. He also lacked Warmoth's cunning, though he seems not to have realized this. "It is really amusing to see Kellogg's ways that are dark and tricks that are vain," a political rival wrote. "I breathe the very air of his Jesuitism." Kellogg had a pompous habit of claiming that he did not really desire power but was compelled by duty, or the people's will, or higher principle, to seek it.

By March 1873, Kellogg was somewhat overwhelmed by the task of organizing his adopted state; he thought of himself, he said later, as "warding off blows." With the help of the U.S. Army and the state militia, he maintained control of New Orleans. But in the rural parishes, where McEneryites seemed to have a monopoly on violence, he was willing, almost eager, to practice appeasement. For Kellogg, buying off Jim Hadnot, one of the McEnery "legislature's" purported members, could be especially useful.

After listening to Hadnot, the Grant Parish Fusionists decided to find out if they could close the deal that the governor and Hadnot had sketched. They appointed two Colfax lawyers, William R. Rutland and Wilson L. Richardson, as a delegation to New Orleans. As former local Republican leaders, Rutland and Richardson were logical ambassadors to Kellogg.

In mid-March, they arrived in New Orleans and found Kellogg at the St. Louis Hotel in the French Quarter. Newly renovated, the immense building opened onto St. Louis Street, where its marble peristyle, topped with a huge illuminated clock, was one of the most imposing landmarks in the city. The state used a suite there as an official residence for the governor. As Kellogg listened, the two Grant Parish lawyers reminded him of what they understood to be his pledge to Hadnot. They explained the agitated state of affairs in their home parish, the concerns of its white citizens, and their belief that only the Fusionists who were currently exercising the powers of local government, especially Nash as sheriff, could guarantee peace and quiet.

They understood that Kellogg had issued commissions to the Republican office seekers in mid-January. But that was no obstacle, the two lawyers explained. Except for Judge Robert C. Register, the Republican who did manage to file his oath of office to Kellogg on March 1, none of the Republicans had yet finished the required paperwork. Thus, none of them was technically in office, and the governor would not actually have to fire his loyalists. He could simply issue new commissions to the Fusionists. They would then be sworn in, and all would be well.

The governor nodded in agreement. "I had it in view to divide the offices, so as to satisfy the people of that parish," he later explained. Register would indeed have to stay on as judge, Kellogg said, and the two lawyers assented. But he promised Rutland and Richardson everything else they asked for. He would commission not only Nash but also the Fusionist candidates for tax collector, clerk, recorder, and most of the police jury. Kellogg even agreed to make Jim Yawn a constable.

In short, Kellogg pledged to put the murderers of Delos White in charge of enforcing the law in Grant Parish. He told Rutland and Richardson that he would have the commissions made out and sent to Colfax; by March 18, the documents were ready and sitting on his desk, awaiting his signature.

William Ward had traveled from Colfax to New Orleans to attend the session of the legislature which began on January 6. He lingered through the battle of March 5 and the conclusion of the legislative session on March 7. It is not clear how Ward found out about Kellogg's plan amid all the chaos. But when he did, he erupted. The new governor, a fellow Republican for whose election Ward and his comrades had labored at the risk of their lives, had offered up Grant Parish to the men who had killed Delos White and tried to steal the local election. How could Kellogg do such a thing?

Ward rushed to the St. Louis Hotel. He told the governor the true significance of what he had done, and demanded that he undo it. Apparently, Kellogg, who had been in Washington at the time of White's murder, knew nothing about the crime or the charges against Nash and Yawn. He listened with what must have been annoyance and embarrassment as Ward filled him in. Realizing his error, but not immediately admitting it, he agreed to reconsider. But first he would give the Fusionists one more chance to argue their case and, perhaps, negotiate a settlement. He asked for another meeting, this time with both Republicans and Fusionists present.

On March 20, Rutland and Richardson returned to the governor's suite, where they were met by Ward, his sidekick Eli Flowers, and William B. Phillips, who had been in New Orleans since fleeing Grant Parish in April 1872. Kellogg gave each side a chance to speak, but the meeting degenerated into a shouting match. The governor told Rutland and Richardson that he would not, upon reflection, commission Nash as sheriff, though he apparently offered the Fusionists other offices. The Fusionist lawyers were not interested. It was either Nash or disaster, they insisted. When the governor repeated his position, they stormed out, warning of bloodshed in Grant Parish.

The way was now clear for William Ward's Republicans to assert their claim to power in Grant Parish. They already had the commissions that Kellogg issued back in January. But they still needed to submit their oaths of office. Ward and Flowers would have to race back to Colfax to make that happen. Taking their leave of the governor, they boarded the next available steamboat. By March 24, they were home.

THE GRANT PARISH COURTHOUSE HAD CHANGED A BIT SINCE THE DAYS WHEN IT housed Meredith Calhoun's horses and mules. Now, instead of being a place where beasts of burden shuffled among the hay, it was divided into a rough courtroom and offices for the judge, sheriff, and other officials. The smell of manure had yielded to the musty odor of piled-up documents and thick leather-bound books: property deeds; marriage, birth, and death certificates; the minutes of tedious police jury meetings.

But it was still basically the structure it had always been: a one-story whitewashed rectangle, about seventy-five feet long by twenty-five feet wide, made of bricks pressed from the Red River alluvium by Calhoun's slaves. The short side of the rectangle faced the river, which was about eighty yards away, over a high berm or levee that had also been built before the war by Calhoun's slaves. There was a hayloft above the ceiling and a crawl space under the floor. The roof consisted of overlapping cypress shingles. There were doors on each end and a couple of windows on each side, with wooden shutters. A grassy field lay all around.

To govern Grant Parish, you had to control this building. Once Ward and Flowers had returned home, the Grant Parish Republicans' first move was to assert control over the former Calhoun stable. Robert C. Register went to see Christopher Columbus Nash. Register informed Nash that he, not Alphonse Cazabat, was going to be the parish judge, and that Nash would have to yield the sheriff's office to the Republican candidate, Daniel Wesley Shaw.* He asked Nash to hand over the keys to the courthouse. Nash, who knew about Rutland and Richardson's trip to see Kellogg, glared at Register with his black eyes and refused.

Late at night on March 25, after everyone in Colfax had gone to bed, a group of Republicans, led by Register and Shaw, crept toward the courthouse. They reached up to a window along its side and tore off one of the boards that served as shutters. Then they hoisted a small colored boy up through the hole. He hopped down to the floor, scurried to the front door, and opened it from the inside. The courthouse was now theirs, as, they believed, it should have been all along. The next day, the Republicans swore their oaths: Dan Shaw became sheriff, Charles Smith became recorder, and three men, Kindred J. Harvey, John B. McCoy, and Lewis Meekins, became police jurors. All of these men except Meekins were white. They promptly sent their oaths to the Kellogg administration in New Orleans, where the secretary of state filed them on March 29.

Fury and alarm consumed the Grant Parish Fusionists. On March 28, Hadnot, Nash, Cazabat, Richardson, and Rutland held an emergency meeting at Rutland's office in Colfax. They quickly concluded that they would retake the courthouse, by violence if necessary, and decided to ask white men to assemble, with their weapons, at the courthouse on April 1. Rutland dispatched messengers to carry the call, secretly, to white farms and stores across the parish. He took the message to Montgomery personally.

---

*Originally commissioned as parish clerk by Kellogg on January 17, Register had been promoted to judge by Kellogg in mid-February, when the previous candidate resigned.

The white supremacists received a huge and unexpected political gift a couple of days later, when a steamboat brought the March 27 edition of the *New Orleans Republican* to Colfax. The *Republican* was both a party sheet and the official journal of the state. Acts of the legislature, decrees of the governor, and other official documents appeared there first. On its March 27 front page was a list of Kellogg's recent appointments to parish offices. At the top of the list was the entire Grant Parish Fusionist slate, headed by "Sheriff" Christopher Columbus Nash.

It was an incredible blunder. Someone in Kellogg's office had mistakenly handed the *Republican* the tentative list of commissions Kellogg made out after his first meeting with Rutland and Richardson—but before his meeting with Ward. Rutland and the other Grant Parish Fusionists knew that the list was erroneous, because they had been at the March 20 meeting in New Orleans when Kellogg refused to appoint Nash. But now they could trumpet the *Republican* list as proof of their claim to power.

Then the Fusionists made a mistake of their own. Their plan to retake the courthouse relied on the element of surprise. But Jim Hadnot couldn't resist boasting about what he was going to do once he reached Colfax on April 1. Not only would he and his comrades reinstate the rightful officeholders, Hadnot announced to one of his Negro laborers, but he was going to personally hang William Ward and the rest of the Republican usurpers, too.

Colored men in Grant Parish had learned to take Jim Hadnot's threats seriously. The laborer rushed to warn Ward, who lived almost a dozen miles up the river in Colfax. On the evening of March 31, he found Ward in bed, suffering from one of his periodic tuberculosis-related illnesses. "Don't you know you are going to be hung tomorrow?" the laborer exclaimed. Ward immediately summoned Judge Robert Register, Sheriff Dan Shaw, Eli Flowers, and Willie Calhoun. They quickly agreed that the threat was real—and that they had to raise a force to meet it.

Register instructed Shaw to swear in a posse. Register, Shaw, and Flowers hurriedly wrote out commission papers, authorizing each "peace conservator" to protect not only the parish officers but also parish records inside the courthouse. At least two white Republicans signed oaths, along with Flowers. Then a white official hastened to the Smithfield Quarters, looking for colored men whom Ward and Calhoun had identified as good candidates for the posse. "Hadnot is coming to kill the colored people," he cried. "Get your gun and come to Colfax."

By the next morning, there were approximately two dozen armed men, most but not all black, guarding the courthouse. They carried shotguns or beat-up fieldpieces; one or two had pistols. No more than a few Negroes in the parish had military-type weapons, such as the muzzle-loading Enfield rifle which had also been standard issue in Ward's now-defunct militia. But at least the courthouse was no longer undefended. If Hadnot wanted it, he would have to fight.

At about 11:00 a.m. on April 1, Jim Hadnot rode into Colfax from the north, pausing three hundred yards from the courthouse at a store owned by a Negro merchant. Hadnot was dressed for battle, with his red sash around his waist, and his rosette pinned to his breast. A sword dangled from his belt, from which a pair of six-shooters jutted. But only Alphonse Cazabat and about fourteen other men, including Hadnot's nephew Johnnie and his sons Gillie, Luke, and Munch, were with him, carrying double-barreled shotguns. To their surprise, they were outnumbered by the courthouse defenders. Hadnot sat down, ordered some whiskey, and considered the situation.

Willie Calhoun had spent the previous night at a friend's place across the Red River in Rapides Parish. His influence in Grant Parish was waning a bit, as his financial situation worsened. In early 1871, Calhoun had defaulted on mortgages worth $15,000 that he had taken out to finance a new agricultural supply store for his Negro tenant farmers. New Orleans bankers were pursuing him in court, attempting to repossess part of the Calhoun estate. In July 1871, Olivia Williams, with William R. Rutland as her lawyer, sued Calhoun for $20,000, claiming he had broken a promise to marry her. Meanwhile, Negroes complained that he was overcharging them at his store. But he was still the richest man in the parish and to many people—himself no doubt included—a major force in local Republican politics. Now he limped into the store and greeted Alphonse Cazabat, whom he had known since before the war, suggesting to Cazabat that he and Register negotiate, using Calhoun as an intermediary. Cazabat replied that Calhoun could tell Register that he was going to get the courthouse back, by force if necessary. When Calhoun conveyed this to Register, he responded dismissively that Cazabat could have the judgeship if he showed him a commission from Kellogg.

While this quarrel proceeded, about sixteen men from Montgomery waited on the northern edge of Colfax. They had answered Rutland's call, but, unlike Hadnot's own squad, the Montgomery men had decided to come to Colfax carrying only sidearms. At about 2:00 p.m., having missed a planned rendezvous with Hadnot, two of the Montgomery men took their handguns and went into Colfax to see what was afoot. Nervously, they rode through the group of armed black men, who eyed them warily but did not disturb them as they passed between the river and the courthouse.

At Wilson L. Richardson's house, they found the Fusionist lawyer, a forty-two-year-old who had served in both the Confederate army and the Rapides Parish government during the war years, barricaded inside, with piles of guns and ammunition, and bars across the doors and windows. The Montgomery men next found Nash, along with Ruffin B. Walker, the Fusionist candidate for parish clerk. They were at the home of Nash's friend George Scarborough.

Though Richardson wanted to stay, Walker, Nash, and Scarborough decided that Colfax was no longer safe for them. The Montgomery men took Walker back to their town, while Nash and Scarborough saddled their horses and headed east, toward the piney woods. Along the way, they were stopped by a group of armed Negroes. One of the black men pointed a gun at Nash and Scarborough. But another Negro, an employee of Scarborough's, recognized his boss and knocked the gun away. Nash and Scarborough were allowed to escape.

Jim Hadnot knew nothing of this. He did realize, though, that it would only be a matter of time before the Republicans came looking for him. He flagged down the next available steamboat to Alexandria. William R. Rutland sent his wife and two children across the Red River to the home of a wealthy planter. They arrived in the evening, shaking like "an aspen leaf in a gale," as the planter's daughter would later recall. "I am crazy with fear," Rutland's wife gasped. Rutland himself stayed in his little white house in Colfax until about 6:00 p.m., when Ward and his men gave him safe passage across the river—on the condition that he leave empty-handed. Probably, they feared he would smuggle out documents from the courthouse. Already, the Republicans had discovered that books and a scal were missing. Reaching a friend's place on the Rapides Parish side of the Red, Rutland gave a vivid report on the "Negro riot," then borrowed a horse and rode to Montgomery, where his family had gone earlier. Fearing that the agitation among the Negroes of Colfax would spread, whites on the Rapides Parish side sank their ferryboats once the Rutlands were safely across.

FOR ALL THE VIOLENCE IN GRANT PARISH SINCE THE WAR, THERE WAS NOT A SINgle confirmed murder or assault by Negroes against whites. But on the night of April 1, 1873, the forbearance of the colored men began to fray. Several colored members of the posse sworn in by Shaw headed for

Rutland's house. Led by Lewis Meekins, they were probably looking for the missing seal and books. The lawyer's house would have been a likely place to stash them. If so, their search soon degenerated into an act of revenge against the leader of the recent Fusionist machinations.

The colored men broke through Rutland's door, brushing aside the two Negro servant women whom Rutland had left behind. They flung open Rutland's trunks, rifled his wife's wardrobe, turned over the furniture, helped themselves to food in the pantry, and took chickens from the coop outside. Inside one of the boxes they overturned was a macabre family keepsake: the tiny coffin containing the embalmed body of Rutland's daughter, who had died in infancy six years earlier. The men left it on the porch and went back to ransacking the rest of the house.

The next morning, Lewis Meekins and his men rode down to Hadnot's property. Hadnot's wife was there, but he was probably already in Alexandria. At Bill Cruikshank's place next door, a caretaker told them that Cruikshank, too, was gone. He had also fled to Alexandria, along with his wife and children. The colored posse searched his house, seizing guns, buckshot, and powder, along with five barrels of pork and a horse. Once they had left, sixteen women and children from Hadnot's extended family fled to the swamps, where they would spend the next two nights hiding, possibly even in some of the same places Meredith Calhoun's escaped slaves had secreted themselves decades earlier.

Meekins's actions troubled some Negroes in Colfax, especially backers of Henry Kearson, who had never liked William Ward or his friends. To them, the raid on Rutland's place was one of Ward's typical excesses—and a dangerous provocation to whites. O. J. Butler, the colored ex-parish surveyor and former U.S. Army soldier who had been Ward's initial connection in Grant Parish, was shocked when he came into Colfax on the morning of April 2 and saw Rutland's house. He accosted Eli Flowers and demanded that he punish those responsible, "to show there is no dirt on the Republican Party." Flowers was in no mood for second-guessing from a political rival—one with whom he had a personal feud based on what Butler considered Flowers's excessive interest in Butler's wife. Flowers pulled a gun and told Butler to get out of town within twenty-four hours.

The actions of Meekins and his patrol may have been violent, but they were not random. They were aimed at people likeliest to organize another attack against the courthouse. Ward was taking no chances; rather, he was thinking like a military man. At the same time that his men were out looking for the leaders of the local white supremacists, Ward tried to extend his little force's defensive perimeter. He sent men to stand guard on the roads into and out of Colfax, with orders to report any threatening movements. It amounted to a blockade against all white men trying to enter town. The Republicans sent out for more recruits from the Negro settlements around town.

Ward's concerns were not ill-founded. On the afternoon of April 2, Negroes spotted armed, mounted white men near Rockford, above the Smithfield Quarters. Robert Register mounted his horse and led a patrol from the courthouse through the quarters. They halted about 250 yards away from the white force and opened fire. The whites wheeled on their horses and shot back. But both sides were using shotguns; the weapons lacked the range or accuracy to do any damage. No one on either side was hurt, and the whites fled.

Militarily insignificant, the incident had an electrifying effect on the local Negro population. Fearing that the clash was only the first of many, Negroes began to flee toward Colfax, where their men, they thought, might be able to protect them. Dozens of men, women, and children raced from their cabins, grabbing their blankets, cooking pots, and whatever food they could lay their hands on, and headed down the dirt road toward the courthouse. By nightfall, there were about 150 colored people camped out on the open ground.

Wilson L. Richardson had doggedly remained in his house at Colfax, bunkered in with his elderly mother and sister. By April 2, as the village filled up with fearful colored people, his position was no longer tenable. That afternoon, a Negro man pushed his way through Richardson's barricaded door, shouting abuse and threatening to kill him. The lawyer, who was armed, cried out, and the man fled. After dark, Richardson, unable to sleep, heard the voice of a Negro man calling him to his front door. He didn't respond. Instead, he ran to the rear door. He heard the sound of gunfire. The man in his yard was shooting into the house.

A white Republican official rushed to the scene, trying to avoid a repetition of the raid on Rutland's house. He ordered three Negro deputies to guard the Richardson place until morning. But the Fusionist lawyer had gotten the hint. On April 3, Richardson and his family packed their things and left, crossing the river into Rapides Parish. O. J. Butler followed. Now the immediate vicinity of the courthouse belonged completely to Ward's Republicans.

BY THIS TIME, WILLIAM R. RUTLAND HAD MADE HIS WAY UP THE RED RIVER TO Montgomery. Born in Kentucky, Rutland was a thirty-seven-year-old Confederate veteran who settled in Lake Charles, Louisiana, after the war and then migrated to Colfax after the establishment of Grant Parish. He took the requisite oath renouncing his Confederate past, registered to vote as a Republican, and moved his family into a white house near the old Calhoun stable. Apparently, Rutland thought he could make a good career as a Republican lawyer in a Republican parish; as recently as August 1871, he had been secretary of the party's parish executive committee. But the growing influence of William Ward scared him, and he shifted his allegiance to Jim Hadnot. For two days after Rutland left Colfax on April 1, 1873, he wandered the streets of white-majority Montgomery, lamenting that his house had been sacked and he was a "ruined man." He and his family had made it across the river just a step ahead of a murderous black horde, he claimed. To this lurid yarn Rutland added the gruesome claim that the Negroes had desecrated his dead child.

Having thus inflamed white public opinion, Rutland pursued a new plan to regain power in Colfax. As a lawyer, it was natural for him to think in terms of legal process, and he came up with a scheme involving the courts. On April 4, he approached a conservative Republican justice of the peace in Montgomery whose claim to office was unquestioned because Kellogg had included him in his January list of appointees to parish offices. In the official's presence, Rutland swore out a criminal complaint against the men he accused of breaking into his house and stealing $2,500 in property.

The list included not only the people who actually had broken in—Lewis Meekins and his band of deputies—but also William Ward, Eli Flowers, Robert Register, and Willie Calhoun. None of these men had anything to do with ransacking Rutland's house. But that was immaterial. The point of Rutland's complaint was to get a warrant for their arrest and, more important, a posse to carry it out. It was a legal fig leaf for an armed counterattack on Ward and his men.

The justice of the peace signed the arrest warrant and deputized a Montgomery man to execute it. He, in turn, swore in a posse and headed downriver to Colfax on the afternoon of April 4. The posse didn't get very far. Just outside Colfax, they spotted some of William Ward's pickets. Everywhere they went, in fact, they saw armed Negroes, and they were not confident that they could fight through them. The men spurred their horses and returned to Montgomery.

On the morning of April 5, William Ward heard that a Negro who had remained behind at the Smithfield Quarters was missing. Ward's first thought was that the man had been taken out and killed by whites. Ward immediately ordered a patrol to check out the rumor. And he put one of his best men in charge of the mission: Benjamin L. "Levi" Allen.

A tenant farmer and one of the few colored men in Colfax who knew how to read and write, Allen had limited military experience: for a few weeks in 1871, he served as a recruiter for Ward's militia unit. But, probably because of that stint, Ward trusted him. In a field just beyond the Smithfield Quarters, Allen and his men saw about twenty armed and mounted white men in the distance. Any hostile presence so close to the quarters was dangerous. The cabins contained supplies, and women were shuttling between the courthouse and the quarters at night with food and blankets for the posse. Allen ordered his men to open fire; apparently surprised, the white patrol shot back, and a sharp skirmish ensued. It ended with no casualties on either side—but the whites once again retreated in haste. They left behind two pistols and saddlebags as they fled.

RUTLAND AND THE WHITE LEADERS OF MONTGOMERY GROPED FOR A NEW PLAN. Seemingly unaware of the fighting near the Smithfield Quarters, they agreed to make a new attempt to enforce their arrest warrant—this time through negotiation. They formed a four-man delegation and drafted what they called a proposal for peaceful resolution of the conflict. According to the document, all armed forces in Grant Parish, white and black, Fusionist and Republican, would immediately disband. All persons who had been driven from their homes would return without any reprisals, and "in future all political topics [would] be avoided in conversation and a more friendly and better feeling be cultivated between the two races." The only condition was that all of the alleged attackers of Rutland's house named in the arrest warrant would turn themselves in.

On the morning of April 5, the four delegates, who were unarmed or carrying only sidearms, headed for Colfax. Along the way, they linked up with Charles Smith, a white Republican parish official. He was a native of Montgomery, and the delegates knew him well. He offered to serve as an intermediary—sparing the men the risk of passing through Ward's pickets. He took their written proposal and rode to the courthouse, where he presented the document to Ward.

Ward eyed the offer, together with Flowers, Register, and others. It was basically a promise of peace in return for the surrender and decapitation of the Grant Parish Republican Party. The Republican leaders did not take the bait—but drafted a polite counteroffer. "We the undersigned pledge ourselves and the men under our control to cease all hostility towards the citizens of Montgomery and use all due politeness towards all citizens of Montgomery and vicinity while in Colfax and afford to them protection while in Colfax," it read. "We will not make any armed demonstration against the people of Montgomery . . . so long as they keep the peace themselves. If any of the citizens of Montgomery join Hadnot then this agreement is not in force any longer."

Leaving Ward—not known as a diplomat—behind, Charles Smith took Flowers and three other men of both races to a parley with the Montgomery delegation. They rode a mile north along the road between Colfax and Rockford, through the Smithfield Quarters, then halted in a field a few hundred yards above the Negro cabins. There, the two sides exchanged greetings. The Colfax group handed over their letter. The Montgomery men perused it. Discussions proceeded for a few minutes. Smith thought some sort of progress was possible.

And then, suddenly, Lewis Meekins rushed in—furious, brandishing his pistols. He jerked the reins of his horse, bringing the animal to an abrupt stop. Jesse McKinney was dead, he cried. Jesse McKinney was dead. White men had murdered him.

JESSE MCKINNEY HAD BEEN BORN IN ALABAMA IN 1834 AS A SLAVE TO WILLIAM Smith. In the years since emancipation, he and his wife, Laurinda, had supported themselves and five children by tilling a patch of the former Calhoun estate as tenant farmers. But Jesse McKinney had taken his shotgun and gone into Colfax on April 3, responding to the calls for help from the courthouse.

On April 4, however, McKinney had decided that the situation was easing, and that he might as well go back to his cabin, about three miles east of Colfax, near a bridge over the Bayou Darrow. At about noon on April 5, McKinney was repairing his fence, no more than twenty-four paces from his front door. As he worked, a group of about a dozen white riders suddenly galloped up. Some of them jumped their mounts over the fence. A man in a white shirt and black vest raised a pistol and fired it at McKinney's head. McKinney let out a ghastly scream, like the wail of a slaughtered pig, and sank to the ground. "I got him, he's dead as hell!" his attacker cried. The group whooped and capered around his body. It had all happened in an instant—right in front of Laurinda McKinney, who was standing on the front porch, with her six-year-old son, Butler. She hugged Butler to her knees and waited for their turn to die.

But the whites rode off, leaving Laurinda to approach Jesse, who was still breathing as gore gushed from his head. With the help of her younger sister, Laurinda put Jesse in a cart and wheeled him to her father's home, where the two women cradled his bleeding head and gave him water. He passed away there about sundown.

Jesse McKinney was not quite dead when Lewis Meekins burst in on the parley between the Montgomery and Colfax delegations. But Meekins didn't know that, and as far as he was concerned these peace talks must be a setup. The men from Montgomery were talking about arresting him and his comrades for burglarizing the Rutland place—and all the while their fellow whites were out shooting innocent Negro men. He aimed one of his guns at the white delegation, trying to decide which of them to shoot first. Eli Flowers made him holster his weapon. But that was the end of the peace conference. The whites had drawn first blood.

As word of McKinney's death spread, blacks flocked to Colfax, convinced they were all vulnerable. By nightfall on April 5, some four hundred black men, women, and children—about one out of every six colored persons in Grant Parish—had crowded into the area around the courthouse.

Ward and his men held a strong, defensible position: the brick courthouse itself, which was almost like a fort. They had sealed off the town; no individual hostile whites could enter. Some of the men in his posse were veterans of Ward's militia unit. Yet the ninety Enfield rifles Governor Warmoth had shipped to that force in 1871 were long gone. The weapons they had now were few and rickety. For ammunition, they had buckshot, including the cache stolen from Bill Cruikshank, but no bullets, and only a limited supply of powder. Meanwhile, the white forces seemed to be maneuvering in a semicircle outside the town, gathering intelligence and trying to stop Ward from sending out for supplies or reinforcements. He was not under siege quite yet, but it wouldn't be long before he was.

Ward sat down and wrote a letter to Jacob Johnson, a colored preacher who lived just across the Red River at Cotile, in Rapides Parish. As a leader among the Negroes of that area, Ward believed, Johnson might come to his brethren's aid in Colfax. It was a long shot, but Ward's growing desperation was clear, even if his spelling and grammar were not. "Dear friend," Ward began.

As I Reserve your ancer you Will Du Me and all hour colord Pepel all the helpe in the world at this time hour Pepel are in trouble and I ask you in the name of hour Liberty and hour Children Writes Come to hour Sistence as many as will and can and that feels that we are Citisens. I can Command all I Lack is helpe. I have Bin in gage 3 days and this day I had a Battle did not amount to But Little. One man I think wounded By all a Count he fell But got off and

Betwean know and Monday we will have heavey times and we are I am in need of all the helpe we can get. If it was Grant Parish men we could manage this but I Seen men today from Win Parish and the Rebels kill Jesey McKiney today and they takeing Charley Harris and Carry him off in the woods today and Jentilmen We are in need off all the helpe We Can Get I hope the Brothers Will Come to each others a Sistence as the Whites does.

Ward signed the note "Very truly yours, Capt. Wm. Ward," and sealed it in an envelope. He handed it to a colored man and told him to get it to Johnson as fast as he could.

Soon, though, Ward's men had another fight on their hands. On the morning of April 6, a small group of his scouts, mounted on mules, spotted a dozen or so armed whites, on horseback, just north of the Smithfield Quarters. The whites had forded a muddy stream, known, fittingly, as Boggy Bayou, and were crossing the old Firenze sugar plantation. The Republican patrol included a white man who held the title of parish clerk. But their leader was colored: Alexander Tillman.

Born on the Calhoun lands in 1843, Tillman had made the most of his liberation from slavery. He had learned to read and write. He had rented a piece of land and planted crops. He had registered to vote and joined the Republican Party, rising to a position on its state committee. In 1868, Tillman worked for the Republicans in Bossier Parish but escaped the horrific "nigger hunt." In 1870, when an enumerator circulated in Colfax, making the first census count in U.S. history that identified Negroes by name, Alexander Tillman made sure he was duly recorded, along with his wife, Chloe. He declared that he owned property worth $170.

Tillman was the last man anyone would have expected to take a prominent role in a force led by William Ward. He had been Henry Kearson's choice to run for state representative against Ward in 1872, and only pulled out in favor of Ward under pressure from the state Republican delegation that came to Colfax. Perhaps that had severed Tillman's ties to the Kearson faction. He may have been fed up with the violence and deceit of the Grant Parish white supremacists. Or possibly he had vowed never to run from white men again, as he had done in Bossier Parish.

Tillman and the rest of Ward's scouts took cover in some willow trees and sent the white parish clerk out as a decoy, betting that the whites would take him for one of their own. The ambush worked. When the white patrol cantered up, the Negroes burst from the trees on their mules and opened fire on the whites. "Mules—mules, by gippity, with niggers on them!" a white man shouted. The colored patrol spurred their mounts, trying to cut off the whites before they could make it to the pine forest across the Boggy Bayou. The whites panicked and galloped desperately for the water, barely pausing to fire back. They plunged their horses into the bayou but found themselves in muck that reached almost to their saddles. A white man felt a sting on his hand and looked down to discover that his thumb had been shot off. "You're lucky it's not your head!" a comrade shouted. Through sheer luck, though, the whites made it over the bayou and into the trees beyond, from which they took a few desultory shots at their pursuers before fleeing up into the piney woods.

Tillman's men stopped at the bayou's edge, permitting the enemy to escape rather than pursue them through the quagmire. In the mud, the Negroes found a token of victory: a straw hat, flown from one of the white men's heads as he dashed away. Heretofore regarded with suspicion by many of the Negroes around the courthouse, at least those who knew of his political past, Alexander Tillman rode back to Colfax as a leader—almost a hero.

SO FAR, THE REPUBLICANS WERE UNDEFEATED. EACH SKIRMISH HAD ENDED WITH the enemy put to flight and not a single friendly casualty. Yet there was no sign of any help from Jacob Johnson. The preacher's place was not far—only eight miles away down the Red River on the Rapides Parish side. If he was sending help, it should have come by now. What William Ward didn't know was that, upon receiving the letter, Johnson had quickly concluded that he wanted no part of any battle.

On April 7, Ward wrote a second letter—this time to Governor Kellogg in New Orleans. He sketched a dire picture of the Republicans' situation and asked him to get U.S. troops sent to Colfax immediately. Then Ward handed it to Willie Calhoun, who was back in Colfax after several days of hiding out in the woods. Things seemed to be settling down a bit; Register had made a brief attempt to open the court (no lawyers appeared), and Negro women and children had begun to trickle back home. Still, Calhoun and Ward agreed that their only hope lay in outside help, preferably U.S. troops.

Calhoun boarded the steamboat *LaBelle*, which followed its normal route down the Red River. As it approached the twin towns of Alexandria and Pineville, however, Calhoun saw a large crowd of armed whites on the Pineville side. Apparently, someone had tipped them off to his presence on board. Calhoun hobbled down inside a cargo hold and closed the hatch. He stuffed the letter into his boot. He could hear men searching above him, until the scuttle opened and a familiar figure loomed over him: Paul Hooe, Michael Ryan's old henchman from the 1868 election.

Hooe had moved up in the world; now the Fusionist claimant to the office of state representative from Rapides Parish, he was lending his aid and authority to a crowd of men headed by Jim Hadnot and Bill Cruikshank, who had fled to Alexandria. The men hoisted Calhoun out of the boat and frisked him. It wasn't long before they had plucked the letter from Ward to Kellogg out of Calhoun's boot and read it thoroughly.

As they pondered how to respond, the whites put Calhoun under the guard of an old acquaintance: Smith Gordon, a physician and planter who had owned 135 slaves before the war and served with Meredith Calhoun on the board of Louisiana's state university. "You ought to be hung," he told Meredith Calhoun's son, standing over him with a pistol.

But Calhoun's captors decided to use him, not kill him. To them, it was axiomatic that Calhoun controlled the Negroes in Colfax. So they would return him to the courthouse, where he would order Ward and his men to disperse. At least that's what he would do if he wanted to live. Later that night, they put Calhoun on a horse and told him to come with them upriver. By 2:00 a.m. on April 8, the column of about forty men had reached a house a few miles below Colfax. They made Calhoun dismount and subjected him to a strip-search, probably more for their own amusement than anything else. Then they all lay down on the porch to sleep.

The next morning, the group got as far as the spot below Colfax where the Red River met the Bayou Darrow. At that point, however, another detachment from Rapides Parish intercepted them. The leader of this group told them it was reckless for such a large body of armed white men to be seen so close to where the Negroes were encamped. There might be bloodshed. The men decided to return to Pineville. Then the question arose: what about Willie Calhoun? Finally, his captors agreed to take him back with them, lest he reveal their whereabouts to the Negroes.

Calhoun spent the night of April 8 in the relative luxury of the Ice House Hotel in Alexandria, where he and the Fusionists reached a new understanding. He could return to Colfax but only if he ordered the Negroes to lay down their arms and give up the courthouse. The "or else" hardly needed to be expressed. On the morning of April 9, Calhoun boarded a steamboat to Colfax. When he got there, he proceeded immediately to the courthouse, where he duly told the men that Jim Hadnot and Bill Cruikshank were in Alexandria and wanted them to disperse.

The courthouse defenders refused. They were still concerned about Hadnot and Cruikshank. But now there was a new threat much closer at hand, they said. One hundred white men, armed and dangerous, were camping out in the piney woods. And they were under the command of Christopher Columbus Nash.

ALPHONSE CAZABAT HAD TOLD NASH TO SUPPRESS THE RIOT IF IT TOOK TWO HUNDRED men. Since he considered Cazabat the duly elected judge, and himself the duly elected sheriff, Nash felt Cazabat's order was legal authority to organize a posse to arrest or, if necessary, attack the illegal armed force at the courthouse. Nash had little respect for the intrinsic fighting ability of the Negroes. But whatever their capability, the Negroes occupied a strong point, the courthouse, from which they could prove difficult to dislodge. His experience in the Civil War taught Nash not to attack until he could bring decisive force to bear. A lot of good Louisiana men had died in that disastrous charge up Cemetery Hill at Gettysburg.

And so he made camp. The planter who had threatened to expel Negro Republican voters from his land in 1872 opened his property to the "sheriff" and what were at first a handful of followers. The planter supplied them with food, blankets, and tents, which they pitched at a place called Summerfield, about three miles north of Colfax. Sleeping in the woods, setting a watch each night, inhaling the aroma of bacon frying over an open fire each morning—it must have reminded Nash of those long-ago days as a rebel soldier on the Rappahannock.

Then Nash set about recruiting. At first it was not easy. Some men just didn't want to get involved. Some were frightened of armed Negroes. Some claimed they didn't want to leave their own homes unprotected. But Nash wasn't taking no for an answer. When his messengers came back empty-handed from Grant Parish's piney woods, he sent them to Rapides, Catahoula, and Winn parishes. He told them to sound the alarm: The Negroes of Grant Parish were going to kill all the white men and take the white women and girls. They were out to found a new race of men through mass rape.

Gradually, Nash's camp began to swell. The first groups came from areas to the north, whence they could reach Nash without passing through Colfax. Nine Winn Parish men arrived, under the command of Jim Bird, an old rebel soldier from Company C of the Twelfth Louisiana Infantry. Next to arrive were sixteen men and teenagers from Montgomery, who entered Nash's camp on April 5, carrying shotguns and muzzle-loading rifles.

By the morning of April 9, when Calhoun reached Colfax, Nash probably had far fewer than the hundred men that the courthouse defenders attributed to him. But he had not yet heard from Rapides and Catahoula parishes, and so he was not yet ready to give up the fight.

• • •

THE LETTER WILLIE CALHOUN HAD BEEN CARRYING FROM WARD TO KELLOGG WAS an intelligence windfall for the white leaders gathered in Alexandria. Not only did it contain Ward's pessimistic assessment of his troops. It also disclosed his strategic plan, such as it was: to summon U.S. troops to save the day. Now the whites knew that their chances to rout the courthouse defenders might be better than they had previously thought, as long as they could prevent them from being reinforced from New Orleans.

White men from the Red River Valley had already been trying to influence public opinion in the state capital, where any decision to dispatch federal troops or state militia would be made. On April 8, the first article about the unrest in Grant Parish appeared in the *Daily Picayune*, headlined THE RIOT IN GRANT PARISH. FEARFUL ATROCITIES BY THE NEGROES. NO RESPECT SHOWN TO THE DEAD. The front-page story purported to be the first-person account of O. J. Butler, who had fled to Alexandria after his run-in with Eli Flowers. Some phrasing, however, such as the use of "Bayonet Legislature" to refer to the Republican-majority body in New Orleans, suggested that the piece was ghostwritten by Fusionists.

Butler described how the rampant Negroes had "plundered" Rutland's house and thrown his dead child's body on the banks of the river. The cause of the affair, the article added, "is the intense hatred [Negroes] bear for the white people of this parish," which Ward and Flowers had stirred up. The *New Orleans Republican* denied Butler's charges, but its tentative tone reflected the difficulty of refuting an eyewitness who was himself a colored Republican. "We are not in possession of all the details," its editorial observed, "but until we hear that the Republican officials of Grant have done something more flagrant than to oust McEnery pretenders to office, we are bound to defend them from the charge of being rioters."

The next day, Rutland arrived in New Orleans aboard the *John T. Moore*. He had more dramatic details for the press. In a *Daily Picayune* article, he portrayed Hadnot's armed foray into Colfax on April 1 as "a mass meeting" that had been called to protest the Republicans' takeover of the courthouse "in a quiet way"—only to be violently dispersed by Ward's illegal posse. He gave a lurid account of his escape across the river, adding that he had learned in Alexandria that his daughter's body had been taken from its coffin and burned.

Rutland marched to the St. Louis Hotel and secured a new audience with the governor. He handed Kellogg what he said was a petition from the citizens of Grant Parish, demanding that something be done to stop the Negro riot. He showed Kellogg his arrest warrant for the men, including Calhoun and Ward, whom he blamed for invading his house. He warned Kellogg that blood would flow unless the governor intervened to restore the Fusionist officers to their rightful positions.

Kellogg must have been irritated. He thought he'd fixed Grant Parish three weeks earlier, and now this excitable fellow Rutland was back, screaming that things had gone from bad to worse. But, still hoping to appease the state's volatile rural whites, he called for his carriage and took Rutland with him to the Custom House to see James Beckwith. Perhaps the U.S. attorney could be of assistance, Kellogg said.

Beckwith's skepticism was immediately aroused when Rutland told him things were so bad in Colfax that no white man could go near the village; if that was true, Beckwith thought to himself, how could Rutland, a white man, know? But Beckwith told Rutland that if he would swear out a criminal complaint under the Enforcement Act, it would be attended to. This was not the answer Rutland wanted. He stormed off, warning, once again, that bloodshed was coming, and declaring that it wouldn't be his fault when it did. Kellogg solicitously took the lawyer to see state and federal military commanders. Those meetings, too, ended inconclusively.

The next day, April 10, Kellogg received lobbyists whom he would have taken much more seriously. The first was J. Madison Wells, the former Republican governor, who was a close friend of Kellogg's. They had first met when Kellogg was doing Andrew Johnson's bidding as customs collector. Wells's granddaughter was even named Cora Kellogg Wells, in honor of the governor. Wells brought a lawyer from Rapides, who read the governor a letter describing the Negro threats to kill white men and violate white women. Then Wells ushered in another of Rapides's leading white citizens, Thomas C. Manning. With Wells standing by to vouch for his reliability, the former attorney for Delos White's murderers assured Kellogg that there was no need to send troops to Grant Parish because, as he put it, "everything would be right."

Between the reports of Negro mischief and Manning's soothing words, Kellogg decided not to send troops, state or federal, to Colfax. A large force would be unduly provocative at this stage, he told himself. He ordered a single officer, the militia commander General James A. Longstreet, to go to Grant Parish to investigate. Kellogg told General William H. Emory, commander of the U.S. Army's Department of the Gulf, based at the Jackson Barracks near New Orleans, that he would like a federal officer to accompany Longstreet. But when Emory demurred, saying that he feared the presence of a federal officer might undercut Longstreet's authority, Kellogg shrugged and went along. An editorial in the *Republican* summed up his thinking. "The opinion was entertained yesterday that the excitement would die away and the parties quietly disperse and resume their ordinary avocations before a force sent from the city could arrive at Colfax," it explained. The next day's *Republican* added that the "better class" of people in Grant Parish considered the unrest "nothing but disaster to the best interests of the state and its people" and that "it is thought that prudent counsels will prevail and no more trouble occur."

Kellogg might not have been able to get troops upriver even if he had wanted to. The state and federal governments had no steamboats. To transport men and supplies, they depended entirely on the white men who owned and operated river-going vessels. And the boatmen, who, like most whites in the state, supported McEnery, were refusing to take either militia or soldiers to the Red River Valley. Longstreet himself inquired with thirty or forty boatmen; all turned him down, protesting that they would lose their business if they cooperated with the Republican government.

But Kellogg could not ignore the situation entirely. Thinking that there was still a chance for compromise, he drew up two new commissions for the sheriff's position in Grant Parish. One was made out in the name of Thomas Montfort Wells, J. Madison Wells's Republican son, who was still aligned with Calhoun and Ward. The other was made out in the name of Samuel E. Cuney, the black Republican who opposed Ward. Surely one of these men would prove acceptable to the contending factions in Colfax. The governor then asked Longstreet to order two top militia officers, Theodore W. DeKlyne and William Wright, to travel up the river. He gave them the commissions and told them to hammer out a settlement.

KELLOGG DID ALL THIS WITHOUT HEARING FROM ANY GRANT PARISH REPUBLIcans. As it happened, William Ward was on his way to New Orleans, a couple of days behind Rutland. Late on the night of April 8, with no sign of help from either Jacob Johnson or the U.S. Army, he decided that he would go to New Orleans to ask the governor for troops. Along with Flowers, Register, Meekins, and others he went to catch the steamboat *St. Mary*. This was an impulsive decision and a risky one—it removed the entire leadership of his embattled posse. But Ward urged his followers to hold out until his return; then, because his illness was acting up again so badly that he could barely walk, Ward asked a friend to help him mount his horse, and he rode down the riverbank to a steamboat landing.

Ward and his group arrived in New Orleans about midday on Good Friday, April 11. They were horrified and angry when they found out that their enemies had beaten them to town and were dominating the press. To counter "misrepresentations" they had read in the *Daily Picayune*, they cowrote a front-page piece for the April 12 edition of the *Republican*. THE SHERIFF IN PEACEFUL POSSESSION, the headline announced—meaning the Republican Dan Shaw, not the Fusionist Nash. The article declared that colored men had committed only "trifling depredations" at Rutland's house, and assured readers that the child's body was intact within its coffin. The authors reported the murder of Jesse McKinney and the abortive peace talks. They detailed the prowling of white patrols. "The Republicans of our parish are deserving of the highest commendation for the moderation and forbearance shown to some bad men living in our midst, who now happily by their own act and on their own motion have left our parish," the statement concluded.

DeKlyne and Wright had not made it out of New Orleans yet; apparently, even their small party had been unable to secure transportation up the river on the night of April 10. That gave Ward and his companions time to go to the Custom House and swear out federal criminal complaints against fifty men they believed to be in the forces arrayed against them. A U.S. commissioner duly issued arrest warrants. And since DeKlyne and Wright were not only militia officers but also deputy U.S. marshals, they could execute the warrants, or at least threaten to. Finally, on April 12, DeKlyne and Wright procured transportation for the trip to Colfax. Robert Register and two Metropolitan Police officers accompanied them. They believed there might still be time to preserve the peace.

HARRISONBURG, THE PARISH SEAT OF CATAHOULA PARISH, LAY SIXTY-FIVE MILES east of Colfax, along the east-west wagon trail that connected to the Natchez Trace. A messenger from Nash reached the town at 11:00 a.m. on Monday, April 7. "The Negroes are striking terror to the white people of Grant," he announced. Within an hour, another courier arrived, repeating the story and asking for armed men from Catahoula to come to Grant Parish's aid.

Nash had chosen the right place to seek reinforcements. There was a strong nucleus of white supremacists in Catahoula Parish, men who had been initiated into the Knights of the White Camellia during 1868, but now called themselves "the Old Time Ku Klux Klan." One of the men, a former Confederate officer who currently held a colonel's commission in McEnery's "militia," gathered up six volunteers, and, with their weapons, the seven rode west toward Colfax, following the Little River rather than the wagon trail to avoid detection. After losing their way and wandering in the piney woods for a day or so, they approached to within about twenty miles of Colfax—where they stumbled upon a white family that had been living in the woods for the last two weeks. After listening to the family's tale of horror, the Catahoulans concluded that they would have to get more men. Two of them were dispatched to Sicily Island, another large town in the parish, carrying a letter seeking more recruits. On the evening of the next day, Thursday, April 10, the remaining five Catahoulans reached Nash's camp.

As the Catahoulans were doing this, the men from Rapides Parish were making their way up the Red River, having finally communicated with Nash's posse and decided that it was safe to link up with them above Colfax. They had tried to force the sheriff of Rapides Parish to join them, so as to lend a patina of legality to their movement. But the sheriff, a white Republican, refused. So the men proceeded up the Rapides Parish side of the Red River; to avoid any contact with the Negroes in Colfax, they crossed the water north of the town, at Montgomery, on a ferry procured by Wilson L. Richardson. They then headed south. On Saturday morning, April 12, they arrived in Nash's camp—a force of about forty-five men headed by David C. Paul, who was not only the Fusionist candidate for sheriff of Rapides Parish but also a former lieutenant in the Confederate army and, more recently, chief of the Spring Creek den of the Ku Klux Klan. About half of Paul's contingent were from Rapides Parish, and about half were returning Grant Parish men such as Bill Cruikshank, Jim Hadnot, Hadnot's nephew and sons, and Jim Yawn.

The previous morning, one of the Catahoulans had led a small patrol to within a mile of Colfax, in order to learn the strength and position of the courthouse defenders. They had found Meredith Calhoun's old sugar mill, a sturdy brick building about two miles northeast of Colfax, undefended. Now Nash's growing posse occupied it as a forward position.

As their strategic situation improved, so did their armaments. On Saturday, C. C. Dunn, who had joined the posse from Montgomery, took a group of about twelve down the river to Pineville, looking for the *John T. Moore*. The vessel was the pride of the Red River, a state-of-the-art boat that traveled between Shreveport and New Orleans each week during the high-water season. It had been custom built for Captain Bill Boardman in 1870 with four boilers, twenty-two-inch cylinders, and a six-stroke engine. It also had a small four-pound cannon cast at a foundry in New Orleans. In lawless times, Boardman wanted the best security for his valuable new boat.

Now Dunn asked Boardman to lend the little artillery piece, which was smaller than the smallest cannon used in the Civil War, to the cause of white supremacy. The men undid the bolts that held it to the *John T. Moore's* iron deck, and mounted it on a wagon for the trip back upriver. The cannon's bore was two and three-quarter inches in diameter. No cannonballs fit such a narrow tube. So, stopping in Montgomery, Dunn and his comrades picked up some two-inch oblong iron slugs made by J. S. Payne, the erstwhile special constable who had been sent to arrest Ward and the other Republican leaders in Colfax. A test firing proved the little gun could indeed work when loaded with this improvised ammunition. And then they took Bob Bernstein, the former Negro slave of a Prussian-born Jewish merchant in the town, and ordered him to drive the wagon down to Nash's camp. By evening, the cannon was at the sugar mill.

Nash and about twenty-five other men stood guard there all night, protecting the cannon and not daring to close their eyes lest they be killed in their sleep by Negroes. They were wide awake at midnight, when the men from Sicily Island arrived. There were eleven of them in all, led by two former Confederate officers. Nash and his men cheered them so loudly that their comrades heard their shouts back at the Summerfield camp.

The last reinforcements to arrive were a detachment of eleven men from Cheneyville, about sixty-five miles to the south along the Bayou Boeuf. Cheneyville was the principal town of the cotton- and sugar-growing region in which Lew Cheney's abortive slave revolt had occurred back in 1837. Memories of that event, and the fear it had sowed, were still fresh in white minds. In Cheneyville, they had heard that William Ward had been campaigning for support across Rapides Parish, making speeches, raising recruits, and conspiring with other Negro leaders. The rumor was that Ward's coconspirators were not going to settle for conquering Grant Parish but, like Lew Cheney in his day, were planning to march on Alexandria and take it by force—then set up a "negro principality" headed by white Republicans including William B. Phillips. When the Cheneyville men, who were also commanded by an ex-Confederate officer, arrived at the sugar house, Nash finally had a force large enough for an attack.

Dave Paul could not contain his joy. He slapped Jim Hadnot on the knee and cried, "I am going to Colfax tomorrow!"

CHAPTER FIVE

BLOOD ON THE RED

A cool dawn broke over the Summerfield camp on April 13, 1873—Easter Sunday. Cooking fires were kindled. Smoke blended with early morning mist. Coffee boiled and bacon sizzled, their smells mingling with those of damp grass and long-needled pine. It was time for the white men who had gathered at Summerfield to make their final preparations. Each of them had at least one weapon; most carried two or more. The most common firearm among them was a simple shotgun, with little range or accuracy. But many also had brought muzzle-loading rifles such as the Enfield. Most of the men also had six-shooters and hunting knives tucked into their belts.

Mounting their horses, the men rode out from Summerfield in the direction of Meredith Calhoun's old sugar mill, which local people called a "sugar house." For just over two miles they traveled through the fresh morning air. They encountered no opposition—saw and heard nothing but the familiar green piney woods and the buzz of mosquitoes. At the sugar house, they met Christopher Columbus Nash, as well as the other men who had spent a wakeful night with him. Once assembled, the force attended to a last piece of business: preparing the *John T. Moore*'s little cannon. They loaded it onto a two-horse wagon and lashed the artillery piece to the back wheels with rope. Then they took off the front wheels of the cart. The result was a reasonable facsimile of a real field gun.

The men watched and waited as the morning sun made its gradual ascent. There were about 165 of them all together. Roughly half of the men were former Confederate soldiers; among their leaders were four former rebel officers, including Christopher Columbus Nash. There were even three former Union soldiers. For these veterans, the pause before an anticipated battle, the time when adrenaline and dramatic notions of duty and honor intensified the flow of blood through their veins, must have felt familiar. Familiar, too, was the fear and outrage at the prospect of

Negro revolt. These men had come to fight for civilization itself—to save themselves from ruin and their women from rape. Either they would control this little chip of the rural South, or it would sink to the level of Africa. There was no middle ground.

Dave Paul, the Klansman who led one of the Rapides Parish contingents, took it upon himself to put their emotions into words. He rode his horse along the line of men, taking a head count and noting down names. Then he drew up in front of the force and reminded everyone in the starkest possible terms what this day was all about. "Boys, this is a struggle for white supremacy," he told them. "There are one hundred and sixty-five of us to go into Colfax this morning. God only knows who will come out. Those who do will probably be prosecuted for treason, and the punishment for treason is death." At the end of his speech, Paul asked anyone who was afraid to die for the cause to step out of line. Some twenty-five men did so.

That left about 140 to make the march to Colfax. They moved out, with Nash in the lead. As if passing over their own Rubicon, they rode across a bridge spanning a bayou and continued down the main road from the sugar house to Colfax, before halting in an open field about fifty yards above the Smithfield Quarters. The Red River was on their right flank, about six hundred yards away. The courthouse stood about three quarters of a mile in front of them. Between it and them stretched the flat ground of the old Calhoun plantation, with the first green shoots of that year's cotton crop poking through the dirt.

Christopher Columbus Nash had heard Paul's oration; he certainly agreed with it. But he also had a tangible goal—the sheriff's office—and if he could get it without bloodshed, well and good. Nash might also have wondered about the staying power of his force. It had not been easy to recruit, and a couple of dozen men had just quit at the last minute. He decided to present the Negroes one last chance to surrender without a fight.

Nash summoned three men: Paul; Charles A. Duplissey, a doctor who had ridden in with the Catahoula Parish contingent; and his own brother, Valentine Nash. He told them to come with him for a parley with the Negroes. The four men took a white flag and rode into the Smithfield Quarters. Most of the ramshackle cabins were abandoned. But Nash caught sight of an ex-slave he knew as one of the "faithful" blacks who had spurned William Ward's Republicans and retained close relations with whites. He asked him to go to the courthouse and call the Negro leaders to a meeting. The man complied.

. . .

WITH ABOUT 150 NEGRO MEN AND A SIMILAR NUMBER OF WOMEN AND CHILDREN crowded in and around the Colfax courthouse, the village resembled one of the refugee camps that sprang up around Union army positions during the Red River Campaign in 1864. The smoke of cooking-fires fused with the stink of human waste and the tang of sweat. Children's cries pierced the air. There was a semblance of organization, with the women running back and forth to the Smithfield Quarters each night for food and supplies, and cooking for the men, who formed a line to receive their chow. But since the departure of William Ward, Eli Flowers, and Robert Register to New Orleans four days earlier, the Negroes had spent more time and energy purging suspected traitors than preparing for an attack.

On April 5, the day of Jesse McKinney's murder, Sam Cuney, the colored Colfax postmaster and bitter political rival of Ward, had left for Alexandria, taking the U.S. mail with him. Cuney said he did this to protect government property against the threat of violence. Cuney came back to Colfax on April 8 but was immediately met with hostility. The colored men found it highly suspicious that he seemed to enjoy free access to the very place where Jim Hadnot and Bill Cruikshank had sought refuge. "You're nothing but a damned spy," one of the courthouse defenders hissed at him.

Fearing for his life, Cuney asked Dan Shaw, the white Republican sheriff, to post a guard at his house. Shaw agreed, but Levi Allen, who was exercising a share of what passed for command authority in Ward's absence, came along later and sent the deputies back to the courthouse. Apparently Allen felt that, with armed whites circulating in the surrounding countryside, he could not spare any men—especially not to protect someone of such questionable loyalty. Cuney fled Colfax on April 10, followed soon thereafter by the town's other colored storekeeper.

As part of their hasty propaganda effort in New Orleans, Ward and his friends had planted an editorial in the *New Orleans Republican*, touting the force they had left behind. "In Grant Parish, it seems there is a local majority of colored men, not only accustomed to the trade of war, but equipped with arms of the most perfect character," the item read. "According to statements most worthy of belief, they are well armed, well disciplined and confident of success. . . . The time is passed, if ever it existed, when a handful of whites could frighten a regiment of colored men."

This report might have been intended to deter an attack on their men. But it was utterly false. In fact, Ward and Flowers were the only ones with significant military experience. Few members of their "regiment" were veterans of anything but Ward's own abortive state militia company. Ward and Flowers had tried to drill their men but gave up after a few sloppy attempts to form them into ranks and march them around the grassy patch in front of the courthouse. They made elementary—but crucial—tactical errors, such as failing to guard the levee so that the whites could not use it to cover a flanking movement along the riverbank.

Whereas nearly every white man in Nash's force was carrying multiple firearms, only a half to two-thirds of the black men had even one gun. Their weaponry was not "perfect," but measurably inferior to that of the whites, and consisted mainly of shotguns and hunting pieces, with at most a dozen Enfield rifles scattered among the ranks. The Negroes only had enough powder and shot for each man to fire about two rounds.

By Saturday, April 12, the men at the courthouse had concluded that an attack was imminent. The colored women who brought them their food and water at night probably had reported the armed whites coming in from other parishes. The courthouse defenders began digging a defensive trench—under the instruction of an itinerant white schoolteacher and peddler of religious illustrations from New York City who had somehow gravitated to Colfax via Chicago and St. Louis. Plunging shovels (probably taken from Calhoun's toolsheds) into the red earth, the Negroes dug through Saturday night and into Sunday morning.

The results were far from ideal. A proper Civil War trench would have been reinforced with heavy timbers and deep enough for a rifleman to stand, or at least kneel, so that he could fire at the enemy from behind a protective wall. At Colfax, the courthouse defenders did manage to excavate a long crescent around their position, enclosing an area about 250 yards square. But the trench was only about two feet at the deepest point. The dirt pile in front of it, reinforced by two-and-a-half-inch-thick wooden planks, created a breastwork only about twenty inches high. In some places, there was no trench at all, just a rough shield made of planks stacked in a zigzag pattern.

The same traveling salesman who designed the trench helped the Negroes rig up three improvised artillery pieces. They secured some lengths of steam pipe, probably left over from a cotton gin or the Calhouns' old sugar mill. Then they plugged the pipes at one end, and drilled vents in them. Effective artillery could have kept the whites at bay as long as powder and shot held out. But these homemade "cannon" were not even on a par with the little four-pound gun from the *John T. Moore*. The freedmen tried a test firing of one on Saturday. As soon as they touched fire to the vent, igniting the powder packed into the pipe, the whole device blew up. They decided to mount the other two on their newly dug breastworks and hope for the best.

On Saturday night, Alexander Tillman addressed the men. The whites were probably coming on Easter Sunday, Tillman said; in all likelihood, there would be a fight. They were short on ammunition, so it was crucial that no one shoot until ordered to do so. The main thing was to stick together, Tillman implored them.

LEVI ALLEN SHOWED NO FEAR WHEN THE NEGRO MESSENGER BROUGHT NASH'S ultimatum on Sunday morning. He mounted his bay mare and rode out to meet the white commander at the Smithfield Quarters, accompanied by a handful of the courthouse defenders. The ex-slave and the old Confederate infantry officer confronted each other, for a moment at least, as equals.

Nash was the first to speak. "What do you depend upon doing in there?" he asked.

"We are doing nothing more than we were before—standing still, as we've been standing," Allen replied. "But I don't want any trouble."

"We want that courthouse," Nash demanded.

"We are going to stand where we are until we get some United States troops or some assistance," Allen countered.

Allen seems to have been puzzled that the whites were ignoring an overture he had made a few days earlier. During Willie Calhoun's visit to Colfax on April 9, Allen had replied to the ultimatum from Hadnot with a letter in which he promised that his men would disband and hand over the courthouse—if Nash's force also put down its arms. Now he asked Nash what had become of the proposal.

Nash's answer made it clear that the whites had no intention of letting armed Negro men walk out of Colfax alive, even if they did surrender the courthouse. Nash told Allen to forget about his past dealings with Hadnot; he alone was in command of the white force. Then Nash offered a deal of his own, a rather different proposition from the one Allen had extended to Hadnot: "If you stack your arms and leave in peace, you will not be harmed," he said.

Allen was far from a seasoned commander or military tactician. He did not know how many of his men would fight if it came to that, but he knew what had happened to Jesse McKinney. And he knew that McKinney's murderers were among Nash's followers. If the freedmen laid down their arms, they would be at the mercy of these killers.

"Colored men have been hurt," Allen answered. "I am afraid to trust the word of any of you. I intend to remain as I am until assistance arrives."

"Then go in there and say to your people that I advise them to get out," Nash said. "I give you thirty minutes to remove your women and children."

Allen wheeled on his horse and rode back to the courthouse. He gathered the men, as well as their women and children, and told them Nash's terms. "There is nothing we can do," he said. The men agreed that they would have to stay and fight. They said good-bye to their families, who gathered up what few belongings they had and fled south through Colfax to the Calhouns' old Mirabeau plantation, which lay on the other side of a thick patch of trees. Many other women and children were already clustered there for protection.

Then came a final plea for surrender—this time from one of Grant Parish's leading colored men. Steve Kimball, a farmer from Montgomery who had been sheltering at Mirabeau during the crisis, came to the courthouse and addressed the freedmen, telling them to lay down their arms and go home. Contradicting Allen, he said they could trust the whites' promises not to harm them. He pointed out that the leaders of the Grant Parish Republicans had all fled, leaving their supporters to face the whites on their own. This was a hopeless situation, he said. But Kimball's plea was refused He asked his friends and relatives to say farewell, since he did not expect to see any of them alive again.

It was also time for the last remaining whites in the courthouse to consider their prospects, Dan Shaw foremost among them. Shaw's personal and political résumés made him a far less controversial figure than William Ward or William B. Phillips, at least in theory, which is probably why the Republicans had named him to balance their ticket in 1872. He was a northern-born Methodist from Ohio, yet he had deep roots in the Red River Valley: Shaw's father was a missionary in Louisiana, and Shaw himself migrated to the state in 1851, at the age of thirty-six. To make a living, he dabbled in cotton planting, which meant he associated in business with white men and had to motivate Negro field hands. He served a couple of years as a sheriff in Rapides Parish before the Civil War; he also represented Alexandria in the state house of representatives after the war. Before the war, he was a Democrat; afterward, he registered Republican. Dan Shaw, in short, had always straddled political fences.

But Grant Parish was now totally polarized along racial lines. Even though Shaw personified the legal authority under which the posse had

gathered at the courthouse, there was no longer any place for an equivocator among the Republican leadership, much less a white equivocator.
After Levi Allen returned from his conference with Nash, Shaw asked
Allen what he should do. Allen looked at the fifty-eight-year-old. He felt
sorry for Shaw, who he knew would probably be worse than useless in a
fight anyway. "Old man, go away and save yourself, if you can," Allen
replied. Shaw fled toward Mirabeau. Kindred J. Harvey and the traveling
salesman followed soon thereafter. His black comrades liked Harvey; he
had stood by them through the entire crisis. But now they warned the
sixty-five-year-old that he would not survive the fight. Only colored men
remained in Colfax.

AFTER ALLEN REFUSED TO CAPITULATE, NASH RODE BACK TO HIS MEN AND BEGAN
using the allotted thirty minutes to organize. He proceeded just as he
must have done during the Civil War, following well-established tactical
principles for attacking a fixed position with a company-sized unit. The
first step was to dismount his men, leaving twenty-five of the smallest
and lightest-armed ones to hold the horses. Nash then assigned a three-
man crew to the cannon, accompanied by the Negro Bob Bernstein, who
would pull the cart. Nash sent a spotter to high ground to help direct the
cannon's fire. He sent three men out to the left of town, about four hundred yards away, to make observations and report them by runner to the
main force. Finally, he formed a skirmish line out of eighteen men carrying the best rifles: modern, quick-firing breechloaders like the ones that
had done heavy damage to Confederate troops in the last years of the
Civil War and were still claiming lives in battles between the U.S. Army
and the Plains Indians. The eighteen skirmishers would march in front
of Nash's main force to clear the way.

At noon, they moved out. The skirmish line patrolled unopposed
down the main street of the Smithfield Quarters, taking control of the
area without firing a shot. Nash and the rest of the force followed. Several Negro women were still there. One of Nash's men ordered them out.
"You see these damned sons of bitches have run off and left you to take
care of yourselves," he said. "Now you women get out of here, and not a
damn one of you will get hurt."

The force advanced 50 yards at a time, beginning about 450 yards
away from the Negroes' trench line. Once the skirmishers had made it
safely to within 300 yards of the defenders, they called for the cannon.
The crew rushed forward. Bernstein followed with the wagon. They set

up the little howitzer in the garden of Willie Calhoun's house. In went the gunpowder, followed by an iron slug and some wadding. Then they packed the missiles in with a ramrod and touched off the fuse.

The first booming shot landed in front of the freedmen's trenches, kicking up a shower of red soil. At the time, several dozen courthouse defenders, exhausted from digging all day and night Saturday, and still apparently unable to believe that the whites really meant to fight, were actually asleep. The cannon fire was a frightful alarm. Minutes later, the steamboat *Maria Luisa* chugged by on the Red River. To the freedmen, its clanging bell seemed to herald the arrival of white reinforcements.

Bullets from the white skirmishers' rifles zipped over the heads of the freedmen. Steadying themselves, a few Negroes returned fire, sporadically, saving ammunition. For the most part, though, the outgunned defenders did not dare raise their heads above the breastworks. The whites soon found that they could make them duck just by pointing their guns at them. The colored men gave one of their remaining improvised cannon a try. It blew up just like the one they tested the day before.

Still, the whites could not inflict a decisive blow. The cannon crew advanced to within 225 yards of the trench, but even from this distance, none of the half-dozen shots they got off did any damage. The whites' rifles were indeed accurate, but they could not hit the Negroes as long as they stayed prone in their trenches or behind the courthouse's walls. On the other side, the freedmen's shotguns were effective only at short range, but they posed enough of a threat to keep the whites from closing in and destroying them.

For two hours, the standoff continued. It was providential, in a way, this mutually assured nondestruction. But the whites had other options. One of the three Union men in their ranks was a certain William Chaney, formerly of the Eleventh Connecticut Infantry Regiment and more recently a fortune seeker in Louisiana. But none of his comrades on April 13, 1873, knew this. Earlier in the week, the same Rapides Parish force that had taken Willie Calhoun prisoner had arrested Chaney as he wandered suspiciously nearby. He told them he was "Ezekiel B. Powell," a Confederate veteran from Virginia. To win his release, he promised to join them against the rioting Negroes in Colfax. He had kept that promise.

Earlier, Nash had sent Chaney—"Powell"—and another man to scout along the riverbank. Keeping the levee between themselves and the battlefield, the pair crept to within 125 yards of the Negroes' left flank. They found the levee completely unguarded. More important, they located a gap in the levee, covered by nothing but a low fence made out of planks. It was behind and to the right of the trench line, as the whites viewed it.

If the whites could bring the cannon to this position, they could fire it directly on the men behind the breastworks.

The two scouts hastened back to Nash with the intelligence. Chaney sketched a plan for outflanking the Negroes from behind the levee. The cannon crew could bring the little gun up to the gap in the levee, with an escort of about fifteen men, he said. As they moved, the eighteen skirmishers would distract the Negroes with rifle fire directly at the trench. Once in position, the cannon crew would load the gun. They would have to stand up from behind the levee, exposed to enemy fire, to do so, which would be dangerous. But the escorts could cover them with a noisy blast of shotgun fire. Chaney's fake credentials helped to sell his plan. "This man is an old Confederate soldier, and he has been down to examine things, and this man says if we can take them trenches we can drive them out," Charles Duplissey of Catahoula Parish said.

Nash agreed, and at about two o'clock he assembled the escort for the cannon crew. He named James Daniels to lead the group. This was probably not a random assignment. Daniels was a former overseer on Andrew Cruikshank's plantation; most of the other men Nash assigned to escort the cannon down the levee also came from the Cruikshanks' and Hadnots' neighborhood. This job belonged to the most committed of Grant Parish's white supremacists.

Still, it was another ex-Union man who showed the most grit as the group moved out. Sidney Shewman, a New Yorker who had settled in Montgomery after the war, was one of the three-man cannon crew. Some buckshot hit Shewman in the heel as he and his comrades took their gun from Calhoun's garden to the riverbank. But he ignored the pain and limped on. No one else was hurt. Once they reached the gap in the levee, the cannon crew loaded the gun with buckshot under the covering fire of their escorts. Then they unleashed their first blast on the colored men.

Some of the hot iron sliced across the abdomen of Adam Kimball, ripping through scar tissue from a burn he had suffered years before. When he looked down, he saw his intestines falling out. In terror, Kimball fled into the courthouse, where he quickly died. Combined with the report of the escort's shotguns, the deadly cannon shot sowed panic and chaos. Dozens of Negroes ran from the trench to the courthouse, clogging the narrow doorway and forcing others to run elsewhere. The whites at the riverbank let out a rebel yell and then charged, shotguns blazing. They halted at the warehouse next to the courthouse, using it for cover as they kept up fire on the retreating Negroes. Meanwhile, the cannon crew moved their gun up over the levee and positioned it about eighty yards away from the front of the courthouse. From this point, they loaded and fired four more blasts at the Negroes before a lucky shot from a black man's gun struck one of the cannon crew, Stephen Decatur Parish, and put him out of action.

By then, though, the rout was well under way. The white skirmish line, followed closely by the main force, rushed forward. About twenty white men remounted their horses to chase Negroes who had not made it into the courthouse and were now heading toward the woods between the courthouse and the Mirabeau plantation—where their anxious wives and children waited, probably even more frightened now that they could hear the sounds of battle. Levi Allen tried to control his men. "Halt!" he shouted. But no one heeded him. Then he spurred his horse and joined their desperate escape.

A white horseman pursued Allen, firing at him as he galloped. Allen made it to the woods, miraculously unharmed. But the freedmen who were attempting to get away on foot were not all so fortunate. Jim Hadnot's nephew Johnnie overtook one of his field hands. The Negro turned and cried, "Master Johnnie, don't kill me!" Hadnot shouted back: "If you had not been here, you would not have been in this thing, God damn you. I told you what I would do if I caught you here." Then he pulled the trigger.

Pinckney Chambers, a fifty-three-year-old freedman who worked for Bill Cruikshank and still lived on his land, was in the trench because the courthouse defenders had made him serve as their water carrier. He and a friend were among the first black men to take flight. A white rider gunned down Chambers's friend; then he turned to Chambers and commanded him to stop running. The ex-slave halted. The white man told Chambers he had a good notion to blow his brains out. Chambers pleaded for his life, explaining that he had been forced into the fight. The man thought it over, then said that if Chambers was telling the truth, he would spare him; but if he found out later that he had lied, he would kill him. He took him prisoner.

But this was a rare moment of restraint. The hunt for fleeing freedmen was almost frenzied. Killing black men even took precedence over saving a wounded white man. When Stephen Decatur Parish got hit, Lod Tanner of Cheneyville rushed to help him. Tanner desperately clenched Parish's severed, gushing femoral artery; he was trying to keep Parish from bleeding to death before a surgeon could come. David Paul saw what Tanner was doing and ordered him to get up and join the pursuit. Tanner objected, but Parish, apparently aware his wound was mortal, told him, "Go along, son."

"If I do, you'll bleed to death," Tanner replied.

"That is all right," Parish insisted. He understood the priorities. Tanner went off with Paul.

But Paul halted his men at the edge of the woods, inside of which colored men were hiding behind trees and bushes. Levi Allen was one of them; he had released his horse and was trying to keep an eye on what the whites were doing. Paul's rage against the freedmen was tempered, somewhat, by his fear of them. Firing at fleeing men in an open field was one thing. Tracking them through the tangled undergrowth and Spanish moss might be something else altogether. "Hold up!" he cried. "We don't know what's in there." Paul turned his group around and headed for the courthouse.

BACK AT THE FORMER STABLE, THE WHITES HAD WHAT WAS LEFT OF THE NEGRO posse surrounded. The entire force had spread out in a semicircle around the building. One group of whites took over a house eighty yards opposite the courthouse's lower door, knocking a plank from its wall so as to be able to fire on fleeing Negroes from a protected position. Another group took over a house from which they could cover the courthouse's upper door. From the nearby warehouse, they could fire through one of the courthouse's windows.

It was approximately three o'clock in the afternoon. Inside the beleaguered courthouse, Alexander Tillman exercised what passed for leadership. There were dozens of colored men crowded inside, many of them wounded, all of them desperate. They were hungry, and their throats were parched. Their ragged clothes were drenched in sweat and spattered with mud and blood. Still, for the first time all day, they managed to put up some effective resistance, firing their weapons through the windows at the whites whenever they had a clear shot.

Nash considered what to do next. He could lay siege to the courthouse, until the Negroes got so hungry and thirsty that they gave up. That had the advantage, potentially, of preventing further casualties on his side or damage to the building, but it would take time. The second option, while much more destructive, might bring the battle to an immediate end: the whites could set the courthouse on fire and smoke the Negroes out. Nash decided that he couldn't wait. The courthouse would burn. The logical place to ignite it was the roof, made of cypress shingles. First, the whites tried to set fire to a wooden cistern-house adjoining the building, in the apparent hope that flames would leap from there to the courthouse roof. But it didn't work. Someone would actually have to carry a flame up to the building, and that could be dangerous given the lingering threat of gunfire from the men inside.

Once again, William Chaney, posing as "Ezekiel Powell," came up with the solution. He and Charles Duplissey took a long bamboo fishing pole from a freedman's abandoned cabin and tied wads of cotton taken from a saddle blanket to one end. Then they went over to a nearby store and took out a square tin can about a third full of kerosene. They doused the cotton wads with the flammable liquid. Now all they needed was someone to take the improvised torch through the crossfire to the courthouse.

One of the white commanders stepped forward and seized the torch. He walked up to Pinckney Chambers, lit the ball of cloth, and handed it, blazing, to the colored man. He ordered him to take it up to the courthouse. If Chambers refused, the white man warned, he would be killed.

Chambers walked toward the courthouse as the shooting continued— on his way to save his own life by endangering those of his friends and neighbors. By some miracle, if that is the right word, he managed to cover the hundred yards or so that separated the white line from the courthouse. On the side of the courthouse facing the river, he touched the torch to the eaves, which were low enough to reach without a ladder. Then he hastened back to the white line, where he was taken to his ex-boss, Bill Cruikshank. "You're a good old nigger," Cruikshank told him. Cruikshank promised to see to it that Chambers made it safely home that night. Another white man laughed and said, "If you're good, he'll keep you for a pet."

Flames leaped from the courthouse into the sky, where clouds were beginning to gather. Inside, Tillman and the others immediately realized what was happening. They desperately tried to put the fire out before it spread to the papers and wooden furniture. They had no water; their only hope was to knock out the blazing patch of shingles. Some colored men went up into the rafters to try, but the whites concentrated their gunfire on them, and they had to back off. The roof began to cave in. The situation was hopeless.

Tillman and a friend, Shack White, who had taken a bullet in the neck, decided that they had no choice but to give up. White could see Bill Irwin through the window. Irwin was well known to the Negroes of Colfax; he was one of the white supremacists from Jim Hadnot's neighborhood. Irwin called out to the men to throw down their arms and come out. "Surrender, Mr. Irwin!" White cried, holding a white shirtsleeve tied to the end of a stick out the window.

Another man tore a page from one of the record books and waved it at the whites. Amid the smoke, the fear, and the noise, the men in the courthouse heard white voices from outside, shouting at them to stack their arms and leave the building. Recognizing Shack White's voice, Irwin called out reassuringly, "I owe you one and I'll pay it." The whites ceased fire. The freedmen complied with their orders, piling their remaining shotguns, pistols, and rifles inside the burning building. Then they headed for the door.

The first dozen Negroes to exit, some of them waving their pocket-handkerchiefs as tokens of capitulation, were met by gunfire. Alexander Tillman took the first bullet but continued running. Bill Irwin shot Shack White dead from close range. Several others were killed or wounded on the spot. Six colored men ran to the nearby warehouse and hid under its floor, where they were quickly discovered and shot dead. Seven men, realizing that the whites had deceived them, ran back into the burning courthouse, lifted up one of the floorboards, and took refuge in the crawl space under the building.

The whites' firing grew so wild that not even they were safe from it. Arranged around the courthouse in a huge, irregular semicircle, they risked hitting each other as they attempted to mow down Negroes. Jim Hadnot saw the danger. He rushed forward, shouting to his men to stop. A bullet hit him from a side angle, striking just below his navel and exiting over his hip. He went down. The Kentuckian Sidney Harris, the third of the Union veterans in the white posse, was hit three times in the back and neck. Several other whites were also wounded, not fatally. "Men, save me, I am shot!" someone cried.

"Cease firing, men!" Nash yelled. "You are shooting our own men!" The shooting stopped. Colored men who had fled the courthouse, and survived, were rounded up and taken prisoner. The whites sat some of them under guard at the base of a pecan tree near the courthouse; they marched others to a nearby field and concentrated them under a cottonwood.

The courthouse fire spread to the wooden gutter that ran along the front eaves of the next-door warehouse. The whites picked two Negroes, Levi Nelson and Baptiste Elzie, to extinguish the flames; one destroyed building, apparently, was enough. It took the colored men about an hour to tear down the gutter and snuff out the fire. When they finished, Nelson asked their captor if they could go. He cursed them and sent them back to the other prisoners. "I didn't come 400 miles to kill niggers for nothing," he said.

Bleeding and throbbing with pain from the wound he had suffered at the courthouse door, Alexander Tillman fled for his life across the open fields between the courthouse and the woods. They were probably the same fields he had played on as a boy. He ran as fast as he could, but it was not enough. About one hundred yards from the blazing courthouse, the whites overtook him. Again and again they fired. Tillman fell as his pursuers crashed down upon him, beating his face and slashing his throat. They kept it up long after he was dead.

By about four o'clock, dead men lay scattered all over Colfax. The wounded moaned and screamed; smoke boiled up from the courthouse. The whites ordered one of the colored men they had just seized, Benjamin Brim, to go back to the courthouse and bring out anyone left inside. A fifty-six-year-old tenant farmer with a wife and four children, Brim braced himself against the heat and entered the courthouse. At first, he couldn't make anyone out in the smoke and stench. Then he noticed that some of the floorboards had been torn up, and found seven freedmen still hiding in the shallow space between the wooden floor and the ground. Brim told them that they would be burned alive if they stayed, but that the whites had promised not to harm them if they came out. Six of the seven agreed to leave; only one refused, telling Brim that he had had enough of the whites' assurances. "I would just as soon be burned up as to come out and be killed," he said. Brim left and returned to the makeshift prison camp with the other six.

David Paul approached the prisoners, accompanied by Jim Yawn. For Yawn, this must have been a satisfying day. Yet his mind burned with the memory of his brother Jeff's death at the hands of William Ward's militia.

Paul and Yawn went up to Charles Duplissey, who was guarding the prisoners. "We got most of them, but the man which we want," Paul said. "We don't see him among the dead." "Examine them carefully," Duplissey replied. "Maybe you can find him there." Paul, Yawn, and Duplissey walked along the line of Negro men sitting on the ground, studying their faces. When they came upon a man with his hat pulled down over his eyes, Yawn pounced. "I got you!" he cried, lifting up the man's hat and grabbing him by the coat. He was sure this was his brother's killer. He took the man twenty feet away, pulled out a gun, and shot him dead.

AS DUSK APPROACHED, RAIN BEGAN TO FALL. THE COURTHOUSE'S FLAMING RAF-ters and hot bricks hissed at the touch of the first drops. One of the whites presented the black captives to Nash. "Captain, here are your prisoners," he said. "What are we to do with them?" Someone suggested shooting them all at once. But Nash said no, not yet. He ordered them marched to Wilson L. Richardson's house near the courthouse. He permitted eight wounded prisoners to lie on the porch, sheltered from the rain. Then Nash sent a prisoner to get water for his Grant Parish contingent.

A measure of calm settled over the whites, as they rested from the long, sweaty afternoon of shooting, riding, and running. Some of the men from Rapides and Catahoula parishes sat down at the old sugar house and enjoyed a meal of raw pork and corn bread. Whiskey began to flow. They could rejoice in the low casualties on their side—a few flesh wounds mostly. Only Parish, of the cannon crew, was confirmed dead. Harris and Hadnot were seriously injured, to be sure. But once they had been set safely on board the *Southwestern*, at about 9:00 p.m., there was not much left to do.

Many whites, especially those from the outlying parishes, began to gather up their guns and go home. David Paul assembled his men from Rapides Parish and told them to follow him. "Every one that came in here with me, I want to go out with me," he said. "Now we have accomplished what we came to do, and I don't want nothing touched. Get on your horses, and let's go."

Nash returned to the prisoners, scolding them like an exasperated master. "If we turn you loose, will you stop this damned foolishness?" he demanded. The Negro men said they would—some even promised to kill William Ward if he ever tried to come back. Satisfied, Nash suggested that they could go home the next morning. The colored men, it seemed, still had some hope of avoiding the fate of Jim Yawn's victim.

But not all of the whites agreed with Nash. Southern men had dealt with captured Negro combatants before—when Confederate forces took colored Union prisoners during the Civil War. More than once they had responded with extraordinary cruelty, most notoriously at Fort Pillow, where rebels had swarmed over the parapets crying, "No quarter!" Any Negro who took up arms against the white man in the antebellum South was guilty of a capital offense: "servile insurrection." Therefore many Southerners approved of, or at least comprehended, the slaughter at Fort Pillow. The *Memphis Daily Appeal* explained that "the sight of Negro troops stirred the bosoms of our soldiers with courageous madness."

To Southern white men, war was a chivalric enterprise, and Negroes were simply incapable of the requisite honor. They could not follow the rules of "civilized" warfare, such as humane treatment of prisoners and respect for the white flag of truce. Any fight with them would therefore be "savage warfare"—a fight to the death in which quarter was neither to be expected nor given. It was waged under the "black flag." When told that one of his officers had taken Negro prisoners in Louisiana, a Confederate general ordered him to remind his men of "the propriety of giving no quarter to armed Negroes and their officers. In this way we may be relieved from a disagreeable dilemma."

To be sure, that approach never became Confederate policy. The government of Jefferson Davis was deterred from mass executions of black Union prisoners because Lincoln threatened to respond in kind against Confederate prisoners. At the very end of the war, the South, in desperation, even authorized the enlistment of Negroes in its army.

Yet as the darkness deepened on the night of April 13, 1873, the "courageous madness" that had gripped the Confederates almost exactly nine years earlier at Fort Pillow took hold of some white men at Colfax. They told Nash that Negroes who were guilty of this kind of defiance had to pay the ultimate price. And given the Negro's instinct for treachery, it was the only safe course of action. "Nash, have you no better sense than to send them old niggers home?" one of his men asked. "You won't live to see two weeks."

Several others spoke up to second the motion. But Nash insisted that the Negroes not be killed. As a prisoner himself during the Civil War, he had depended on the two sides' adherence to the rules of war; that experience may have sensitized him to the risks of the "black flag." He also had at least two practical reasons to prevent further bloodshed: it would help avoid further trouble for him with the federal authorities; and it would boost the legitimacy of his claim to the sheriff's office. Even after everything that had happened, he still hoped to govern Grant Parish, black and white.

Nash went down to the river to meet with some other men. Perhaps he felt that he had given an order, and that his orders would be followed. If so, he had forgotten that, for all its military trappings, and for all the legalities in which he sought to cloak it, his force was not really a hierarchical organization, much less a lawful one. It was a mob. He had no means of enforcing commands the men felt like disobeying.

Not long after Nash left, around 10:00 p.m., a group headed by Bill Cruikshank, who was armed with a shotgun and riding his white horse, took charge of the prisoners. Cruikshank told the colored men that they were being transferred to the sugar house for the night—en route to jail later in Alexandria. Then he explained how they would march: two armed, mounted white men would ride close behind each pair of black men, in a kind of cavalcade. Cruikshank called the prisoners by name, pairing them off and assigning them to the various white guards. He pointed to William Williams. "I want [Levi] Nelson and you," he said, "and if you run I will shoot hell out of you."

"Go on, we won't hurt you," another white man offered.

"Are all the beeves yoked up?" Cruikshank asked, as if the Negro men were so many head of cattle. They were ready, someone answered. "All right, march!" Cruikshank ordered. The line of men moved off into the night.

Near the front of the column, Clement Penn had taken charge of Etienne Elzie and another colored man. Penn was a veteran of the Louisiana unit that had defended the Red River Valley against Delos White's New York cavalry during the Union invasion of 1864. Penn had gotten his revenge on that Yankee interloper in September 1871, when he joined Alfred Shelby and Christopher Columbus Nash in the attack on White and William B. Phillips in their home. Right now, however, Penn was thinking about the time three years earlier when Elzie had pushed Penn off his perch atop a bale of cotton. Penn told Elzie he was going to get even for that insult. He pointed a gun at the colored man's head. Etienne Elzie begged for his life. Penn ignored him and pulled the trigger.

Bill Cruikshank shot Levi Nelson and William Williams, making a sport out of lining them up so close to each other that he could kill them with a single bullet. Nelson played dead, but Williams cried out and a white man came along to silence him with six more shots. Another man aimed a weapon at Meekin Jones. "If you shoot me, you're shooting an innocent man!" Jones cried, and darted over a nearby fence. The bullet meant for him struck and killed someone else. Like Cruikshank, Wash Brannon's captors decided to see if they could kill both him and another man with one shot. The other man was killed, but Brannon was only wounded and played dead. A white gunman rode his horse over him to make sure he was not alive; he managed to remain still.

As all this was going on, Benjamin Brim walked alongside Baptiste Mills, near the back of the column. They heard gunfire up ahead.

"Are you shooting the prisoners?" Brim asked his captor.

"Shut up. We're only shooting the wounded," the white man answered.

Brim knew it was a lie. The sound of firing and shouting came closer, working its way back from what Brim guessed was a distance of fifty or sixty yards up ahead. But before he could try to escape, he heard a click behind him as his captor cocked his six-shooter. Brim turned to beg for his life—and felt a blast of pain as a bullet entered his face, just below the left eye. Mills, too, went down. As Brim lay on the ground, he felt a second bullet pierce his back and exit through his side.

Miraculously, neither man was dead. The bullet to Brim's face had gone through his nasal passages and out under the angle of his jaw; the shot to his back had bypassed his vital organs. The shot that hit Mills only wounded him slightly. Once they realized that they had a chance to live, the two men got to their feet. Mills fled, but Brim struggled to keep up.

The eight injured prisoners on the porch also heard the shooting. Some of them had multiple gunshot wounds. Weak and exhausted as they were, their fear energized them and they got up to escape. This took the four whites guarding them by surprise. One guard shouted that they were getting away. Another white man answered that they should just shoot them all. The whites opened fire, rushing chaotically after the wounded Negroes as they staggered into some nearby brush.

The whites, following the fleeing wounded, were now headed toward Benjamin Brim. He pitched forward on the ground, playing dead. The blood gushing from the wound in his face had begun to coagulate in his nose. Brim felt as if he were suffocating. He tried to blow the gory mass out, thinking that he might not be heard amid the din. But he was wrong. A white man on horseback noticed the sound. "This nigger's not dead!" he shouted. He fired at Brim's back.

Brim lay still. Blood poured from his three gunshot wounds. He must have drifted in and out of consciousness as the night wore on. The rain resumed, and the cool wetness on his skin refreshed him. Gradually, the sounds of the roaming whites faded out. He felt safe enough to make another escape attempt but could not haul himself upright. Brim had to crawl, usually managing to go about twenty yards at a stretch before collapsing in exhaustion and pain.

By the time dawn broke Monday morning, Brim had reached a ditch at the side of a road. Lying there, he saw white men and women walking and riding through Colfax. As the sun traveled higher in the sky, they plundered the dead of anything valuable, and they looted the freedmen's homes. They took beds, wagons, mules, horses. They fed their animals on grain left at the abandoned Smithfield Quarters.

Still fearing discovery, Brim covered himself with weeds and waited in the ditch until nightfall. Then he crawled another five hundred yards until, at last, he reached a friend's cabin. He collapsed, drenched in blood and clinging to life.

THE NEGRO WOMEN OF COLFAX HAD WITNESSED MUCH OF THE SLAUGHTER, AND some simply could not stay away from the scene. They crept back after dark, close enough to see and hear the whites shooting the prisoners.

Anna Elzie hid in tall weeds just a few yards from the spot where Clement Penn marched her husband, Etienne. She saw and heard him plead for his life, but she did not dare intervene. And then she saw Penn coolly raise his carbine and fire. Her man fell almost at her feet.

In the morning, they returned to the battlefield, looking for their kinsmen. Along the road from the Mirabeau plantation, Virginia Davis met a white man who laughed and told her, "You'll see plenty of dead beeves."

"Why did the niggers turn against the whites?" a second white man scolded Rebecca Jones. "Go and see your husbands!"

At the ruined courthouse, another of the whites sneered, "Listen to the cows bellowing over the dead bulls!" Amid the taunts, the black women found their men. Lank Pittman had been partially eaten by dogs. Shack White was stripped to the waist, his flesh burned. Etienne Elzie's head was a bloody pulp.

So many corpses could not simply be allowed to lie in the open and rot. For one thing, the whites needed to get rid of the evidence of what they had done. But who was going to bury the bodies? The whites would not touch Negro dead. In fact, at least one of them refused to aid the living. Richard Grant, a planter who lived just across the river, came to Colfax on Monday, having watched the fight from his front porch on Sunday. As he toured the scene, one of the wounded called to him for help. Grant heard his cries—and kept walking.

On Sunday night, white men demanded that a colored woman who had come to the field to find her husband go out and get Negro men to bury the dead. She tried but soon realized they had all fled. On Monday morning, Nash and several other whites rode by the home of William Kimball, a Negro who had been at the courthouse on the previous day but had escaped. One of the men with Nash saw Kimball and aimed his gun at him. "He was at the courthouse!" the gunman cried. Nash slapped the rifle down. "By God, you are doing too damned much killing!" he said. "You have got to stop. This sort of business will get us into trouble."

Then Nash addressed Kimball politely. "Mr. Kimball," he said, "this is a horrible business." He told him to go get the bodies. Kimball did not dare say no. But after Nash was gone, Kimball never buried anyone. There was no one to help him because almost all the other Negro men were hiding in the woods. Several had actually taken refuge in a nearby pond; they remained in the water for two days. As of Tuesday morning, April 15, when deputy U.S. marshals Theodore W. DeKlyne and William Wright arrived from New Orleans, only about four men had been recovered by their families and buried.

Participants in Sunday's slaughter kept a close watch on DeKlyne and Wright as they approached Colfax on horseback. Three armed white men from Rapides Parish intercepted them on the road and followed them into town, where they were joined by Dennis and Tom Hickman, two brothers who had helped Cruikshank gun down the prisoners. As Kellogg's emissaries rode among the decomposing bodies, they were met by another white man who introduced himself as a messenger from Sheriff Nash. The sheriff, he said, wanted to see DeKlyne.

Escorted by the Hickmans, DeKlyne rode to Nash's camp about a mile and a half outside Colfax. Nash first wanted to tell the deputy U.S. marshal what had happened and why. Nash knew the truth, of course: his men had shot unarmed black men as they fled the burning courthouse, trying to surrender; Hadnot and Harris had probably been killed by friendly fire; and blacks had been taken out and murdered in cold blood on Sunday night. He knew all of this because he had tried, and failed, to prevent it.

But Nash was not about to tell any of that to DeKlyne. When the deputy marshal came to see him, Nash greeted him and confirmed the details of his meeting before the fight with Levi Allen—to prove the lengths to which he had gone to avoid bloodshed. He conceded that he had no commission as sheriff from Kellogg, but insisted that his claim to office was legitimate, based on the list he had seen in the March 27 *Republican*. He told DeKlyne that the Negroes had triggered the worst of the slaughter when they shot Hadnot and Harris after waving a flag of truce. Surely DeKlyne, an old military officer himself, could understand how that evil deed inflamed Nash's men.

Nash also made it crystal clear that he had no intention of submitting to arrest. If that was why DeKlyne had come to Colfax, he said politely, the deputy marshal must understand that he would be resisted.

DeKlyne took his leave of Nash and began trying to organize the burial of the dead. There were only a handful of men to do the digging and a huge heap of corpses. An individual grave for each was out of the question. It would have to be a mass burial, making use of the grave that the dead themselves had, in a sense, already dug: the trench around the courthouse. With the help of a few local Negroes who finally stepped forward, DeKlyne and his little delegation heaved the cadavers in.

And when that was done, they shoveled the rich, red soil of the old Calhoun place on top of them.

CHAPTER SIX

BLACK-LETTER LAW

On the evening of April 22, 1873, the leading colored men and women of New Orleans crowded the St. James African Methodist Episcopal Church on Roman Street, in a quiet residential section north of the French Quarter. Founded by free people of color in 1844, St. James became an abolitionist stronghold in a city decidedly unfriendly to that cause. By 1851, the congregation had erected its small but opulent Victorian Gothic chapel, set back from the unpaved street, with white walls and soaring white steeples. St. James was an architectural pearl, emblematic of the free people of color's prosperity and solidarity. It was the logical place for New Orleanians of African descent to gather and express their grief, and their fury, at the horror in Colfax—and to consider what, if anything, they might do about it.

Thomas Morris Chester addressed the assembly. The Pennsylvania-born son of an escaped slave mother and a free black father, Chester had been an active abolitionist before the war—an advocate of colonization in Liberia, where he lived for several years. He spent part of the Civil War in England, lecturing on the evils of slavery, and then worked as a war correspondent in Virginia for the *Philadelphia Press*. After the war, he found his way to New Orleans, became a lawyer, and dabbled in Republican politics. He later became a general in the state militia.

Powerfully built, with a pair of intense dark eyes set off by a high forehead and a thick, curly beard, Chester offered his audience the first public narrative of the massacre from an authoritative member of their own race. It was a rhetorical tour de force that took his listeners from the peaceful occupation of the courthouse to the gunning down of fleeing black men—many of whom, he said, were "on fire to the waist."

Chester's account was far from precisely accurate: he claimed that a white man had torched the courthouse roof and that Christopher Columbus Nash had personally blocked the door of the burning building. As a moral statement, though, Chester's oration rang true. "On

Easter Sunday," he thundered, "when the Christian world was chanting anthems in commemoration of the resurrection of the world's Redeemer, when from every sanctuary the gospel of love and peace was proclaimed, it was then that angels veiled their faces, and devils howled at the bloody and revolting scenes that were enacted on the banks of the Red River."

Yet Chester had no new ideas for how his community could deal with the outrage. He ended up advocating trust in powerful whites. "We appeal to the government which made us free men and citizens, and especially to the administration of President Grant, which we assisted in placing in power, to protect us in our liberties and lives from the wrath of our Democratic neighbors," he concluded. The assembly voted to endorse and publish Chester's statement, then filed out of the little church and into the night.

THE COLORED PEOPLE OF NEW ORLEANS WERE FORTUNATE IN ONE THING: OF ALL the white men in the city who might be receptive to their pleas, the most receptive was the U.S. attorney assigned to prosecute the massacre. What distinguished James Roswell Beckwith from the vast majority of whites in Louisiana—and most whites in the country as a whole, probably—was his belief that men and women of African descent were human beings. There was nothing political or expedient about Beckwith's attachment to this idea, which he had probably absorbed as a youth in Cazenovia. It was just a part of who he was. "I know if I had been there," in the Grant Parish courthouse, he said, "I should have hurt just as many [whites] as I could and just as fast as I could, under the law of self-preservation." When black people were killed in cold blood, Beckwith believed, they had a right to swift and equal justice.

The U.S. attorney pored over the Colfax Massacre file in his barracks-like office at the Custom House, growing more and more committed. He assigned all of his office's other work to his deputy and devoted his own time exclusively to the Grant Parish case. "It has never been my portion," Beckwith wrote Attorney General George H. Williams, "to be connected with the prosecution of a crime so revolting and horrible in the details of its perpetration and so burdened with atrocity and barbarity. Protection from repetition in the future demands the prompt and severe punishment of the guilty."

His investigation moved swiftly. On May 9, Beckwith convened a new grand jury, most of whose members were men of color, and began laying out the evidence—more than enough, Beckwith felt, to warrant indictments. There was DeKlyne and Wright's account, now buttressed by firsthand testimony from Levi Allen, who had emerged unhurt from hiding in Colfax and accompanied the deputy U.S. marshals back to New Orleans. Beckwith had statements from the Grant Parish Republicans—William Ward, Eli Flowers, and Robert Register—who had come to the Crescent City before April 13. John J. Hoffman had found Negro survivors of the massacre who would be willing to testify. And Hoffman had identified twenty-three additional potential witnesses, whites from Catahoula Parish who had seen and heard the Catahoula Klansmen organizing their ride to Colfax.

Hoffman himself was Beckwith's star witness before the grand jury. In a closed session on June 11, the Secret Service agent revealed the grim details he had gathered working undercover among perpetrators of the massacre. He produced dozens of their names. He described not only the extent of the killing but also its racially tinged sadism. The agent noted that the whites had mocked and taunted their black prisoners, calling them "beeves" before gunning them down. He confirmed that the killers slashed with their knives at some victims who had not been immediately dispatched by bullets. Hoffman reported the drunken boasts of men like Paul Hooe, who had come to the slaughter with the Rapides Parish contingent. Intriguingly, Hoffman revealed that Judge Thomas C. Manning of Alexandria had helped organize the white forces. Manning's plea to Governor Kellogg not to send troops in the week before Easter Sunday was apparently a deliberate deception, part of a plan to buy time for the assault on the courthouse.

Of all James Beckwith's radical notions, his most audacious was that a white man should face the same "severe punishment" for murdering a black man that a black man would surely face if the roles were reversed. In Louisiana in 1873, that penalty would be death. Beckwith was determined to seek capital punishment for the authors of the Colfax Massacre—and, in a state where black people had been routinely whipped and shot by whites for generations, with total impunity, that was unheard of. The fact that he hoped to send white men to the gallows based on the testimony of black witnesses was utterly revolutionary.

But if Beckwith was going to have any chance of pulling that off, he would have to be careful, very careful. He must be a lawyer—"the noblest work of science." He could not indulge his emotions. Unlike Thomas Morris Chester, he did not have the luxury of rhetorical excess. He could not allow himself to focus exclusively on the horrific facts of the case; he also had to face the technical legal questions it posed.

The most pressing of these was: what crime, exactly, could he charge?

Men had been murdered in Colfax; there was no disputing it. Ordinarily, however, prosecuting murder was not the U.S. attorney's job. State governments had the primary responsibility to investigate and punish criminal offenses, except where some provision of the Constitution provided clear authority for federal action.

The Enforcement Act, adopted on May 31, 1870 (and the subsequent amendments toughening it), marked a bold departure. The legislation assumed that the Fourteenth and Fifteenth amendments to the Constitution made people of color American citizens and recognized their civil rights, among which was the right to vote on equal terms with whites. It also assumed that the post–Civil War amendments empowered Congress to criminalize acts by private individuals or groups—such as the Ku Klux Klan—that interfered with the exercise of those rights. The new phenomenon of racist terrorism against an emancipated Negro population, which the Southern states were either unwilling or unable to stop, had created an exception to the usual rule.*

Ambitious and noble as they were, the post–Civil War amendments and the Enforcement Act were, like all legal texts, open to interpretation. Beckwith was too good a lawyer not to recognize this. But to him, the fundamental issue in the Colfax case was nothing less than the true meaning of the Civil War.

AT THE WAR'S END, THE FEDERAL COURTS CONSISTED OF LITTLE MORE THAN THE Supreme Court in Washington and forty-six district judges spread out over thirty-six states. The Supreme Court both ruled on appeals and helped district judges conduct trials: each justice was assigned to one of nine geographically defined "circuits" and spent months each year "riding circuit," dealing mostly with the arcana of admiralty law or interstate commerce.

---

*Section 6 of the Enforcement Act made it a federal crime, punishable by ten years in jail, for "two or more persons [to] band or conspire together, or go in disguise upon the public highway, or upon the premises of another, with intent to violate any provisions of this act, or to injure, oppress, threaten, or intimidate any citizen with intent to prevent or hinder his free exercise and enjoyment of any right or privilege granted or secured to him by the constitution or laws of the United States, or because of his having exercised the same."

Section 7 provided that if any common-law crime were committed in furtherance of such a conspiracy—that is, if Klansmen committed assault, robbery, or burglary in the process of violating civil rights—the perpetrator would face the penalty for that offense set by the state where the crime occurred. This made it possible to sentence Klansmen to death when their conspiracies resulted in murder. It was Beckwith's legal avenue to capital punishment.

The Civil Rights Act of 1866 flooded the federal courts with new business as the freedmen sued to protect their rights as citizens. In late 1869, Congress authorized President Grant to appoint nine new circuit judges to help with the workload. These new judges were not limited to hearing appeals, as today's circuit courts are; rather, they sat on trials, including jury trials of both civil and criminal cases. In time, this came to include many Enforcement Act trials. The Republican-controlled Congress also created the circuit judgeships so that Grant could fill them with Republicans to counter the conservatism of Southern district judges, some of whom had been appointed by Andrew Johnson.

The new judges soon faced constitutional questions related to the Enforcement Act and its use against the Ku Klux Klan. In October 1870, Klansmen burst in on a Republican campaign meeting in Eutaw, Alabama, revolvers blazing and whips flaying. They killed four men of color and wounded fifty-four others. In prosecuting the case, *United States v. Hall*, the U.S. attorney in Alabama, John P. Southworth, became one of the first Justice Department officials to attempt a practical definition of the rights protected by the Enforcement Act. Southworth's indictment assumed a broad interpretation of the post–Civil War amendments: that the "privileges or immunities" of citizenship protected in the Fourteenth Amendment included the rights enumerated in the Bill of Rights. Accordingly, Southworth reasoned, the "rights and privileges" covered by the Enforcement Act must also be those in the Bill of Rights. In two separate counts, Southworth's indictment charged the Klansmen with conspiring to violate two of the Republicans' First Amendment rights: freedom of speech and freedom of assembly.

Southworth's approach matched the expectations and constitutional principles of many members of the Republican Congress that had drafted the Fourteenth Amendment. But the Klansmen's defense lawyers denied that it was correct. They argued that the Bill of Rights was mainly intended as a limitation on Congress's power. The First Amendment said that "Congress shall make no law" abridging freedom of speech or assembly. It did not say anything about states—which therefore remained free to define the rights of their citizens within their boundaries. The great chief justice John Marshall had said as much in the seminal 1833 case of *Barron v. Baltimore*. And nothing in the Fourteenth Amendment overturned that basic understanding. Furthermore, the defense argued, the prosecution did not allege that the *state* had done anything wrong in this case. Alabama had not passed or enforced a law that discriminated against the freedmen. Instead, the colored men killed at Eutaw were victims of violent crimes by private individuals. And fighting crime was the state's job.

If accepted by the court and applied across the Fifth Circuit, which included not only Alabama but Florida, Georgia, Mississippi, Louisiana, and Texas, the defense arguments would have crippled federal protection of freedmen in that vast segment of the former Confederacy. Still, the defense's narrow construction of the Enforcement Act was hardly far-fetched—especially in a constitutional culture inherently suspicious of federal power and still largely defined by pre–Civil War concepts and traditions. *Barron v. Baltimore* was a powerful precedent, one of the great constitutional rulings of the age.

William Burnham Woods, the Grant-appointed circuit judge for the Fifth Circuit—and a former Union army officer—presided over the case. He accepted Southworth's view of citizenship and federal power. "By the original constitution," Woods conceded, "citizenship in the United States was a consequence of citizenship in a state," but thanks to the Fourteenth Amendment, "this order of things is reversed." U.S. citizenship was primary, and its fundamental attributes—the "privileges or immunities" of citizens—were, indeed, defined by the Bill of Rights, Woods ruled. Congress could criminalize conspiracies that prevented people from speaking or assembling freely.

Furthermore, no "state action" was required to trigger the exercise of federal power, as the defense had contended. Woods ruled that "denying the equal protection of the laws includes the omission to protect, as well as the omission to pass laws for protection." The federal government thus had the power to protect freedmen not only from discriminatory state legislation but also from "state inaction, or incompetency." In other words, the federal government could fill the power vacuum that the Klan was trying, with alarming success, to create through murder and intimidation of Republican state and local officials across the South. According to Woods, the Fourteenth Amendment was a shield against anarchy as well as tyranny.

Woods's opinion, issued in May 1871, helped federal prosecutors combat the Klan in Alabama, Georgia, and Mississippi. Then the action moved to the Fourth Circuit (encompassing the Carolinas, Maryland, Virginia, and West Virginia). In the late fall of 1871, mass Ku Klux Klan trials opened at Columbia, South Carolina.

One of the first cases was *United States v. Crosby*. On the night of February 1, 1871, a mob of Klansmen led by Allen Crosby arrived at the York County, South Carolina, home of Amzi Rainey, a mulatto freedman.

Klansmen burst into Rainey's house, beat his wife unconscious as she clung to her young child, raped one of his daughters, and shot another in the head—miraculously, the latter was not seriously wounded. They dragged Rainey out of the house, clubbing him on the head, neck, and shoulders, shouting that they were going to kill him. Finally, they let him run for his life when he swore never to vote Republican again. Then they moved on to whip and intimidate other Negroes in the neighborhood.

U.S. attorney Daniel T. Corbin proceeded under a theory much like the one that Southworth, his Alabama counterpart, had adopted: that the Fourteenth Amendment had nationalized citizenship, and that the rights of citizens were defined by the Bill of Rights. He indicted Crosby and other Klansmen on charges including two counts of conspiring to deprive Rainey of his constitutionally guaranteed privileges and immunities, and one count of violating his right against unreasonable searches and seizures, protected by the Fourth Amendment of the Bill of Rights. The main difference between *Crosby* and *Hall* was that Corbin also alleged a conspiracy to violate both Rainey's individual right to vote and that of Negroes in the community generally. The right to vote, Corbin argued, was not part of the Bill of Rights but had been established by the Fifteenth Amendment.

Wade Hampton, a leading South Carolina Democrat, raised ten thousand dollars to assemble a crack team of defense lawyers: former U.S. senator Reverdy Johnson of Maryland, a lion of the Supreme Court bar who had argued, and won, the 1857 *Dred Scott* case on behalf of Scott's master; and Henry Stanbery, who had served as attorney general under Andrew Johnson. They immediately filed a motion challenging the entire constitutional and legal basis of the indictment against Crosby and the other Klansmen, employing the same arguments that the defense in *Hall* had articulated—buttressed by their greater rhetorical skill, political clout, and personal prestige.

Presiding over the case was Hugh Lennox Bond, the new circuit judge for the Fourth Circuit. Bond was a Methodist, a die-hard Union man, and a Republican, who led the Association for the Moral and Educational Improvement of the Colored People in Baltimore. Bond knew Reverdy Johnson, his fellow Marylander. He knew that he and Stanbery were using this case to get the Enforcement Act before the Supreme Court, where they thought—accurately, Bond feared—that the justices would strike it down. Under the legal procedures of the time, Johnson and Stanbery's Klan clients would have no right to appeal to the high court if they were convicted. But they could get the case there if Bond and George Seabrook Bryan, the conservative district judge who shared the two-man bench with him, disagreed on the defense motion.

In his heart, Bond likely favored a sweeping affirmation of the Enforcement Act based on a broad theory of national citizenship. But Bryan would never agree to that. If Bond insisted on it, he would provoke a split—and give Johnson and Stanbery their Supreme Court case. The Klan trials would be paralyzed until the Supreme Court acted. So, instead, Bond struck down most of the indictment. He rejected U.S. attorney Corbin's argument that the Fourteenth Amendment incorporated the Bill of Rights, as well as his claim that the Fifteenth Amendment created a constitutionally protected right to vote.

Yet Bond did uphold two counts of the indictment that charged Allen Crosby with conspiring to prevent black voters generally, and Amzi Rainey specifically, from voting. He found authority for these counts not in the Fifteenth Amendment, or any other post–Civil War law, but rather in Congress's inherent power to protect federal elections. That power, he said, had always existed. "It is a power necessary to the existence of Congress," Bond explained. Bryan had to agree. Bond's clever, pragmatic ruling preserved a narrow but sufficient basis for federal prosecution of Klansmen in the Fourth Circuit. Cases proceeded to trial and, most of the time, to guilty pleas or convictions.

As President Grant's second term began in March 1873, then, the Supreme Court had not yet addressed the constitutionality of the Enforcement Act. The prevailing law on the issue was still defined, albeit not uniformly, in the lower courts—by judges such as Woods and Bond. And their rulings had, for the most part, preserved federal authority to use the statutes against white terrorists.

But the Supreme Court would not remain uninvolved in the momentous debate over the post–Civil War amendments. On the morning of April 14, 1873, as Benjamin Brim lay in the weeds of Colfax, soaked in his own blood, the Supreme Court announced a ruling that would redefine the Fourteenth Amendment's scope and meaning—and complicate James Beckwith's prosecution of the Colfax Massacre.

THE COURT'S DECISION CONCERNED A GROUP OF CONSOLIDATED LAWSUITS FROM Louisiana known as *The Slaughterhouse Cases*, which began because Henry Clay Warmoth kept his promise to modernize Louisiana. For decades, butchers in New Orleans had routinely herded steers, sheep, and pigs through the streets and, after they killed and gutted them, dumped the offal in the Mississippi—just upriver from intake pipes that supplied the city's drinking water. And for decades, people in New Orleans had been complaining about it. Finally, in March 1869, Warmoth signed a new law creating a central abattoir under the exclusive control of a state-chartered corporation. The slaughterhouse would be located across the Mississippi from the city and downstream from its water intake pipe. As of June 1, 1869, all butchers would have to slaughter their animals at this location, under the watchful eye of a state inspector.

The slaughterhouse law was a sensible measure, similar to laws in New York, San Francisco, and Boston, as well as several European cities. But New Orleans's Democratic press and politicians furiously attacked it. The legislation, Democrats claimed, was a corrupt insider deal, an "odious monopoly" that would enrich Warmoth and his cronies by oppressing humble butchers, white men who traced their ancestry to the French region of Gascony. The *Daily Picayune* called the law "an outrageous bartering away of birthrights."

The Democrats' true objections were political and racial. Partly, they were angry that the new slaughterhouse would be open to all butchers, regardless of race. Mostly, however, they were simply determined to obstruct any legislation adopted by the biracial Republican-majority legislature, whose acts were, in the words of the *New Orleans Bee*, "of no more binding force than if they bore the stamp and seal of a Haytian [*sic*] Congress of human apes instead of the once honored seal of the state."

John Archibald Campbell led the legal assault on the slaughterhouse law. Before the Civil War, Campbell, born in Georgia, had been an associate justice of the U.S. Supreme Court. In 1857, he was part of the six-justice majority in *Dred Scott*. When hostilities broke out, though, he resigned and became the Confederacy's assistant secretary of war. After the war, Campbell settled in New Orleans, nursing a deep resentment of Reconstruction and an even deeper loathing for people of color. "We have Africans in place all around us," he wrote to his daughter. "They are jurors, post office clerks, custom house officers and day by day they barter away their obligations and duties." He once mused that white "insurrection" would be preferable to Reconstruction.

Filing his cases before the most conservative judges he could find, Campbell launched a series of lawsuits whose main purpose was to harass Warmoth's government. The Louisiana Supreme Court, dominated by Warmoth appointees, generally overturned Campbell's lower-court victories, but the costs to the state—in time, dollars, and loud, hostile coverage in the New Orleans Democratic press—were substantial.

Campbell's legal arguments were as creative as they were insistent. Representing the butchers, Campbell portrayed the slaughterhouse law as a modern-day version of royally ordained trade monopolies in medieval England. It violated the butchers' "right to exercise their trade," he asserted, which made it both a form of involuntary servitude banned by the Thirteenth Amendment and an abridgement of the "privileges or immunities" of citizenship protected by the Fourteenth Amendment.

Campbell, like most of white Louisiana, supported the Black Codes and bitterly opposed the Fourteenth Amendment. Now, however, he claimed that the Thirteenth Amendment protected white butchers as well as black freedmen, and that the Fourteenth "secures to all protection from state legislation that involves the rights of property, the most valuable of which is to labor freely in an honest avocation [*sic*]."

The Louisiana Supreme Court made short work of Campbell's case, as usual. But since it raised constitutional questions, Campbell had a basis for an appeal to the U.S. Supreme Court. There, he repeated the arguments he had made in the Louisiana courts, and embellished them. His brief called the carpetbaggers the "foulest off-spring of the war." In an obvious allusion to the (unproven) charges that the slaughterhouse law was a product of corruption, he added that "the misfortune is that the issue of the bonds and shares in the companies find their way in large parcels among those whose official duty it is to protect the public honor and credit." Referring to Negro suffrage, Campbell wrote that "whatever ambition, avarice, usurpation, servility, licentiousness, or pusillanimity needs a shelter will find it under its protecting influence." Meanwhile, he noted, "a large portion of the dominant population had been disfranchised."

Justice Samuel Freeman Miller wasn't having any of this. Miller was fifty-seven years old and hailed from Kentucky, a former slave state. He turned against the peculiar institution as a child, when he saw his colored nursemaid whipped for some supposed transgression. After leaving his first career—medicine—to practice law, Miller joined the movement to amend Kentucky's state constitution to provide for gradual abolition. In 1850, after it became clear that proslavery forces would win, he left for the free soil of Keokuk, Iowa. There, he manumitted the last of his own slaves and became a prominent Republican member of the bar. Abraham Lincoln appointed him to the Supreme Court in 1862.

As a physician, Miller had studied cholera and was one of the first Americans to argue that the illness was caused by contaminated water. He also did not much care for John Campbell, disdaining both Campbell's support for the South during the war and his subsequent efforts against Reconstruction. "I have never seen nor heard of any action of Judge Campbell's since the rebellion that was aimed at healing the breach he contributed so much to make," he wrote privately. "He has made himself an active leader of the New Orleans democracy. Writing their pronunciamientos, arguing their cases in our Court, and showing all the evidences of a discontented and embittered old man, filled with the disappointments of an unsuccessful partisan politician."

On the Supreme Court, Miller struggled for five votes to uphold Louisiana's law. The justices first heard oral arguments in *The Slaughterhouse Cases* in January 1872. Only eight members of the Court were present, because Justice Samuel Nelson was ill. The justices divided four to four; the Court ordered reargument in February 1873. By this time, Nelson had resigned and Justice Ward Hunt had replaced him, so the Court was at full strength. Hunt gave Miller a fifth vote for his opinion.

On April 14, 1873, Miller read it to a near-empty courtroom. He began by reminding those present that this would be the Court's first authoritative interpretation of the post–Civil War amendments—a matter of "far-reaching" importance. And then he proceeded to shred John Archibald Campbell's case.

Louisiana's slaughterhouse law was an exercise of the state's traditional power to protect public health and safety, Miller said, and Campbell's claim that it subjected the butchers to "involuntary servitude" was basically preposterous. The purpose of the Thirteenth Amendment was to abolish "the institution of African slavery, as it existed in about half the States of the Union," he wrote, "and its obvious purpose" was to forbid slavery's reemergence. These self-evident points were "all that we deem necessary to say on the application of that article to the statute of Louisiana, now under consideration," Miller concluded.

The question of the Fourteenth Amendment was more complicated, Miller conceded. But as he had done with the Thirteenth Amendment, the justice analyzed the Fourteenth in light of its purposes. It had been adopted, he said, to counter the Black Codes in ex-Confederate states. Its framers felt "something more was necessary in the way of constitutional protection to the unfortunate race who had suffered so much," Miller pointed out. The amendment was not, in short, designed to protect white butchers from inconvenient but defensible state public-health regulations.

Miller still had to address Campbell's broad argument: that the plain language of the Fourteenth Amendment, whatever its framers' intentions, had the effect of nationalizing citizenship—black and white—and putting the states "under the oversight and restraining and enforcing hand of Congress," such that "every member of the empire shall understand and appreciate the fact that his privileges and immunities cannot be abridged by State authority." Campbell's sweeping definition of privileges and immunities encompassed not just the Bill of Rights but "the personal and civil rights which usage, tradition, the habits of society, written law, and the common sentiments of people have recognized as forming the basis of the institutions of the country."

This was tricky. Miller sensed, correctly, that Campbell's true agenda was to turn every grievance of the South's former ruling class into a federal court case against the Reconstruction governments. Yet the justice knew that many of the Fourteenth Amendment's own authors saw it as both expanding the content of citizenship and strengthening federal power vis-à-vis the states.

Miller tried to find a middle ground. Though it imposed "additional limitations on the States," and conferred "additional power on . . . the Nation," he wrote, the Fourteenth Amendment was not meant to overthrow federalism, as Campbell insincerely contended. "Under the pressure of all the excited feeling growing out of the war," he declared, "our statesmen have still believed that the existence of the State with powers for domestic and local government, including the regulation of civil rights—the rights of person and of property—was essential to the perfect working of our complex form of government." U.S. citizenship and citizenship in a state were still two different things, each with its own corresponding privileges and immunities, the justice said.

Miller might easily have ended his opinion there, having shown that the Louisiana law was within the state's power and did not abridge the privileges and immunities of American citizenship—whatever they might be. But he felt compelled to rebut Campbell's expansive notion of citizenship in detail, by offering examples of the true privileges and immunities of national citizenship.

And this was the part of his ruling that would ultimately entangle Beckwith. Prosecutors in Enforcement Act cases had based their charges against the Klan on a broad notion of privileges and immunities that encompassed the Bill of Rights. But in the context of this very different case, Miller defined the phrase to include only "those rights which depended on the Federal government for their existence or protection"—meaning those which could not have existed but for the creation of a federal government by the states' ratification of the Constitution in 1789. For Miller, this included the right to seek a writ of habeas corpus, to travel freely from state to state and through American ports, or the right to come to Washington to assert a financial claim on the federal government.

Only these relatively arcane privileges and immunities "are placed by [the Fourteenth Amendment] under the protection of the Federal Constitution," Miller said. Everything else—including the rights spelled out in the Bill of Rights—"must rest for their security and protection where they have heretofore rested": on the states. Any other interpretation, he declared, "would constitute this court a perpetual censor upon all legislation of the States, on the civil rights of their own citizens."

Writing at a moment when it was widely believed that Grant's crackdown on the Ku Klux Klan had slain the dragon of white terrorism, Miller was not thinking about the impact of his ruling on the Enforcement Act. He undoubtedly thought he was striking a blow for the legitimacy of the post–Civil War Republican governments of the South, inasmuch as he was instructing recalcitrant Southern whites to live under the laws made by legislatures chosen through universal suffrage. His sympathy for the freedmen permeated his opinion, which noted that, during the war, colored soldiers in the "armies of freedom" had "proved themselves men." He quite plausibly thought both white and black citizens could vindicate their rights under state law at a time when Louisiana's constitution—drafted by a mixed-race convention under the watchful eye of a Republican Congress—was arguably more progressive than the U.S. Constitution. The Republican lawyer who represented the state in *Slaughterhouse* had urged just such a view on the Court.

But Miller went too far. In destroying Campbell's extreme and self-serving view, Miller substituted a definition of privileges and immunities so cramped that it emptied the clause of practical meaning. It was fine for him to say that it protected access to the ports, but the Klan had not killed any colored men in the South for exercising that right. As one of the four dissenting justices complained, Miller's view could make the Fourteenth Amendment "a vain and idle enactment, which accomplished nothing, and most unnecessarily excited Congress and the people on its passage."

Clever Democratic lawyers in New Orleans quickly recognized Miller's opinion as a potential silver lining for them in Campbell's defeat. Yes, the perfidious slaughterhouse monopoly had been upheld; that was a shame and a disgrace. But the Enforcement Act might have been dealt a serious blow. Miller had not only emptied out the Fourteenth Amendment's "privileges or immunities" clause, he had declared the primacy of state citizenship over national citizenship. This was the opposite of the position William B. Woods had articulated just two years earlier in *United States v. Hall.*

Beckwith, too, spotted the issue. Less than two days after he found out about the massacre at Colfax, he sent a telegram to Attorney General George H. Williams, asking for an official copy of Miller's *Slaughterhouse* opinion. The decision had been reported in the New Orleans press. But Beckwith wanted to be absolutely sure of what it said. He was concerned, he wrote Williams, because the decision "is believed here to limit the criminal jurisdiction of federal courts under recent acts."

AND *SLAUGHTERHOUSE* WAS NOT JAMES BECKWITH'S ONLY HEADACHE-INDUCING obstacle. In one crucial respect, the Colfax case was quite unlike the South Carolina or Alabama Klan prosecutions. Those cases centered on incidents in which blacks had been attacked by surprise while in their homes or attending clearly peaceful political gatherings. It was hard enough to wedge these incidents into the legal paradigm of the Enforcement Act, which required federal prosecutors to frame their cases in the artificial language of violated civil rights—rather than murder, rape, or assault. In the Colfax case, the defense team could depict the killing as the unfortunate, but hardly unprovoked, consequence of an armed clash. In fact, they would probably portray it as R. G. Hill, the steamboat passenger, had in his letter to the *New Orleans Times:* a wild Negro "riot" stymied in the nick of time by Grant Parish's rightful officeholders.

Even if the jury did not accept that interpretation, the difficult fact was that there had been a fight—albeit a brief and highly unequal one—between the whites and the blacks. The victims were genuine, but not necessarily as innocent as Beckwith might have preferred. The Colfax Massacre was most properly categorized as a war crime, but political and legal realities did not permit dealing with it in those terms. No one wanted to consider the possibility that a new war was under way in the Deep South, much less that the old one had never really ended. Beckwith had no choice but to work within the legal framework of the Enforcement Act.

Beckwith's solution was to focus his case on two of the most sympathetic black victims. The first was Levi Nelson. Nelson had quit the fight early, been taken prisoner as he fled, and then obeyed an order to put out the fire at the warehouse. Bill Cruikshank marched him out at night with the other defenseless prisoners and tried to kill him, and another man, with a single bullet. No matter what the provocation, shooting prisoners was an outrage, and who better to make that point to the jury than a surviving eyewitness?

The second victim was Alexander Tillman. Tillman, of course, was dead, so he could not testify. But unlike others killed in the massacre, there was no doubt about who he was; he had been positively identified by DeKlyne and Wright. Like Nelson, he had tried to surrender when the whites torched the courthouse, but they shot him, rode him down in the fields, and then savagely finished him off. The wounds in his body, and its position—hundreds of feet from the courthouse—proved that he had been slaughtered when he was fleeing and posed no threat to anyone. Tillman's well-known political activities would make it easier to charge that he had been singled out for attack because he had exercised rights protected under the Enforcement Act. And, finally, Tillman's murder gave Beckwith a legal basis for seeking the death penalty.

Beckwith's indictment contained thirty-two separate counts, covering 150 handwritten pages. Its structure was complex but logical. The first half—counts 1 through 16—was based on section 6, the Enforcement Act's anticonspiracy provision. Counts 1 through 8 charged the white perpetrators with "banding together" to "injure, oppress, threaten, or intimidate" both Nelson and Tillman, so as "to prevent or hinder" their "free exercise and enjoyment" of various rights guaranteed by the Constitution or federal law.

In specifying these rights, Beckwith necessarily improvised, doing his best to fit within both the precedents set by Judges Woods and Bond, and Miller's new *Slaughterhouse* opinion. In count 1, Beckwith charged the defendants with banding together to violate the colored men's "right and privilege peaceably to assemble." In count 2, he charged a violation of their "right to keep and bear arms for a lawful purpose." The case for these two counts, which were based on rights protected in the First and Second amendments of the Bill of Rights, respectively, was, indeed, harder to make after *Slaughterhouse*. But the ruling gave him plausible reasons to try. In enumerating the privileges and immunities of citizenship that the federal government *could* still protect, Miller had specifically mentioned "the right to peaceably assemble and petition for redress of grievances." As for the right to bear arms, *Slaughterhouse* had said nothing one way or the other.

Count 3 spoke of the two men's right not to be deprived of life and liberty without due process of law. This resembled a claim Campbell had made on behalf of the butchers in *Slaughterhouse*, only to be rejected by Miller. However, the right to due process was not only in the post–Civil War Fourteenth Amendment but also in the prewar Fifth Amendment. And though he dissected privileges and immunities, Miller had dismissed Campbell's due-process claim briefly, saying only that "under no construction of that provision that we have ever seen, or any that we deem admissible, can the restraint imposed by the State of Louisiana upon the exercise of their trade by the butchers of New Orleans be held to be a deprivation of property within the meaning of that provision." To Beckwith, this must have left open the possibility that the Fourteenth Amendment could protect a due-process right for men who were not resisting paying a fee to slaughter their cattle, but who themselves had been imprisoned, beaten, and killed like animals.

Count 4 cited Tillman and Nelson's right to the same legal protection "for the security of their persons and property . . . that is enjoyed by white citizens." Beckwith derived this from the Civil Rights Act of 1866, which guaranteed "all persons" the same right "to make and enforce contracts, to sue, be parties, give evidence, and to the full and equal benefit of all laws and proceedings for the security of persons and property as is enjoyed by white citizens, and shall be subject to like punishment, pains, penalties, taxes, licenses, and exactions of every kind, and to no other." In Beckwith's view, the allegation flowed from the simple and obvious fact that the white mob at Colfax would never have treated the Negroes this way if they had been white men.

Count 5 was more general. It spoke of an enterprise to violate the men's "rights, privileges, immunities and protection as citizens of the state of Louisiana and the United States . . . on account of their race and color and for the reason that they, being such citizens, were persons of African descent and race and persons of color and not white citizens." Count 6 charged the men with banding together to punish Nelson and Tillman because they had voted on Election Day, November 4, 1872, at which both state and federal offices had been contested. Count 7 charged them with combining to prevent the Negroes from voting in any future elections. These two counts could have been valid either under the theory that the Fifteenth Amendment created a right to vote or under Judge Bond's ruling in *United States v. Crosby*.

Count 8 charged the violation of "every, each and all and singular of the several rights and privileges granted or secured to them respectively by the constitution and laws of the United States." It was vague, but Beckwith thought that its advantage lay precisely in its generality. It was a catch-all charge that said, essentially, "Whatever rights Levi Nelson and Alexander Tillman may have under the Constitution or federal law, the conspirators violated them."

Counts 9 through 16 were almost identical to counts 1 through 8, the only difference being the substitution of the phrase "combined, conspired and confederated" for "banding together"—in case the defense tried to quibble over that linguistic nicety.

Beckwith based counts 16 through 32 on section 7 of the Enforcement

Act—its penalty provision. They repeated the first sixteen counts but added that, in carrying out their unlawful enterprise, the conspirators had murdered Alexander Tillman. If the jury found them guilty on any one of these sixteen counts, the defendants would hang.

Beckwith was anticipating every conceivable defense objection—and giving the jury so many different ways to convict that they would take at least one. Given the ambiguous text of the Enforcement Act and the uncertainties created by *Slaughterhouse*, the indictment was a credible effort. In crucial respects, it was similar to indictments used to convict Klansmen in other states. Moreover, as a good real-world practitioner, Beckwith was probably anticipating that William Woods, the Republican author of *United States v. Hall*, would preside over this trial as circuit judge. To be sure, in *Slaughterhouse*—now binding precedent—the Supreme Court had not embraced Woods's broad view of U.S. citizenship. But given Woods's record, Beckwith had every reason to hope he would find a way around that problem.

The grand jury approved the indictment in *United States v. C. C. Nash, et al.* on June 16. In addition to Nash, it named ninety-seven other defendants. They were all "men of evil minds and dispositions," the indictment averred. But everything Beckwith had done so far was easy compared with his next tasks: to organize a manhunt across the pine-cloaked hills and meandering swamps of northwestern Louisiana, locate almost one hundred accused killers, capture them, and bring them to New Orleans to face justice.

CHAPTER SEVEN

MANHUNT

Carried down the Red River by the *Southwestern*, Jim Hadnot and Sidney Harris had reached Alexandria late on Easter night, after the killings. The town's leading doctor took them in. Harris seemed stable, but the physician must have been unnerved when he examined Hadnot. Judging by powder burns on his shirt, the soft lead bullet had been fired from as close as thirty feet. It made a neat round wound in Hadnot's flesh upon impact, chewed up his insides, and exited through a large, jagged hole. Trying to keep the wounds open so that the pus would drain, the doctor might have repeatedly packed and unpacked them with wads of a cotton thread known as charpie. This was common Civil War–era practice but nearly useless against the inevitable infection. Lying in the doctor's house, feverish and in intense pain, Hadnot clung to life until four in the morning on April 15.

The death of a white man after combat with Negroes sent fresh waves of outrage through the Red River Valley. The fact that the deceased was an avatar of white supremacy, considered by most members of his race to be Grant Parish's duly elected state representative, only heightened collective fury. Hadnot's passing "at this time and under its peculiar circumstances can but throw a pall of grief and regret over our whole people," the *Louisiana Democrat* declared. "Persecuted and hunted down for the past three years by the barbarians who have murdered him at last, he goes to his last home, sleeps his last sleep, amid the regrets and the sorrows of a family and a people who knew him but to love and honor him."

On Wednesday, April 20, under a cold, steady rain, Hadnot's family and friends tramped with his coffin to his homestead on the eastern bank of the Red. There, his sons and nephew laid him deep within the copper-hued loam. As the assembled whites uttered prayers, their grief was probably already turning vengeful.

Grant Parish's white supremacists saw Willie Calhoun, William B. Phillips, and William Ward as the ultimate culprits in the "Negro riot."

The three of them were in New Orleans, long gone. But Robert C. Register, the Republican parish judge, had returned to Colfax with DeKlyne and Wright on April 15—and stayed after they went back to the Crescent City. Register, fifty-six years old, had never actually studied law, but he had worked as a detective and a tanner, and traveled widely in North and South America, including a sojourn in Shreveport, whence he had escaped in an open boat at midnight during the election violence of 1868. Worldly and tough, Register was not a hothead like William Ward, an idealist like Delos White, or a political impresario like William B. Phillips. But as far as Grant Parish's white supremacists were concerned, he bore responsibility for the courthouse takeover, and he would be their first target.

BRAVING THE CHILL AND THE DAMP, UNUSUAL FOR THAT TIME OF YEAR, REGISTER camped in the woods behind the Smithfield Quarters. His wife, Emily, remained at home in Colfax with their four children, who ranged in age from four to fifteen. On the night of April 20, Emily Register saw armed men loitering in the neighborhood and sent word to her husband. Register, issuing instructions from hiding, sent his fifteen-year-old son to ask the men what they wanted. They dismissed the boy. Frightened, his wife and children fled to the Smithfield Quarters, where a colored man took them in. Register soon joined them, but when he saw fires burning in the distance, near his house, his wife urged him to flee.

Register did not go back to the woods; instead, he crept to within a few yards of his house, where he took cover as fifteen armed men, carrying torches, approached the little wooden structure. They knocked on the door and called his name. When no one answered, all but four of the group left. The remaining men took one of their torches and touched it to the wood structure. Though moist from the rain, the structure was soon burning brightly. The arsonists stood there, guns at the ready, watching the blaze until there was nothing left of the house but ashes and smoldering timbers.

Unaware that Register was watching them, the men probably had it in mind to ambush and kill the Republican leader as he rushed to save his home. If so, they were disappointed. Well after midnight, the group proceeded to the nearby home of a white physician, where they demanded that his mulatto wife tell them where they could find some meat and whiskey.

· · ·

THE NEW CAMPAIGN TO KILL OR EXPEL REPUBLICANS THREATENED TO SPREAD. About fifty miles up the Red River from Colfax, a Vermont-born former Union army officer and Freedmen's Bureau agent named Marshall Harvey Twitchell dominated the little town of Coushatta. Twitchell and a group of fellow Yankees had transformed Coushatta into a prosperous agro-industrial center, complete with a steam-powered cotton gin, sawmill, and gristmill. Twitchell treated his colored workforce with respect, providing a school and new homes for freedmen; conditions were so favorable to Negroes that many of them moved from other parishes to live in Twitchell's domain. And they made Coushatta a Republican stronghold: with the help of Negro votes, Twitchell became a state senator.

A few days after the massacre, a letter from Colfax arrived at Twitchell's house in Coushatta. Dated April 16 and signed "A true frend," the missive purported to be from a conscience-stricken participant in the Easter Sunday slaughter. "I was in the fite at Colfax and if the lord will forgive me for that I wil never bee gilty of such a thing agane," the mystery correspondent wrote. He warned Twitchell that two men from the Coushatta area had taken part in the killing, and that they, together with Grant Parish men, were planning to attack Twitchell's town next. "You are in great danger," the man wrote. "They entind to kill all the yankees and Nigger officers you had all better make your escape as men enuff will come to do the work in a few minnits."

Twitchell took the warning seriously, especially after local white Democrats in Coushatta advised him that a force from Colfax was coming to "clean out" Republicans. The Democrats assured Twitchell that he and his family would be safe if they kept indoors and that only a few "troublesome niggers" would be killed. But Twitchell was not easily cowed. He told the Democrats that "there would be no surrender as at Colfax," and that he "could make the Red River valley a desert before the affair would be over."

The Coushatta Democrats consulted among themselves and decided to stay on Twitchell's side in case of invasion. Then the Vermonter put the word out to all Coushatta Republicans, black and white: get your weapons and prepare for war. He sent couriers toward Colfax to warn any prospective invaders that they would have a fight on their hands. The attack from Colfax never came—but when the threat had passed and Twitchell visited his mother, she told him that he looked like he had aged ten years.

• • •

ON APRIL 21, AT ABOUT 6:00 P.M., THE STEAMBOAT *B. L. HODGE* PULLED INTO COL-
fax, carrying two companies from the Nineteenth Infantry Regiment of
the U.S. Army. Governor Kellogg asked for troops late at night on April
15, after he received the first credible reports that there had, indeed,
been a violent clash at Colfax. Alarmed—and no doubt cursing his own
misjudgment—Kellogg wired General William H. Emory at the Jackson
Barracks. He told the army commander that Grant Parish was "in a state
of insurrection," and that "conflict has occurred between two bodies of
armed citizens." Emory promised to send a company from Baton Rouge,
which was the closest camp to Colfax.

This was already far too late to stop the killing, as both Kellogg and
Emory would learn in the next few days. In any case, no boat would take
the Baton Rouge–based troops. Many boat operators were in league with
the white supremacists on the Red River, but they claimed intimidation—
that their steamers would be boycotted and their businesses ruined if
they helped U.S. soldiers. Stymied in Baton Rouge, Emory ordered two
companies from New Orleans to prepare for the trip. They, too, were
stalled by hesitant steamboat operators. The army was not able to charter the *B. L. Hodge* until April 18; the boat was not ready to go until the
night of April 19. The attack on Robert C. Register's house took place
about twenty-four hours later, when the *B. L. Hodge* was still on the river
between New Orleans and Colfax.

On April 21, the smoking ruins of Register's house and the charred remains of the courthouse were clearly visible to the blue-uniformed soldiers as they hoisted their gear and trudged up the riverbank into Colfax.
The air must still have been tinged with the rank odor of dead men, but
the silence of the place was what most impressed Captain Jacob H.
Smith, the detachment's commanding officer. The village, he wrote to his
superiors, was "almost totally deserted."

Accompanied by a surgeon and a fresh shipment of medical supplies,
Smith had orders to help any remaining wounded and to bury any bodies. The surgeon found ten victims in need of treatment, only two seriously wounded (men like Benjamin Brim who had been shot, but not
killed). Soldiers sent to look for unburied dead found the body of Jesse
McKinney, which had lain at a neighbor's house since his murder on
April 5. The corpse was decomposed and partially eaten by vultures. Until the troops came, McKinney's family and friends had been afraid to
venture out and bury him. In their absence, a flock of the black carrion
birds had taken over the little cabin where he lay.

Word soon reached Smith that armed whites in the area were threatening to attack his force, and Smith took the rumors seriously. He had only about 150 men. Though armed with modern rifles, they were camped in unfamiliar territory at the end of a long supply line. As a precaution, he asked Emory for artillery, which he proposed to fire at dawn and dusk each day, so as to "give all to understand that steamboat cannon would not be available for any resistance to me."

Smith need not have worried. On the evening of April 25, a representative of the local community, bearded and stout under his old rebel's slouch hat, marched up to Smith's camp at Colfax and extended his hand in greeting. Christopher Columbus Nash told the army captain that he was the sheriff, a claim which Smith seems not to have wasted any time disputing—though by this time he had heard plenty from local Negroes about Nash's role in the Easter carnage. Nash assured Smith that he would use whatever influence he had to pacify the area, and offered to return later to discuss the events of April 13 in detail. Before he left, however, Nash invited Smith and his officers to a meeting with the "principal gentlemen of the country," so that they could "exchange courtesies."

Nash's tactful approach reflected his understanding that taking on the U.S. Army would be self-defeating; it would surely provoke all-out federal military retaliation. He must indeed have used his influence to keep white vigilantes in order, because, over the next few days, overt violence ceased in Grant Parish. "Since my last letter nothing has transpired of an unusual character and the riot is only spoken of as an occurrence of the past," Smith wrote Emory on April 29. "The negroes are rapidly returning to their work with some degree of confidence they will not be molested."

For the time being, white supremacists from both the Red River Valley and other parts of the state devoted their energies to a different fight: the battle for public opinion. Some McEneryite papers, such as the *Shreveport Times*, saw no need to mince words. "We shall not pretend to conceal our gratification at the summary and wholesome lesson the negroes have been taught in Grant Parish," the paper declared. But cooler heads understood that it wouldn't help their cause if Americans, and their representatives in Washington, believed that the McEneryites in Grant Parish were a bunch of murderers. They neither celebrated nor denied the slaughter. Rather, they tried to convince newspaper readers and public officials, in the North and the South, that the white posse's actions in Colfax on April 13, while regrettable, had been necessary, lawful, and righteous—a case of justifiable homicide.

Hardly a day went by without some new apologia in the Louisiana press, most of which was under the control of white Democratic editors and publishers. A favorite tactic was to present ostensible Republicans as witnesses for the defense. On April 27, Samuel E. Cuney, the colored former postmaster of Colfax, issued an open letter in Alexandria denouncing alleged Negro threats against his life in the days leading up to the fight. The statement listed three well-known Rapides Parish white supremacists as witnesses; it quickly found its way into the *New Orleans Daily Picayune*.

On May 3, the *Daily Picayune* published an account of its correspondent's trip to Colfax, under the dramatic headline A RIDE WITH SHERIFF NASH. It hailed Nash's purported exploits, claiming that "after the murder of Mr. Hadnot, he rode up alone to the door of the courthouse and broke it open with an axe. He is a man of character and has the respect of all here, with many devoted friends." Accompanying the story was the text of a letter purportedly handed by Nash to Captain Smith during their meeting. In it, Nash emphasized that he was the "duly elected and legal sheriff." He recapitulated what he said were his repeated efforts at reasonable compromise before the fight on April 13, which were rebuffed by rioters who threatened to "drink [his] blood."

On May 18, thirty white men assembled at a place called Big Creek, in the piney woods of Grant Parish. Nash was there, along with Bill Irwin, the Cruikshanks, Johnnie and Gillie Hadnot, and other participants in the mayhem on Easter Sunday. They drafted an open letter addressed "to President Grant, Congress and the People of the United States at Large." Published on the front page of the *Daily Picayune*, the manifesto depicted the entire history of the four-year-old parish as a time of unrelieved white suffering at the hands of Willie Calhoun, William B. Phillips, William Ward, and their Republican "clique." These men's thirst for money and power, the letter argued, was the true cause of the recent Negro riot, which, after several attempts at a peaceful settlement by the whites, had culminated on Easter Sunday in the ultimate treachery: the shooting of Jim Hadnot under a false flag of truce. After such a deed, "the rage of the men knew no bounds," the letter said, adding: "While it is to be deplored that such a collision had to take place, yet its necessity was apparent; for if it had not taken place all the white men would have been killed and the white women taken by the negroes."

The flag-of-truce story was the white supremacists' rhetorical trump card. It fell on receptive ears in the South, but recent events made it seem like a theme that would resonate up North as well. Far from Colfax, in the desolate "lava beds" of Northern California, the U.S. Army had been engaged since late 1872 in a bitter guerrilla war with the Modoc

Indians. The Modocs fought so skillfully that the army commander, General Edward R. S. Canby, consented to peace talks with them. On Good Friday, April 11, 1873—two days before the Colfax Massacre—Canby met the Modoc leader, "Captain Jack" Kientopoos, under a flag of truce. Captain Jack suddenly opened fire, killing Canby and several others. The atrocity was front-page news across the country; the army refused to negotiate again with the Modocs, and Captain Jack was hanged not long after his capture.

In the white supremacist press, the Negro men of Grant Parish became "Louisiana Modocs." "According to the laws of war every man in Colfax Court-House had forfeited his life by this treachery," the *Daily Picayune* contended, "just as certainly as the Indian chief who has just slain Gen. Canby." Probably the most florid variant of this argument, however, was the account by George W. Stafford, who led the Cheneyville contingent on Easter Sunday. Published on May 14 in the *Louisiana Democrat*, Stafford's article fused the themes of white chivalry, Negro treachery, and Indian savagery into a single fierce polemic, its most incendiary phrase set off in italics. He wrote:

> In regard to the ferocity displayed by some men, so commented upon by the northern press, I would say it happened after seeing the treacherous assassination of friends and near relatives, and before condemning would simply say, "Put yourself in his place." If you want a further reason, it means a "war of races." To the most observant mind it must be apparent that in a war of races under such circumstances *there can be no quarter. Vide* Modoc war. Exceptions to this rule may be made by our race before being maddened by loss of friends or kinsmen; after that the black flag must prevail.

The tale was powerful—but false. Jim Hadnot had been fatally shot in the side; if the courthouse defenders had deliberately fired at him they would have struck him frontally. He was hit by a bullet, a fact mentioned in steamboat passenger R. G. Hill's on-scene report; the Negroes used birdshot and buckshot. Sidney Harris, Hadnot's comrade, was hit in the back and neck. (Harris, who had not seemed mortally wounded when he arrived at Alexandria, took a turn for the worse and died in early May.)

Notably, there were several different versions of the blacks' purported treachery. On the night of the battle, whites in Colfax told R. G. Hill that Hadnot and Harris were shot when they reached the door of the courthouse—which was already burning—having gone there in response to the Negroes' display of a white flag. The *Daily Picayune* reported on April 16, however, that "several detachments of men advanced" upon seeing the flag of truce, only to be met by fire from within the building. After that, the newspaper said, the whites set the building on fire and shot the blacks as they ran out.

Stafford's version, the most elaborate of all, began with Negroes hanging a white flag out a window of the burning building. At that point, Stafford wrote, the whites gave a white flag to a black prisoner, "Isaiah," and sent him to tell the Negroes to come out. A "squad" of blacks, crying "Don't shoot! We are whipped!" ran out of the courthouse and surrendered unharmed. But Alexander Tillman "and his band of outlaws and assassins" were bent on revenge and shot Hadnot. Stafford did not explain how he had identified Tillman through the smoke and flames, not to mention the brick walls of the courthouse. Nor did he explain how Negroes inside the courthouse could have taken such precise aim amid the haze.

At least some whites in the Red River Valley were willing to admit that this story was a lie. On April 28, a New Orleans correspondent of the *Cincinnati Times and Chronicle* filed a report based on statements by a "gentleman" of "wealth and high social position" from Rapides Parish. The "gentleman" said that the whites had "poured fire" on the blacks as they fled the burning courthouse. "Hadnot sprang in front of his men, and shouted to them to stop, as the negroes had surrendered," the "gentleman" recounted. "He fell dead, shot by his own men; whether purposely or accidentally it cannot be determined. The negroes were not firing then. Men from his own gang tell me this is the true statement of the flag of truce story." If anyone deserved the title of "Louisiana Modocs," it was Nash's posse.

WHILE WHITE SUPREMACISTS IN COLFAX WERE LYING LOW, THOSE ELSEWHERE turned once again to violence. In St. Martin Parish, deep within the swampy south-central part of the state, Knights of the White Camellia founder Alcibiades DeBlanc called a boycott of state taxes in protest of Kellogg's "usurpation." He formed a heavily armed six-hundred-man militia, ousted Republican local officials, and went about setting up his own state within the state. Kellogg vowed to crush DeBlanc. His state militia arrived in St. Martinville, the parish seat, on May 4, only to be fought off by DeBlanc's men. Federal troops followed, and DeBlanc and his men fled into the surrounding bayous rather than engage the U.S. Army directly.

Retaliation from the white supremacists came swiftly, in the form of an attempted assassination of Kellogg. On May 7, as the governor approached his carriage, which was parked on a street corner in New Orleans, a stranger accosted him and demanded to know if he was indeed the "usurper" Kellogg. "I don't know you, Sir," Kellogg replied, and got into the carriage. As it was driving away, the stranger produced a pistol and fired a single shot; the bullet whizzed so close to the governor's neck that he actually felt "a tingling" as it went by. Things were clearly getting out of hand. On the next day, General Emory wrote to his superiors asking for reinforcements, warning that the state was near anarchy. Kellogg echoed that view in his own letter to Grant on May 13.

Ever since his inauguration on March 4, Grant had avoided the Louisiana mess. Apparently pleased at Kellogg's triumph on March 5, and reluctant to be accused of meddling in Southern affairs, Grant had taken a long postinaugural vacation, traveling to St. Louis and his home town of Galena, Illinois. He left Attorney General Williams in charge of the administration's Southern policy. The quickening pace of violence in Louisiana showed that this passive approach was no longer viable.

On May 22, Grant issued a new proclamation intended to establish governmental authority in the state once and for all. Three months earlier, he had offered Congress a chance to call new elections or to reach some other solution if it wished; by its subsequent inaction, the president now wrote, Congress had "tacitly recognized" Kellogg as the rightful governor. He was therefore inclined to do the same explicitly, calling Kellogg's election "duly certified by the proper local authorities." Invoking his constitutional authority to protect a state "against domestic violence" at the request of its governor, he ordered all "turbulent and disorderly persons to disperse and retire peaceably to their respective abodes within twenty days." On May 31, McEnery yielded, insisting he was governor but ordering all of his followers to "obey the peremptory order of the president." New Orleans settled down. Republican officials returned to their offices in St. Martin Parish as the state militia, backed by U.S. troops, finally captured DeBlanc and ten of his men.

Paradoxically, the one place in Louisiana where the president's proclamation did not have its intended pacifying effect was Grant Parish.

ON MAY 17, TWENTY-SIX DAYS AFTER HIS TROOPS' ARRIVAL IN COLFAX, CAPTAIN Jacob Smith reported that the situation was peaceful and his men were no longer needed. He suggested that they move downriver to Pineville, a larger and, for the soldiers, more comfortable town. Smith assured his superiors that this would not affect security in Grant Parish. "If necessary," he wrote, "I can be back within four hours." On May 21, Smith received word that his plan had been approved.

The army's presence had helped deter Nash and his followers from violence. Prosecution witnesses among the local population, black and white, were relatively safe. Once the troops left, however, trouble began. Among all the Negro Republicans of Grant Parish, perhaps none was more hated by white supremacists than Lewis Meekins, who had led the raids on the Rutland and Hadnot homes before the massacre. His testimony could have helped Beckwith immensely—but he showed up dead on June 10, the day after the first meeting of the Republican-dominated police jury, of which Meekins was a member.

Then there was Dan Shaw, the would-be sheriff under whose authority the Republican posse first gathered at the courthouse. Shaw had traveled a strange and dangerous path since Levi Allen let him flee the imminent battle on Easter Sunday. After sundown on April 13, he had returned to Colfax from his refuge—Henry Kearson's house on the Mirabeau plantation. But when he arrived, Nash's men took him into custody. Shaw appears to have remained under the sway of the Nash posse for the next couple of weeks.

On April 29, at a store just across the river from Colfax, Shaw sat down with Alphonse Cazabat and signed a statement, which was supposed to give the public his version of events but actually read as if Cazabat had written it. In the document, Shaw purportedly conceded that Nash had won the November 1872 election. He denounced the "riotous" Negroes who assembled at the courthouse, and claimed that he had warned them to lay down their arms, lest they be killed, "as they most certainly deserved."

Once U.S. troops arrived, Shaw's story changed. In a conversation with John J. Hoffman of the Secret Service, he indicated that he would testify for the prosecution. Whether Shaw knew who Hoffman actually was is not clear. But in his reports to Secret Service headquarters, Hoffman said that Shaw would be a government witness. Then, as soon as the troops left, Shaw disappeared. On June 1, Hoffman reported his belief that Shaw had "either been killed or driven out of the country. . . . No trace of him can be found from which fact it is argued that Shaw has been foully dealt with."

James Beckwith remained determined to arrest all the men he had indicted. But, as he wrote Attorney General Williams, "the very character of the crime charged," a hanging offense, "will make resistance or escape certain." His conversations with Hoffman only reinforced his impression that they were dealing with men who would sooner flee or fight than face trial in a federal court and possible capital punishment. Hoffman reported that Paul Hooe, among others, had already disappeared. Beckwith felt that there was no chance of bringing in the alleged perpetrators without military aid—specifically, cavalry, or at least mounted infantry. Only men on horseback could keep up with the elusive culprits.

Beckwith began lobbying for mounted troops even before the grand jury finished its work. On June 11, Hoffman wrapped up his testimony at the Custom House and left immediately for Washington, carrying confidential papers from Beckwith for Attorney General Williams. The first document was a preliminary list of nearly one hundred men who were to be indicted. The second document was a letter introducing Hoffman to Williams as the Secret Service detective "employed in the investigation of the Colfax Massacre," and noting, "I have requested him to call on you, and explain matters much more fully than has been done by letter— the difficulties of arrest, etc. He has rendered very efficient service, and fully comprehends the situation, the details of which you should know." The need for mounted troops was one of the Secret Service man's main talking points.

By regular mail, Beckwith sent a letter of his own to Williams, apparently timed to reach Washington when Hoffman did. It laid out the realities facing Republican federal and state officials in Louisiana. "The nature of the country where the accused reside (involving three parishes) is such, that it is perfectly useless to attempt the arrest of the accused with infantry as a posse," Beckwith wrote. In theory, the Louisiana state militia could supply a mounted posse. But neither Governor Kellogg nor the U.S. marshal, Stephen B. Packard, had enough cash to equip and transport such a force, which would need to feed not only itself but a large number of horses, pay a steamboat crew, and fuel the vessel.

Therefore, Beckwith wrote, the U.S. Army must conduct the operation. "Cannot the War Department be induced to permit the mounting of some infantry to aid in the arrest?" he asked Williams. "If this cannot be done, the prosecution might as well be abandoned, as the worst of the accused will secrete themselves in the pine woods in the rear of the parishes where they reside and defy arrest."

Beckwith had every reason to expect that this request would be granted. On April 18, Williams had publicly and unequivocally declared that Beckwith was to "spare no pains or expense to cause the guilty parties to be arrested and punished, and, if military aid is necessary to execute any United States process," then General Emory "has been instructed to furnish it."

• • •

GEORGE HENRY WILLIAMS WAS BORN IN NEW LEBANON, NEW YORK, ON MARCH 23, 1823. His father was a shoemaker and a farmer, but Williams had loftier ambitions. After reading law and earning admission to the New York State bar in 1844, he borrowed money from friends and headed west. His first stop was Ft. Madison, Iowa, where he became an active Democrat and, in 1847, won election to a local judgeship. One of the lawyers who practiced before him was Samuel. F. Miller, the future Supreme Court justice. In 1852, he served as an Iowa presidential elector pledged to the Democrat Franklin Pierce, who, as president, made Williams chief justice of the Oregon Territory in 1853.

Williams was a pro-Union, antislavery Democrat, and he did as much as, or more than, any other man to keep slavery out of the Pacific Northwest. One of his first rulings as chief justice in Oregon came in the case of a Missouri slave who had been brought into the territory, where slavery was prohibited, by his master. The slaveowner freed the Negro man and his wife but kept ownership of their children, apparently intending to raise cash by selling them in Missouri. The father sued for his children's freedom, and Williams ruled in his favor, holding that the territory's statutory ban on slavery trumped the master's claim that the U.S. Constitution protected slave property in free territories. In short, Williams took the exact opposite of the view that the Supreme Court would adopt in *Dred Scott* four years later. After Williams left the bench, his published "Free State Letter" was a highly influential argument against slavery during Oregon's debate over a new state constitution. Thanks in large part to its impact, Oregon banned slavery when it entered the Union in 1859.

Williams became a Republican during the Civil War. The Oregon state legislature sent him to Washington as a senator from that party in 1865. In the Senate, he aligned with the Radical Republicans, helping to draft both the Reconstruction Act of March 1867 and the Tenure of Office Act. Alleged violations of the latter law, which barred the president from firing any cabinet member without the Senate's approval, would form the basis of the 1868 impeachment case against Andrew Johnson. Though Williams was not reelected to the Senate in 1870, President Grant appointed him to negotiate with Great Britain over the U.S. government's claims for damage the Union suffered at the hands of British-built Confederate warships.

By 1871, Williams was a solidly built forty-eight-year-old with a brown beard trimmed in the then-popular style known as "cavalry whiskers." As a widower, he was one of the most eligible men in Washington. He attracted a second wife, Kate Hughes George, who encouraged Williams's dreams of higher office—but alienated many with her gossip and conspicuous consumption. Still, Grant picked Williams to succeed Amos Akerman, the attorney general whom the president fired on December 11, 1871.

Many suspected that Akerman's ouster reflected Grant's disenchantment with his pursuit of the Ku Klux Klan under the Enforcement Act. The crackdown on white terrorism in the South was, indeed, Akerman's signature issue. He had personally supervised the arrest and trial of the Klan's leaders in South Carolina. Secretary of State Hamilton Fish, the leading conservative voice in Grant's cabinet, disdained Akerman's approach, remarking in his diary that Akerman had the Klan "on the brain . . . it has got to be a bore to listen twice a week to this thing."

But that was not Grant's view. Akerman's firing had more to do with his lack of support for the railroad companies, the Republican Party's most powerful constituency. Williams, a West Coaster, was a known friend of the transcontinental railroads. His antislavery background and his Senate record suggested that he would actually continue Akerman's policies on the Klan. Shortly after the Senate confirmed him in January 1872, Williams sent letters to Justice Department officials in the South telling them that "the Department has no intention of abandoning proceedings against any persons who may have rendered themselves answerable to the laws of the United States," adding that it was his wish to "vigorously prosecute them to a conviction." Working through the backlog of indictments accumulated under Akerman, Williams actually increased Klan convictions from 128 in 1871 to 456 in 1872.

As 1872 wore on, though, Williams began to modify his stance. Ostensibly, the problem was money. Congress gave the Justice Department $3.2 million for fiscal 1872, which began in October 1871. But the department spent $3.5 million, much of it on Enforcement Act cases, which were especially expensive because prosecutors often had to pay transportation costs and per diem allowances for dozens of witnesses. Under pressure to cut spending, Williams began urging U.S. attorneys to limit prosecutions of alleged white terrorists.

This was not totally new. Akerman himself, citing financial limitations, had urged prosecutors to use discretion in taking on the Klan. But Williams was also responding to the fact that in the election year of 1872, the Liberal Republicans and their Democratic allies portrayed "excessive" spending on anti-Klan activity as proof that the administration's real concern was not the rights of freedmen but enriching Republican bureaucrats and political clients. Administration opponents also took aim at Williams's lifestyle, which included a spacious home on Rhode Island Avenue and a fancy carriage known as a landaulet.

Under pressure, Williams accused U.S. attorneys of "frivolous and vexatious prosecutions," and told them to drop more and more Enforcement Act cases. Akerman had instructed South Carolina's federal prosecutor to bring only the most egregious instances of white terrorism to trial. In the second half of 1872, Williams went further, ordering him to limit trials to the smallest number of cases "necessary to preserve the public peace and prevent future violations of the law."

In the aftermath of a peaceful and, for the Republicans, victorious 1872 election, Williams cut back further on new Enforcement Act prosecutions. On February 5, 1873, he sent a letter to a U.S. attorney in North Carolina directing that "no case be prosecuted . . . unless the public interest imperatively requires it." Answering an inquiry from a federal prosecutor in Georgia, Williams wrote that he had suspended Klan cases in the Carolinas "with the view of determining hereafter as to whether or not it will be necessary to proceed with them. Violations of said acts will be prosecuted as heretofore," Williams added, somewhat contradictorily, but

> it is hoped that all persons concerned in combinations to resist the laws or to violate the rights of other persons have seen or soon will see the folly of such a course and that the necessity of punishing men for such acts has to a great extent ceased in all parts of the country. All that is desired upon this subject is that Ku Klux and similar combinations of persons shall be abandoned, and the rights of all persons respected, and when this is done obviously there will be little need for proceeding any further with criminal prosecutions under said acts.

Williams penned this optimistic letter on April 15, 1873—just twenty-four hours before he got the first reports of the slaughter at Colfax.

BECKWITH WAS WELL AWARE OF THE ATTORNEY GENERAL'S POLICY. BUT IT DID not seem to present an obstacle in the Colfax case. Not only had Williams explicitly promised Beckwith all the money and military support he needed; the slaughter had so aroused public opinion in the North that it seemed to fit within Williams's proviso that U.S. attorneys should prosecute when the "public interest imperatively requires it."

The attorney general felt otherwise. After meeting with Hoffman on

June 16, he wrote to Beckwith at length. He did not order him to give up on the case—but strongly suggested that it be scaled back. "I should doubt the expediency of undertaking to arrest or convict all the persons indicted," he wrote. "It seems to me the better course would be to select from the number six, eight or twelve of the ringleaders and most responsible parties and direct all your efforts to their arrest and conviction; for it would be impracticable to prosecute all who were concerned in that affair, and the conviction of the prominent men and leaders would have all the desired effect to vindicate the law and induce the future observance of it by the people."

Beckwith must have been chagrined, but Williams had a point. A trial of nearly a hundred men might present impossible problems of organization and security. If, indeed, Beckwith managed to convict and hang a dozen of the worst conspirators, it would have a powerful impact. The attorney general's next words, though, were devastating. "I would suggest that you ascertain where the persons you would prefer to convict reside," he wrote, "and quietly make arrangements for their arrest. I do not think it is desirable or practicable to put any more troops at this time into the state. Therefore you must not expect to be supplied with mounted men." Beckwith was free to use the infantry to help in the arrests, Williams noted, adding helpfully that the U.S. attorney might procure horses for them "in the localities where the arrests are to be made."

This was incredible. In the immediate aftermath of the massacre, it had taken U.S. troops in Louisiana days to hire a steamboat. Now, Williams was blithely proposing that they politely ask the people of Grant Parish for horses. The attorney general wrote that he doubted the accused in Grant Parish would show "any disposition to resist." But if any did get away, so be it. "If those persons who were guilty of instigating the massacre were driven out of the country and compelled to stay by the pendency of prosecutions, it would perhaps be as well for all concerned as though they were convicted," Williams wrote.

On June 18, the attorney general promised Beckwith he would take the matter up with President Grant when the latter returned from his vacation home at Long Branch, New Jersey, but it appears that Williams never actually did. In Louisiana, the summer yellow fever season was approaching—time for Governor Kellogg and General Emory, and his troops, to leave New Orleans. In fact, within two weeks of Williams's last letter, Emory started to pack up his headquarters for the trip up the Mississippi River to Holly Springs, a hill town near the Tennessee-Mississippi border.

Suddenly, the Colfax Massacre case, to which James Beckwith had devoted every waking hour for the last two months, was on the brink of collapse.

AS THE FEDERAL OFFICIALS DITHERED, A LOUISIANA STATE PROSECUTOR DECIDED that he would act. J. Ernest Breda was a thirty-two-year-old lawyer of French descent. Though he had fought for the Confederacy during the war, he took a loyalty oath at the end of the conflict and became a staunch Republican. In January 1873, Kellogg commissioned him as district attorney for the Ninth Judicial District, a multiparish jurisdiction that included Grant Parish. Breda was one of the few whites in the Red River Valley who disapproved of the murders on Easter Sunday. He was pleased when he heard that federal indictments had been issued in New Orleans on June 16—but grew frustrated as the days went by and the expected arrests inexplicably did not materialize.

On July 7, he convened a state grand jury at Colfax, in the old Calhoun warehouse next to the ruined courthouse. In all likelihood, the grand jury consisted entirely of colored men, with at most a few white Republicans. Over the course of the next two days, Breda laid out evidence and secured indictments against 140 men. After the grand jury adjourned on July 9, he wrote Beckwith to explain what he had done and to inquire whether his state prosecution would interfere with the federal case. Beckwith sent back a brief note telling Breda that he should probably keep his indictments a secret.

The state prosecutor obliged, but, inevitably, word leaked out. When Breda came back to Colfax on July 24 for the scheduled resumption of court, he was met by between sixty and seventy men, armed with knives and revolvers. Breda recognized many in the mob as participants in the slaughter on Easter Sunday. Defiantly cursing and mocking the federal officials in New Orleans, they shouted that as long as they were going to be prosecuted anyway, they might as well kill a few more "Negroes and radicals." To prove the point, someone in the mob fired his revolver at Robert C. Register, who escaped, as did Breda, who left Colfax just before dark.

On the morning of August 4, Republican police jurors attempted to hold a meeting in Colfax. At first, only three men, two white and one colored, were present. The police jury president, Kindred J. Harvey, the elderly white Republican who had served for a while in William Ward's posse at Colfax, called the meeting to order and proceeded to the first item of business: two other Republicans had commissions from Kellogg entitling them to open seats in the legislative body, including the vacancy created by Lewis Meekins's death. The new men were seated, but that was as far as Harvey got. The police jury took a recess at noon, whereupon a gang of armed men—probably Fusionists infuriated at the installation of two more Republicans—stormed in. They waved their guns and told Harvey they would kill him. The old man fled. At two o'clock, the remaining four police jurors reassembled, duly recording in the minutes the fact that Harvey had been "forced to leave to save his life." They then proceeded to the next agenda item: construction of bridges over three local creeks.

Breda, the state prosecutor, was frightened—and angry. U.S. troops were just thirty miles away in Pineville. But they had made no move to intervene. What was the point of the army's presence? Breda wondered. As far as he could tell, he wrote later, they were there for the "amusement and companionship of the sportsmen who killed Negroes in Colfax." On August 11, Breda sent letters to Beckwith, Packard, and Attorney General Williams, telling them the federal government must act, lest it become a laughingstock.

Breda's words must have stung the U.S. attorney, who was still seething over his Washington boss's refusal to supply a mounted posse to capture the indicted men. If it had been up to Beckwith, cavalry would have long since swept up the Red River Valley. But the quixotic state prosecutor's outburst probably helped reinforce Beckwith's resolve. Breda's correspondence demonstrated the dire human costs of the attorney general's policy. At the same time, it showed that the state was helpless to enforce its own laws. There was simply no alternative to vigorous federal prosecution.

BECKWITH REFUSED TO GIVE UP. HE COULD MAKE NO ARRESTS DURING THE SUMmer months. But at least he could use the time to work on a new plan, in conjunction with the U.S. marshal, Stephen B. Packard. Packard, who had been born in Maine but came to New Orleans as a Union officer, was not only a key federal law enforcement official but also the chairman of the Louisiana state Republican Party. A well-known "radical," he had first made a name for himself at the 1867 Louisiana state constitutional convention, where he advocated disenfranchising not only high-ranking rebels but all former members of the Confederate army. More recently, Packard had helped direct the Custom House Republicans' battles with Henry Clay Warmoth.

By the first week of September, the Republican officials had come up with a revised proposal. The new plan called for no new cavalry, only a shift of one infantry company from Pineville to Colfax, and another from Baton Rouge to Harrisonburg, in Catahoula Parish. These U.S. troops would simply provide backup. The actual arrests would be made by two dozen picked state militiamen from New Orleans, who would be deputized by Packard as a federal posse and transported north on the new state boat, the *Ozark*. All Washington had to do was sell the expedition thirty days' worth of food and fodder on credit and provide cash to cover steamboat fuel and a pilot's wages.

Now it was the U.S. military's turn to disappoint. Attorney General Williams conveyed Beckwith and Packard's new plan to Secretary of War William W. Belknap, but Belknap replied that the War Department's budget was "barely sufficient for the imperative wants of the Army," and that selling supplies, on credit or otherwise, was impossible for technical legal reasons. General Emory in New Orleans objected that the plan conflicted with what he understood to be an official policy of minimizing army involvement in politically sensitive missions. Having been called upon to deal with the battle between the Custom House and Warmoth in January 1872 and the Fusionist coup attempt in March 1873, Emory had grown cynical about the state's politicians, Packard very much included. On September 14, he wrote the marshal, "I have no more right to equip and man the *Ozark*, or charter a steamer to aid in the execution of civil process than I have to pay the salaries of the judges and marshals of this district from the appropriation for the support of the Army." His troops would be happy to assist the U.S. marshal—just as soon as Packard came up with a way to pay for their transportation himself.

This bureaucratic runaround consumed most of September and the first week of October. Packard and Beckwith, and Governor Kellogg, wrote anxiously to Williams, asking for the War Department's final decision, not knowing that it had been delayed in part because a clerk had lost an important letter from Emory to Belknap. Finally, Belknap wrote Williams with the War Department's official answer: no money for food, fodder, fuel, pilots, or anything else. Emory's troops were standing by as always in Pineville and Baton Rouge, ready "to move on the marshal's requisition." On October 16, Williams cabled Beckwith with the bad news.

Washington had broken the promises it had made in the immediate aftermath of the massacre. There would be no federal cavalry sweep, not even the more modest thirty-day joint state-federal campaign that Beckwith, Packard, and Kellogg had devised. But Beckwith would not abandon the case. As long as there was hope of capturing even one Colfax conspirator, he was determined to persevere.

Beckwith and Packard went back to the drawing board. They came up with a plan for a relatively brief trip—ten days or so—by the two dozen mounted state militia men under federal authority, in the person of deputy U.S. marshal Theodore W. DeKlyne, who would command the expedition. Army companies would not deploy to Harrisonburg or Colfax. But a few U.S. infantrymen—no more than Packard could feed and equip himself—could lend support in Grant Parish and other places close to their Pineville base. It might be too little, and it was definitely much later than Beckwith would have preferred. Still, it was better than nothing.

On October 21, the party assembled on the docks in New Orleans. The waterfront on the Mississippi was jammed with boats of every description—from little skiffs to giant, gleaming packet steamers. Bobbing in this immense lineup of vessels was the *Ozark*, a seven-year-old, 152-foot, shallow-draft wooden sternwheeler built to haul cargo up and down the Red and the Mississippi. The *Ozark*'s original owners ran into financial trouble and sold it at a May 1873 U.S. marshal's sale for $1,410. Packard must have spotted the boat and suggested that Kellogg acquire it from the new owners, so as to end the state's dependence on politically hostile boat operators. Aware of how desperate the governor was for river transportation, the new owners let him have it for $4,500.

Kellogg had to pay an additional $1,337 out of his own pocket to renovate the boat so that it could serve the militia, a contribution that demonstrated the governor's strong personal stake in establishing respect for the law in the most violent rural parishes of Louisiana. As it floated at the waterfront, the spruced-up *Ozark* bore the grand title of "state boat." There was a brig on board to hold the hoped-for prisoners.

DeKlyne led the men on board: a second deputy marshal, a hired boat crew, and twenty-five state militiamen, wearing blue uniforms and shouldering rifles. Their horses came next, along with enough hay to feed them at least until the expedition could find a place to graze upriver. Once everything was ready, the *Ozark*'s two boilers sputtered to life, its wheel churned the brown water, and, just over six months after Christopher Columbus Nash's posse had left dozens of Negro men dead on the grass in Colfax, James Beckwith's effort to bring the guilty to justice was at last under way.

NEWS OF THE *OZARK*'S MISSION TRAVELED UP THE RED RIVER. IN THE COTTON fields of the valley, Negroes had begun the harvest. As they labored, the colored men and women sang a new song that both spread the information and expressed their joy: "The Ozark's a'coming," they chorused, "move along children, the Ozark's comin', move along."

But among whites, the long-anticipated intelligence meant it was time to rally to the protection of the Colfax perpetrators. As soon as word reached the junction of the Red and the Mississippi, about eighty miles or so east of Colfax, messengers rode to spread the alarm through Rapides, Grant, and Catahoula parishes. By October 22, when the *Ozark* was still only halfway to Colfax, the warning had already reached Alphonse Cazabat in Alexandria. The would-be judge of Grant Parish packed his saddlebags, said good-bye to his friends, and fled. Oscar Watson, the young man with the twin six-shooters, lit out for Texas. Farther north, in Winn Parish, Jim Bird, leader of that parish's contingent on April 13, changed his hiding place from a Masonic lodge to a church, where he slept near the pulpit. In Cheneyville, wanted men spent their nights at a campsite in the swamps. By day, they worked on their farms, keeping one eye on a hill where a spotter hung a white tablecloth from the flagpole as long as the coast was clear. At the first indication of an approaching posse, he would hoist a red tablecloth—the signal for everyone to get back into the swamp.

The *Ozark* finally reached Pineville in the late afternoon of Thursday, October 23. DeKlyne immediately sent a courier to the U.S. troops' commander, the newly promoted Major Jacob Smith. Citing General Emory's standing orders to supply troops at the request of the U.S. marshal, DeKlyne asked Smith to detail a company to help execute arrest warrants in Grant Parish. He invited Smith to discuss the matter with him over dinner on board the *Ozark* at 5:30 p.m. Having heard a few stray revolver rounds—mingled with curses from angry whites—as he steamed up the Red, DeKlyne apparently did not think it wise to step off the boat himself.

Over dinner with Smith, DeKlyne laid out his plans. His first move would be a raid on Colfax itself, where, according to John J. Hoffman, the Hadnots and other leaders of the massacre were still to be found. The Secret Service man's report was now many weeks old, but it was the best intelligence DeKlyne had. The *Ozark* would head out at 6:00 a.m. on the twenty-fifth, with the U.S. troops on board. Meanwhile, the mounted militia, led by DeKlyne, his deputy, and two state officers, would ride overland to Colfax. Unless the militia met with armed resistance, the soldiers would stay on the boat, their only jobs being to make a show of force and to guard any prisoners the militia might take. The trip would last eight days.

• • •

AT THE APPOINTED HOUR, THE TWO FORCES MOVED OUT, THE *OZARK* CHUGGING up the river and DeKlyne's improvised cavalry pounding the red dirt trails that connected Pineville with Colfax. The Hadnots and Cruikshanks lived about halfway down that road, so the posse could be upon them relatively soon—if they were home. Having lost the element of surprise, DeKlyne and his men would be very lucky if their quarry had not already fled. But the suspects might be confused by the fact that the U.S. and state troops had headed in different directions.

They were not lucky at the late Jim Hadnot's place. His son Gillie Hadnot was living there, but he saw the posse coming and ran out the back door into the woods. He was last seen dashing into some thick forest about one hundred yards away. DeKlyne left his deputy and ten militiamen to search, and galloped off with the rest of the posse to Jim's nephew Johnnie Hadnot's house, three miles up the river.

Johnnie was still at home and still unaware of the militia's presence. DeKlyne positioned himself with the majority of his squad on a nearby hill and sent Private Henry Hule of the state militia to Hadnot's house. Hule was a former resident of the area, and he and Hadnot knew each other. Apparently, Hule was in civilian clothes, because Hadnot thought nothing was amiss when his old friend showed up unannounced and asked him to accompany him to meet someone. When they arrived, De-Klyne declared, "John P. Hadnot, you are my prisoner."

Eager to strike again before word of Hadnot's arrest spread, DeKlyne sent four men another mile up the road to Andrew Cruikshank's farm. Andrew was nowhere to be found, but the squad came back with an even bigger prize: his brother Bill. They found him calmly sitting at his home, next door to his brother's place.

Once the entire posse had reassembled, DeKlyne took his prisoners and rode to the house of Bill Irwin, Shack White's killer. Irwin, too, had let his guard down and had to submit to arrest. By 4:30 p.m., the posse and its detainees were in Colfax, where, the next day, DeKlyne picked up Austin P. Gibbons, one of Nash's men, as he sat on his front porch. Donas and Prudhomme Lemoine, also indicted, turned themselves in at Robert C. Register's house. DeKlyne placed all six prisoners on board the *Ozark*, watched by the U.S. soldiers, and pondered his next move.

Meanwhile, in Alexandria, the whites' initial mood of confident preparedness was turning darker. The arrival of Kellogg's biracial posse from New Orleans suddenly changed the balance of power. Its mission could only embolden the local Negroes, people believed, and stir their worst instincts. Shortly after the *Ozark* arrived in Colfax, vivid rumors of a horrific new Negro rampage in Grant Parish began to circulate among whites in Alexandria. Most shocking of all, the cry of rape went up from two white women in Colfax—or, to be more precise, from white men speaking on their behalf. According to them, on the night of Saturday, October 25—the day the *Ozark* had left Pineville for Colfax—a group of armed black men broke into the home of a thirty-five-year-old planter's wife and her seventeen-year-old daughter. The white females were the sister and niece of the white Republican leader Thomas Montfort Wells, William Ward's ally. After ransacking the house, the intruders seized both women, dragged them to some nearby woods, and raped them as a thirteen-month-old white child wailed in terror.

In early versions of the story, it was not spelled out who had committed this vile crime—black state militiamen or local Negroes incited by the militia's presence. As the Rapides Parish white supremacist leaders later explained, however, such details hardly mattered. The main point was that the arrival of Kellogg's men had set the stage for abuses far worse than the ones they came to punish. "We all believe," a former local judge wrote in a letter to the press that was published as far away as Chicago, "if they were not the perpetrators, they instigated the negroes to the horrid deed of infamy."

In Alexandria, the town fathers ordered the fire bell rung and called a meeting of the white population for Tuesday, October 28. Michael Ryan presided. Fortune had not, in the end, smiled on Ryan's 1868 bid for Congress. The U.S. House investigated the election and declared his Republican opponent, Joseph Newsham, the rightful winner. Ryan stayed in Alexandria, nursing a grudge against the Republicans and getting ever more deeply involved in white supremacist activities.

Under Ryan's guidance, the town meeting approved "resolutions" condemning the "detestable outrage of rape" and demanding that the U.S. troops go to Grant Parish to deal with the real danger—Negro depravity—that Kellogg's men were ignoring in their pursuit of the Colfax heroes. The resolutions blamed the crime on the militia and on "bad negroes [who] commit crimes, assured in their own belief of immunity from punishment by the presence of these uniformed men." White people should remain calm, but "if those having or claiming authority do not dispense equal justice to both races, we shall take care of ourselves and those to whom we owe protection." The assembly called for "immediate and decided steps to avenge the outrage in such a way as shall in all time prevent a repetition of similar crimes."

A three-man committee presented the document to Lieutenant Charles A. Vernou of the U.S. Army in Pineville. Vernou later reported that it struck him as "the irresponsible utterances of a mob, rather than (as purported) the calm appeal of law-abiding citizens taking council for the preservation of peace." Vernou thought Ryan and the others might be trying to stir up white violence, against either DeKlyne's posse or U.S. troops, or both. If they did, Vernou informed his visitors, they could expect to be dealt with severely. "The duty of the officer commanding this Post would be clearly evident," he told them. Meanwhile, they could report any alleged rape to the proper authorities. It would help, Vernou noted, if Alexandria's white leaders showed the "same indignation . . . at all similar outrages, without regard to race or party politics."

It was never clear exactly what happened to the women. Vernou found that claims of state militia involvement or encouragement were indeed "false and exaggerated." But he confirmed that the seventeen-year-old had been violated, he believed, by a local black man acting alone. Eventually a twenty-six-year-old Negro named Hamp Henderson was identified as the alleged rapist. The Republicans knew Henderson as the alleged murderer of a colored woman in 1867—and a traitor to his race with close ties to Hadnot's crowd. In fact, the *New Orleans Republican* charged that Henderson had helped block one of the Negroes' escape routes during the Colfax Massacre. Thomas Montfort Wells believed that Henderson had been put up to the attack on his family by Fusionists intent on driving out Colfax's last few white Republicans.

Hamp Henderson would never get to tell his side of the story. A black Republican posse captured him and turned him and several of his friends over to the authorities in Colfax. On Sunday, November 9, a white mob broke into the jail, seized the Negroes, and dragged them to the Plaisance plantation. There, not far from the spot where men of color had first voted for president in 1868, the whites shot Henderson and four other Negro men dead, quenching their thirst for vengeance in the age-old manner.

IN COLFAX, DEKLYNE WAS UNAWARE OF THE RAPE STORY OR THE LYNCH-MOB mentality swirling among the whites of Alexandria. He was focused on executing his arrest warrants. At noon on Sunday, October 26, his men galloped up to the George Hickman home. All three indicted Hickman brothers were long gone. The posse searched from the closets to the chicken coops but found no one. Still, the posse managed to capture

Clement Penn before DeKlyne concluded that there was nothing further to be accomplished in Colfax. On Wednesday, October 29, DeKlyne decided to take the *Ozark* upriver to Montgomery.

As the boat moved, warnings crackled on the grapevine. "Darling we have just heard from the troops," C. C. Dunn's wife wrote him in a letter dated simply "after dark." Dunn, who had brought the little cannon from Pineville to Colfax in time for the fight on April 13, was hiding with his twenty-two-year-old son Milton, who had accompanied him on that day. "They are between here and Christie's. . . . I am uneasy about Milton tonight. I think he is too careless. You and Milt leave your present hiding place. I don't think you are safe there. . . . Don't come Saturday night. You will not be safe. Nothing more [from] me now."

Dunn would have been a good catch. The man DeKlyne wanted most, though, was Christopher Columbus Nash, whom local whites had concealed—until DeKlyne got a tip that Nash was camping at St. Andre Bluff, on the east bank of the Red about two-thirds of the way back down the road between Montgomery and Colfax. This was roughly a mile west of Summerfield, the same spot where Nash had raised his posse back in April.

DeKlyne quickly organized a raid. The militiamen galloped toward Nash's hiding place, guns drawn. But the old Confederate soldier had vowed back in April that he would never be taken alive. He leaped onto his horse and made a dash for the Red, the hooves of the posse's mounts thudding on the turf behind him. Nash plunged his horse into the copper-tinted water and spurred it on; the animal carried him all the way across to Rapides Parish. The posse opened fire, but their bullets splashed ineffectually around the rider and his mount. Nash emerged on the far shore—soaked but safe. In the coming days and years, whites in Grant Parish would swear that he turned to face his pursuers, taunting them with a defiant wave of his old slouch hat.

That was DeKlyne's last, best shot at his main target. On October 31, he ordered the *Ozark* back to Pineville. During his one-week presence, white and black Republicans had enjoyed a rare interval of security. Things had been so peaceful that Eli Flowers, William Ward's friend, announced that he would accept Governor Kellogg's commission as the new Grant Parish supervisor of voter registration. But almost as soon as state and federal forces were gone, white vigilantes struck in Colfax.

Edmond Ware was a nineteen-year-old freedman, the son of Negroes first brought to the Red River as slaves by William Smith. He had been wounded on April 13 but survived; it was widely known that he was a prospective prosecution witness. Possibly, whites also suspected him of helping DeKlyne track down his quarry. On November 3, three heavily armed white men accosted Ware. One of the men remarked to another, "Ed has been talking about you." "What have you been saying about me?" the second white man asked Ware. Ware said he hadn't told the authorities anything. "You're a damn liar," came the reply. One of the whites passed a revolver to his companion, who promptly killed Ware with a single shot. Then they burned his body and threw it into the Red. Later that day, the three gunmen found Eli Flowers and told him to get out of town. He left for New Orleans on the next steamboat, his tenure as supervisor of registration over after only four days.

WHEN THE *OZARK* PULLED INTO PINEVILLE ON THE LAST DAY OF OCTOBER, THE militia and the U.S. troops disembarked, except for a few soldiers who guarded the prisoners. On November 1, DeKlyne and his posse crossed the Red to Alexandria and searched the countryside within a six-mile radius of that town. They found none of the men they were seeking. Still, DeKlyne was not ready to give up; key figures in the conspiracy remained at large in Rapides and Catahoula parishes.

Hoping to capture them, DeKlyne decided to take his militia to Harrisonburg, the capital of Catahoula Parish, on the *Ozark*. They would get off there and send the boat back to Pineville. Then the posse would return overland from Harrisonburg to Pineville, scouring the Catahoula and Rapides countryside along the way. Upon their return, they would board the *Ozark* once again and head for New Orleans. A squad of U.S. soldiers, one sergeant and eight privates, would guard the prisoners as the boat went to and from Harrisonburg. It probably seemed wiser to keep the detainees on the boat than to leave them behind in Pineville, where there was too much risk that the local population would try to help them escape.

The *Ozark* left Pineville for Harrisonburg on Monday, November 3. As in Colfax, local white supremacists in Pineville and Alexandria took the boat's departure as a sign that they could once again operate freely—and violently. The last gray puffs from the steamer had barely disappeared over the horizon when Michael Ryan convened another mass meeting of whites in the town hall of Alexandria. "We denounce the military and naval expedition which has recently made its appearance," their new manifesto said. "We deeply sympathize with all those who have recently been arrested and dragged from their peaceful homes."

With these angry words still fresh on the page, three heavily armed white men rode in search of Loyd Shorter, a forty-three-year-old leader of Alexandria's colored community. During slavery, Shorter, a mulatto, had been a dining-room servant in the plantation home of Bill and Andrew Cruikshank's father, who had brought him from Maryland when the Cruikshanks migrated to Louisiana. Since the war, however, Shorter had joined the Methodist Church and served as president of the Philip Sheridan Republican Club. Alexandria's white supremacists hated him for that. Still less did they appreciate the way he proudly rode through town on a fine saddle horse. But his ultimate crime, they believed, was fingering several Rapides Parish participants in the Colfax Massacre to DeKlyne's posse. Once DeKlyne was gone, they decided to make him pay.

The white men found him on the outskirts of town, riding his horse with one of his nine children behind him on the saddle. "Loyd, you must come with us," one of the men told him. "You go home to your mother and tell her not to be uneasy about me," Shorter told the boy, adding that he should be sure to give his mother the names of the white men with whom he would be traveling. Shorter knew what was coming. The men led him into the swamps, where one of them produced a revolver and killed him.

Shorter's murder was especially audacious; though the state militia was gone, the U.S. Army was still just across the river in Pineville. Certainly the killers went to great lengths to conceal their deed. They hacked off Shorter's hands and feet, disemboweled him, and buried his entrails. They poured kerosene on the corpse and set it on fire. When the fire went out, they weighted the partially charred, hollowed-out body with stones and threw it into the Bayou Rapides, a tributary of the Red. They chased the horse of which he had been so proud into the water and shot it dead. Then they sent Shorter's wife a letter, with fifty dollars enclosed, telling her that he was safe in Arkansas and would not be coming back.

Shorter's death became known when his charred, mutilated corpse washed up in the Red River. Soon thereafter a colored man whom the whites believed to be a witness in the case was also found dead. After that act of intimidation, no other witness would come forward, and any possibility of a real investigation ended. When a third black man was taken from the Alexandria jail and murdered, the *Louisiana Democrat* sarcastically reported that he had "gone up Salt River to look for Loyd Shorter."

WHEN DEKLYNE AND THE MILITIA APPEARED IN CATAHOULA PARISH, LOCAL MEN who had taken part in the Colfax Massacre issued death threats to a half-dozen Republicans, accusing them of having said that anyone involved in the Easter slaughter should be captured and hanged. It is possible that their real crime, in the eyes of the white vigilantes, had been to talk with John J. Hoffman. The authors of the death threats specifically blamed James W. Forsyth, the president of the parish Republican executive committee, for supposedly inviting the *Ozark* into Catahoula Parish.

When he heard about the threats, Forsyth, a tough Irish immigrant, confronted his enemies. The parley became heated. The "Colfax men" again charged that Forsyth had called in the *Ozark*. Forsyth countered that if there was any violence against him and his fellow Republicans, they would respond in kind. The conflict was eventually defused when the Republicans promised not to help DeKlyne arrest anyone in Catahoula, and the Colfax men promised not to kill the Republicans.

After that, DeKlyne and his men had no chance. Leaving Catahoula Parish empty-handed, they decided to try one last raid back in Rapides Parish. At 2:00 a.m. on November 11, they descended at a gallop on Alexandria. The men surrounded the houses of several wanted men. But each time, the suspects had escaped just before the militiamen arrived.

There was nothing more to do. At noon on November 12, some twenty-two days after the *Ozark* first left New Orleans, DeKlyne put his posse and their seven prisoners on board the steamer and headed back down the Red River. A U.S. Army officer in Pineville reported that "the smoke from her chimneys was still in sight, when the fugitives began to return to their homes."

The expedition had fallen far short of Beckwith's original goals and had triggered a loud and sometimes bloody white backlash. The failure to capture Nash was especially disappointing. But given its limited resources, DeKlyne's force had managed to arrest a respectable number of targets: seven men, including some of the worst offenders, such as Bill Cruikshank, Johnnie Hadnot, and Bill Irwin. If Attorney General Williams meant his suggestion that Beckwith should pick "six, eight or a dozen" of the ringleaders for prosecution as a quota, then it had at least been partially filled.

CHAPTER EIGHT

LOUISIANA ON TRIAL

The Orleans Parish Prison loomed behind a row of scraggly trees, on a barren stretch of dirt road between the Treme Market and Congo Square in the French Quarter. Some of the most savage thieves and murderers in the South were incarcerated there, awaiting trial or hanging. Plastered and painted to resemble granite, the three-story brick building was made up of two wings—each approximately sixty feet long by seventy feet wide. Alarm bells were mounted on the roof. There were two strong iron doors in front—and it was through that grim entry that state militiamen and deputy U.S. marshals escorted the seven Grant Parish prisoners on November 14, 1873. They took them to their new home on the second floor: a drafty ten-by-twelve-foot cell, with hard beds, a bare floor, and iron bars across the windows. A cheap framed painting adorned the drab walls.

But before the doors clanged shut behind them, the prisoners had been given an opportunity to speak to the Crescent City press. The *New Orleans Times* printed their statements on November 15. Burly, self-confident William J. Cruikshank described himself as the fifty-year-old owner of 2,500 acres valued by the tax assessor at seventy-two thousand dollars. He denied being in Colfax on the day of the massacre, claiming that, because of threats against him and his family by the Negroes, he had fled to Alexandria two weeks before Easter and remained there through April 13. John P. Hadnot, nineteen years old, explained that armed and dangerous Negroes had come to his house on April 3, looking for his uncle Jim. They left a note saying that William Ward would pay fifty dollars for the elder Hadnot's head. Austin P. Gibbons said that he left his place near Colfax on April 6, because of the "threats of the Negroes to kill every man, woman and child in the parish," and did not come back until April 16.

At fifty-three, Donas Lemoine was the oldest of the group. He said that he, too, left Colfax on April 5 and did not come back until after Easter, except for two brief visits to get feed for his horse. His twenty-nine-year-old stepson, Prudhomme Lemoine, said he could prove that he was in church at Cloutierville, twenty-nine miles away, on the day of the massacre. Bill Irwin said that he was actually a deputy sheriff appointed by Robert C. Register. Clement Penn noted that he was home when he was arrested, adding, "That is all I have to say."

These statements left more than a few questions unanswered. One didn't have to parse the words of Hadnot, Penn, and Irwin, for example, to see that they did not deny being in Colfax on the day of the massacre. And none of the declarations had any legal significance, because they were not made under oath, and never would be: in 1874, the defendant in a federal trial not only was allowed to remain silent—but had to. According to the old common-law assumption, the accused's testimony would be self-serving and thus inherently suspect. Only confessions were admissible. The real purpose of the Grant Parish prisoners' statements was political.

BY THE FALL OF 1873, THE WHITE SUPREMACIST MOVEMENT IN LOUISIANA WAS sputtering like an aging steamboat. McEnery still claimed to be governor, but with each passing day the danger grew that whites might resign themselves to Kellogg for a few more years. Some white leaders actually considered a political alliance with top members of the New Orleans colored elite. Nothing came of it, but the short-lived "Unification" movement showed that the campaign to oust Kellogg and "redeem" Louisiana needed new energy and new ideas.

Out of this lull emerged the Committee of 70, an organization of prominent New Orleans lawyers, businessmen, and politicians who backed McEnery. Eschewing open advocacy of violence, the Committee of 70 tried to keep the "governor's" cause alive through aggressive propaganda in Louisiana, and a lobbying effort in Washington aimed at winning McEnery recognition, or at least sympathy, from Congress.

The New Orleans lawyer Robert Hardin Marr chaired the Committee. Fifty-three years old, Marr had a thin, angular face, high cheekbones, and an uncommonly large pair of ears set off by a shock of short black hair. He looked eerily like the young Abe Lincoln, but the two had little else in common. Marr moved to Louisiana in 1845 and later married his first cousin. He was too old to serve in the Confederate army, but his passion for the Lost Cause was fervent. When the Union reoccupied New Orleans in 1862, Marr refused to swear allegiance to the United States, and the Yankees expelled him to rebel-held Louisiana. After the war, he devoted himself to such causes as the readmission of Southern lawyers to practice in the federal courts, until he joined the McEnery campaign in 1872.

Marr had one talent Louisiana's white supremacists desperately needed: a silver tongue. He had a knack for recasting their most regressive racial ideas and aggressive political demands in honeyed terms of state sovereignty and constitutional traditionalism. He sensed that there was still much political hay to be made—in both the North and the South—by insisting that the real problem in Louisiana was not white resistance but the corrupt and dictatorial carpetbagger regime.

As soon as the Grant Parish prisoners reached New Orleans, Marr volunteered to represent them. Their statements upon arrival show his unmistakable influence. For Marr, the defendants were the perfect cause to reenergize white supremacism in Louisiana. Theirs was the story of every white man who had tried to stand up in self-defense against the carpetbaggers and scalawags and their ignorant Negro dupes—or who had only dreamed of doing so. And Marr was going to use this trial to tell it—not only to the jury but to the city of New Orleans, the Southern states beyond, and the entire United States of America.

Many New Orleans lawyers were eager to help Marr and reap the free publicity that would come from representing such popular clients. Marr picked the best and most politically dependable, starting with Ezekiel John Ellis, a fellow member of the Committee of 70. Just thirty-three years old, John Ellis, as he was called, was a young star in the Louisiana Democratic Party. A Confederate officer in the Civil War, he was captured by U.S. troops in February 1863 and spent the rest of the war at the Union prison on Johnson's Island in Lake Erie—with Christopher Columbus Nash. But while Nash wandered central Louisiana after his release, Ellis went back to his home parish of St. Tammany, opened a law practice, and won election to the state senate, in which he served from 1866 to 1870. The *New Orleans Bee* described him as a "brilliant orator" and a "stump speaker par excellence."

Ellis and Marr were masters at lobbying, speech making, and press manipulation. But they would be going up against a first-class legal technician in James Beckwith, and so they would need someone just as good for drafting motions, preparing defense witnesses to testify, and cross-examining the prosecution's witnesses. Marr picked a brilliant Massachusetts-born attorney named William R. Whitaker. Whitaker had come to New Orleans with the Union army, then stayed on after the war as one of the conservative Republicans who staffed the Custom House during the Johnson administration. By 1872, he had gone over completely to the white supremacist camp, serving as legal counsel to both the Democratic Party state committee and Warmoth's voter registration operation.

Some 120 people said they would come from the Red River Valley to testify for the defense. It would not be cheap to bring them to the Crescent City. The defense had other costs, too: printing, stenographers, and, of course, lawyers' fees. And something had to be done to make the prisoners comfortable behind bars. A January 18, 1874, story in the *Daily Picayune*, headlined OUR MODERN BASTILLE, called their cell in the Orleans Parish Prison a "vile dungeon" where the "horrors of close confinement" had turned them into "mere wrecks of men."

Marr and his allies launched a fund-raising drive. With newspapers urging readers to contribute and local performers lending their talents to the cause, the campaign soon became a kind of festival, raising thousands of dollars at a time when even the wealthy in Louisiana were still feeling the economic effects of the war. Mrs. R. K. Gibbs of Mansfield, near Shreveport, donated $105. In Alexandria, the town's thespians staged a benefit before a full house. In New Orleans, "Dr. Mehav" filled Exposition Hall with his "Grand Prestidigitation Performance" on behalf of the prisoners. The Shakespeare Club and Orleans Dramatic Association put on Edward Bulwer-Lytton's comedy *Money* at the Varieties Theatre—admission, one dollar.

Thanks to the donations, liberally spread around among their already sympathetic prison guards, the Grant Parish defendants were soon enjoying hotel-like conditions in their prison. And the defense chartered a steamboat, the *St. Mary*, to carry witnesses to New Orleans from the Red River Valley free of charge. "All their expenses will be paid in New Orleans whilst there," the *Louisiana Democrat* reported. There was, of course, a fine line between helping witnesses from a poor, rural parish do their civic duty—and buying their testimony. The defense team was not afraid to cross it.

As the defense fund swelled in New Orleans, Louisiana's white supremacists took their campaign on behalf of the defendants all the way to Washington, D.C. On February 25, 1874, a stern-looking man with neatly combed black hair and a trim gray beard knocked on the front door of the White House. It was John McEnery, accompanied by Robert Marr. McEnery wanted to discuss the Colfax Massacre case. Informed that the president was busy, McEnery left a petition from the "citizens of Grant Parish," pleading for executive clemency on behalf of the defendants. The document explained that the blame for the massacre lay with Radical Republicans who "did not scruple to excite the ignorant colored population by speeches of the most virulent character."

Attached were the signatures, or *X*'s, of some 391 men, both white and colored, proof that the Grant Parish prisoners enjoyed support across racial lines. The list included Wilson L. Richardson of Colfax and, not surprisingly, several men who had been indicted for the massacre, but who had so far avoided arrest.

Rather more unexpected were the names of the Negroes: among them were Shack White and Henry Hall. Both men were dead. They had been killed at Colfax on April 13, 1873.

The name of Jesse McKinney was on the list as well.

PRESIDENT GRANT PAID NO HEED. HE SENT THE DOCUMENT OVER TO THE JUSTICE Department, where it was filed and forgotten. Beckwith never saw it, but he needed no reminders of his opponents' zeal. Death threats had started coming to his office early in the case and never seemed to stop. Some of the notes and letters stated their intimidating purpose bluntly: let the Grant Parish prisoners go, or you will be killed. Others pretended friendly advice— a word to the wise suggesting that it might be in Beckwith's interest to drop the Colfax case. All went into the wastebasket of his cramped second-floor office at the Custom House. But the menace must have taken a toll on him.

The Justice Department squeezed every penny in Beckwith's puny budget. He had to write Attorney General Williams personally for permission to hire a court stenographer. Williams consented but otherwise offered no special financial assistance; Beckwith had to supply $150 of his own money for printing and the services of an extra clerk. These were troubled, distracting times for the attorney general. On December 1, 1873, President Grant had nominated him to be chief justice of the United States, in place of Salmon P. Chase, who had died in May. Williams had immediately come under attack from his many political enemies, who dug up an accusation that his handsome landaulet carriage had been paid for with $1,600 of Justice Department money. The actual evidence for this charge was murky—Williams had earned a legitimate fortune in Oregon—but the anti-Grant press began to deride him as "Landaulet Williams." By Christmas, it was clear that Williams's nomination was dead; two days after the New Year, he withdrew. The episode undoubtedly reinforced Williams's skittishness about staying within his budget.

Perhaps the only person Beckwith could count on was Catherine, with whom he had recently moved to a brick town house at 182 Canal Street, at the busy corner of Canal and Dryades streets, across the wide boulevard from the French Quarter and a few blocks south of the Custom House. Beckwith's wife had long since grown used to her husband's workaholism and sleepless nights. She made his work ethic a part of her novel *The Winthrops*, writing of Fred Houghton's earnest, but futile, "attempts to 'leave the office behind him when he came home,'" which "won him as much approbation as if he had been successful." Hers was the role of Fred Houghton's wife, "Frankie Winthrop," "whose own pen copied pages of the documents needed in some emergency."

Recent news had not been all bad for Beckwith. On November 14, as the Grant Parish prisoners arrived in New Orleans, General Emory split the army forces stationed at Pineville and sent half of them to Colfax. The attacks on J. Ernest Breda and Robert C. Register, as well as the murder of Edmond Ware and the lynching of Hamp Henderson, had apparently convinced Emory that the peace could not be kept in Grant Parish by troops stationed four hours away. The new garrison amounted to only a few dozen soldiers. But their presence might deter white violence and thus encourage prosecution witnesses to testify in New Orleans when the time came.

The deputy U.S. marshals had also brought in two more of the ninety-eight suspects named in the indictment—without army assistance or extra money from the Justice Department. They arrested sixty-two-year-old Alfred C. Lewis shortly after New Year's Day, 1874, while he was on a visit to New Orleans. When Theodore W. DeKlyne went back to Colfax in mid-February to gather prosecution witnesses, he stumbled upon Tom Hickman, who peacefully submitted to arrest. Now there would be nine defendants, not seven—far too few to suit Beckwith, but at least a bit closer to the maximum of twelve that Williams had suggested.

There was one problem Beckwith had not been able to overcome: he would have to make his case based on almost no testimony from white witnesses. He had lined up Robert C. Register and his wife, Emily, along with Willie Calhoun and the two deputy marshals, DeKlyne and William Wright. But these were Republicans long since written off by most of the white community. The defense could brand them as partisans. What Beckwith needed were people like the defendants themselves to swear on the Bible and tell the jury what had happened—and that it was wrong.

Dozens, perhaps hundreds, of white people in the Red River Valley knew their neighbors had shot Negro prisoners in cold blood on Easter Sunday. They had watched Nash's men assemble, load weapons, saddle horses. They had heard them boast later. Yet, except for the Registers and Calhoun, not a single white person came forward to denounce it. They approved of what had been done. And if any of them did not—well, they could consider the attacks on Register and J. Ernest Breda, and the expulsion of the Grant Parish police jury president, Kindred Harvey. John J. Hoffman's Catahoula Parish witnesses backed out.

Prosecutors in the South Carolina Ku Klux trials used confessions or testimony from Klan insiders who had turned state's evidence in return for leniency. Early in his investigation, Hoffman had suggested to Beckwith that some of the guilty parties in the Colfax massacre, too, might also testify for the government—if the U.S. attorney gave them immunity from prosecution and assumed the risk that the jury might dismiss testimony from turncoats. That potential source of information had also dried up. In fact, the list of defense witnesses included some whites who had actually helped the Negroes on Easter Sunday but later switched sides.

Most damaging of all for Beckwith, Dan Shaw opted to testify for the prisoners. As the would-be sheriff under whose authority the mostly colored posse had assembled at the courthouse, Shaw could have helped the prosecution establish that the Negroes had gathered for a lawful purpose. But Shaw was a weak and frightened man. After meeting with Bill Cruikshank at the Orleans Parish Prison, he accepted the defense's offer of $1.50 per day to cover his "expenses" in New Orleans, up to a total of $150.

Defying deep-rooted tradition, Beckwith would have to rely on the testimony of Negroes. In the antebellum South, no Negro, slave or free, could testify against a white man in any case, much less a capital one. This prohibition had been nullified by the federal Civil Rights Act of 1866, the Fourteenth Amendment, and Louisiana's 1868 constitution. But law was one thing—and prejudice quite another. By no means had the white men of Louisiana, some of whom would be on the jury, conceded that a colored man's word could, or should, be trusted in a court of law. Beckwith, clearly, had no margin for error. If eleven jurors voted to convict and the twelfth refused, a mistrial would be all the U.S. attorney would have to show for his months of effort.

Beckwith could offer his witnesses a small per diem and transport to New Orleans at government expense. He would have to hope that these modest inducements, together with the Negroes' thirst for justice and the loud but unenforceable threat of subpoena, could overcome their fears. Christopher Columbus Nash and his men still roamed freely; no Negro who testified could feel completely safe in Grant Parish, even if there was a small U.S. Army encampment in Colfax.

ON FEBRUARY 23, 1874, THE APPOINTED DAY FOR THE BEGINNING OF THE TRIAL, the morning temperature in New Orleans hovered around fifty degrees— quite chilly for southern Louisiana. Beckwith knew that the deputy marshalls had summoned dozens of colored men and women, and arranged for them to travel to the city by steamboat. And sure enough, when he arrived at the Custom House, the sidewalk was crowded with these colored witnesses, dressed in their rough plantation finery: ill-fitting suits for the men, calico dresses for the women.

Their next few steps would take them into the Custom House—the largest building in the United States. The seventy-five-foot-tall irregular trapezoid had been authorized by Congress in 1845, in part to handle the heavy flow of trade through New Orleans, and in part to provide a visible symbol of U.S. sovereignty over the lower Mississippi Valley, which was then close to hostile Mexican territory. During the Civil War, the cavernous, unfinished building contained both the Union army's headquarters and a makeshift prison for captured Confederates, including two thousand men seized during the Red River Campaign. Construction resumed after the war, and by 1874 the building—though still not complete—housed not only a huge team of customs inspectors and duty collectors but also the post office, Beckwith's office, and the federal court.

The Custom House's exterior walls were made out of huge gray blocks of granite from a quarry in Quincy, Massachusetts. A wide staircase, also granite, led to the entrance. Four immense Egyptian-style columns with lotus-blossom capitals crowned the doorway. The heavy iron front door swung open to a three-story-high chamber with a floor made of cool, gleaming black and white marble from New York. As they entered, the colored men and women of Grant Parish would have felt their eyes drawn to the light pouring through the building's glass ceiling, which was fifty-four feet above the floor, supported by fourteen white Italian marble columns. Each column was decorated with carved images of Mercury, representing New Orleans's commerce, and Luna, representing the crescent-moon shape of the city. Even New Orleanians found it imposing. For the Negroes from the old Calhoun lands, it must have been startling.

Still, in they came, walking through the chamber and up the sweeping staircase at its rear. At the top of the stairs, they turned left and took a few steps down a short marble-floored hall to the courtroom. This, too, was a grand space—its soaring thirty-six-foot ceiling a visible symbol of the law's loftiest intentions. There were high-backed wooden chairs for spectators, separated from the defense and prosecution tables by a stolid railing of carved mahogany. To the left of the lawyers was the jury box. At the head of the massive room loomed the judges' bench, fashioned from wood as dark and rich as the paneling on the high wall behind it.

An uneasy reunion of the Grant Parish population took place as the colored men and women took their seats in the spectators' section, alongside the mostly white people who had come to testify for the defense. The rest of the seats were taken up by people from the city, including leading men of politics and the bar. The men of the New Orleans press huddled at the defense table. "Much popular interest has been manifested in the proceedings," the *Daily Picayune* observed, in a rare understatement. At 11:00 a.m., when the court crier bellowed "All rise," the huge audience rose like a human wave. A door connecting the judge's chambers to the courtroom opened, and William B. Woods ascended the bench in his black robe.

BORN IN NEWARK, OHIO, IN 1824, WOODS WAS A TALL, CRAGGY-FACED MAN WITH A thick beard and sterling credentials—legal, political, and military. He was the valedictorian of Yale's class of 1845. His hometown elected him mayor in 1856; the next year, voters sent him to the state legislature, where he rose quickly to the leadership of the Democratic caucus. As a Democrat, Woods opposed Lincoln's election and resisted a measure to finance a Union contingent from Ohio after the rebels fired on Fort Sumter. But he soon changed his mind. Woods's switch was crucial to the solidification of Ohio's support for the Northern war effort—and signaled his sincere dedication to the Union cause. He spent the next three years in the army, rising to the rank of general and serving with Grant at the siege of Vicksburg. After the war, he became a Republican and settled in Alabama, where he grew cotton, practiced law, and served as a state judge. Woods's ruling in *United States v. Hall* reflected his transformation in the crucible of the Civil War.

The trial had been delayed at Beckwith's request until the final week of February (after Mardi Gras) because it was the earliest date at which Woods would be able to make the trip from his home in Mobile. This assignment was not without danger for the Republican jurist, who had also met with threats and verbal abuse in New Orleans. Beckwith had insisted that the Justice Department pick up the tab for a verbatim transcript of the trial in part because Woods thought a clear record was his best protection against charges of bias and manipulation.

As soon as Woods gaveled the court to order, defense counsel were on their feet, asking the court to let Judge Edward H. Durell, the federal district judge for Louisiana, preside as well. Under the practice of the day, a two-man bench was permissible; in theory, it would help the defense because if the two judges disagreed on any legal issues, that would create the basis for an appeal to the Supreme Court. But Durell and Woods were like-minded Republicans, so it was unlikely this was the defense's real motivation. More likely, they wanted to get Durell in front of the white members of the jury. For New Orleans whites, Durell was the villainous judge who had ruled in Kellogg's favor during the 1872 election crisis.

His very presence could recall that episode and tilt them against Beckwith's case. Woods said he would leave it up to Durell. The judge, bitter that his political enemies had started impeachment proceedings against him in retaliation for the election decision, was in no mood to help. He sent word that he was ill.*

That left Woods to rule alone on the first defense motions, just as Beckwith had wanted. The defense mounted technical attacks on the indictment, claiming that it was invalid because it did not state explicitly that it was found by twelve grand jurors who had taken the proper oath, and because all the grand jurors were Republicans. The second of these objections was transparently specious. The first was pointless even if true; at most, it would delay the trial for a few days. The U.S. attorney did not even bother to argue against the motions, and Woods swiftly overruled them.

Then the defense raised a more serious challenge—to the all-important jury pool. The defense wanted to maximize the number of white Democrats on the panel; Beckwith wanted Republicans, preferably colored Republicans. Under the established procedure for federal cases in Louisiana, two court-appointed freeholders—prominent registered voters and property owners—would comb the registration rolls and pick 250 voters, "without regard to race or color." The names would be written on slips of paper, mixed up in a box, and selected at random. As each man was called, the defense and prosecution would question him, accepting and rejecting potential jurors until they had settled on twelve. This was the procedure Woods planned to follow. It was to Beckwith's advantage, since the two court-appointed freeholders were Republicans: former mayor Benjamin F. Flanders and John R. Clay, a colored politician.

But the defense cited an 1840 federal law requiring that a jury in a federal case be chosen by a process "as near as practicable" to that prescribed by the relevant state. In Louisiana, state law called for the sheriff to draw a jury pool by lot from all the registered voters of the parish. If this procedure were followed, it would help the defense, since two-thirds of the registered voters in New Orleans were white, and almost all the whites were Democrats.

Woods heard arguments from both sides and overruled the objection. The defense's preferred method would involve going through thousands of names. And that would be "impracticable," he concluded. Like it or not, the defense would have to deal with the jury pool selected by Flanders and Clay.

*Durell did sit on the trial for three days—after Woods ruled on the defense motions. But Durell made no legal rulings and then abandoned the bench for the remainder of the case. His presence had no legal impact.

Having failed to thwart Beckwith's indictment on technical grounds, and having failed to reshuffle the jury pool to its advantage, it would have been logical for the defense to try a broad constitutional attack on the trial—as the defense had done in both *United States v. Hall* and the South Carolina Klan trials. Given the result of *The Slaughterhouse Cases*, Beckwith was anticipating such an attempt. Yet the Colfax defendants' lawyers did nothing of the kind. Probably they felt there was no point in trying with Woods on the bench. Under the procedural rules of the time, a decision against them by Woods alone would not be appealable to the Supreme Court; it would stand as binding precedent across the Fifth Circuit.

Whatever the reasons, the defense's failure to make constitutional objections was a huge, if tacit, concession. It meant that the lawyers were accepting that the indictment alleged a real offense, and that the federal court had the power to try their clients for it. They were conceding that their clients' only legitimate path to freedom was through a "not guilty" verdict.

OVER THE NEXT TWO DAYS, BOTH SIDES WOULD ASK PROSPECTIVE JURORS whether they had already formed an opinion about the case, whether they had spoken to their friends and family about the guilt or innocence of the prisoners, and what their feelings were about capital punishment. Those whose answers were not to the liking of one side or the other were dismissed.

Each side also used peremptory challenges, dismissing prospective jurors not because of their responses or for any stated reason at all—but because of how they looked, their facial expressions, the way they sat in the witness chair. The defense likely used its allotted peremptory challenges to remove men of color. Beckwith would have had to make subtler calculations. Was this man's address in a Democratic neighborhood? Did that one's Northern origins make him a likely Republican? The defense objected to more prospective jurors than Beckwith did. Yet under Woods's direction, the process moved swiftly. By midday on February 24, the twelve-man jury was in place.

Nine of them were white. Frederick Frye must have seemed like a potential ally to Beckwith. A Republican lawyer, he was originally from Bridgeport, Connecticut, where he volunteered for the U.S. Army in 1861. He rose to the rank of major and then settled in New Orleans after the war, serving as a state judge during the Warmoth years. Howard Millspaugh was a sixty-one-year-old white Republican who ran a confectioner's shop.

Arthur Perrot was a printer of unknown political leanings. His father, Gaspar, was a French-born butcher who died when Arthur was a boy, leaving him to be raised by his mother, Irma. James Simpson was an ex–U.S. soldier, possibly a favorable indicator for the prosecution.

However, the defense had managed to seed the jury with five white Democrats: Thomas McDonald; Henry Long, who had once served as a deputy coroner in the city; Lawrence Kenney, an Irish-born grocer; Charles Evans, a store clerk; and Peter Ramos, a former deputy sheriff, born in Louisiana of Mexican parents. He had married an Irish woman in Ireland during the Civil War and then moved back to the city with her and their child in 1866.

There were three jurors of color: Simeon Esnard Jr. was the mulatto son of a prominent shoe manufacturer from Cuba. Louis P. Fonteneau Jr.'s name suggested French, or possibly Haitian, heritage. John O. Egana was the son of a wealthy landowner from Spain and his colored mistress. He worked for the federal government as an inspector of customs. All of the jurors were in their twenties or thirties, except for Millspaugh, who was sixty-one, and Kenny and Ramos, who were in their early fifties.

Woods ordered court officers to sequester the jurors in the Custom House, under close watch to make sure that they did not speak with any outsiders about the case. At 5:00 p.m., after the clerk finished the tedious three-hour task of reading the indictment, court adjourned—with James Beckwith set to make his opening argument the next morning.

WHEN COURT OPENED AT 11:00 A.M. ON FEBRUARY 25, BECKWITH WAS SHARP AND energetic. For the moment, at least, the legal preliminaries and courtroom maneuvers were over. At long last, he could tell a jury—and the world—just why this crime was so awful, and why it had consumed him for almost a year. He could speak for the voiceless victims of the Colfax outrage. He could lay out an alternative narrative to the one that had been printed over and over again in the white supremacist press.

Beckwith began coolly, mastering his indignation. He started not with the horrible facts of the case but with its legal underpinnings. He explained the Enforcement Act and how Congress had intended it to protect all citizens from violations of basic constitutional and civil rights. Then he moved on to the law of conspiracy—what it meant to "band together" to commit a crime. Reading from legal texts, he told the jury that it was not necessary to prove that any of the defendants had actually pulled a trigger on Easter Sunday in order to convict them of the conspiracy counts in the indictment. "When an armed body of men shoot into a crowd, they are all guilty of murder," he explained, "and any one who aids and abets and doesn't try to help stop it is also guilty." He reviewed the definition of *murder* in Louisiana law, a crucial point if the jury was not only to convict, but to hang, the defendants.

The jury was focused, attentive. Beckwith moved on to the origins of the troubles in Grant Parish. He recounted the dispute over local offices, the Republicans' occupation of the courthouse, Hadnot's threats to oust them, and the mustering of a posse under Dan Shaw to defend the building. He hammered home the point that the Negroes had been lawfully in possession of the courthouse. Not even attempting to deny that they had been armed and had expected a fight, he argued that any resort to arms on their part had been purely defensive, authorized by the sheriff, and thus legitimate. He described how the whites shelled the trench, driving the colored men into the courthouse. In "graphic and poetic" terms, as the *Daily Picayune* put it, he told how the building was torched and how the whites fired on the surrendered Negroes as they fled the smoke and flames. He ridiculed the whites' claim that the colored men had fired on a flag of truce. To the contrary, he said, the evidence would show that the whites' firing grew so wild that they hit Jim Hadnot with one of their own bullets.

Beckwith's voice boomed in the cavernous courtroom—his hands slashed and chopped the air. His narrative had reached the moment when the whites marched approximately forty prisoners into the night and shot them in the backs of their heads. He promised the jury that they would hear firsthand testimony from one of the survivors, Levi Nelson, the very man mentioned in the indictment. Nelson would tell them how he was hit by three bullets and then crawled away, bleeding, into the night. He would tell them about the others who had not been so lucky as to survive.

The men who committed these acts, Beckwith concluded, were murderers, plain and simple. They had claimed to strike in the name of civilization, white civilization. They may even have believed that. But, he thundered, "they can hardly be deemed human."

Beckwith returned to his seat and prepared to call his first witness. His plan was to present the case in roughly three stages. First, he would bring on witnesses to prove the lawfulness of the Negroes' presence in the courthouse. Then, he would present testimony proving that there had been a massacre, and that at least sixty men, including Levi Nelson and Alexander Tillman, had been gunned down in the horrific manner he had just described. Finally, he would bring on witnesses to identify the defendants as the parties responsible for the carnage.

The sequence was not precisely chronological, but it allowed Beckwith to start with his white witnesses, as well as his best-educated colored witnesses. Robert C. Register was the first to take the stand, explaining that he had been the parish judge in late March 1873, and that he had urged Sheriff Dan Shaw to organize a posse in response to Hadnot's threats. He described Hadnot's arrival on April 1 at the head of an armed band and the various skirmishes initiated by white groups—as well as the murder of Jesse McKinney. The colored men, he swore, had "no aggressive designs." He had been absent on April 13. But when he returned with the deputy U.S. marshals to Colfax, he saw "some of the limbs protruding from the earth."

Willie Calhoun limped into court the next day, February 26, basically unchanged by events. He was certain that he was in the right, and was eager to get even with the men trying to wrest control of the parish away from him and his allies. At Beckwith's prompting, Calhoun recounted Cazabat's threats to Register and his own seizure by a mob at Pineville. He emphatically identified Bill Cruikshank and Bill Irwin as members of the crowd that kidnapped him and snatched the letter from William Ward to Governor Kellogg.

DeKlyne and Wright were vivid and compelling as they told of coming upon the killing field at Colfax, of the half acre filled with dead, and of the horrible wounds on Alexander Tillman's body. William Ward, who had been living in New Orleans lately and serving as Grant Parish's representative in the state legislature, repeated Register's account, emphasizing that he, Calhoun, and Register had helped Shaw swear in a mostly—but not entirely—colored posse, and adding that the colored men who flocked to the courthouse after Jesse McKinney's murder had been "half-starved" with "no design to attack anyone or be aggressive."

Levi Allen identified Tom Hickman, Alfred Lewis, and Bill Irwin as participants in the attack on the courthouse. He confirmed that Hadnot was hit by his own men. He refuted any notion that the Negroes had coerced Shaw into deputizing them, noting that on the morning of the fight the would-be sheriff had left Colfax of his own accord. He said that his final words to Shaw were "Go ahead old man, save yourself."

Levi Nelson's testimony was riveting, as Beckwith had promised. Under the U.S. attorney's gentle prodding, he told his life story, beginning with his birth on the Calhoun lands and the years he worked as a slave for Meredith Calhoun, and continuing right through the fateful day in April when he ran to the courthouse, because he heard that "Hadnot's men were going there." The colored men were lying in the trench when the shooting began on April 13, Nelson recalled. One of the whites' bullets passed through Nelson's hat, and another hit him in the shoulder. He saw Bill Irwin and Bill Cruikshank at the fight; he told the court how Irwin had shouldered his weapon and shot Shack White down as White left the blazing building, trusting in Irwin's promise that the Negroes would not be harmed.

And then he brought the jury right up to the moment when Nash and his men debated whether to kill the "beeves." Finally, two mounted white men marched him out with another Negro. The first shot hit Nelson in his neck, "stunning me and dropping me." The next one killed his companion. But Nelson realized that he was still alive. He lay on the ground, feigning death, until finally the whites were gone and he could crawl from the field. "This is the scar made by the bullet which struck my neck," he testified.

Nelson recalled specifically that he saw each of the defendants that night, except for Alfred C. Lewis. Beckwith asked him if he could point out the men in the courtroom. Calmly and deliberately, Nelson stepped down from the witness stand, walked over to the defense table, eyed the men, and laid his hand on each one's shoulder. Cruikshank. Irwin. Penn. Hadnot. Hickman. Gibbons. The Lemoines. "As he did so, a thrill ran through the entire courtroom," the *New Orleans Republican* reported, "for the act declared the men murderers."

AND SO IT WENT FOR THE REST OF THE PROSECUTION CASE. ONE AFTER ANOTHER, Negro men and women raised their right hands, swore to tell the truth, and described the horrific things they—and the dead—had endured in Colfax. Alabama Mitchell testified that he huddled under the floorboards of the courthouse, emerging only to see Alexander Tillman fired on by whites who had promised to spare the Negroes' lives. Annie Elzie recounted how she watched in terror as a white man ignored her husband Etienne's pleas for mercy and then fired a rifle at him from point-blank range. She unhesitatingly pointed to the murderer in the courtroom: "Clement Penn is the man and there he sits," she said. Jackson Thomas testified that the whites made him carry water to the wounded Negro prisoners, and that, as he did so, he heard Bill Cruikshank say "Kill the niggers."

Through it all, William R. Whitaker counterattacked, bombarding the prosecution witnesses with questions designed not only to confuse them but also to remind the jury of the defense's version of the truth. Wasn't it true that the letter Willie Calhoun was carrying contained a vivid description of fighting between whites and blacks at Colfax, proof that the Negroes' purposes there were anything but peaceful? Calhoun said he hadn't read it. What about C. C. Nash and Alphonse Cazabat? Hadn't they acted as sheriff and judge, based on commissions from Governor

McEnery, for weeks prior to March 25, without Willie Calhoun so much as squeaking in protest? With his characteristic hauteur, Calhoun answered that he refused to recognize them as legitimate officeholders. Then how, Whitaker asked, did Shaw and the Republicans come into possession of their offices?

Beckwith leaped to his feet, objecting. This was a dangerous line of questioning: if the court allowed it, the defense could turn the trial into a debate over who the rightful officeholders in Grant Parish were. This case was about the allegations in the indictment, he told the court, not a trial for tenure of office. Woods sustained the objection—but only in part. The defense team could not try to show that Nash and Cazabat were actually entitled to office. But they could try to prove that the men who assembled in Nash's posse thought they were. It was only fair to allow them to argue a benign motive, Woods ruled, since the indictment accused them of intending to violate Nelson's and Tillman's rights.

It was a small, but significant, victory for the defense, and Whitaker exploited it to the hilt in cross-examining Ward's sidekick, Eli Flowers. Whitaker first got Flowers to admit that he had given a speech to the colored men before he and Ward left Colfax, which the lawyer was quick to portray as haranguing ignorant Negroes. Whitaker asked about the military drills he and Ward had run. How was that consistent with a peaceful assembly? Flowers denied that they had drilled, or that they were all armed with Enfield rifles, as Whitaker also insinuated. He also denied that the Negroes had set up pickets around the town, but when the defense lawyer asked if they had built cannon out of old pipe, Flowers had to concede that, yes, they had.

There was an inconsistency in the picture the defense was painting of the Negroes at Colfax: both a rioting mob bent on rape, robbery, and murder and a disciplined military force complete with a written roster. But the general point—the Negroes were anything but peaceful—was a strong one for the defense and struck right at what Beckwith knew was his Achilles' heel.

The defense also exploited Beckwith's other big weakness: the fact that many of his witnesses were poorly educated people of color, with only a rudimentary command of simple math or formal English, and little or no experience or knowledge of the law and its formalities.

Levi Nelson's testimony was devastating for the defense—and so Whitaker had to attack it, hard. How could you be sure you saw Bill and not Andrew Cruikshank? The Hickmans look alike, too. Are you positive you saw Thomas? What time was it exactly when you saw Prudhomme Lemoine? What time was it when you crawled away? And by the way, what were the Negroes doing converting gas pipes into artillery? The rapid-fire questions left Nelson struggling to keep up.

"It was evident that Levi knew exactly what he was saying," the *Republican* reported, "though he had a halting way of expressing himself. Questions as to distance, time, locations, numbers and such would prove difficult for almost anyone to answer under the circumstances; when a man's life is in great danger his mind is not likely to closely observe things generally so as to fix circumstances in his brain and make him a fluent witness."

For all that, the defense failed to shake Nelson's basic story; he never backed off. As the witness stepped down after several hours of testimony, Beckwith could claim his best day of the case so far. The prosecutor got another break later that afternoon, when Baptiste Elzie, Etienne Elzie's brother, was on the stand. Backing up Nelson's account, he detailed his own experience as one of the few prisoners to survive; he, too, swore that he had seen the defendants at the scene of the crime. On cross-examination, though, Elzie admitted that he had a pair of pistols with him when he went to Colfax to join Shaw's posse. At that point, Woods intervened, exercising his judge's prerogative to question the witness.

"What did you have in your hands when you were shot?" he asked Elzie.

"Nothing," Elzie responded.

Over and over, prosecution witnesses told the court in detail what had happened in Colfax. Again and again, they identified the defendants as the men they had seen imprisoning and killing Negroes on Easter Sunday. Each time they did so, the defense insinuated that they were lying or covering up the true, violent nature of the colored assembly at the courthouse. The witnesses held firm, though they sometimes stumbled.

Whitaker cross-examined Levi Allen for hours, trying to get him to admit that the Negroes were little better than an illegal militia, and that he had been their military boss. But Allen, who could read and write, did not buckle. He denied that the men had been assigned ranks; he was called "captain" but had no military experience. When Whitaker shoved a piece of paper at him that he said was a "muster roll" of the Negro force, he answered that he had never seen it before.

Beckwith saved the dramatic highlight of his case for last. On March 3, Benjamin Brim entered the courtroom. He had miraculously survived his multiple gunshot wounds in the face and back, and Beckwith had found him, probably through John J. Hoffman's investigation. Now he was at the Custom House to tell his story, a large, muscular, dark-skinned man with pus still oozing from the spot in his cheek where a white man's

The Colfax Massacre caused a sensation in the Northern press. *Harper's Weekly* provided this artist's rendering in its May 10, 1873, issue. The two white men on horseback are probably meant to represent deputy U.S. marshals Theodore W. DeKlyne and William Wright, who made the first official report on the slaughter. (*Courtesy of HarpWeek LLC*)

Three generations of Louisiana planters: William Smith (top left), the South Carolinian who bought thousands of fertile acres on the Red River; Meredith Calhoun (top right), who built the estate into a modern agro-industrial complex, worked by hundreds of slaves; and William Smith Calhoun (bottom), who planned a new order built from white capital and black votes. (*U.S. Senate Historical Office/Hemphill Family Collection/Hemphill Family Collection*)

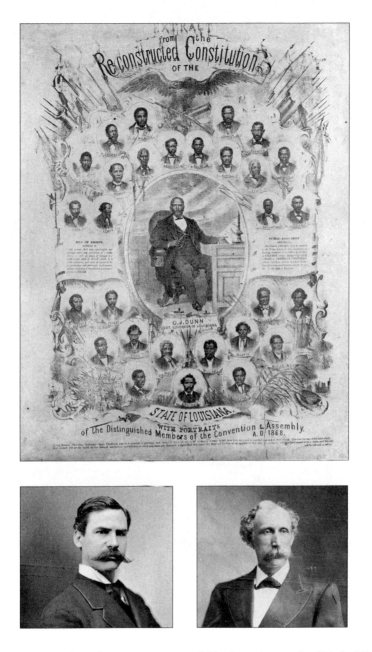

Reconstruction ushered in a new era of black voting and office-holding in Louisiana, but its governors were white Republicans. Elected in 1868, Henry Clay Warmoth (left) was charming and pragmatic, but clashed with President Grant; his successor, Vermont-born William Pitt Kellogg (right), was aloof and overwhelmed by the political chaos of his adopted state. (*Courtesy of the Louisiana State Museum / Library of Congress / Library of Congress*)

Christopher Columbus Nash (top left) led the assault on the courthouse at Colfax. Robert H. Marr (top right) headed the legal defense team at the Colfax Massacre trials in New Orleans. Marr later urged White League troops into battle against the Louisiana state militia on September 14, 1874. Fighting raged in front of the giant U.S. Custom House. (*Melrose Collection/Illustrated Visitor's Guide to New Orleans, 1879/Library of Congress*)

Privately convinced of the Grant Parish defendants' guilt, Judge William B. Woods (top) made sure they nevertheless got due process through two trials in New Orleans. As attorney general, George H. Williams (bottom left) vacillated in enforcing laws against white terrorism, but fought hard against defense lawyer Reverdy Johnson (bottom right) at the Supreme Court. (*Collection of the Supreme Court of the United States/Library of Congress/Library of Congress*)

Justice Samuel F. Miller's (top left) ruling in the Slaughterhouse Cases uninten-
tionally weakened the Fourteenth Amendment; he resented the appointment of
Morrison R. Waite (top center) as chief justice in 1874. Justice Joseph P. Bradley's
(top right) ruling in the Grant Parish trial crippled federal law enforcement in the
South. The Waite Court (left to right): Bradley, Stephen J. Field, Miller, Nathan
Clifford, Waite, Noah H. Swayne, David Davis, William Strong, Ward Hunt.
(*Collection of the Supreme Court of the United States*)

Grant Parish erected an obelisk in honor of the fallen white men of the "Colfax Riot" in 1921. It still towers over Colfax Cemetery today. The little cannon that blasted the Negro defenders of the courthouse is now a treasured heirloom on the Littlepage family's farm outside of Colfax. A state historical marker commemorating the "riot" stands in front of the modern courthouse. (*Melrose Collection / Author photo / Avery Hamilton*)

U.S. Attorney James Roswell Beckwith in a photograph taken many years after the Grant Parish trials. "I am not so constructed that I can look with calmness on such horrors," he said. "I would rather be that poor wretch burned to a cinder in the ruins of the courthouse than stand as the apologist for the crime that caused it." (*New Orleans* Daily Picayune)

bullet had pierced it. For an hour, he told the jury what hell had been like: the roundup of the prisoners; the captor who told him the whites were only shooting the wounded; the burst of pain as the bullet smashed into his face; crawling to safety; the looting of the dead.

The defense lawyers tried the same hectoring approach with Brim that they had used on the other colored witnesses, eliciting from him the admission that he had been armed when he came to Colfax. But that was as far as Brim would be pushed; he battled back, reminding his inquisitors that he had long since been disarmed by the time the whites marched him out to the slaughter. For Beckwith, it was a powerful coda. He brought in Chloe Tillman, who briefly told the jury that her late husband left behind two children; the prosecutor presented proof that Alexander Tillman had voted on November 4, 1872, as alleged in the indictment. And then, after seven long days of testimony, Beckwith rested his case.

ON THE AFTERNOON OF MARCH 4, THE DEFENSE ROSE. WILLIAM R. WHITAKER made no effort to deny that prisoners had been killed. But he did intend to explain and to justify it. Beckwith had tried to convince the jury that the Negroes in Colfax had been attacked by a lawless white mob. In truth, Whitaker argued, the only mob in Colfax had been a black one. Negro provocations and Negro threats had forced the whites to fight. It was because of the Negroes' treacherous firing on the flag of truce, which felled Hadnot and Harris, that the blood of the white men had boiled over, with such unfortunate consequences. But, in any case, Whitaker said, only two of the white men in court, Bill Irwin and Johnnie Hadnot, had even taken part in this defensive battle, and the evidence would show that both of them had left Colfax before the slaughter of the prisoners began, Irwin returning home and Hadnot accompanying his wounded uncle on a steamboat to Alexandria.

The first defense witness was Wilson L. Richardson, who described fleeing across the river on April 2, in fear of his life because of the Negro riot. Charles Smith, the white Republican who facilitated the abortive peace talks between whites from Montgomery and Ward's men, asserted that he had narrowly escaped from a gang of armed blacks yelling, "Kill the damned white son of a bitch." Smith claimed that Alexander Tillman, far from being an innocent victim, was the architect of the Negroes' military-style trench. O. J. Butler and Sam Cuney, the colored men who had opposed the Negro posse from the beginning, said that they, too, had been run out of town because they refused to go along with William Ward's violent designs.

The defense called its army of alibi witnesses, some of whom were men and women of color. Two of Alfred Lewis's Negro servants swore that he was home all day on Easter Sunday, as did colored employees of Tom Hickman. Bill Irwin's Negro servants swore that he had returned home by Sunday night. But for the most part, the witnesses were white friends and relatives of the accused. Several such men and women put Prudhomme Lemoine in church on Easter Sunday and said that Donas Lemoine and Austin Gibbons were at a farm miles away from Colfax, where they supposedly killed a hog. Maurice and Benjamin Kraft testified that on the day of the fight, Clement Penn was sitting on a tree limb outside their store on the Rapides Parish side of the river. Penn watched the battle from there, they said, though he visited the town briefly on the night of the thirteenth to help take out a wounded white man.

The dramatic climax of the defense testimony came when Whitaker called on J. C. Morantini to describe how the Negroes had violated the sacred flag of truce. Morantini lived on the Rapides Parish side of the Red River, on a spit of land just opposite Colfax. He had aided William R. Rutland when the lawyer fled Colfax on the night of April 1. His version of the flag story was the most colorful yet. The whites, he said, had taken a large white banner, attached to a pole, and carried it with them as they approached the burning courthouse. They got to within seven or eight paces of the building when suddenly they were met by a volley of at least twenty shots. From his front porch across the river, Morantini saw the flag totter and fall—only to be snatched up by someone else before it hit the ground. After this, he saw the Negroes escape their stronghold, unhurt.

"Were you there all the time from the time you heard this first volley immediately following the flag of truce, until the firing ceased?" Whitaker asked Morantini.

"I was looking at it all the time," the witness replied.

"You didn't see any Negroes shot then?"

"I did not."

The defense case was an exercise in mass perjury, but coherent and, if believed, effective. In a March 7 editorial, the *Daily Picayune* crowed that "the case assumes a very different character," now that the jury was hearing from the defense witnesses—including some Negroes and white Republicans. There was abundant evidence, the *Daily Picayune* said, of the Negroes' "fierce and unappeasable thirst for war and bloodshed." The defense must indeed have benefited from the fact that so many of its witnesses were Negroes, rounded up through what Beckwith suspected to be a combination of intimidation and bribery. This gave the defense a cross-racial hue that the prosecutor simply could not match.

Beckwith would have to dismantle the lies one by one. He would have to conduct the cross-examination of his life.

Beckwith believed in the old lawyers' maxim that "alibis fail because of their perfection." With that principle in mind, he demanded that each alibi witness explain in detail where, when, and how he had seen a given defendant on the day or days in question. When did you first find out about the fight at Colfax? he would ask. And who told you? When a witness responded evasively—insisting that he could not recall anything about the events at Colfax except that a particular defendant was not involved—Beckwith would consider his point made. Benjamin Kraft eventually conceded that he was "not too positive" about seeing Clement Penn up the tree after all. Others could not manage to keep their stories consistent with those told by others. Richard Grant, for example, confidently said he had been with Penn on the Rapides Parish side of the river the whole day but had not seen him in a tree.

Beckwith drilled one hole after another in J. C. Morantini's story. He asked who had first told Morantini that a fight was coming in Colfax. "Two colored men, sir," he implausibly replied. Morantini's porch was hundreds of yards away from the courthouse, across the Red River and behind buildings and trees. Smoke from the burning courthouse and burning gunpowder shrouded Colfax. "Could you tell white men from black men at that distance?" the prosecutor asked him.

"I believe I could."

"How long a pole was this the flag was on?"

"I should judge about five or six feet long."

"How big was the flag?"

"Not very large; about three or four feet long, and two and a half feet wide."

A flag that size would have looked like a postage stamp from where Morantini was standing, if he had seen it at all.

"Where did you first see that flag?"

"Near the courthouse."

"Did you see it anywhere before they advanced with it?"

"No."

And so it went. On redirect examination, Whitaker tried to shore up his witness. He asked where Morantini had seen the two colored men who had told him of the fight. He met them at a store, he said. They bought meat there.

"Are you a clerk at the store?" Beckwith countered.

"No," Morantini conceded.

"How do you know they got meat there?"

"I do, sir."

BECKWITH'S MOST IMPORTANT TARGET BY FAR WAS DANIEL WESLEY SHAW. SHAW'S claim to the sheriff's office was the source of the Negro posse's legality, but now he had come to swear that the posse had no basis in law. If the jury believed that, Beckwith had no case.

Shaw took the stand on the morning of March 5. On direct examination, he stuck to the defense story. The Negroes under Ward organized themselves like a military unit, complete with drilling and lists of companies. He claimed that they quickly overthrew him and kept him prisoner. He tried to escape twice, but both times armed Negroes brought him back. He was told he'd be shot if he tried it a third time. He testified that he urged the blacks to disarm and go home and take the case to the courts, but that they ignored him. Shaw even said that Nash had beaten him in the November 1872 election by a three-hundred-vote margin. "The white men were a posse under Nash," Shaw testified. "The colored men were not a posse under me."

On that note, Shaw finished his direct testimony. It was just before noon. Then Beckwith did something unusual. Whereas he had immediately tackled all the other defense witnesses, he asked the court for permission to postpone his cross-examination of Shaw until later that night, after he had reviewed certain documentary evidence. Woods agreed.

Actually, there was no need for Beckwith to review the document he had in mind. He was quite familiar with it. As Shaw surely knew, it was Shaw's letter of resignation as sheriff of Grant Parish, published in the *Republican* on September 10, 1873. This letter told a very different story from the one Shaw had just given under oath. "In obedience to an order of court I at one time summoned a posse to protect the judicial records and officers of court from the threatened violence of the mob," Shaw's letter declared. "The courthouse was burned and the posse cruelly exhausted and buried near the courthouse yard." In resigning, Shaw accused Kellogg of "ignor[ing] all appeals for protection."

William B. Phillips had ghostwritten the letter for Shaw in New Orleans, and William Ward had delivered it to Kellogg, during a moment when Shaw had escaped the influence of the Grant Parish Democrats and was apparently susceptible to the schemes and, probably, the bribes of the Grant Parish Republicans. Phillips's purpose at the time was to embarrass Kellogg by pointing out how little had been done to arrest and punish the perpetrators of the massacre. But whatever the letter's origins, it bore Shaw's signature, and it contradicted his testimony.

The delay in cross-examining Shaw was probably a ploy by the U.S. attorney. Shaw knew that the letter was in the public domain, and that Beckwith was going to confront him with it. But now he had to sit and fret for several hours about the painful grilling to come. At 7:00 p.m., after the recess for supper, when the witness was good and anxious—and plenty tired, too—Beckwith would start hammering him.

When the evening came, Beckwith put Shaw back on the stand. He began gently, asking Shaw to tell the court when he had arrived in Grant Parish—1869. Then he asked whom Shaw had replaced as sheriff when Warmoth appointed him in 1870. "Delos White," he replied. By eliciting the murdered man's name, Beckwith deftly reminded the jury of the crime committed by Christopher Columbus Nash in 1871, which had started Grant Parish on its long, violent spiral toward the bloodbath of Easter Sunday.

Then he asked Shaw if he thought Nash had won the sheriff's office in a fair vote. Shaw admitted that he didn't think the 1872 election was fair. He acknowledged that there had been no need to defend the courthouse for the first week after the Republicans entered it. That became necessary only when Hadnot issued his threats; at that point, Shaw conceded, he had indeed made out papers deputizing a mostly colored posse—just as Beckwith's witnesses had testified.

Beckwith was gaining momentum. Now he asked Shaw whether Nash had ever demanded that Shaw give him back the courthouse before Easter Sunday. It would have been the logical thing to do, especially since the defense insisted that the whites had exhausted all peaceful alternatives before launching their assault. But no, Shaw said, Nash had never made such a demand to him. And when your Negro deputies refused to obey you, and held you against your will, Beckwith asked, did you ever think to revoke their commissions? No, Shaw conceded, he had not.

Then Beckwith maneuvered Shaw into another damning admission. What did you do, and whom did you see, after you returned to Colfax from the Mirabeau plantation? he asked. Well, Shaw said, he had gone back to the courthouse, where he was detained by a group which included Bill Cruikshank—now Shaw was placing Cruikshank at the scene of the crime. Shaw said that he saw Nash that night, too, but Nash did not ask for the sheriff's office. Nash never demanded the office, Shaw admitted.

Shaw's story was collapsing, and it was taking down much of the other defense testimony with it. Now Beckwith moved in for the kill. He produced Shaw's letter of resignation. Shaw squirmed. "I was called on to write a narrative of the Red River Valley troubles but would not undertake the task," he said. "One was written for me, and I signed my name to it, but said it was incorrect." Having established that Shaw was the sort of man who would do something like that, Beckwith slipped in a quick aside about the cash Shaw was getting from the defense. Shaw admitted he saw Cruikshank at the parish prison, and that he had told Willie Calhoun just a few days earlier that he would not testify for the defense unless he got $1.50 a day, retroactive to December 8. "Mr. Cruikshank and the attorney told me I must not leave New Orleans," he added glumly.

By this point, Beckwith must have had even the most pro-defense members of the jury wondering if there was anything Shaw wouldn't do or say out of fear or greed.

Now, about that letter, Beckwith said. "Yes, it is correct in the main statement of facts," Shaw acknowledged. "I still say that I was detained in Colfax by force used by the colored people."

But it was no use. Shaw was totally broken. Beckwith had just one last matter he wanted to raise. Shaw testified earlier that, after the fight, he had been detained by the white men at the same house where Jim Hadnot lay wounded.

What did Hadnot's wound look like? Beckwith wanted to know.

"It was a large one, as if made by a bullet," Shaw said. "The clothing was powder burned."

The Negroes' buckshot could never have inflicted such an injury.

BECKWITH'S BRILLIANT CROSS-EXAMINATION OF SHAW BLEW A HUGE HOLE IN THE defense case. But William R. Whitaker was a worthy rival. He probably anticipated that Beckwith would get Shaw to admit that Cruikshank had arrested him on the night after the slaughter. He had a witness waiting in the wings to provide an innocent explanation for Shaw's sighting of Cruikshank. The witness, B. F. Stuart, claimed that Bill Cruikshank was in Rapides Parish during the whole period of unrest in Grant Parish, except for a few hours late on April 13 when he and Stuart popped into Colfax to recover property that rioting Negroes had stolen from Cruikshank—and to help one of the Negroes, a man who used to work for Cruikshank on his farm, escape the fighting. This was a lie. It clashed with Cruikshank's November 14, 1873, statement to the press, in which he claimed not to have been in Colfax *at all* on April 13. But it might have helped repair some of the damage Beckwith had done.

Then the defense reached for some documents of its own. The first was the March 27, 1873, edition of the *New Orleans Republican*, which Whitaker tried to introduce to prove that Nash had been the duly commissioned sheriff—or that Kellogg had deliberately created confusion about title to the office. This was a flat violation of Woods's previous ruling, in which the judge had forbidden them to argue that Nash was the rightful sheriff. Woods ruled the newspaper out, but not before an extended discussion of its contents in front of the jury.

Beckwith had seen that maneuver coming. The defense's next document, though, caught him by surprise. On March 10, the defense produced the letter William Ward had sent to the Negro preacher Jacob Johnson on April 5, 1873, begging him for reinforcements. Apparently, Johnson gave the letter to the white landowner on whose property he lived. Sensing its potential importance, the landowner then forwarded it to the defense team.

It was a perfect rejoinder to Beckwith's cross-examination of Shaw. Now the jury could read for itself Ward's militant language about standing up for the rights of all colored men, his claim to be "in command" of his forces, and his signature: "Captain William Ward." None of this was easy to reconcile with the picture Beckwith was trying to paint of a lawful posse under the authority of Dan Shaw.

Beckwith was in a bind. He had several rebuttal witnesses ready to call after the defense rested. Most of them were Negroes who would contradict the defendants' alibis, but he also planned to call William B. Phillips and Ward, to recount the meeting at which Kellogg refused to commission Nash as sheriff. He could strike Ward from the witness list and let the defense version of the letter's significance go unrebutted, or he could proceed with Ward's testimony and hope that the colored politician would explain to the jury that the letter reflected the Negroes' desperation, not their aggression.

Beckwith chose the latter option. The result was a disaster for the prosecution: on cross-examination, Ward denied any knowledge of the letter. He swore that he did not know who Jacob Johnson was. He said he had been too sick with "rheumatism" to write anything on April 5. "Flowers did all my writing for me," he claimed.

There was no way to tell just why Ward lied; perhaps his pride would simply not let him admit to so many childish spelling and grammar mistakes. But with his obviously false words, Ward hurt the credibility of Beckwith's entire case. Whatever the reasons for Ward's perjury, white jurors would be all too likely to attribute it to his race: if this Negro, a member of the state legislature, would lie under oath, they must have thought, what about all the other Negro men and women the prosecution had presented? But there was nothing Beckwith could do about that now. At 8:00 p.m. on March 10, Beckwith told the court he was through with his rebuttal. He would have to use his closing argument to repair whatever damage Ward had inflicted. At least he would not have to wait long: summations were set for the next morning. Beckwith would go first, followed by the defense lawyers, then the prosecutor's rebuttal.

The *Daily Picayune* told its readers to get ready for a memorable show: "It will undoubtedly be one of the most eloquently argued and discussed cases for many years," the paper reported.

THE PUBLIC HEEDED THE *DAILY PICAYUNE*'S CALL. WHEN WOODS GAVELED COURT to order at 10:00 a.m. on March 11, 1874, the high-ceilinged room was full. The jury looked "fresh," the *Republican* reported, suggesting that the "change from prosy testimony to speech making was welcome to them." Maybe the twelve men were simply excited that the trial would soon be over. They had been sequestered for more than two weeks. Woods had let them out of the Custom House only once, on March 4, when he gave them permission to see the Firemen's Parade. The U.S. marshal rented three carriages, put a deputy in each, and drove the jurors through the rutted streets.

The prisoners, by contrast, did not look well. The constant tension of the trial, the *Republican* noted, "naturally tells on them."

Certainly Beckwith was reaching the end of his stamina. When the trial began, the temperatures outside had been unseasonably cool; but for the last week, the mercury had hovered near the eighty-degree mark, heating up the interior of the poorly ventilated Custom House. His weariness was evident to everyone.

Beckwith spoke from the opening of court until 1:30 p.m., with a half hour lunch break at noon. He stuck to the evidence, methodically going over all of the testimony on both sides, showing the jurors how the facts and circumstances added up to one inevitable conclusion: all nine defendants had conspired to deprive Levi Nelson and Alexander Tillman of their rights, and the conspiracy had culminated in horrific violence. They deserved to hang. The U.S. attorney's recapitulation of the facts showed "an extraordinary memory," the *Republican* observed, "because he made no notes during the entire trial." The reporter was struck by the mildness of Beckwith's demeanor and rhetoric in comparison to his opening statement: "At times he was very emphatic, although it was plain to see that, physically, he was nearly exhausted, as might have been expected, having prosecuted this case without assistance." Probably Beckwith was conserving energy for his rebuttal.

ROBERT H. MARR OPENED FOR THE DEFENSE AT 1:30, HAVING RETURNED FROM Washington three days earlier. He began by assuring the jury that he would not even attempt to match the intemperate "insinuations" of the U.S. attorney; nor would he "employ the language of passion, or appeal to their political feelings." Rather, Marr promised, he would talk about the case calmly. Could the charges even be true? "No," he scoffed. The prisoners were accused of violating the rights of Nelson and Tillman, but "the prisoners, as well as most of the whites of Grant Parish, did not know there were two Negroes in the world named Levi Nelson and Alex Tillman." The posse under Nash—of which most of these defendants were not, of course, members—did not attack the Negroes entrenched in the courthouse to violate their constitutional rights, "but to defend their endangered families and their devastated property."

Then Marr launched into the constitutional argument that the defense had failed to make at the beginning of the trial. It was of dubious propriety to argue questions of law before the jury, a fact-finding body. But Marr gambled that Beckwith and Woods would not try to stop him if he kept it short—and he was right. "This affair is entirely out of the general government's jurisdiction," he noted, "and ought to be brought before a state court which is the only one that has jurisdiction." Then he quickly moved on.

Finally, Marr showed what he really meant by calm and dispassionate. "The truly responsible ones are those miserable people who out of pure self-interest have whipped up the ignorant Negroes and called them to arms—until the moment of danger when they abandoned them to their fate," he cried. There was no need to name "those miserable people." Every right-minded white man and woman in Louisiana knew Marr was talking about William Pitt Kellogg and all the other scalawags and carpetbaggers who propped up his usurper's government. An acquittal would strike a blow against them. But a guilty verdict, Marr said, "would give the signal for civil war and riots in the entire state, because the blacks would feel supported and would not know how to stop."

Marr sat down at 3:20. William R. Whitaker came next. With Marr having roused the jury's emotions, Whitaker's task was to flatter their intellect and to supply them with the ostensible factual basis for an acquittal. Speaking until the court adjourned at 4:00 p.m., and then for three and a half more hours the next day, Whitaker went over the prosecution case point by point, arguing that not only Ward but also Flowers and Levi Nelson had repeatedly perjured themselves. "I have never seen a trial in which the witnesses called were less worthy of belief," he intoned. The pro-defense *New Orleans Bee* praised the "young and ardent advocate for the defense," but even the *Republican* had to admit he was "excellent."

At 2:00 p.m. on March 12, Michael Ryan rose. Added to the defense team as a sop to the defendants' home region, Ryan had turned into a bit of a problem for the defense during the trial. The defense team found scant legal work for Ryan, and when they put him on the stand as a witness, his testimony amounted to little more than a vague rant. Now, however, they gave him a token ten minutes to address the jury. Ryan used the time to take a personal shot at Beckwith. "If there is a hell as Beckwith so ardently believes," Ryan roared, "he will get there sooner or later because the Christian who sends others to eternal fire deserves it himself." He accused Beckwith of forgetting the biblical injunction to "judge not lest ye be judged." "You don't need the brilliance of Mr. Beckwith to tell virtue from crime," he harrumphed.

And then it was time for E. John Ellis. Like Marr, his colleague, Ellis began by disavowing any attempt to tug at the jury's heartstrings. He declared that he wasn't going to appeal to the "pity" which the jurors might be feeling for the defendants. That would "degrade" both him and them. "No," Ellis insisted, "I want that justice be done and that the jury be able to say after hearing me these men are innocent or guilty." He meandered through the defense testimony and the salient incidents of the case. It all led to the same conclusion that Marr had reached: "The true and only guilty parties are the ones who instigated the disorder, who put weapons in the hands of ignorant negroes and told them: 'Come fight for your rights, you'll never be free men if you don't rid yourselves of the whites.'"

"Are they criminals who, after having tried all means of conciliation, defended themselves with the disadvantage of fewer numbers and responded to force with force?" Ellis cried. He was, seemingly, forgetting the defense's alibi argument. But he could not forget the much more powerful fear of every decent white man in Louisiana—the ultimate fear that had so justly and correctly motivated the white men at Colfax. "If Mr. Beckwith is to be believed, the blacks of Grant Parish are all little saints," Ellis roared. "If that's true, then what about the horrors that followed the invasion of the Metropolitan Police in Grant Parish? Wasn't a young girl raped by black bandits?"

There it was: the specter of interracial sexual violence—an image so emotionally charged that Ellis had to assume that it would stir even the most ardently Republican of the white jurors. "His words produced a profound impression and all who heard them were moved," the *Daily Picayune* observed.

Beckwith was down to his last chance to produce an impression of his own.

AT 7:00 P.M. ON MARCH 12, 1874, JAMES R. BECKWITH HAULED HIMSELF TO HIS feet and, once again, addressed the jury. Every seat in the courtroom was still occupied, "mostly," the *Republican* noted, "by citizens who take an interest in the history of Louisiana." He reviewed the events in Grant Parish, emphasizing how clear it was in hindsight that the whites, far from seeking to avoid conflict, had been preparing for it and threatening it almost from the beginning. The key fact, he noted, was William R. Rutland's effort to swear out an arrest warrant against the alleged invaders of his home. He hoped to cloak the coming attack in some legality, however threadbare. The very time and place of the ultimate conflict was calmly selected by the whites, Beckwith argued. "The fight was a violation of law by the assaulting party," he said. "Nash could have opened it or delayed it as he chose. The Negroes, as shown, were only on the defensive. But Sunday was chosen and the one most reverenced of the year, Easter Sunday, for the motive that they might not be interrupted from without."

Beckwith decided to ignore William Ward's embarrassing testimony. Instead, he shifted to the offensive and attacked Dan Shaw. And, even more audacious, he compared the white Shaw unfavorably to a colored man, Levi Allen. He recounted Nash's ultimatum to Allen, followed by the thirty-minute interval during which the women and children fled. "That half hour was the stillness before the storm, and here occurred the incident that counsel have chosen to comment on with a sneer," Beckwith said. "Levi Allen was in command, and that dark hour when the conference broke up and death was in sight, and this poor miserable man Shaw—and may I never again see a man look as he did on the stand—said 'What shall I do now?' Levi Allen told him, 'Old man, go away and save yourself, if you can.' There is more merit, more manhood, more chivalry in that sentence than can be conceived. Consider the importance of the presence of Shaw. He was their civil head and when Allen in his self-abnegation and in the face of the bitter force against him told him to save himself, his skin might be black, but he possessed a soul far whiter than any of the horde that attacked him. . . . [H]e may have never had another good impulse; but at that moment when he told Shaw to go, the man was grand, and signified the possession of inherent manhood."

Now it was Beckwith's turn to sneer at the defense case. A simple fact disproved the contention that the killings had somehow been justified, he argued. Once the Negroes had been driven from their trench and were trapped in the courthouse, there was no need for any further shooting by the whites: "A siege would have caused it to be vacated." The flag-of-truce story was a patent lie, he scoffed: "A marvelous man, Morantini, who did his duty to humanity by watching the fight from across the river, says he saw it." Morantini had testified that it looked about two and a half feet by three or four feet in size. "If it appeared that large to him," Beckwith said, "it must have been as large as the mainsail of a schooner."

"The Negroes that Shaw swore in had faith in his right, as did those who followed Nash and believed that they were right," Beckwith added. "But suppose they were wrong, as the counsel would have you believe, did that give Nash the right to slaughter them?"

Beckwith still had to deal with the race of his witnesses. He decided to confront the issue head-on, casting himself as someone who, like the white jurors, had had doubts about the reliability of Negroes. "All testimony must be valued according to the source from which it comes," he told the jury. "This is the first time, and God grant it may be the last, that all testimony has been from colored men. Aside from their lack of intelligence, I was apprehensive that by their aggressive sense of wrong and their disposition to exaggerate, a vindictive feeling might be manifested. But of all the witnesses placed on that stand and confronted with their murderers, not one of them manifested in any instance that degree of malice that a white man would. I confess I don't understand it. Add to this, when it came to the test of identification, when it must have occurred to them that it was almost certain death to exercise the moral courage to point out one after another of the accused, the spectacle is beyond my comprehension. Nine out of ten white men would have preferred that the criminals go unwhipped of justice rather than take the responsibility of risking their peace hereafter. Each one told his story with an intelligence that astonished me."

Beckwith had one last plea to make: a plea on his own behalf. He had to address the doubts about himself that the defense had so assiduously sown throughout the last two weeks. His passion was insincere, the defendants' counsel claimed, proof of his partisan motives. Though the jurors had not been reading them, the white supremacist papers had attacked Beckwith as well, with the *New Orleans Bee* claiming that he had "alienated the esteem and the sympathy of everyone through his vehemence and his imprudent words."

Now Beckwith reached deep within his soul and found a voice so eloquent, and so resonant with moral fervor, that it might have belonged to one of the orators at that long-ago abolitionist rally under the apple trees in Cazenovia. "We are all exhausted by this long trial," he said, "long in time, but short for the crime that has been committed, and short for the interests of justice, law and humanity. I should have gladly escaped any participation in it, have been glad to have shirked my duty, and if I had known what it was to have been, to have abdicated my position. I am not so constructed that I can look with calmness on such horrors as we have listened to. . . . I would rather be that poor wretch burned to a cinder in the ruins of the courthouse than stand as the apologist for the crime that caused it. I would rather go to the bar of God with the chances of the souls of the sixty-four or sixty-five human beings so inhumanly butchered than carry to God a soul so debased as to defend such a crime."

"While history lives the massacre of Colfax will never be forgotten," Beckwith boomed, "and the slaughter of those helpless men only be compared with the fearful deeds of Philip and Alva in the Netherlands.* I must now leave the case with you, and I trust and hope—and I say it on my conscience, my motive is only the administration of justice; nothing but to enforce the law—that your verdict will be said to have done justice between these parties and the sixty-three or sixty-four lives they have taken. . . . I would call your attention to this, that someone is responsible for this crime, and someone must be punished, or justice is dead." And at 10:40 p.m., three hours and forty minutes after he began, James Beckwith left the jury to ponder that challenge.

WILLIAM BURNHAM WOODS HAD GOVERNED THE TRIAL WITH A LIGHT TOUCH. IN-deed, after the first few defense motions, there had not been many objections raised by either side. But it was no mystery where the judge stood. This was the same transplanted Ohioan who had sustained the indictment in *United States v. Hall.* He had helped Baptiste Elzie, the Negro prosecution witness, with a sympathetic question when the defense was bearing down on him. On the biggest evidentiary issue of the trial, the defense's attempt to introduce the March 27 *Republican* as proof of Kellogg's sinister double-commissioning of sheriffs, he had sided with Beckwith. It was not Woods's job to help Beckwith, much less to try to win the case for him. But he apparently concluded that he could not let the jury start its deliberations without at least trying, as subtly as possible, to nudge

*In 1567, King Philip II of Spain ordered Fernando Alvarez de Toledo, Duke of Alva, to subdue the rebellious Dutch. He did so through mass executions.

them in the direction of a conviction. Anything more interventionist would have violated his judicial oath; anything less would have violated his sense of decency.

On Friday, March 13, Woods ascended the bench at the usual time— 10:00 a.m.—and began his charge to the jury with the relevant provisions of the Enforcement Act, which he called "a just and wholesome" law. Then he addressed the defense's repeated contentions that the case was a Republican vendetta. "This is simply a prosecution against the accused for an alleged invasion of the lawful and constitutional rights of others," he told the jurors. "You will therefore dismiss entirely from your minds the idea, if any such idea has found lodgment there, that the prosecution is in the interest of any political party or faction. It is in the interest of the whole people: It is in the interest of peace, public security and of public order." In a clear effort to counter the defense's racial appeal, he said, "It is your duty and mine to administer the law without regard to persons, and to do equal justice to all classes of citizens. Come then, to the consideration of this case with minds free from prejudice and determined to render a just and true verdict according to the law and the evidence."

For what must have seemed to the jurors like the millionth time, Woods went over the story once again. To be sure, the alleged firing on a flag of truce remained disputed, Woods said. But almost none of the other facts was; he lingered with special emphasis over two details. The first was that when the deputy marshals arrived in Colfax two days after the fight, they "found fifty-nine dead bodies. They showed pistol shot wounds, the great majority in the head and most of them in the back of the head." And the second was that "the only white men injured from the beginning of these troubles to their close were Hadnot and Harris.* The court-house and its contents were entirely consumed . . . there is no evidence that either Nash or Cazabat, after the affair, ever demanded their offices, to which they had set up claim."

"The real controversy between the prosecution and the defense," Woods pointed out, "is touching the purpose and intent of [the whites'] banding and conspiring." The case hinged on this question: if, as the prosecution said, the whites' motive was to violate the Negroes' rights, then the men were guilty. It made no difference that the colored men may have been armed. Their right to assemble for a peaceful and lawful purpose included the right to do so with guns, as long as they used them

*Woods apparently forgot that a third white man, Stephen Decatur Parish, had also been killed.

defensively. Marr was incorrect to suggest that the case belonged in state, not federal, court, Woods continued. "The law under which this prosecution is carried on," he said, "was framed for the express purpose of punishing just such acts as these. No man or body of men has the right thus to take into their hands the summary administration of what they may suppose to be justice." Nor did it make any difference, legally, that the whites might not have known that Tillman and Nelson were among the Negroes at the courthouse, as Marr had argued. "If the intent applied to the crowd, and Tillman and Nelson were part of the crowd, that is sufficient to sustain the indictment," the judge said.

"Gentlemen of the jury," Woods concluded, "the case is now committed to your hands. It is one of magnitude to both the prosecution and the defense. On your verdict may depend the peace and order of the State; on it do depend the liberties and lives of the prisoners at the bar. Give it your best deliberations. Though you may be convinced that a most atrocious and appalling crime was committed at Colfax on Easter Sunday last, though you may believe that white men engaged in that terrible affair left the neighborhood on that Sunday night with hands red with the blood of helpless prisoners, that alone is not a ground for a verdict of guilty. You must be clearly satisfied that the precise crimes described in this indictment, or in some of its counts, were committed by one or more of the prisoners at the bar. If you are not so convinced, you must acquit. On the other hand, if you are persuaded by the evidence that the prisoners, or any of them, banded or conspired with the intent laid in this indictment, or in any of its counts, I trust you will have the courage, I trust there is enough good and lawful manhood among you, to say so by a verdict of guilty.

"And I pray God to lead you to a true and just conclusion."

Displaying none of the emotions that must have been churning inside of them, the jurors quickly elected the Republican Howard Millspaugh as their foreman and filed out to the next-door jury room. It was just after noon on March 13, 1874. Along with the crowd of spectators, the men of the New Orleans press, the defense lawyers, and the defendants, James Beckwith watched as the jurors disappeared behind the door. For three weeks, he had argued, demanded, and pleaded in front of those twelve men. All day, each day, he had done everything he could think of to get them to believe what he believed: that a horrible crime had been committed and that these nine defendants had to pay for it. Now, there was nothing he could do but wait.

CHAPTER NINE

A JUSTICE'S JUDGMENT

For the rest of the day, and all that night, the jury's silence taxed even the unflappable Judge Woods. After they had deliberated for roughly twenty-four hours, he called the twelve men back to his courtroom to ask if they were approaching a verdict. Not yet, foreman Howard Millspaugh answered. The jury stayed mute until late the next night, March 15, when Woods, who had remained at his chambers, finally gave up and went back to his hotel. Physically and mentally spent, James Beckwith used the time to try to get out of a counterfeiting trial set to begin in April. He telegraphed Attorney General Williams, asking him for five hundred dollars to hire a substitute. AM EXHAUSTED AND SICK FROM OVERWORK IN THE GRANT PARISH MASSACRE CASE, Beckwith wrote. But Williams, still pinching pennies, denied the request.

Suddenly, on the evening of March 16, the jury sent a note to Woods, informing him that they had something to announce. The judge quickly dispatched couriers to find Beckwith and the defense lawyers. At the same time, the deputy marshals went to get the defendants at the parish prison. By 8:00 p.m., the courtroom was open, with everyone assembled in front of Woods's high bench.

The judge opened the envelope, scanned the page inside—and then, at last, read it aloud. Woods's words must have left Beckwith nearly choking with frustration: The jury had acquitted Alfred Lewis. On the other eight—Cruikshank, Hadnot, Irwin, Penn, Hickman, Gibbons, and the two Lemoines—the jurors were deadlocked. Woods, seemingly shocked, asked the jury twice if they were divided as to the facts of the case or were in dispute over the meaning of his instructions. No, came the reply, we simply cannot agree.

Beckwith had labored to build a case that no reasonable man of any color or party could deny. Woods had kept the jury sequestered, insulating them from the passions swirling outside the Custom House's thick granite walls. On the last day of the trial, he had begged them to cast aside prejudice and consider the case coolly and courageously. Yet, in the end, race had apparently dictated the outcome. The white-majority jury had split 9–3 "not guilty" for Penn, the Lemoines, Gibbons, and Irwin—with the only "guilty" votes coming from the three men of color. The vote to acquit Cruikshank, Hadnot, and Hickman had been 11–1, with John O. Egana, who was not only colored but also an employee of the Republican-dominated Custom House, casting the only "guilty" vote. There had been "but little discussion" among the twelve, a juror later told the press.

Woods turned to Beckwith. Would the U.S. attorney consent to a mistrial? There was no alternative. Yes, he replied. The defense followed suit. Woods declared a mistrial and ordered the clerk to record it in the minutes of the court. He sent the defendants back to the parish prison. The lawyers stayed behind, pondering the prospect that, after a trial lasting nearly four nerve-racking weeks, they would soon have to come back to the same courtroom and do it all over again.

IN THEIR CONFIDENCE, THE WHITE SUPREMACISTS OF NEW ORLEANS PROBABLY never expected anything but outright acquittal for all nine defendants. Soon, though, they realized that the hung jury might be a blessing in disguise. The eight remaining defendants' extended martyrdom and the prospect of a second trial meant new opportunities to exploit the case politically. The Committee of 70 resumed its campaign, distributing a pamphlet that repeated once again that the Negroes had waved a false flag of truce; it noted that Captain Jack of the Modocs had been hung "for such an offense." William Ward, a "full-blooded Negro," was portrayed as "the real murderer" in Colfax.

New Orleans's white leaders circulated a petition addressed to Woods, asking him to grant bail to the eight remaining defendants. As of March 27, it had been endorsed by four hundred commercial firms; pages of individual signatures stretched eighty feet when pasted together. A seven-man delegation headed by Joseph Wilmer, the Episcopal archbishop of New Orleans, presented the document to Woods, but the judge resisted, aware that the defendants would disappear into the piney woods if freed. "I do not wish in the least to prejudge this case," he wrote to Wilmer's delegation, "but it is one of such moment to the people of this state that I have been compelled to refuse bail." He pledged to make sure the prisoners were comfortable, and to start the second trial promptly. Beyond that, the judge would not go: "I cannot conscientiously, in a case of this magnitude, grant bail as yet," he repeated.

A new fund-raising committee sprang up and announced that the Orleans Dramatic Association would stage a benefit performance of Friedrich von Schiller's *The Robbers,* starring the popular actress Minna Doyle, at the Varieties Theatre. The show netted $1,073.95. The *Daily Picayune* provided prospective jurors reasons to disbelieve prosecution witnesses at a second trial. On April 18, it carried a letter from "Civis" in Colfax, recounting the lurid tale of a murder attempt by Negroes against the white tax collector of Grant Parish. Supposedly, he had been attacked with an ax while he slept, as part of a plot by the brother of "the notorious raper, Hamp Henderson." Even worse, the letter continued, the Negroes had schemed to blame their crime on Christopher Columbus Nash and "all engaged in the Colfax affair of last April." This, "Civis" argued, showed "the animus of the ignorant voudous and semi-barbarians among whom we live and whom the United States Court in New Orleans will soon call again to swear away the lives of the best citizens of the State."

The letter from "Civis" fit into a wider campaign of witness intimidation. On April 6, Paul Hooe and George Marsh, both of whom had taken part in the massacre, accosted a Negro prosecution witness in Alexandria. "Oh, you son of a bitch!" Marsh shouted. "You sworn against me, did you?" Marsh stabbed the man twice, then started beating him. Hooe also kicked and pummeled the victim as a crowd looked on. Lieutenant Charles A. Vernou of the U.S. Army watched from the front porch of the nearby Exchange Hotel, accompanied by his new Louisianan bride. The brazen attack was probably staged to remind both Vernou and local Negroes of how little he could do to protect colored witnesses.

The message sank in. A Republican reported the attack to U.S. marshal Stephen Packard but declined to sign the letter, "for fear that his death might be an example as Loyd Shorter . . . was on Bayou Rapides, in this parish."

THE WHITE SUPREMACIST PRESS SOON BEGAN TO CHARGE BECKWITH AND HIS allies in the Custom House with manipulating the jury pool for the second trial. The *Daily Picayune* noted that it was composed "principally of the octoroon class." "On its very face the panel is a fraud," the *New Orleans Bulletin* complained, "for the proportion of Negroes is altogether too large to have been the result of chance, and the character of some of the men is such as to excite astonishment and disgust."

These were exaggerations, of course, but the articles probably contained a kernel of truth. With Benjamin F. Flanders and John R. Clay, partisan Republicans, assembling prospective jurors, it was hardly far-fetched that they would favor the prosecution. Sure enough, when the two-hundred-plus names appeared publicly before the scheduled opening of the second trial on May 18, half of them belonged to men of color. Of the whites on the list, many had connections to the Republican-dominated state and federal bureaucracies. One was a white captain in the Metropolitan Police, which was under Kellogg's personal control. Another white Republican volunteered for the jury pool after being told to do so by one of Packard's deputies. The defense could still exclude jurors, for specific reasons or through peremptory challenges. But the disproportionate number of colored and white Republican potential jurors would force the defense to use its allotted challenges faster—while Beckwith could focus his on white Democrats. He was sure to get a jury more to his liking than the one in the first trial.

Neither the press nor the Grant Parish prisoners' lawyers ever produced any direct evidence that Beckwith connived to shape the jury pool. But given the results of the first trial and the white supremacist campaign of intimidation, it is easy to imagine that he would have felt justified in doing so—or in looking the other way as someone else did.

THE SUPREME COURT OF THE UNITED STATES ADJOURNED ON MAY 4. IT WAS THE time of the year for Associate Justice Joseph P. Bradley to "ride circuit" in the federal courts of the Deep South. At 8:00 a.m. on May 14, he boarded a train at the Baltimore & Potomac Railroad Station on the Mall in Washington. On May 17, it reached Manchac, Louisiana, a tiny port on the northern shore of Lake Pontchartrain, and Bradley switched to a steamboat for the trip to the Crescent City. Arriving in New Orleans at 1:00 p.m., the justice had plenty of time to check into his hotel, rest up, and pay a call on Woods—who probably briefed him on the court's agenda, starting with the Grant Parish case scheduled to open the next day.

When the judges' chambers door swung open at 11:30 a.m. on May 18, and the cry of "All rise!" rang out in the cavernous Custom House, two men, Woods and Bradley, emerged and mounted the great black bench.

Woods, the bearded, battle-scarred Civil War veteran, towered over the balding Bradley, whose smooth cheeks, thin lips, bulbous nose, and intense, bright eyes made him seem a tightly wrapped little package. But in their profession, Bradley, sixty-one years old, was the giant, one of the most eminent lawyers of his generation.

The oldest of twelve children, Joseph Philo Bradley had risen to the pinnacle of the judiciary from the depths of rural poverty. His family scratched wheat and rye from the rocky soil of a farm in Berne, New York. As a child, Bradley worked hauling homemade charcoal sixteen miles to the market in Albany. Reading was Bradley's escape; his parents encouraged it, as did his uncle, the village librarian. A highlight of his youth came in December 1828, when a relative loaned him *Bonnycastle's Algebra*. "I hardly ate, drank or slept until I knew that book from beginning to end," Bradley later wrote. By the time he was sixteen, Bradley was already earning extra cash as a schoolteacher and land surveyor.

But he felt that he was wasting his life. In late 1831, while threshing buckwheat with his father, he announced a plan to leave home for New York City, so that he could earn money for an education. With a twenty-dollar loan from his father, he set out, but arrived in Albany just ten minutes after the last New York–bound boat of the winter had left. He spent a few days reading in the state library and watching sessions of the legislature, then returned home. Along the way, he met the Berne village dominie—the Dutch Reformed Church's minister. He poured out his story, and the dominie felt sorry for him. He took Bradley under his roof and prepared him for college.

In September 1833, Bradley entered Rutgers, the Dutch Reformed college in New Brunswick, New Jersey, with a $250 scholarship to study theology. He was a twenty-year-old freshman in a homespun suit, joining the sixteen-year-old sons of New Jersey's upper class, but his brilliance did not go unnoticed. The friends he made at Rutgers—including a future U.S. senator, Frederick Frelinghuysen, and a future president of the American Bar Association, Cortland Parker—would remain his lifelong political allies. He gained admission to the New Jersey bar in 1839 and later became general counsel to the Camden and Amboy railroad company, known as "the Monopoly" because it dominated New York–Philadelphia freight traffic. During more than two decades with the firm, Bradley handled everything from Supreme Court cases to complicated financial transactions.

As a young man, Bradley supported the Whigs, the party of Senator Henry Clay, the Great Compromiser from the border state of Kentucky, who tried to hold North and South together for their mutual economic benefit, despite their dispute over slavery. By the 1850s, however, the Whigs were in decline, and Bradley followed Frelinghuysen and Parker into the Republican Party, running unsuccessfully for Congress in New Jersey on the party of Lincoln's ticket in 1862. In 1868, Bradley was a presidential elector from New Jersey pledged to Grant.

In addition to his legal ability, it was Bradley's party loyalty and support of the federal government's constitutional authority to issue paper money—a major issue at the time—that prompted Grant to pick him for the Supreme Court in 1870. Some New Jersey political enemies objected to a man from the "monopoly," but he was confirmed easily. Soon, he was considered one of the Court's brightest members. He owned a personal library of sixteen thousand volumes, read Hebrew and hieroglyphics, and was a serious student of mathematics, philosophy, and history. Bradley wrote essays on "Truth," "Self-Control," and "Experience." He drew up a precise model of Noah's Ark and calculated the exact date of the Crucifixion at April 7, AD 30. George Williams once found Bradley poring over immense sheets of paper covered with algebraic formulas and asked the justice what he was doing. "Calculating the transit of Venus," Bradley replied.

But for all his erudition, Joseph Bradley seems never to have been troubled by slavery. To some extent, this reflected Bradley's own geographic and religious origins. On his family's farm, the plight of the Negro must have seemed remote indeed. Unlike Cazenovia, Berne was not a hotbed of abolitionist creeds. The Dutch Reformed Church, which dominated the Albany area (and Rutgers), condoned slavery. And New Jersey, Bradley's adopted home state, was probably the most pro-South of all the Northern states, in part because its factories did a brisk trade with Southern plantations. New Jersey did not enact gradual abolition until 1804; the law slowly reduced the slave population from its peak of 12,422 in 1800 to a mere handful by the eve of the Civil War.

There were still a few hundred slaves in New Jersey in 1845, when its tiny Anti-Slavery Society brought suit in the state supreme court to free them. A young lawyer from Newark, Joseph P. Bradley, defended one of the slave owners. When the abolitionist lawyer argued that slavery violated not only New Jersey's constitution but the Ten Commandments, Bradley countered with a learned discussion of the institution in biblical times. Bradley asserted that New Jersey slaves lived "among the farmers, in their families, like their children," where they were "better off than if they would be free." In fact, he noted, since the few slaves left in the state were all over forty, abolition would cast them "adrift upon the world." Bradley won the case. On July 17, 1845, the court voted 3–1 to uphold slavery. The only dissent came from Chief Justice Joseph Coerten Hornblower—Bradley's father-in-law.

It is the lawyer's lot to represent clients with whom he disagrees or even abhors. For Bradley, the "New Jersey Slave Case," as it was known, was not such an occasion. Up to the start of the Civil War—and even after it—he consistently, publicly, opposed abolition. In December 1860, with war looming, he proposed constitutional amendments that would have allowed slavery in a fixed portion of the Western territories and let slave owners seek compensation in federal court if Northerners refused to return their fugitive slaves. This was "simple justice," he said. Bradley, who regarded abolitionists as "little better than the rebels of the South," called his plan a true expression of Republicanism.

When war came, Bradley supported the North unreservedly. But he considered it a struggle for Union, not Negro freedom. Campaigning for Congress in October 1862, he declared to a Newark audience that "this cause of ours is a holy cause—the cause of civil freedom—the cause of human rights." He added, "In saying this, I do not refer to the question of domestic slavery; I am speaking of the great mission of this country." He assured his audience that once the Union was saved, he was willing to let the South run its own affairs. "I do not . . . hate the Southern people or their institutions," Bradley said. "I do not care a straw about their institutions, comparatively."

This attitude persisted even after the war. Bradley passed through New Orleans in April 1867, when he was still a private lawyer. The lingering anger of the whites toward the North was so intense that even a tourist could feel it, but Bradley was not unsympathetic. After all, he noted in a letter home, "they have lost their field hands, and will be obliged to hire laborers at large prices." Criticizing "little informed" Northerners who failed to appreciate such dilemmas, he repeated his hosts' complaints "that the Freedmen's Bureau is an engine of mischief, that it teaches the Negroes to be discontented; gives them false notions and utterly incapacitates them from labor. This is the great question of the day—how to restore the labor of the Southern States to a normal condition."

Three years later, Bradley returned to New Orleans, riding circuit as a Supreme Court justice for the first time. During this sojourn, he aided John Archibald Campbell's effort to overturn Louisiana's slaughterhouse law. Bradley granted Campbell a "writ of error" authorizing his appeal to the high court, wrote an opinion declaring the slaughterhouse law unconstitutional, and ruled that it could not be enforced until the full Supreme Court decided Campbell's appeal.

Bradley admired the white supremacist lawyer, whom he considered the "*beau* idea of forensic perfectness." When a majority of the Supreme Court voted in April 1873 to uphold the slaughterhouse statute, Bradley dissented. His opinion echoed not only Campbell's constitutional arguments but his broader denunciation of "carpetbagger" rule in the South. Bradley called the Louisiana law "one of those arbitrary and unjust laws made in the interest of a few scheming individuals, by which some of the

Southern States have, within the past few years, been so deplorably oppressed and impoverished."

MOST OF THE SPECTATORS PACKED INTO THE CUSTOM HOUSE FOR THE START OF
the second trial of the Grant Parish prisoners on May 18, 1874, were men
and women of color. The *Daily Picayune* mockingly reported that they
"seemed wonderfully and strangely interested in this case," which, the
paper said, they could not hear from where they were sitting, and would
not understand anyway. More likely, the Negroes had come because they
knew exactly what the case meant to them: this was Beckwith's last
chance to get justice for the victims of Colfax and to salvage the rule of
law in Louisiana.

Things began well for the U.S. attorney. As expected, the defense
lawyer William R. Whitaker rose to challenge the jury pool. As in the first
trial, he argued that the selection process was unlawful because it was
not similar enough to the process used in Louisiana state courts. His
most significant new objection was that prospective jurors had not been
picked "without regard to race or color," and that three men had been
admitted to the jury pool even though they had improperly volunteered
"with a view to sitting on this cause."

Bradley, with Woods silently concurring, overruled all the objections.
Whitaker persisted, demanding that he be allowed to interrogate every
member of the jury pool to determine his race. He claimed that 120 of
them were Negroes. Bradley told him it would be a waste of time to
"trace the descent and lineage of the jurymen." He did let Whitaker question John R. Clay, the colored freeholder who had helped put together
the list. Clay testified that it actually contained slightly more whites than
blacks, after which Bradley told Whitaker that he was through. "The
facts that you have shown do not affect the panel and we therefore declare it good," Bradley said.

For the rest of the day, and into the next morning, Beckwith and the
defense team battled over the selection of twelve men. The defense asked
each prospective juror if he had ever held a federal, state, or local office;
if he belonged to any political organization whose object was to help the
prosecution win the case; and who had suggested his name as a juror.
Beckwith occasionally consulted what appeared to be detailed notes that
he kept in a small leather-bound notebook.

Beckwith rejected a white coal merchant born in Connecticut, who
said he already had a "fixed opinion" on the case; he also turned away
the owner of the iron foundry that manufactured the little cannon Nash's

posse fired at the Negroes on April 13, 1873. Woods helped the defense by excusing a twenty-three-year-old Irish-born streetcar driver who had one brother in the police and another working in the Custom House. The defense rejected a police captain, as well as a thirty-two-year-old mulatto shoemaker who had been born free before the war; a thirty-six-year-old mulatto professor of languages; and a thirty-two-year-old Prussian-born clerk in the state government.

By 12:50 p.m. on May 20, the jury was complete, and Beckwith had to like what he saw. Five of the men had direct or indirect associations with the Custom House or the Republican-controlled city police. John R. Beals, born in Maine in 1821, had worked as an assistant assessor of internal revenue until just five weeks before the trial began. Alexander McKee, fifty-three, was an Irishman who shared living quarters with a police sergeant. Timothy Kelly, thirty-three, was a customs inspector, also born in Ireland. And Jacob Wolf and E. S. Curry were two of the Republican recruits to whom the defense so heatedly objected. A sixth juror, George D. Wright, forty, a railroad fireman, seemed a likely prosecution vote, since he was born in Massachusetts. Only three jurors—James Mulvey, a twenty-two-year-old Irish-born drayman who lived with his mother; John C. Gantz, a forty-six-year-old butler, born in France; and Charles Bernard, also French—had no apparent pro-prosecution attributes.

As to the race of the jurors, there was some debate. At least nine were white. The *Daily Picayune* reported that "as far as can be determined by the eye, three are colored, light mulattoes." One of these "light mulattoes" was Florville Foy, a renowned marble cutter and sculptor who built tombs for the St. Louis cemetery. Foy was born in Louisiana in 1825; his father was from France and his mother a free woman of color. In the 1850 U.S. Census, he declared himself mulatto—and reported owning two slaves. In 1870 he told the census taker he was white. The other two possible men of color were Sidney Brunet and Joseph Dastugue. But the *Bee* listed Brunet as white; the *Republican* claimed that Brunet was the only colored man.

Having failed to have his way in jury selection, Robert H. Marr rose to make the constitutional challenge that he had been unwilling, or unable, to present in the first trial. Marr knew that Woods would reject it, since he had explicitly told the jury in the first trial that the indictment was perfectly constitutional. But Marr also knew of Bradley's role in *The Slaughterhouse Cases*. That litigation had shown that the justice was sensitive to the concerns of the Southern people, and he might be persuaded to rule that this court had no right to hear this case. If he did, there would be a division of opinion, the trial would be halted, and—most important—the South would at last have its Supreme Court case on the Enforcement Act.

Bradley was not in the courtroom; he had ducked out during jury selection. But Marr wanted him back in. "We ask that Judge Bradley be requested to sit so that in case of a difference of opinion we may have the benefit of the opinion of the Supreme Court of the United States," Marr announced.

Woods tried to deflect Marr. "I would be glad to have Justice Bradley sit with me in this case," he replied, "but at present I do not see that you have raised any point."

Marr then proceeded to lay out his motion, but Woods responded that it was out of order. The defendants had already pled not guilty, implicitly accepting the legality of the indictment, the judge said. Marr would have to wait until some actual testimony was introduced, then object to that. Marr disagreed with Woods, Beckwith rose to argue the point—and, at that very moment, Bradley strolled back into the courtroom and rejoined Woods on the bench.

Woods whispered in Bradley's ear, filling him in on what had just occurred. The justice then announced that he concurred with Woods: Marr's motion was out of order.

Marr was not finished. He explained to the court that he was not moving to quash the indictment, which might indeed be out of order. Rather, he intended to challenge the very authority of the federal court. As far as he understood, "it was eminently proper" to raise such a jurisdictional challenge at any time. "The interests of the people are so great in this matter, and my duty to my clients is such that I feel bound to urgently press this matter for the united determination of the court," Marr pleaded.

Bradley considered that. "Let the case go on," he said. As both Marr and Beckwith undoubtedly noticed, the justice had not said no.

BECKWITH MADE HIS OPENING ARGUMENT ON MAY 20, FOLLOWING THE SAME outline as the first trial. He questioned the same witnesses: Register, DeKlyne, Calhoun, Ward. It was not until the morning of Thursday, May 21, that the prosecutor brought on his first new witness, a black man whose still-visible wounds proved the horrors he had been through in Colfax. He was followed by Kindred J. Harvey, whom Beckwith had located and summoned to bolster his thin roster of white witnesses.

Woods had been by himself on the bench when that day's session began. But as Harvey was testifying, the door suddenly opened—and Bradley returned. The justice kept his silence, but when Harvey stepped down, he made an announcement: upon reflection, it would indeed be proper for Marr to challenge the jurisdiction of the court at this point in the trial. The defense lawyer could proceed immediately if he wished.

Beckwith tried to object, but Bradley overruled him. Marr leaped to his feet. He was ready. He had been hoping and preparing for this moment for months.

Marr argued that section 6 of the Enforcement Act, the statutory foundation of Beckwith's indictment, was unconstitutional. To be sure, it had been enacted to enforce the Fourteenth and Fifteenth amendments, and the Fourteenth Amendment could be taken to mean that the federal government, for the first time, had undertaken to protect the life and liberty of U.S. citizens, as well as their rights to assemble peacefully, keep and bear arms, and the rest of the rights guaranteed by the Bill of Rights. But a crucial distinction must be made, Marr argued: The amendment only provided that "no State" shall pass laws violating those rights. "It does not provide against personal aggression—the infringement of those rights by individuals," he said. That remained the responsibility of state criminal law. And "personal aggression" was essentially the offense with which the U.S. attorney had charged his clients. The Fourteenth Amendment only triggers federal action to "protect the citizen against the aggression of the State, of organized power."

Marr's second point had to do with section 7 of the Enforcement Act. It permitted the federal government to adopt the state punishment for any felony committed in the course of a conspiracy that violated section 6. This was the basis for Beckwith's plea for capital punishment. But federal prosecutors could not relabel murder cases as civil rights cases, Marr insisted. Among other problems, "It does not affect all the citizens of the United States equally—it is not equal," he said. In some states, Marr noted, the punishment for murder would be imprisonment for life, in others ten years, and, he added portentously, "death in Louisiana."

Concluding his speech, Marr read aloud from *The Slaughterhouse Cases*.

Bradley listened. When Marr finished, the justice remarked that he had heard Reverdy Johnson and Henry Stanbery make some of the same points; then he flattered Marr by noting that the New Orleans lawyer had raised issues that even those two luminaries had missed. The court would take the matter under advisement, Bradley concluded.

Beckwith had been uneasy from the moment Bradley arrived in New Orleans. He, too, would have remembered the justice's role in *Slaughter-*

house—how Campbell played on Bradley's long-standing instinct to appease Southern whites, how the justice had accepted Campbell's extreme position. For Beckwith, the justice's presence was becoming a "nightmare," as he wrote to Attorney General Williams.

Bradley's response to Marr did nothing to allay Beckwith's anxiety. The justice's willingness even to entertain Marr's motion had been alarming. His sympathetic mention of Johnson and Stanbery, the Ku Klux Klan's lawyers, was positively horrifying. Bradley was referring to an 1871 Supreme Court case, *United States v. Avery*, in which the Klan lawyers argued that the Court should strike down section 7 of the Enforcement Act—for reasons similar to those Marr had just stated. Unwilling to decide such a sensitive issue in the middle of the Klan trials, the justices had dismissed *Avery* on a procedural technicality.

But Bradley was implying that the Grant Parish trial might provide a good vehicle for the Supreme Court to reexamine that issue and others. If that happened, and if the Court decided in Marr's favor, it might upset not only Beckwith's plans to send the Colfax defendants to the gallows but also the entire federal statutory scheme aimed at white terrorism in the South.

THE NEXT MORNING, MAY 22, BRADLEY, ACCOMPANIED BY WOODS, CALLED THE court to order and got right down to business. The defense had raised a grave question, Bradley intoned—"too grave to be passed upon without mature deliberation and consideration that could not be given during the progress of the trial." Therefore, he and Woods would not rule on it. The trial could proceed, Bradley said. If any or all of the defendants were convicted, however, the defense could raise its objections anew. They would be proper because the law allowed a convicted defendant or the court itself to move for "arrest of judgment." "I will hold myself ready to come and sit with Judge Woods and pass upon the matter, on a motion for arrest of judgment," Bradley announced.

With that, the justice rose and walked out; the next day he caught a steamer to Galveston, Texas. Bradley did not return to New Orleans during the rest of the Grant Parish trial.

Beckwith was angry that the court had permitted Marr to challenge his indictment in the presence of the jury, writing to Williams that this could only sow "confusion and complication." But Marr openly boasted that the justice had compared his arguments to those of Johnson and Stanbery. In his view, Bradley had all but promised to certify a division of opinion if anyone was convicted; that, in turn, would guarantee a

Supreme Court case. "The skies are brightening for the Colfax prisoners," the *Louisiana Democrat* reported. Their lives, Marr told the paper, "are now safe."

OVER THE NEXT TWO WEEKS, WOODS HELD COURT EVERY DAY, EXCEPT SUNDAY, from 9:00 a.m. to 5:00 p.m., with a half-hour break for lunch. If anything, the second trial was more grueling than the first. Midday temperatures in New Orleans rose above ninety degrees, turning the Custom House into a huge granite sauna. Beckwith called eighty-nine witnesses, thirty-nine more than he had put on in the first trial. "Apparently bringing forward these additional witnesses [is] to cumulate evidence against the prisoners who were said to have been engaged in the fight," the *Daily Picayune* observed—correctly. Beckwith was padding his case against the prisoners' alibis. Some thirty-two prosecution witnesses swore that they had seen Donas Lemoine at the fight; eighteen swore against Johnnie Hadnot and Bill Cruikshank. Beckwith was especially determined to leave no doubt about Cruikshank. One of his new witnesses was Pinckney Chambers, who told how he had been ordered to set fire to the courthouse to save his life—and how Cruikshank then kept the white men's part of the cruel bargain by escorting him out of town after the killing was over.

The defense team countered with twenty new witnesses of their own, increasing their total from seventy-nine in the first trial to ninety-nine in the second. Trying to turn the case into a trial of the bloodthirsty Negro William Ward, the defense harped on his letter to Jacob Johnson, bringing in the preacher to testify that he had indeed received it. Another new witness was the doctor who treated Jim Hadnot's bullet wound. Whitaker asked him if Hadnot had said anything on his deathbed about how he was shot. Why yes, the doctor replied. Beckwith leaped to his feet, objecting. Whitaker's ploy was transparent: the doctor would testify that Hadnot had confirmed the flag-of-truce story—and Beckwith, of course, could never cross-examine the dead man. "A man who could not be a witness in this case cannot now be permitted to give his evidence through a second person, even though it was a dying declaration," Beckwith told the court. Woods ordered the doctor not to answer.

The testimony was mostly a grinding repetition of the first trial, though Dan Shaw did adjust his story again. This time he said that perhaps he had seen Andrew Cruikshank, not his brother Bill, Sunday night in Colfax. Yes, Levi Allen had told him to go and "save himself" before the fight, but now Shaw recalled that Allen added, "God damn you."

In the infernal heat, both sides began "to show the effect of the constant and long continued mental strain," a newspaper reporter wrote. Beckwith and his opponents did not like each other's politics, and, increasingly, they did not like each other, period.

The hostility boiled over on May 26, while Wade Ross, one of Beckwith's new witnesses, was on the stand. In response to Beckwith's questions, Ross testified that he saw the Lemoines, Johnnie Hadnot, and Tom Hickman at the fight in Colfax. E. John Ellis, on cross-examination, demanded that Ross specify the time, manner, and place in which he had seen each defendant. The harsh barrage of questions caused Ross to waver, so Beckwith asked the court for permission to question him again. He had barely begun when Whitaker objected that Beckwith was leading the witness.

"Well," Beckwith blurted out, "this has been the most beastly cross-examination that I have ever listened to." *Beastly* was a strong word in the mid-nineteenth century and not appropriate for the courtroom.

Ellis was on his feet immediately, shouting at Beckwith. "Mr. Beckwith, what was that, sir?" he demanded. "You will please repeat that remark of yours. I did not quite hear you."

Beckwith, refusing to face Ellis, muttered: "I was expressing my disapproval of your mode of examining witnesses."

Marr piped up, as if he were Ellis's second in some schoolyard tussle: "He used the word 'beastly.' That is what it was, 'beastly.'"

"Did you, Mr. Beckwith, apply the term 'beastly' to this examination?" Ellis asked, his words rich with mock outrage.

"It was rather a hard term, I'll confess," Beckwith replied. "I did not mean it." He rose sheepishly to his feet and faced the court. "I retract the word," he said. "I was angry. I try in all cases to treat opposing counsel as gentlemen should be treated."

Woods commanded both sides to stop arguing, but Ellis took a last shot. "I warn you, Mr. Beckwith, to understand that such language is not to be used again in connection with me," he fumed. Beckwith's outburst was a gift to the defense—a chance to make him seem like a fanatic to the jury. Ellis, with his theatrics, had made the most of it.

Beckwith compensated the only way he knew how: by delivering an effective rebuttal to the defense's case. On June 3, Beckwith called Thomas Johnson, a Negro and former Calhoun plantation slave driver who was now a Republican member of the Grant Parish police jury. Johnson testified that he saw defense witness Sylvester Dubois in Colfax on Easter Sunday, despite Dubois's testimony that he and the defendant Donas Lemoine were at his house. When the defense lawyers insisted that Johnson was lying, Beckwith called their bluff. He agreed to stage a lineup in open court. On June 4, five men entered, and the defense asked Johnson to pick Dubois out of the group. Without hesitation, Johnson fingered the right man.

Beckwith called Willie Calhoun to counter J. C. Morantini's tale of white men shot while carrying a huge white banner up to the courthouse. If anyone knew Colfax, it was the town's founder. Beckwith had hired the *Daily Picayune*'s mapmaker to sketch the area. He spread the map on a table in front of the jury. Then he produced a set of toy blocks and asked Calhoun to arrange them on the map as if they were the buildings and other landmarks of his old plantation. With this ingenious model, Calhoun showed that from where Morantini supposedly had been standing, he could never have seen the fantastic scene he described.

The prosecution and the defense staggered to the end of the testimony, like two boxers holding each other up at the final bell. But Beckwith was ahead on points.

THE THRONG OF SPECTATORS FOR CLOSING ARGUMENTS ON JUNE 5, 1874, WAS SO huge that deputy U.S. marshals began to worry that someone in the crowd might exploit the chaos to help the prisoners escape. So they moved the defendants from their usual spot next to their lawyers and put them in a corner of the courtroom under heavy guard. They stood there anxiously as Beckwith rose to sum up his case against them one last time.

As in the first trial, he began with the law, telling the jury of the "necessities" that had caused Congress to adopt the Enforcement Act. He hammered on the point that the Negroes in Colfax had assembled not only for a lawful purpose, as Dan Shaw's posse, but also in self-defense, because of Jesse McKinney's murder. He contrasted this with the manifestly violent purposes of Nash's force. And he attacked the alibi witnesses, noting the contradictions among their various stories. "Too many cooks spoiled the broth," he scoffed. Of course, he told the jury, any white man who testified truthfully did so at the risk of his life.

It was a solid performance, more polished and less emotional than his closing in the first case—perhaps the "beastly" exchange with Ellis had reminded him to keep his cool. Earlier in the case, a white supremacist newspaper had mocked Beckwith as a "Methodist preacher." Now, though, even the *Daily Picayune* had to acknowledge that his speech "seemed the result of careful study and preparation." The *Bulletin* conceded that he was "actually interesting," "animated and forcible." Beckwith framed the case just as he felt it had to be framed: even if the Negroes had been on a rampage, they didn't deserve to be taken out two by two and shot in the head.

Marr followed Beckwith, his stridency betraying just a hint of desperation. "The blood of these murdered Negroes rests on the hands of Ward, Flowers and Register," he declared, "men who were so anxious for their offices that they broke into the courthouse, summoned the Negroes from miles away and prepared to defend the courthouse they had stolen. They thought they were commanders, organized their Negro army, drilled, equipped and furnished them, and prepared to reign as sovereigns without the least authority. They treated with the white men, signing their names as 'leaders of the Negroes.'"

No such words appeared on the "treaty" with Montgomery, for the simple reason that some of the Republicans who signed it were white. But Marr sought emotional, not factual, authenticity. "Their threats, their robberies, the evil intentions, soon awoke the white people," he continued. "Then it was that, with cowardly haste, these arch-villains fled from Colfax in the night-time, leaving their victims to fight for 'the United States.' And yet, some say that the white men ought to have left this assembly alone. If they had, it would be there now; the whites could get no end. It was only then, when challenged to arms, that the whites engaged in a battle."

"Was there no conspiracy amongst the blacks?" Marr roared. "Was this assembly a peaceful assembly? Is the system of perjury displayed by the witnesses for the prosecution, perjury thirsting for blood, no conspiracy? These questions must be asked before any blame can be attached to the prisoners." A flutter of applause went through the audience as he finished.

The next day, Whitaker spoke. After weeks of working in the heat, he appeared faint but still managed a three-hour oration, arguing that the case was outside federal jurisdiction—and the jurors could acquit on that basis alone. "Whether you murder a Negro or a white man," Whitaker said, "you go before [state] Judge Atocha, and not the United States Court." In effect, Whitaker was asking the jurors to nullify Beckwith's evidence—and thereby backhandedly admitting that his evidence was strong.

Yet on Monday, June 9, the last day of arguments, E. John Ellis closed with a similar appeal. As 1,500 spectators listened, he told the jury that most of the counts in the indictment were not valid federal offenses. Besides, Ellis argued, Christopher Columbus Nash and Alphonse Cazabat had acted as sheriff and judge for so long prior to the Republicans' courthouse takeover that none of the men who had responded to their call for a posse could be blamed for doing so. He repeated Marr's claims that the Negroes had robbed, threatened, and murdered innocent people, and as he did, whites in the audience once again clapped. Ellis fed on their approval. He was "heated, caustic, passionate and pleasant all at the same time," the *New Orleans Bee* reported. "He inspired fury and indignation equally."

When Ellis finished, "a murmur of appreciation ran through the room," as one of the reporters present put it, and his supporters could no longer contain themselves. They erupted in applause. Woods banged his gavel, then ordered one of the loudest members of the audience before the bench and cited him for contempt of court.

For four hours that afternoon, Beckwith poured out his rebuttal, followed by Judge Woods's charge to the jury. But neither statement could quite erase the powerful message of that applause for Ellis: these were the sentiments of the community to which the jurors would return after rendering a verdict.

At 6:00 p.m. on June 9, the twelve men retired to begin their deliberations.

ELLIS CELEBRATED THE TRIAL'S END BY JOINING JOHN MCENERY AT A POLITICAL rally in downtown New Orleans. "Ellis! Ellis!" the throng cried. He obliged with a few remarks, apologizing for his hoarseness after so many days in court. For the other participants in the trial, there was nothing to do. Woods stayed in his chambers until late Monday, June 9, playing "set back," a card game, with William Pitt Kellogg. "The lives of eight white men were being balanced between life and death at that very time in the neighboring jury room," the *Bulletin* complained, "as the Judge watched for 'ace' and 'right bower' to turn up."

At first, the jurors were anything but united. In their little room next to the court, every fact about every defendant seemed to be in dispute. A particular sticking point, though, was the defense's insistence that they were supposed to be judges of the law as well as the facts. Woods had told them the opposite. He had instructed them almost precisely as he had instructed the jury in the first trial: disregard any suggestion that the court lacked jurisdiction, or that you are to judge anything but the factual evidence.

Two jurors were still not sure what to do with these conflicting demands, so at 9:00 a.m. on June 10, the whole jury asked for a new meeting with Woods. Woods reread his instructions—and that seemed to settle the issue. For the next nine hours or so, the jurors debated among themselves. At 7:30 p.m., they sent a new message to Woods. They had a verdict.

Beckwith and the defense lawyers were having dinner at various places around New Orleans when they got the word. Within minutes, they were back in the Custom House courtroom. Shortly after 8:00 p.m., the prisoners entered, guarded by deputy U.S. marshals. Cruikshank, Gibbons, Hadnot, Hickman, Irwin, Penn, and the Lemoines looked nervous, their lawyers, gloomy. If Beckwith expressed emotion, it did not register with any of the newspaper reporters who recorded the scene.

At 8:30, the jury filed in, seemingly more tense than the prisoners, with whom they avoided eye contact.

"Gentlemen, have you agreed upon a verdict?" Woods asked.

Alexander McKee, the foreman, answered for the group: "Your honor, we have brought in a qualified verdict, which we have written out. I will read it."

McKee adjusted his glasses. He moved closer to one of the gaslights that dimly illuminated the vast room. But he was simply too anxious to read the page he held in his trembling hands. He asked a fellow juror for help.

E. S. Curry stepped forward, took the document from McKee, and declared: "We find Cruikshank, Hadnot and Irwin guilty of combining and conspiring on the first sixteen counts, and we recommend them to the mercy of the court. D. Lemoine, J. B. P. Lemoine, Gibbons, Hickman and Penn are not guilty."

Astonishment creased the faces of the few dozen spectators who had heard about the coming verdict in time to see the jury deliver it. But they stifled any impulse to cry out. At the defense's request, Woods polled the jury. One after another, each man averred that this was his verdict. All eight defendants had been acquitted of murder. Five of them had been acquitted of all charges. But three of the most clearly culpable defendants—Cruikshank, who organized the slaughter of prisoners, and Hadnot and Irwin, who never denied being in Colfax on Easter Sunday—had been found guilty of conspiring to violate the Negroes' civil rights. Each faced ten years in jail and a fine of five thousand dollars.

The verdict was clearly a compromise, hashed out among twelve men sworn to do impartial justice—but frightened of what might happen to them no matter what they decided. Beckwith was dismayed at what he considered a "beggarly" result. He suspected that the defense's arguments against the court's jurisdiction had confused the jury and made them shrink from convicting the men of murder. He wrote to Attorney General Williams that the result showed the "inadequacy of the courts to make law respected." He might have been too much the "rectifier of injustice" to see how much he had actually accomplished. There would be no perfect justice, that was true; but there would not be total impunity either. The rule of law was vindicated, however minimally. James Roswell Beckwith had not exactly triumphed—but he had won.

WHITE LOUISIANA REACTED WITH FURY. THE VERDICT, SAID THE *DAILY PICAYUNE*, "could not be honestly and conscientiously found in such a case." The *Bulletin* printed the names of the twelve jurors, so that "our community may know" them—and, presumably, take revenge. The outcome of the trial, the paper opined, "is only another proof of the fearful fact that Southern white men have no rights that Republican officials are bound to respect."

Beckwith wanted to retry the five acquitted defendants on different indictments, but, having failed twice to convict them, he grudgingly consented to their release on bail. On June 11, wealthy New Orleanians came up with ten thousand dollars for each man, and the Lemoines, Penn, Hickman, and Gibbons left the court amid handshakes and backslaps. The defense, trying to free the other three, asked Woods to hear several motions for a new trial, based on alleged flaws in the jury pool and the fact that one of the jurors had a criminal record. As the defense undoubtedly knew, none of these arguments stood much of a chance with Woods. The only real question was: what will Justice Bradley do?

Woods cabled the justice about the verdict as soon as it was rendered. Woods told both Beckwith and the defense lawyers that he doubted Bradley would, in fact, return to New Orleans, but that he might mail his ruling. When Marr reminded him that the justice had promised to return in case of any convictions, Woods allowed that this was possible.

Beckwith treated himself to the hope that Bradley would not rule in favor of the defense after all. The jury had acquitted all defendants on all the murder charges, so the issue that seemed to interest Bradley— whether a federal court could punish someone for a state felony—was gone. As for the conspiracy counts on which the three men had been found guilty, Beckwith was confident that they were supported by precedent. "There will doubtless be a motion in arrest of judgment," he wrote to Attorney General Williams, "which under the verdict I am satisfied cannot prevail."

Beckwith tried to find a place to lock up Cruikshank, Hadnot, and Irwin; normally, federal prisoners went to the Louisiana state penitentiary in Baton Rouge. But it was notoriously easy to escape. He was still working on this problem when Woods returned to New Orleans from a week back in Mobile. On the morning of June 20, as a tropical rain clattered on the roof of the Custom House, a messenger brought Woods a telegram in his chambers. It was from Bradley. The justice said he was nearly finished with his opinion and would mail it in a few days. He would have communicated sooner, but there had been an illness in his family. To Woods, this could mean only one thing: the justice was going to overturn the convictions.

He confided the news to Beckwith, who scrambled to think of some way to stop Bradley. All he could come up with was a long shot. There was some doubt, legally, as to whether Bradley could rule in absentia. Beckwith thought that his decision would be invalid unless Bradley was actually on the bench in New Orleans. At least he was prepared to make that argument, and to take the issue to the full Supreme Court if necessary.

Beckwith cabled Bradley, informing him that he would resist a mailed-in ruling. It was provocative for a mere U.S. attorney to issue such a challenge to a Supreme Court justice. Bradley accepted it. At 7:00 a.m. on June 24, he once again went to the Baltimore & Potomac station and boarded a New Orleans–bound train. At Lynchburg, Virginia, he switched to a sleeping car. "This was the hottest day I have known," Bradley wrote in his diary—but not hot enough to stop him. On he went, through Atlanta and Montgomery and Mobile, until at 11:00 p.m. on June 26, "a cool evening along the Gulf," as Bradley described it, he pulled into New Orleans.

At 9:00 a.m. on June 27, a Saturday, Woods entered the Custom House courtroom, alone, and announced that he was ready to rule on the defense's motions for a new trial. His opinion was lengthy and detailed, but utterly unsurprising. One by one, he rejected the defense arguments, emphasizing his own strong belief that the "prisoners have had a fair and careful trial before a patient and intelligent jury."

But his declaration took on an almost valedictory quality when he made his next announcement. The case was still not quite over. Court would adjourn until 12:00 p.m., at which time Justice Bradley would rule on the defense's motion for arrest of judgment.

THE SCENARIO THAT JAMES BECKWITH HAD DREADED FOR WEEKS PLAYED OUT right on schedule. At the stroke of noon, Bradley and Woods reopened court before an expectant throng. Marr rose and read his motion. And then Bradley began to speak. The justice had labored over his opinion for more than two weeks, scratching it out in spidery longhand on sheet after sheet of legal-sized parchment. He cared enough about it to trek halfway across the country in a sweltering railroad car to deliver it in person. Yet, in court, he read his opinion in a flat, emotionless, voice.

"The main ground of objection" to Beckwith's indictment, Bradley began, is that section 6 of the Enforcement Act, "is municipal in character, operating directly on the conduct of individuals, and taking the place of ordinary state legislation; and that there is no constitutional authority for such an act, inasmuch as the state laws furnish adequate remedy for the alleged wrongs committed."

A constitutional challenge to the statute required a constitutional analysis. When the Constitution guarantees a right, Bradley explained, Congress can enact laws to enforce it. That much had been established before the Civil War, when the Court upheld Congress's power to protect slaveholders' property rights by sending federal marshals to round up escaped Negroes. But, he added, "one method of enforcement may be applicable to one fundamental right, and not applicable to another." To decide this case, he would have to figure out if the Enforcement Act was not only authorized by one or more of the post–Civil War amendments but also properly tailored to their purposes.

As he read, Bradley tinkered with his draft. He had spotted a misspelling, perhaps, or a missing comma. Without interrupting his flow of words, he motioned with his quill to Woods, who passed him an inkpot. The justice dipped the pen in the ink, fixed the mistake, and kept on reading.

A crucial distinction must be kept in mind, Bradley explained. When, as in the Fourteenth Amendment, the Constitution protects certain rights "only by a declaration that the state or the United States shall not violate or abridge them," it is not creating new rights but merely protecting existing rights from official violation. "For example," he intoned, "when it is declared [in the Fourteenth Amendment] that no state shall deprive any person of life, liberty or property without due process of law"—a right guaranteed in the original Bill of Rights—"this declaration is not intended as a guaranty against the commission of murder, false imprisonment, robbery or any other crime committed by individual malefactors so as to give Congress the power to pass laws for the punishment of such crimes in the several states generally." Rather, Congress could only intervene "against arbitrary and unjust [state] legislation."

In *Slaughterhouse*, Bradley thought that unjust state legislation included laws like the Louisiana abattoir "monopoly." But now he seemed to accept *Slaughterhouse*'s more limited conception of federal power and adapted it to the issue that was before him: an alleged conspiracy by *nonstate* actors to violate constitutional and legal rights.

Having established that *Slaughterhouse* covered this case, but without yet saying exactly how, Bradley took up the Thirteenth Amendment, which prohibited slavery and gave Congress the power to enforce the ban—no mention of the states. The implication, he said, was that Congress itself could indeed punish individuals for violating the Thirteenth Amendment, which he saw not only as the narrow abolition of chattel slavery but also as the broad "bestowment of liberty on . . . millions of people." In his view, Congress had quite properly exercised this power in the Civil Rights Act of 1866, which attempted to eliminate racial inequalities in citizenship.

Bradley was being consistent with his well-known dissenting opinion in the 1871 case of *Blyew v. United States*, which involved the murder of a ninety-year-old blind Negro woman by whites in Kentucky. The only witnesses were two men, both colored. But Kentucky law at the time banned testimony against whites by people of color. The U.S. attorney took over the prosecution, citing the Civil Rights Act's provision allowing federal intervention where state courts refused to treat Negroes the same as whites. A majority of the Supreme Court said this was a misapplication of the Civil Rights Act, because the law protected the *victim*, not the witnesses. And the victim was dead, so there was no case. In his strongest statement ever in support of the rights of the Negro, Bradley wrote, "To deprive a whole class of the community of this right, to refuse their evidence and their sworn complaints, is to brand them with a badge of slavery."

In *Blyew*, both the Court majority and Bradley had said that the Civil Rights Act was primarily enacted to benefit the freedmen and should be interpreted in that light. But neither had said that it could *only* be invoked by people of color. Now, in the Custom House courtroom, Bradley added that limitation. The law was aimed at only one category of offense, he said: crimes motivated by racial prejudice. "The duty of Congress," he explained, "in the creation and punishment of offenses is limited to those offenses which aim at the deprivation of the colored citizen's enjoyment and exercise of his rights of citizenship and of equal protection of the laws because of his race, color or previous condition of servitude." Everything else was up to the states.

Bradley then applied the same reasoning to the Fifteenth Amendment, which Congress had cited as authority for the Enforcement Act. He said that the Fifteenth Amendment created a right to vote without being discriminated against on the basis of race, color, or previous condition.

Congress could protect this right "not only as against the unfriendly operation of state laws, but against outrage, violence and combinations on the part of individuals, irrespective of state laws." Once again, though, the key was racist intent. Congress could outlaw only acts which "have for motive the race, color or previous condition of servitude of the party whose right [to vote] is assailed," Bradley declared.

For Bradley, in short, no murder, arson, assault, or robbery was a federal offense unless it was a hate crime. Without this distinction, he continued, "we are driven to one of two extremes—either that Congress can never interfere where the state laws are unobjectionable, however remiss the state authorities may be in executing them, and however much a proscribed race may be oppressed; or that Congress may pass an entire body of municipal law for the protection of person and property within the states, to operate concurrently with the state laws, for the protection and benefit of a particular class of the community."

THE TIME HAD COME TO FIND OUT EXACTLY WHAT BRADLEY HAD IN MIND. "I WILL now proceed to examine the several counts in the indictment, and endeavor to test their validity by the principles which have been laid down," the justice said. "These have been so fully enunciated and explained, that a very brief examination of the counts will suffice."

Not surprisingly, given his remarks about the Fourteenth Amendment, Bradley threw out counts 1 and 2, which charged conspiracy to violate the Negroes' First Amendment right to assemble, and their Second Amendment right to bear arms, respectively. Protecting these rights was the "prerogative of the states," Bradley averred. Count 3 charged a conspiracy to deprive the Negroes of life and liberty without due process of law. In *Slaughterhouse*, Miller and the majority had left open the possibility that the privileges and immunities of citizenship might include such a due-process right. Beckwith had hoped his indictment might thread this legal needle. But now Bradley said no. The right to due process was an "old" right that the Fourteenth Amendment protected only against the state, not individuals or mobs. Cruikshank, Hadnot, and Irwin might have killed Alexander Tillman. But "every murderer . . . does this," the justice said.

Count 4, Bradley conceded, was relatively solid. It charged conspiracy to deprive the Negroes of "the free exercise and enjoyment of the right and privilege to the full and equal benefit of all laws and proceedings for the security of persons and property which is enjoyed by the white citizens." Bradley correctly noted that Beckwith derived it not from the Fourteenth Amendment but from the Civil Rights Act, which

Bradley had just said was a valid exercise of Congress's power to enforce the Thirteenth Amendment.

The problem was that Beckwith had not expressly alleged a racial motive, Bradley said. Bradley conceded that "such a design may be inferred from the allegation that the persons injured were of the African race, and that the intent was to deprive them of the exercise and enjoyment of the rights enjoyed by white citizens. But it ought not to have been left to inference; it should have been alleged." This was the first time any federal court had ever ruled that the Thirteenth Amendment *required* explicit allegation of racial motive in an Enforcement Act case. The U.S. attorney could not have known he was bound by this newly minted rule. Yet Bradley enforced it strictly—and retroactively.

Now Bradley came to count 5, in which Beckwith *had* expressly alleged a racial motive: it charged the defendants with conspiring to violate Tillman's and Nelson's rights "by reason of, and for and on account of the race and color of" the two men, "and for the reason that they . . . were persons of African descent and race, and persons of color, and not white citizens."

But first Bradley paused to add another complaint against the previous count: it was too vague. "It seems to me that such a general and sweeping charge," he said, "without any specification of any laws or proceedings, does not amount to the averment of a criminal act. It is not merely informal, it is insufficient."

That became Bradley's reason to dismiss count 5, which charged the men with conspiring to "hinder and prevent" Nelson's and Tillman's "respective free exercise and enjoyment of the rights, privileges, immunities and protection granted and secured to them" as citizens of the United States and of Louisiana. These words, Bradley announced, were "open to the same charge of vagueness and generality as the fourth" count. That was also the fatal flaw in the allegations contained in count 8, he quickly added.

Counts 6 and 7 charged a conspiracy to prevent the Negroes from voting in the future—and to punish them for having voted in November 1872. They were based on section 6 of the Enforcement Act. And now it was section 6 that Bradley attacked. Congress had not expressly limited it to voting rights violations motivated by race. "The law on which this count is founded is not confined to cases of discrimination," Bradley said. "It is general and universal in its application," meaning that it could also protect whites. "Such a law is not supported by the constitution."

Of course, Bradley alone could not strike section 6 down. Only a majority of the Supreme Court could do that. But even assuming section 6 was valid, Bradley added, these two counts of Beckwith's indictment were invalid, because they did not explicitly say that the conspiracy against Nelson and Tillman was racially motivated. "It should, at least, have been shown that the conspiracy was entered into to deprive the injured persons of their right to vote by reason of their race, color or previous condition of servitude," he said.

Bradley was almost finished. "The next eight counts on which the verdict was found are literal copies, respectively, of the first eight, so far as relates to the language on which their validity depends. The same observations apply to them which apply to the first eight," he said. All sixteen counts were gone. And if there were no valid charges, there could be no valid convictions.

"In my opinion," Bradley concluded, "the motion in arrest of judgment must be granted." The guilty verdicts must be overturned.

The courtroom erupted in applause. "A Daniel come to judgment!" someone cried.

BECKWITH WAS DUMBFOUNDED. HE HAD JUST HEARD A SUPREME COURT JUSTICE declare that three men who had been found guilty of one of the greatest crimes Beckwith had ever known should go free because of drafting errors in the indictment against them. This was the injustice Bradley had traveled half a continent to correct.

William B. Woods had known more or less what to expect, but he must have been almost as dismayed as Beckwith. Over the course of two tense and difficult trials, Woods had upheld the indictments, remaining steadfast despite intense political pressure and threats of violence. Now Bradley had just told the world, in effect, that Woods had not known what he was talking about. He had made a mockery of Woods's entire effort.

And Bradley had also implicitly repudiated Woods's signature ruling, *United States v. Hall.* This must have been especially galling—albeit for reasons that Woods would never express publicly.

As he pondered *Hall* back in the fall of 1870, Woods had sought the guidance of the Supreme Court justice for his circuit: Joseph Bradley. He wrote Bradley explaining that a mob, not the then-Republican government of Alabama, was to blame for the violence, and asking if such a case belonged in federal court. Yes, Bradley answered, an ordinary riot would have been only a state offense, but the Klan attack was intended "to intimidate persons and prevent them from exercising the right of suffrage, guaranteed to them by the fifteenth amendment," and that made it a federal crime.

Bradley said nothing about racial intent in that letter, and on March 12, 1871, he wrote Woods even more emphatically that the Fourteenth Amendment protected fundamental rights not only against state action but also against state *inaction*. That meant that the federal government could step in not only when a state passed discriminatory legislation but also when a state—like Alabama—was too weak to protect citizens' rights. "Federal rights," Bradley wrote, "must be protected whether it interferes with domestic laws or domestic administration of laws."

Two months later, Woods issued his ruling in *United States v. Hall*, taking much of his opinion verbatim from Bradley's March 12 letter.

Bradley's opinion in New Orleans on June 27, 1874, was certainly not in the spirit of his *Blyew* dissent, but, in a formal sense, the two were consistent. *Blyew* was about a state law—Kentucky's ban on Negro testimony—not mob violence. The U.S. attorney in that case *did* allege that the witnesses were forbidden to testify "on account of" race. Had Bradley retreated from the sweeping notion of constitutional rights in his *Slaughterhouse* dissent? That, too, could be explained: he had lost that case and was bowing to Supreme Court precedent.

What Bradley could not easily account for was his double-crossing of Woods—the contradiction between this ruling and his 1871 letters. But as long as Woods kept quiet about it, Bradley would not have to explain.

When the applause for Bradley died down, Woods spoke. "I regard the opinion of Judge Bradley with appropriate deference," he said. "But my opinion on the validity of the indictment has been carefully formed and is of long standing. I regret to disagree with my learned brother." It was the only time in Reconstruction that a lower-ranking federal judge publicly disagreed with his circuit's Supreme Court justice on a civil rights issue. There would be a certificate of division of opinion. The Supreme Court would get the case. That was the most Woods dared to do.

The U.S. attorney was helpless, furious. The unfairness must have been more than he could bear. The defense had slept on its rights during the whole first trial, not even raising the constitutional objection that Bradley had just sustained. Of course, the fact that it had ended in a mistrial meant that, legally, the first trial counted for nothing. But surely it meant something morally. And Bradley had struck Beckwith's indictment down without even suggesting how a valid one might have been drafted. Grant Parish was riven by racial, political, economic, and social conflict, all of which contributed to the Colfax Massacre. How, exactly, could Beckwith—or any U.S. attorney—prove beyond a reasonable doubt that racism, and no other motive, caused it?

Beckwith stood. Words began to form on his lips—a last-ditch motion, perhaps, or an objection of some kind. Bradley silenced him with a glare. "I am not through, Mr. Beckwith," he said.

There was still the question of what to do with the prisoners. In theory, they could be held until the Supreme Court ruled. As long as they were behind bars, Beckwith might empanel a new grand jury and seek a new indictment to Bradley's specifications. Once the men were out, however, that would be futile.

Bradley wanted them released. He granted a defense request for bail, setting it at five thousand dollars each—only half of what Woods had made the five *acquitted* defendants post. Thirty prominent New Orleanians raced to the Custom House with the cash, and by about 3:30 p.m., Bill Cruikshank, Johnnie Hadnot, Bill Irwin, and their lawyers were out on Canal Street. Hundreds of people rushed up to them, smiling, cheering, and reaching out to shake the hands of their heroes.

The Grant Parish prisoners' defense fund bought the three men new clothes and tickets back to Colfax on board the *Bart Able*, a handsome 206-foot sidewheeler whose staterooms were a decided improvement over the *Ozark's* brig. Word of their triumph preceded them, and their trip home quickly turned into a victory tour. At Pineville, their supporters staged a loud salute with cannon fire. The steamer piped a cheery whistle blast of its own, and the three men stepped ashore, surrounded by exultant friends.

ALL ACROSS LOUISIANA, THE WHITE SUPREMACIST PRESS HAILED BRADLEY'S RULing, crowing that it was much more than a victory for three individual defendants. Rather, it effectively suspended federal law enforcement in Louisiana and the rest of the Deep South, so that white men could now resist Negro abuses without interference from the likes of James Beckwith. Before Bradley's ruling, the *New Orleans Bulletin* observed, "the white people have passively endured the most intolerable wrongs on the part of the deluded negro, and the latter has become insufferably arrogant and insolent." But now, the paper continued, the "negro will . . . understand that if he violates the rights of the white man he . . . can no longer invoke the strong arm of the Federal Government to protect him in wrong and outrage upon the rights of others." The *Bulletin* later published the entire text of Bradley's opinion on its front page.

Joseph Bradley probably didn't read any of these articles; he got on a northbound train to Washington within an hour after he ruled. But Bradley was proud of his opinion. Upon returning to the nation's capital, he took the unusual step of ordering printed copies sent to his colleagues on the Supreme Court, members of the cabinet, congressional leaders, and major newspapers and law journals. He mailed one each to five federal judges across the Fifth Circuit, to guide them in Enforcement Act cases until the Supreme Court ruled.

One of those who got a copy was Bradley's old friend from Rutgers, the Republican senator Frederick Frelinghuysen of New Jersey, a strong advocate of Negro rights who had helped draft the Fourteenth Amendment. Apparently troubled by the damage the ruling could do to federal law enforcement, he wrote Bradley to suggest that he preferred the expansive view of national citizenship and federal power that Bradley had seemed to embrace in *Slaughterhouse*.

On July 19, Bradley replied to Frelinghuysen from his vacation in the fresh green hills of Stowe, Vermont. He breezily conceded that Frelinghuysen might have a point, but added, "My own mind is rather in the condition of *seeking for truth*, than that of dogmatically laying down opinions, and I am very glad the Louisiana case is now in a position where it can be brought before the Supreme Court, and receive the deliberate and well-considered judgment of the whole court."

Actually, with transitory exceptions such as *Blyew*, Bradley had always advocated benign neglect of the South on racial issues. The Joseph Bradley who steered between "extremes" in his Grant Parish opinion sounded very much like the Joseph Bradley who, on the eve of the Civil War, had sought to reconcile Northern and Southern whites at the expense of the Negro.

And now Bradley seemed to speak for many white people, North and South. The financial panic triggered by the collapse of Jay Cooke & Company on September 18, 1873, had plunged the once-exuberant North into depression, leaving Northern voters concerned more with their own welfare than the rights of distant Negroes. "The truth is, our people are tired out with this worn out cry of 'Southern outrages,'" a Republican officeholder wrote. "Hard times and heavy taxes make them wish the 'nigger,' 'everlasting nigger,' were in hell or Africa." Northern papers that had bemoaned the Colfax Massacre only a year earlier now praised Bradley's ruling: the *Chicago Daily Tribune* called it "a masterly exposition of the absurd assumptions and usurpations under the Ku-Klux act."

The would-be governor John McEnery gave a speech suggesting that Bradley had consulted with the White House and that his decision reflected administration policy. This was false; yet McEnery was right in the sense that not even the president could ignore the political climate. Prior to Bradley's ruling, Grant had refused to send troops to help Republicans in three of Louisiana's neighboring states. As a result, Texas Democrats drove a Republican governor from office on January 15, 1874. In Arkansas, a local war between two claimants to the governorship cost dozens of lives before it ended on May 15, 1874, in victory for the anti-Reconstruction contender. On July 4, 1874, a white mob in Vicksburg, Mississippi, broke up a Negro Republican celebration, leaving several colored men dead. The rampage was intended to intimidate voters ahead of a local election, and it did: the Democrats won.

BACK IN THE CRESCENT CITY, JAMES BECKWITH READ AND REREAD BRADLEY'S opinion, growing angrier and angrier. He grumbled in a letter to Attorney General Williams that it seemed Bradley had not even read the indictment but "exhibited a determination to demolish the law where he feels equal to the task, and to demolish the indictment where he cannot wrestle successfully with the law. . . . If the demolished indictment is not good, I am incompetent to form a good one." Beckwith asked Williams if he should even bother prosecuting white terrorism until the Supreme Court ruled. As he probably expected, the attorney general replied, "I do not think it is advisable."

Beckwith had no illusions about what this would mean for Louisiana. Even before Bradley's ruling, he had seen indications that white supremacists were preparing for a violent campaign on a scale not seen since 1868. Yet unless and until the Supreme Court overruled Bradley, Republicans, white and black, could be targeted with impunity. The result, Beckwith predicted, would be five hundred murders by the November election.

CHAPTER TEN

"IF LOUISIANA GOES . . ."

Bradley's decision had a swift, bloody, impact on Grant Parish. On July 25, 1874, whites gathered in Colfax for a big outdoor barbecue in honor of the former defendants. They were surrounded by indicted men who had been in hiding but were now free again to enjoy slabs of pork and bottles of whiskey with their neighbors. The *Louisiana Democrat* billed the party as a "Wake Up Jake" affair, a reference to a minstrel song, then popular, about Jake, a railroad fireman who turned into "de debil when he gets upon a bender." But a new newspaper in Alexandria, the *Caucasian*, called it a "mass meeting for the purpose of organizing the White Man's Party for the Fall campaign."

As the shadows lengthened, the mood shifted. The anger in them all took hold; three of the Hadnots and some friends galloped through the Negro "quarters," firing pistols randomly as their horses' hooves tore up the freedmen's vegetable patches. About six miles from town, the gang encountered a Negro named Frank Foster, on his way to get water. The whites called on him to halt and ordered him to walk in front of them as they rode. Foster complied, but the situation must have reminded him too much of the way colored men had been marched to their deaths on Easter Sunday. After a short distance, he tried to run away. The whites spurred their horses and gave chase. They overtook Foster and hurled him to the ground, shooting him with their pistols and plunging a dagger in his throat. His body was left, sprawled and bloody, on a dirt road.

The group rode on to the cabin of another Negro, Jim Cox, where they demanded a gourd of water. Cox was an old man, polite by nature, and, no doubt, also well aware that a challenge on his part would be unwise. But when he brought the water, the white men shot him and cut his throat. The knife slashed his neck so hard it nearly severed Cox's head from his body.

News of the murders spread immediately. Negro men grabbed their shotguns and a few possessions and fled to the woods. The coroner, a Negro Republican named Henry Deshazier, was supposed to go to the crime scenes to inspect the dead, but he told Captain Arthur W. Allyn of the U.S. Army's detachment in Colfax that he was afraid to investigate the murders alone. Allyn sent a blue-uniformed officer with him. Deshazier and the officer found that one of the killers had left the sheath of his knife by Jim Cox's body; several colored people recognized it as the property of one of the Hadnots. It was more than enough evidence for a warrant.

By this time, there was a new sheriff in Grant Parish: John B. McCoy, a white Republican appointed by Governor William Pitt Kellogg in March 1874, shortly after the beginning of the first trial. McCoy had served in a Union guerrilla unit during the war and now lived with a Negro woman in his piney woods cabin. He had to be tough, and he was. But even McCoy "could no more have arrested those men than he could have captured the city of New Orleans," Allyn reported. So the army helped him execute the warrants.

On July 28, Sheriff McCoy brought two prisoners before Judge Robert C. Register, who was holding court in the warehouse next to the former courthouse site. Register asked the complaining party to step forward, but even with U.S. troops present, not a soul dared to testify. The Negroes of Colfax had, indeed, been taught a lesson by the Easter massacre—and by the trials in New Orleans. Register had no choice but to dismiss the case.

For the rest of the summer of 1874, armed white men roamed Colfax and its environs, forcing a dozen Republicans, black and white, to take refuge in Allyn's camp. New attacks broke out across the state. After a siege by white vigilantes, the Republican government of Natchitoches Parish, next door to Grant Parish, resigned en masse on July 27. Five Negroes were lynched that same month in the town of Lafayette. Republican officials in Iberia Parish fled on August 12. And down in St. Martin Parish, a mob led by Alcibiades DeBlanc, the founder of the Knights of the White Camellia, forced out the Republican parish judge.

By late August, Governor William Pitt Kellogg was growing desperate. He wrote a long, alarming report to Attorney General Williams, blaming the violence on Bradley's opinion, which, he wrote, "was regarded as establishing the principle that hereafter no white man could be punished for killing a negro, and as virtually wiping the Ku Klux laws off the statute books." Kellogg also cited the widespread belief that Grant's hands-off approach in Texas and Arkansas meant that he would write off Louisiana, too. With General Emory having left the state because of yellow fever season, there were only 130 U.S. troops in Louisiana. Kellogg warned that unless the army came back soon, his government could fall. "If Louisiana goes," Kellogg wrote, "Mississippi will inevitably follow and, that end attained, all the results of the war so far as the colored people are concerned will be neutralized, all the reconstruction acts of Congress will be of no more value than so much waste paper and the colored people, though free in name, will practically be remitted back to servitude."

THE WAVE OF MURDER AND INTIMIDATION IN THE SUMMER OF 1874 WAS THE WORK of a new organization: the White League, a successor to the Democratic Party and the Knights of the White Camellia. (Though this was not yet public knowledge during the Grant Parish trials, two of the White League's key organizers in New Orleans were the defense lawyers Robert H. Marr and E. John Ellis.) The league was founded on the belief that the Republicans could be defeated only if Negroes were ousted from politics through intimidation, and so it fused political and paramilitary action, operating on both fronts more or less openly. Its first manifesto, published in March 1874, proclaimed that "there will be no security, no peace, and no prosperity for Louisiana until the . . . superiority of the Caucasian over the African in all affairs pertaining to government is acknowledged and established."

The righteous stand of Grant Parish's white men was a major theme of White League propaganda. During the first half of 1874, the White League launched several provincial newspapers, including the *Caucasian*, which began publication in Alexandria the day after the hung jury in the first Colfax trial. Edited by George W. Stafford, who led the Cheneyville contingent at Colfax, the *Caucasian* made Christopher Columbus Nash into a chivalric superhero. A front-page story in the paper recounted the supposed travails of a bankrupt Mississippi planter and his family who were repeatedly waylaid by savage Negroes as they traveled across Louisiana to their new home in Texas. Each time, the arrival of Sheriff Nash sent the Negroes fleeing in panic. The article concluded with a prayer asking God to "help and keep Sheriff Nash, who, we hear, is driven from his home and hunted like a wild beast, for protecting the helpless."

By late summer, the White League had fourteen thousand men under arms in the countryside. Units drilled openly all along the Red River, including in Coushatta, the stronghold of the Republican Marshall Harvey Twitchell. Throughout August, the league issued threats to local Republican officials. The first shots were not fired until August 25, however, when armed whites killed two colored men in a scuffle at a boat landing about ten miles from Coushatta. One of the Negroes had fired back before he died, killing one white man. The cry of Negro revolt went up throughout the Red River Valley, and armed White Leaguers descended on Coushatta, arresting the entire Republican political leadership, except for Twitchell, who was visiting New Orleans. On Saturday, August 29, they murdered three prominent local Negroes, including one whom they tortured over a fire before killing him. Then, on Sunday morning, they expelled six white Republicans, including the sheriff, to Texas, escorted by thirty armed guards.

By the middle of Sunday afternoon, the group had reached a point about thirty miles south of Shreveport. The "guards" called a halt, supposedly to let the horses rest. In fact, it was to allow a prearranged rendezvous with a lynch mob from DeSoto Parish, headed by a white man with the significant nickname of "Captain Jack" Coleman. When the white Republicans saw Captain Jack's gang rushing toward them, they attempted to flee, but Captain Jack's men shot three of them down. The other three were captured, robbed of their cash and jewelry, and then shot to death execution-style. All six of the murdered white Republicans were then buried in shallow graves.

The Coushatta Massacre, as it was called, set a bloody precedent: for the first time white terrorists in the South had killed members of their own race en masse. Outrage spread in the North—and panic set in among Louisiana's white Republicans. "Unless protected by military force," a Kellogg administration official wired Attorney General Williams, "every white Republican in Louisiana will be either murdered or driven from the state before November."

Word of the crisis reached James Beckwith in New York, where he was halfway through a planned sixty-day vacation with Catherine. Beckwith, the only Louisiana Republican official in the North at the time, was dispatched for consultations with President Grant himself, who was summering at the family retreat in Long Branch, New Jersey. The town fathers of the little shore settlement had given the president a cottage on a bluff overlooking the ocean, and he turned it into the "nation's summer capital." It was the first time that the U.S. attorney met the president, and little or no information about the encounter survives. But apparently it went well; the two men followed the same moral compass. Beckwith cabled Kellogg that he had left Long Branch feeling confident that the federal government would "crush" the White League.

Beckwith's next stop was Washington, where he met with the secretary of war, who promised that troops would be made available to protect the Red River Valley. On September 5, Beckwith sent the attorney general a memorandum recommending new troop deployments to battle "the spirit of violence and resistance to the law in Louisiana." The problem, though, was that the army was already spread terribly thin, with most of its cavalry units committed to the Great Plains. It was up to Attorney General Williams to put Grant's wishes into practice, and all he was able to do on short notice was to move Captain Arthur Allyn's infantry company from Colfax toward Coushatta—which prompted Beckwith to remind Williams that if the soldiers left Grant Parish, "all of the witnesses in the late massacre trial will be killed." Meanwhile, the attorney general instructed U.S. attorneys in the South "to proceed with all possible energy and dispatch to detect, expose, arrest and punish the perpetrators of these crimes." Since Bradley's ruling was still the law in the Fifth Circuit, the order was little more than empty rhetoric.

IN NEW ORLEANS, THE CRESCENT CITY WHITE LEAGUE EMERGED AS THE URBAN counterpart to the organization's rural units. It enrolled twenty-six infantry companies and two artillery batteries—a total of about 1,500 men—by the first week of September. They carried no weapons as they marched in formation up and down the city's streets. But new rifles were headed their way, secretly, every day. Kellogg's police seized them by the wagonload, and still the guns flowed in. On September 8, 1874, officers boarded the *City of Dallas,* a newly arrived steamer, and found six crates of Springfield muskets. On September 13, Kellogg's men seized the steamer *Mississippi,* which was carrying another huge shipment of modern repeating rifles.

What happened next was the closest the country would come to the resumption of full-scale civil war during Reconstruction. The White League's leaders reacted to the unexpected loss of their expensive guns by advancing the date of their planned overthrow of Kellogg's government. The putsch began on the morning of September 14, as a huge crowd of White Leaguers gathered at the statue of Henry Clay on Canal Street. White Leaguers threw up barricades across the major downtown streets, D. B. Penn, John McEnery's "lieutenant governor," declared himself acting governor. (McEnery was out of the state.)

At 11:30 a.m., Robert H. Marr emerged and addressed the throng at the Clay statue, then led a delegation to the statehouse, which Kellogg refused to receive. When Marr returned, he reported the snub and asked the men what they should do: endure the "usurpation," or rise up and drive out the usurper. "Hang Kellogg!" "We'll fight!" "Call out the troops!"

the white men cried. Marr told them to go home, get their weapons, and come back at 2:30 p.m., at which point their "military" leaders would give them their marching orders.

That afternoon, hundreds of White Leaguers, claiming to be the legal state militia under "Acting Governor" Penn, battled mostly Negro Louisiana police and state militia on Canal Street. The decisive moment came when five companies of White League troops broke through the smoke, pierced the din with a rebel yell, and charged into Kellogg's militia. The militia, surprised and outgunned, broke and ran. When the one-hour battle was over, the White League had lost twenty-one dead and nineteen wounded; Kellogg's side counted eleven dead and sixty wounded, among them James Longstreet, the militia commander, who had been thrown from his horse and hurt his right arm. But despite their higher body count, White League troops seized strategic points in the city and recaptured their confiscated weapons from the *Mississippi*.

The remnants of the state militia took refuge in the state arsenal. The thick-walled building would have been hard for the White League to take by force, so they resorted to more subtle means. E. John Ellis, the "acting assistant adjutant general" of White League forces, issued an offer of "amnesty" to any militiamen who would lay down their arms and depart the scene. By the next morning, September 15, the state forces had accepted the offer and deserted. It was an ignominious way to lose, but the deserters were simply following the example set by Governor Kellogg, who had fled to the basement of the Custom House as soon as the first shots were fired.

The white population of New Orleans celebrated Kellogg's downfall by staging an "inauguration" for Penn at the statehouse, accompanied by wild rallies and celebrations in the French Quarter. "This is the happiest city in the universe," the *Bulletin* declared. And when word of the White League triumph in New Orleans reached Grant Parish, local white supremacists treated it as their signal to strike, too. Bill Irwin, out on bail, killed two Negroes eight miles from Colfax. On September 18, the Grant Parish White League issued an ultimatum to Judge Robert C. Register, Sheriff John B. McCoy, and the other Republican officeholders: resign in four days or be forced out. A group headed by the recently acquitted Tom Hickman kidnapped the Republican tax collector, a former Union cavalry officer from New Orleans whom Kellogg had installed along with Sheriff McCoy. The mob gathered weapons and spoke openly of lynching Register and attacking the U.S. Army. They called in men from neighboring parishes. Captain Allyn prepared his forces; he discreetly alerted local Negroes to help dig trenches and bring their weapons to aid the troops if necessary. Allyn ordered his drummer to sleep next to him in his tent, so as to be able to sound an alarm on a moment's notice.

But the White League had overreached. President Grant had declined to intervene in Texas and Arkansas partly because they were white-majority states and Republicans' legal claims to office were relatively marginal. Louisiana, though, was one of three black-majority states in the South (along with Mississippi and South Carolina) that were critical to the Republicans' future. And Grant had already staked his credibility on Kellogg's government by recognizing it in May 1873.

On September 15, after meeting with his cabinet and with Beckwith, who had followed the president to Washington, Grant gave "turbulent and disorderly persons" in Louisiana five days to disperse. On September 17, General Emory returned to the city at the head of a column of troops, the beginning of a huge new infusion of U.S. forces that would bring three infantry regiments, an artillery battery, and the famed Seventh Cavalry Regiment, along with navy gunboats and marines, to Louisiana. On September 19, the White League, unwilling to risk a direct battle with federal forces, surrendered, and Emory reinstated Kellogg to his office.

Grant's action also quelled the White League uprising in the parish that bore the president's name—though its impact was necessarily delayed by slow communications. Captain Arthur Allyn did not learn of the president's proclamation until several days after it had been issued. But when he did, he wrote to Dr. John J. Compton, the man who had chased Levi Allen from the courthouse on April 13, 1873—and who was now in charge of the local White League. Allyn informed Compton of Grant's position and suggested "in a spirit of peace and harmony" that the League's behavior "might be construed as seditious." Compton got the hint. By September 21, white forces in Grant Parish had demobilized.

But the Grant Parish White Leaguers declined to rescind the other decisions they had reached in their assembly of September 18. C. C. Dunn, who brought the little cannon to the fight on Easter Sunday, would still be their nominee for state house of representatives in the November elections. Wilson L. Richardson would be their candidate for parish judge. And their choice for sheriff was still Christopher Columbus Nash.

A SUPERFICIAL PEACE PREVAILED IN NEW ORLEANS AND IN THE RED RIVER VALLEY. Republicans, propped up by the U.S. military, governed in both locations. James Beckwith returned to the Crescent City on October 1 and threw himself into the investigation of the Coushatta Massacre. He wrote Williams that the "details are more horrible and inhuman than the newspaper accounts of the crime." General Emory sent troops to help deputy U.S. marshals arrest the Coushatta suspects. Federal lawmen received no help from local residents, who were so intimidated that they did not dare point out any of the wanted men. Still, by the third week in October 1874, the deputy U.S. marshals had arrested fifteen men implicated in the massacre.

Of course, this would be a pointless exercise unless there was some valid law under which they could be prosecuted. Hence Beckwith also wanted Williams to ask the Supreme Court to accelerate the Grant Parish case. If it acted soon, and if it reversed Bradley's ruling, he might once again be able to prosecute the culprits, not only in Coushatta but also in Grant Parish. He wrote Williams to impress upon him the linkage between Bradley's ruling and the White League's offensive. The White League, Beckwith explained, "sprang into life or received their only vitality from the action of Justice Bradley in this case and if his views of the legislation in question are correct, some new expedient must be resorted to, to maintain quiet and protect the helpless in the late slave states."

IN A SECOND LETTER, BECKWITH ASKED THE ATTORNEY GENERAL: "WILL THE case of *U.S. v. Cruikshank, et al.* be brought on for trial in the Supreme Court soon? It is important that the questions involved be settled early, if any further prosecutions are to be carried on under the act. I am very much embarrassed by Justice Bradley's action in that case. If unreversed, jurors will make it an excuse to acquit under the popular belief that jurors are judges of the law and fact. A belief so general that it is difficult to overcome, particularly when jurors apprehend personal danger or inconvenience in the event of a verdict of guilty."

On October 20, Williams wrote Beckwith informing him that the administration would not seek accelerated Supreme Court action. He explained that there was another crucial Enforcement Act case pending. Two white Kentucky state election officials had been indicted in federal court for refusing to register a Negro man to vote, even though the only reason he did not qualify was that a third white official had refused to accept his offer to pay a $1.50 poll tax. A federal prosecutor charged the officials with violating sections 3 and 4 of the Enforcement Act, which punished state officials for denying qualified voters the right to vote. The officials, represented by the old Klan defense attorney Henry Stanbery, argued that sections 3 and 4 were unconstitutional.

Williams's decision was probably influenced by the devastating political news he and his fellow Republicans had just received. On October 13, Ohio and three other midwestern states held midterm elections, and Democrats scored a landslide, capturing thirteen of Ohio's twenty seats in Congress. Alarmed by this result, the attorney general was pursuing a defensive strategy. Sections 3 and 4 of the Enforcement Act were less controversial, politically, than section 6, the anti-Klan conspiracy provision at issue in the Grant Parish case. Consequently, the Kentucky case, known as *United States v. Reese*, was probably more winnable for the government than the Grant Parish case.

Beckwith was worried. Potential witnesses in the Coushatta Massacre would be as intimidated as those in the Grant Parish trials. The White League's show of force in New Orleans meant that jurors would be drawn from a city whose population either supported the league or was thoroughly cowed by it. He wasn't going to put any jurors or witnesses through a trial before the law was settled. Beckwith tried to explain to Williams that his plan contradicted his previous orders to bring the Coushatta killers to justice. "Any trial in the present circumstances will be simply an expensive mockery," he wrote Williams on October 27.

But the attorney general would not budge. He coolly informed Beckwith that he "agreed" with him that there would be no point in prosecuting anyone. "Persons hereafter arrested for offences like that described in the Cruikshank case should not be tried until the decision of the Supreme Court is had, and I advise that they be admitted to bail," he wrote.

WILLIAMS SENT THIS LAST LETTER TO BECKWITH ON NOVEMBER 7, FOUR DAYS AFter the 1874 midterm election, which was another disaster for their party. The Democrats gained an incredible 81 seats in the U.S. House of Representatives, creating a Democratic majority of 169 to 109 over the Republicans, who had previously held a two-thirds majority. Eighty-nine Democrats in the new House hailed from Southern or border states.

In Louisiana, the election took place amid disorder and fear. Kellogg controlled New Orleans; U.S. troops controlled the areas that they occupied. But the White League dominated almost everywhere else. The state registrar of voters informed the press that registration was way down in the Red River Valley because Negroes were "afraid to exercise their rights." In Colfax, the presence of troops kept overt violence to a minimum, but the bloody events of the recent past deterred many Negroes from registering to vote. Captain Allyn noticed that colored men fled to the woods every time anyone fired off his shotgun a few times. None of them voted in the parish outside of the area directly patrolled by troops, and even within that area, two or three colored men told Allyn that they would not vote for fear of what would happen once the troops withdrew. And, of course, the massacre on Easter Sunday 1873 eliminated dozens of Republican voters. From a normal level of about 700 in previous years, the total number of registered black voters in Grant Parish fell to 441 in 1874—whereas 473 whites registered.

Adding to the Grant Parish Republicans' woes was the fact that they splintered into two factions. William Ward had returned to Colfax, accompanied by William B. Phillips. Ward ran for state house of representatives, teaming up with Phillips, who ran for judge. But Willie Calhoun opposed his former allies; he had been persuaded to run against Ward by Kellogg's moderate white Republican friends in New Orleans. They wanted to deny Ward the parish's seat in the state house because he was aligned with Kellogg's colored Republican rival, P. B. S. Pinchback. Calhoun put together a full slate of candidates in opposition to the Ward-Phillips ticket. Ultimately, Calhoun only got a handful of votes, but that may have been enough to cost Ward the election.

In fact, the dispute among Republicans became so intense that it may have caused an episode of postelection violence more spectacular than anything the whites actually committed in Colfax. On November 7, William Ward appeared at the old Calhoun warehouse, now being used as the parish courthouse. The apparent purpose of his visit was to meet with his opponents within the Republican Party, but the old cavalryman also brought his pistols with him. Waiting for him inside the building was the incumbent parish judge, Robert C. Register. Perhaps Register was going to attempt some mediation, but soon Ward and a white man were yelling at each other. They pulled their guns and opened fire—in full view of Register and a number of other witnesses. Ward was hit three times, his foe twice, but neither man was seriously injured.

Now that blood had been spilled, there was no controlling Ward and his Negro supporters. Late that night, they attacked the home of Gustave Radetzki, the Republican tax collector, who had backed Ward's opponent at the fight earlier in the day. They set the place on fire and shot at Radetzki and his family as they fled. Two of the attackers were later arrested for arson and sentenced to six months' probation. William Ward, indicted for his part in the shooting, fled to New Orleans—where he would later claim a seat in the legislature.

The parish was ungovernable. "The local authorities are paralyzed with fear," an army officer reported. "And the same remark applies to the citizens themselves. They are afraid and refuse to assist the officers of the law in the execution of their duties." Even the U.S. troops in Colfax were losing deterrent power. Angry whites threatened to kill William B. Phillips in the presence of army officers; Phillips fled to New Orleans again.

The state returning board, controlled by Kellogg's allies, ended up throwing out the returns from Grant Parish, alleging widespread voter intimidation. The board did the same in ten other parishes. After wrangling over the count for six weeks, the board announced on Christmas Eve that the state house of representatives was evenly divided 53–53 between Republicans and Democrats—with five seats still in dispute. Those would have to be decided by the house itself when it convened in January.

THE TENSION SPAWNED BY SEPTEMBER'S VIOLENCE NEVER FULLY DISSIPATED IN New Orleans, and the November results only deepened the city's anxiety. The White League, still in possession of its weapons, was emboldened anew by the Republicans' defeat in the November elections. Once again, league units began drilling day and night.

One of the White League's first targets was that most visible symbol of "Negro rule" in Louisiana, the integrated public schools of New Orleans. The league did not attack the schools openly; with federal forces occupying the city, that would have been too risky. Instead, it worked through gangs of supposedly spontaneously organized "boy regulators" (some of whom appeared well above high school age), which would barge into classrooms and demand that all the nonwhites leave. Among the colored students forced to get up from their desks and flee were the two sons of P. B. S. Pinchback, the most prominent Negro politician in the state.

These open acts of intimidation were frightening enough. But Republican officials soon discovered an even more unsettling reality: their communications were mysteriously finding their way into the hands of people like Robert H. Marr. It turned out that White League sympathizers controlled the Western Union office and were sending their leaders copies of all cable traffic between the Custom House and Washington. The league, it seemed, was everywhere. James Beckwith and other officials found themselves obliged to send their messages in code, and for the first time since he came to New Orleans in 1860, Beckwith expressed real fear. "We are surrounded by an armed camp with a force exceeding by far the federal land forces now in the city, and that force flushed with the victory of the 14th of September," he wrote Williams in December. The situation was "volcanic," he reported; "anarchy in January is inevitable."

President Grant was not oblivious. On December 7, 1874, he devoted much of his annual message to Congress to Louisiana. Despite his election defeat, Grant refused to apologize for his policies in the state. He acknowledged that federal intervention in state affairs was unwelcome, insisting that he had sent troops to Louisiana only with great reluctance. The real fault, the president argued, lay with those white Southerners who excused or participated in racist violence. "Treat the negro as a citizen and a voter, as he is and must remain, and soon parties will be divided, not on the color line, but on principle. Then we shall have no complaint of sectional interference."

Privately, Grant worried that he had been misled by past reports from Kellogg, Emory, and the Custom House officials. Seeking a fresh perspective, he secretly sent Philip Sheridan to New Orleans. He told the cavalry general who had established Reconstruction in the state back in 1867 to size up the situation and authorized him to take command of the army in the Gulf states if he saw fit. The general checked into the St. Charles Hotel in New Orleans on New Year's Day, 1875.

Just three days later, Beckwith's prediction of chaos proved prophetic. On January 4, the state legislature convened, with the first item of business being the distribution of the five disputed seats. Fifty-two Republicans and fifty Democrats answered the roll call—but the instant it ended, a White Leaguer, Louis Wiltz, offered a prearranged flurry of motions, which Democrats seconded and approved by acclamation. Before anyone knew what had happened, Wiltz had had himself sworn in as Speaker, and the Democrats had voted in all five of their contenders for the disputed seats—including the Colfax Massacre perpetrator George W. Stafford.

Wiltz summoned gangs of toughs, declared them "sergeants at arms," and ordered them to detain Republicans who were trying to get out of the building so as to deprive the session of a quorum. Wiltz asked for help from the U.S. Army security detail at the statehouse, which reluctantly obliged, and the Democrats appeared to have won the day. With control of the house, the white man's party could impeach Kellogg and his lieutenant governor; the senate, still controlled by Republicans, would not convict them, but senate Democrats could prolong their trial by parliamentary maneuvers, during which time they would be suspended from office, and Wiltz would act as governor.

Republican members of the house marched into Kellogg's office to tell him what had just happened. Kellogg then informed General Emory of the true state of affairs and asked for troops to remove the five Democrats who had been installed as members of the house of representatives. At 2:00 p.m., soldiers escorted them out—followed by the entire Democratic caucus, which boycotted further proceedings.

Monitoring these events from the St. Charles, Phil Sheridan concluded that he would have to take over command from Emory. He sent an urgent cable to Grant.

I THINK THAT THE TERRORISM NOW EXISTING IN LOUISIANA, MISSISSIPPI AND ARKANSAS COULD BE ENTIRELY REMOVED AND CONFIDENCE AND FAIR DEALING ESTABLISHED BY THE ARREST AND TRIAL OF THE RINGLEADERS OF THE ARMED WHITE LEAGUES. IF CONGRESS WOULD PASS A BILL DECLARING THEM BANDITTI THEY COULD BE TRIED BY A MILITARY COMMISSION. THE RINGLEADERS OF THIS BANDITTI, WHO MURDERED MEN NEAR HERE ON THE FOURTEENTH OF LAST SEPTEMBER, AND ALSO MORE RECENTLY AT VICKSBURG, MISSISSIPPI, SHOULD IN JUSTICE TO LAW AND ORDER AND THE PEACE AND PROSPERITY OF THIS SOUTHERN PART OF THE COUNTRY BE PUNISHED. IT IS POSSIBLE THAT IF THE PRESIDENT WOULD ISSUE A PROCLAMATION DECLARING THEM BANDITTI, NO FURTHER ACTION NEED BE TAKEN, EXCEPT THAT WHICH WOULD DEVOLVE UPON ME.

Sheridan's analysis was characteristically blunt and logical. The White League's attempted seizure of the house was the latest sign that the law—local, state, and federal—had broken down in Louisiana. And in the absence of civilian law, martial law might work. Grant's reaction was favorable, though he did not immediately adopt Sheridan's suggestion: THE PRESIDENT AND CABINET CONFIDE IN YOUR WISDOM AND REST IN THE BELIEF THAT ALL ACTS OF YOURS HAVE BEEN AND WILL BE JUDICIOUS, Secretary of War Belknap cabled Sheridan.

But Grant was a weakened president whose political opponents had convinced many that he wanted to impose military "tyranny" on the South. Sheridan's proposal, and the supposed military "invasion" of the Louisiana legislature, triggered some of the harshest condemnation Grant had yet faced. Most alarming for the president, the outcry was not limited to Democrats or Southerners. In Boston, a crowd at Faneuil Hall repudiated the army's action in New Orleans. The Ohio and Pennsylvania legislatures condemned the alleged invasion of their Louisiana counterpart. Senator Carl Schurz of Missouri, who had joined the Liberal Republicans in 1872, gave a speech suggesting that Congress itself might be the next legislature invaded, and calling Sheridan's proposal "so appalling that every American citizen who loves liberty stands aghast."

Even Beckwith felt that the time had come for some sort of decisive change in policy by Grant. He wrote to Williams again, warning of the spreading anarchy in New Orleans, and expressing his concern that the president, under pressure, might yield to demands for new elections in the state. That, he said, would simply embolden the White League, and then "the entire army of the United States would be inadequate" to save the state. He called instead for legislation that would allow a provisional government to serve out Kellogg's term, so that a new government could be picked in the 1876 elections. Beckwith argued that this solution would "dispose of a lot of disreputable political hacks on both sides" and give a "chance for a reputable Republican administration" to show what it could do. Best of all, he added, it would quiet the state and relieve Grant of a chronic irritant in national politics.

Though it undoubtedly would not have endeared him to Kellogg, Beckwith's idea made sense. In a calmer time, it might have received at least some consideration. But Grant was in a fighting mood. He blamed the troubles in Louisiana squarely on violent whites—and on Congress for failing to find a solution on its own. In a January 13, 1875, message to Congress, he quoted the description of the Colfax Massacre that William B. Woods had read to the jury—the first time Grant addressed the atrocity personally. "Fierce denunciations ring through the country about office-holding and election matters in Louisiana," Grant wrote, "while every one of the Colfax miscreants goes unwhipped of justice, and no way can be found in this boasted land of civilization and Christianity to punish the perpetrators of this bloody and monstrous crime."

Grant's resolve helped change the debate. Republicans rallied behind him, and the Democrats conceded they could not overthrow Kellogg. William Wheeler, a Republican congressman from New York, negotiated a peace agreement under which the Louisiana Republicans conceded the state house of representatives and the Democrats promised not to impeach Kellogg. White Leaguers considered it a sellout; black Republicans were bitter that Democratic control of the house meant ousting black representatives. But the pact held.

Still, Grant's message was self-contradictory. Many of the obstacles to the Grant Parish prosecution had been raised by his War Department, army officers, and attorney general. Grant probably knew little of these details. But his lament was a confession of impotence. His administration could have used the Enforcement Act more aggressively against white terrorism, even after defeating the Klan in 1872. But now, thanks largely to Bradley, the president did not even have the option. And he would not get it back—unless and until Bradley's colleagues overruled him.

Grant, like everyone else, would have to wait for the Supreme Court to decide.

CHAPTER ELEVEN

THE COURT SPEAKS

Washington had probably never looked more like the capital of a great nation than it did in the early days of 1875. After three years of renovation, the city was no longer just an overgrown Southern village. Muddy streets had been graded and paved. Wastewater that once reeked in a downtown canal flowed through a modern sewer system. Gaslights shone in the night. The project had bankrupted the city, but, as *Harper's New Monthly Magazine* put it, the streets were "covered with the most noiseless and perfect pavements in the world, and embowered in the greenest borders of grass-plots, inclosed with panels of post and chain or graceful palings, and planted with trees."

The spruced-up city was also transformed politically. The Republicans had lost the election, which meant that the House of Representatives to be sworn in on March 4, 1875, would be controlled by the Democrats. The white man's party would soon be able to cut the Grant administration's budget and investigate myriad White House scandals—real or contrived. And for the first time since Andrew Johnson's administration, Democrats would also have a say in Reconstruction policy.

The lame-duck Republican Congress made a last effort to entrench Negro freedom in federal law. Lawmakers tried, and failed, to toughen the Enforcement Act. They also took up the civil rights bill that had been debated since Grant's first term. It guaranteed all citizens access to hotels, restaurants, theaters, steamships, and railroad cars, regardless of race—a proposal so controversial that the Republicans had not dared push for it during the 1874 campaign.

No one spoke more eloquently in favor of the civil rights bill than the dwindling band of colored Republican congressmen from the South. On February 4, 1875, Representative John Roy Lynch of Mississippi implored his white fellow lawmakers to imagine his life. "Think of it for a moment," he said. "When I leave my home to come to the capital of the nation to take part in the deliberations of the House and to participate

with you in making laws for the government of this great Republic . . .
I am treated, not as an American citizen, but as a brute. Forced to oc-
cupy a filthy smoking-car both night and day, with drunkards, gamblers, and criminals; and for what? Not that I am unable or unwilling
to pay my way; not that I am obnoxious in my personal appearance or
disrespectful in my conduct; but simply because I happen to be of a
darker complexion."

Lynch also made a constitutional argument. Opponents of the bill, including some Republicans, had objected that it ran afoul of the Supreme
Court's interpretation of the Fourteenth Amendment in *The Slaughterhouse Cases*. But Lynch said that he had read Justice Samuel F. Miller's
opinion several times and was convinced that the civil rights bill was
perfectly consistent with it. The Fourteenth Amendment not only concerned the "privileges or immunities" of U.S. citizenship, which Miller
had, indeed, eviscerated. It also had a clause guaranteeing the citizens of
each state the "equal protection of the laws." And, Lynch argued, Miller
had specifically said this clause should be interpreted in light of the
Fourteenth Amendment's purpose to abolish "laws in the States where
the newly emancipated negroes resided, which discriminated with gross
injustice and hardship against them as a class." Surely that included
laws segregating public accommodations, Lynch suggested. "The constitutional right of Congress to pass this bill is fully conceded by the
Supreme Court," he concluded.

The Republican Congress passed the bill, and President Grant signed
it into law on March 1. The Civil Rights Act of 1875 was the high-water
mark of Reconstruction. Still, the debate over the Fourteenth Amendment was far from over. The issues Lynch had addressed were similar to
those in *United States v. Cruikshank*, which was scheduled for two days
of argument before the Supreme Court, beginning on March 31, 1875.
The Grant Parish case, too, was about the meaning of American citizenship. The political survival of the Republican Party in the South was at
stake—along with the freedom of four million men, women, and children of color.

AT 10:00 A.M. ON MARCH 31, AS THE SUPREME COURT CRIER SHOUTED THE TRADI-
tional prayer—"God save the United States and this honorable court!"—
nine black-robed justices filed into their courtroom, the semicircular
former Senate chamber on the second floor of the Capitol. It was the
same hallowed place where Henry Clay, Daniel Webster, and John C. Calhoun had debated.

The members of the Court settled into a row of nine high-backed chairs behind a long mahogany bench, which was raised about a foot above floor level and set off from the chamber by a sturdy balustrade. At the bench was a little silver box of snuff, first installed for members of the court by Chief Justice Roger Brooke Taney (the author of *Dred Scott*). Behind the justices, a row of eight Ionic marble columns stood along the chamber's east wall; amid the columns was an arched space decorated with thick curtains and crowned with a bronze sculpture of a bald eagle in flight. Spectators sat along the chamber's west wall, about fifty feet away from the justices. Between the justices and the public were the lawyers and members of the press.

The chief justice of the United States, Morrison Remick Waite, occupied a place of honor in the middle of the row of justices. A short, thickset Republican attorney with a bristly iron-gray beard, the fifty-seven-year-old Waite had been confirmed by the Senate only fourteen months earlier. He had been nominated by Grant, who noticed Waite because of his work on an arbitration that resulted in a $15.5 million payment from Great Britain for damage done to the United States by British-made Confederate warships.

Waite's path to the middle chair had been awkward. Salmon P. Chase's death in May 1873 created a vacancy in the chief justice's chair, which Grant waited to fill until Congress returned in the fall. In the interim, Justices Samuel F. Miller and Noah H. Swayne campaigned for the job, and Joseph Bradley's supporters urged the president to choose him. No associate justice had ever been elevated before, and Grant did not want to break that precedent. Yet, of the first four men to whom he offered the job, two declined, and two, including George Williams, met with insuperable opposition in the Senate.

Finally, on January 19, 1874, Grant sent Waite's name to the Senate. At the time, he was almost unknown outside his home state of Ohio. The *Nation* said that Waite stood "at the front rank of second-rate lawyers." Ebenezer Rockwood Hoar, a member of Congress whom Grant had also considered for the post, called Waite "that luckiest of individuals known to the law: an innocent third party without notice." The Senate unanimously confirmed Waite on January 21, 1874, but his new colleagues treated him coldly. Miller wrote privately that he found Waite "pleasant" but "mediocre." In letters home, Waite, who actually was an able lawyer— the son of a distinguished judge—described himself as "anxious."

Only one justice immediately reached out to Waite: Joseph Bradley, who invited him over to dinner on Waite's first Friday night in Washington. This was the start of a close relationship, in which Waite often agreed with Bradley and seemed to defer to his superior legal learning. The two men had much in common. Like Bradley, Waite had been a Whig before the Civil War. Even after Waite joined the Republican Party, his main concern was preservation of the Union, not the abolition of slavery. In 1862, Waite had run unsuccessfully for Congress as a conservative Republican in his hometown of Toledo. Waite's slogan, "Union for the Sake of the Union," could have been Bradley's motto in his failed Newark race that same year.

The eight associate justices were arranged on either side of Waite, according to seniority. At Waite's immediate right sat Nathan Clifford, the senior associate. Clifford, seventy-one years old, was a Democrat from Maine of immense pride and, at three hundred pounds, even greater girth. He had presided over the Court between Chase's death and Waite's confirmation, and insulted Waite by offering to continue running things until the new chief justice felt able. Clifford was generally passive in oral arguments, his chubby face twisted into a perpetual sneer. His demeanor only changed when there was a large crowd in the gallery. Then he would make a point of interrupting counsel with questions and sitting back with a look of satisfaction as they struggled to answer.

To Waite's left was Noah Swayne, the second-most senior associate, who had coveted Waite's job. The alternating pattern continued with Miller, Stephen J. Field, and Bradley sitting in a row to Clifford's right— and David Davis, William Strong, and Ward Hunt lined up on Swayne's left. Swayne and Davis, neither of whom spoke much during arguments, liked to pool their pennies and send messengers out to buy stick candy. The two big men would occasionally get up and lean against the marble columns during oral arguments, munching the sweets as they took in the proceedings. Field fought tedium by sending Court pageboys out to fetch him large stacks of law books. He would make a show of leafing through a few of the tomes, hurl them to the floor with a loud thud, and send out for another batch. Bradley sat with his eyes closed; but this was a trap for the unwary. He was concentrating, not sleeping. Of all the justices, Bradley and Miller were the sharpest and most active questioners from the bench.

GEORGE WILLIAMS HAD BEEN IN NO HURRY TO REACH THIS MOMENT. THE ATTORney general's reluctance to argue the Grant Parish case was consistent with his equivocation on the Enforcement Act and his generally defensive response to the country's growing anti-Reconstruction mood. It probably also reflected his intimate knowledge of the nine men who would decide the case. He needed five votes to win, and based on the record of the current Court, it was hard to see where they would come from.

Bradley, of course, had ruled against the government in New Orleans. Waite was likely to follow his new friend. Clifford was a Democrat, unlikely to do the Republicans any favors in this case. Field, also a Democrat, had dissented in *Slaughterhouse*, arguing that the Fourteenth Amendment broadened the rights of American citizens. But he had done so because of his opposition to government regulation, not his sympathy for the freedmen. David Davis, an Illinoisan, had been close to Abraham Lincoln. But he had soured on Grant's Reconstruction policies and, in 1872, angled, in vain, for the Liberal Republican presidential nomination.

There was the faintest hope that Samuel F. Miller, because of his long-standing support for the rights of the Negro, might side with the government, and that if he did, he could form a bloc with Swayne, William Strong, a Grant appointee from Pennsylvania, and the junior associate, Ward Hunt, another Grant appointee from New York, that would be strong enough to win over one of the other five. But even if Miller had intended *Slaughterhouse* as a rebuff to Southern Democrats, *legally* the ruling offered them much ammunition in this case, as Marr's success before Bradley in New Orleans had shown.

At a time when the whole country seemed to be turning against Reconstruction, Williams would have to give Miller powerful reasons to distinguish this case from *Slaughterhouse*—and to support the administration. The attorney general could no longer count on his friendship with Miller. They had met in Iowa before the war; they lodged together at the National Hotel in Washington for six years after the war, during Williams's Senate term. In the last year, however, Miller had soured on Williams, believing that he had urged Grant not to appoint Miller as chief justice so that Williams himself could get the job. "He had the shuffling of cards and stacked them for his own benefit," Miller wrote to a friend.

The government's written brief, filed on February 11, 1875, showed that Williams was indeed thinking defensively. Instead of a strong case for the Enforcement Act's constitutionality, it offered a narrow, technical apologia. Citing unspecified "difficulties" with most of Beckwith's indictment, the brief began by conceding that the government would defend only four counts: counts 6 and 14, which alleged a conspiracy to deny Nelson's and Tillman's right to vote, and counts 8 and 16, which contained Beckwith's catch-all allegation of a conspiracy to violate the men's constitutional rights generally—probably the vaguest of his charges.

The brief argued that the counts were valid under section 6 of the Enforcement Act, but not because section 6 was a proper exercise of Congress's power to protect the right of colored men to vote under the Fifteenth Amendment. Williams did not mention the Fifteenth Amendment at all. Rather, the brief suggested that section 6 was rooted in Congress's inherent authority to protect elections for its own members. This claim was hardly far-fetched; it resembled the rationale Judge Hugh Lennox Bond had embraced in *United States v. Crosby*, though Williams's brief strangely did not cite that opinion.

Even more puzzling, Williams did not show how this case could be distinguished from *Slaughterhouse*. Rather, he argued that it was *consistent* with Miller's ruling—but not for the reason John Roy Lynch had suggested in the House: equal protection. Instead, Williams linked Congress's power to protect the right to vote at federal elections to the "privileges or immunities" guaranteed by the Fourteenth Amendment. Given that the right to vote in federal elections had existed only "since 1789," Williams argued, it belonged on the truncated list of federally guaranteed privileges and immunities that Miller proposed in *Slaughterhouse*. And *that* was a valid basis for section 6. The rest of the government's twenty-seven-page brief consisted of a review of British precedents and obscure legal treatises intended to show that Beckwith's indictment was properly drawn under the common law of conspiracy.

Williams's approach was not necessarily misguided. Given that the Court was probably leaning against him, he might have decided that his best bet was to ask it for as little as possible. Also, he had been distracted and somewhat rattled by the uproar in January over Philip Sheridan's remarks—in the middle of which he had had to make a difficult oral argument in *United States v. Reese*.

But, even as a modest plea, Williams's brief was not terribly convincing. The Court made this clear on March 29, 1875—two days before the *Cruikshank* argument—when it ruled in *Minor v. Happersett*. Virginia Minor, a women's suffrage leader in Missouri, claimed that a state official's refusal to register her to vote violated the Fourteenth Amendment, because the right to vote was one of the privileges and immunities of U.S. citizenship. Minor's argument was similar to the argument in Williams's brief—and, in a unanimous opinion by Chief Justice Waite, the Court rejected it.

His central legal claim rebuffed by the Court in another case, Williams made one last effort to postpone *Cruikshank*. Late into the night on March 30, 1875, he asked the Court and the lawyers for Cruikshank,

Hadnot, and Irwin for a delay, citing the "excited" political condition of the country. His opponents were not interested. The legal and political climate favored them. In fact, the Court had originally set argument for January, as the defense requested, but later put it off until after *Reese*, as Williams preferred. That was all the delay the attorney general would get.

THE FIRST DAY OF ARGUMENTS DID NOT GO TERRIBLY WELL FOR THE GOVERNment. Williams sent the solicitor general of the United States, Samuel F. Phillips, to speak first for their side; the attorney general was saving himself for rebuttal the next day. Though a talented lawyer and a familiar face to the court, Phillips made little impact during his allotted three hours. Sticking to the text of the government's brief, he contended simply that the handful of counts in the indictment were "legal and regular." As the Associated Press's Supreme Court reporter put it, Phillips's presentation was "of a legal and technical nature entirely." None of the justices bothered to ask him anything.

After lunch, it would be Robert H. Marr's turn. His brief had been clear and passionate—and relied heavily on *Slaughterhouse*. "If the Enforcement Act, particularly this sixth section, shall be held by this Court to be within the constitutional power of Congress," he wrote, "then, indeed, will the government have been completely revolutionized, by the mere conferring of power upon Congress to enforce the provisions of the recent Amendments. All the serious, far-reaching and pervading consequences, so forcibly depicted in the Slaughterhouse Cases, will be realized; and we shall have taken a fatal departure from the structure and spirit of our institutions." He pleaded with the Court, the "great conservative department" of government, as he called it, to prevent such a catastrophe: "The shackles will have fallen in vain from four millions of blacks, who were born slaves, if fetters more galling are to be riveted on so many more millions of whites, who were born free."

Standing before the justices, Marr conceded that the post–Civil War amendments had limited the traditional autonomy of the states, requiring them to make Negroes citizens and voters. But the amendments were "nowhere leveled against individuals" like Cruikshank, Hadnot, and Irwin, Marr argued. To say otherwise, he intoned, would put the federal government in the business of policing almost the entire spectrum of human behavior, leaving nothing for the states to do. "The continuance of the state governments and the liberties of the people are at stake in your decision," Marr told the justices.

Eager and confident though he was, Marr could not hope to brief and argue such an important case by himself—nor was it in his interest as a provincial lawyer with little Supreme Court experience to do so. So he ceded most of his side's argument time to more seasoned Supreme Court practitioners, of whom the first to address the Court, immediately after Marr, was David Dudley Field. A balding, silver-haired New Yorker with a bushy mustache, Field was one of the most respected legal minds in the country, the author of a much-admired new legal code in his home state—and, at seventy, the older brother of Justice Stephen J. Field. (Ethical norms of the time allowed a justice to rule on a case in which a family member was involved, just as it was acceptable for Bradley to sit in judgment of his own circuit court ruling.) Field now lent his awesome prestige to the cause of three obscure white supremacists from tiny Grant Parish.

Field reminded the justices of the political debate over Reconstruction and, by implication, of the recent election, which showed that the country was turning against it. To be sure, Field said, insincerely, "a political argument addressed to the Supreme Court would . . . be out of place." But the country had so recently ratified the post–Civil War amendments that it was appropriate to "appeal to the knowledge of the men around us, to our fellow-citizens of the whole nation, to bear us out in the assertion that the people did not suppose they were thereby changing the fundamental theory of their government."

Then he recast Marr's arguments in an even more extreme and threatening form. "If the view of the other side was to prevail," he told the Court, "then the whole domain of personal and political rights was transferred to the federal government." This was a wild exaggeration; the government's brief actually made a narrow defense of the Enforcement Act. Before Field could go much further, Miller interrupted, asking what Field thought should happen in the *Reese* case, according to his argument. "If Congress had no right to pass any affirmative legislation," the justice queried, "what remedy would have occurred to the Kentucky Negroes?"

It was an obvious question. Field, and Marr before him, had argued that Congress could only prevent the states from enforcing discriminatory laws. But what about a case in which individual state *officials* discriminated, without formal authorization? Surely, in that case, there could be federal intervention.

Field, in an almost incredible lapse for a lawyer of his stature, admitted to Miller that he did not know about *Reese*, which had been argued before the Court on January 13. But at that moment, Bradley opened his eyes. Normally severe with unprepared lawyers, he helped his colleague's brother, explaining to him that the "Negroes had been deprived of the right to vote through the neglect or refusal of the State officers to take from them the poll tax which they had tendered, and the negroes had sought their remedy under the enforcement act." Responding to Bradley, Miller added that Kentucky had passed no law denying Negroes the right to vote, and therefore, under Field's argument, they would be without any redress.

The discussion let Field recover: the Negroes could press charges in a state court, he said—and then, perhaps unintentionally, revealed the racial animus embedded in his case. "If eight hundred thousand voters cannot secure the rights to which they had been declared entitled," he told the court, "then that is the best argument that they are not worthy of them." No one on the Court disputed the point.

THE COURT RECONVENED THE NEXT MORNING, APRIL 1, FOR A FINAL ROUND OF arguments. In the audience sat several of the Republican senators who drafted the Enforcement Act; they were there to see a showdown between Reverdy Johnson, Marr's second distinguished cocounsel, and Attorney General Williams. Now seventy-eight years old, Johnson was never an attractive man, and the years had bloated the bags under his eyes and elongated the jowls that hung beside his minimal chin. But Johnson still had the rich, clear voice that had enhanced his advocacy ever since his days as President Zachary Taylor's attorney general. And he knew his way around the Supreme Court. When he addressed the justices, Johnson liked to stand on the spot where Daniel Webster had uttered his famous line, "Liberty and Union, now and forever, one and inseparable!" in 1831.

Whereas Field bombastically played to the Court's fears of "despotism," Johnson gave a cool textual analysis of the post–Civil War amendments. Standing where Webster had stood, he explained that the Thirteenth Amendment had ended slavery, but without making the Negro a citizen. The Fourteenth Amendment had made him a citizen, but without guaranteeing him the right to vote. The Fifteenth Amendment had remedied that, but it was "designed merely to provide that there was no distinction in the franchise between the white and the black man." Each amendment was a modest step toward formal equality between the races. None of them could justify an extension of federal power like section 6.

Johnson, like Field, distorted the government's brief, claiming it would "elevate the black man above the white man." This was "extraordinary," he said. The country could not possibly have intended this. And now, Johnson declared, the Court must do its "duty" to preserve the balance between state and federal power, lest such a disastrous doctrine prevail. "This tribunal," he told the Court, "is the keystone of the arch upon which rests all our institutions, state and federal."

FINALLY, THE TIME HAD COME FOR GEORGE WILLIAMS TO ADDRESS THE JUSTICES. During Grant's second term, the attorney general had probably done as much as anyone to dilute the practical impact of the Enforcement Act. His policy on white terrorism, based on the notion that leniency toward Southern extremists would induce their respect for the law, was a failure. His bungled brief to the Court in this case had left the government groping for a way to win.

Yet, for all his uncertainty and strategic errors, George Williams had always had fairly consistent views about Negro rights. He had left the Democratic Party because he opposed slavery; he had fought to keep slavery out of Oregon. And he was a partisan Republican. He knew that his party, already in trouble with Northern voters, would be finished in the South unless it could at least threaten federal intervention on behalf of its Negro voters. He took pride in his legal skills. He was not going to lose this case without showing the Court what he could do. He wasn't going to lose it without a fight.

And so Williams began his presentation by reminding the Supreme Court of one obvious fact that no one else had yet thought to mention: there had been a mass murder in Colfax, Louisiana, on April 13, 1873, and the perpetrators were trying to get away with it. "The parties appearing as defendants in this court," Williams said, "have been tried and convicted. The question is whether these guilty parties should go unwhipped of justice." Beckwith's indictment was imperfect, Williams argued, but essentially valid. Marr and Field and Johnson were trying to make it sound as if American citizens hardly had any rights to speak of, except what their respective states granted them. This couldn't be. After all, "the original constitution recognized the right of the slaveholder to property in his slaves and the Supreme Court decided that Congress had the right to pass a law to protect him in those rights. If the time ever comes when as liberal a construction shall be given to laws designed to protect human freedom as had always been given to laws designed to protect human slavery, then the doctrine of the government in this case would be admitted."

It was an effective beginning. Williams had shown the Court that there was another side to the story of Reconstruction. But Williams still had to demonstrate that the Constitution authorized Congress to enact section 6. To do that, he tried to take advantage of the well-known fact that, as a senator, he had helped enact the post–Civil War amendments, the Civil Rights Act of 1866, and the Enforcement Act. Recounting their legislative history, he explained to the Court that "by the Thirteenth and Fourteenth Amendments, and the civil rights bill, the people of the United States intended to secure to the colored man, under the protec tion of the United States, the right to make contracts, to sue, to hold property, and the various other rights of citizenship." His opponents in this case "contended that the Fourteenth Amendment was nothing more than an empty formula and amounts to nothing—nothing but empty and vain words"—but this had to be wrong. "Even before the adoption of the late Amendments Congress had the power to protect the right to vote for presidential electors," Williams argued.

Williams seemed to be preparing to restate the argument of his brief, the argument similar to the one dismissed in *Minor v. Happersett:* that the right to vote was one of the "privileges or immunities" guaranteed by the Fourteenth Amendment.

Joseph Bradley cut him off. "Suppose Congress should enact a law making it a felony to steal the property of another," Bradley asked. "Congress has the undoubted right to punish the stealing of the property of the government, or of property in the service of the government, but beyond that the law would be unconstitutional. Now, when a law is so framed that one part is constitutional and another unconstitutional, and the two are so bound together as to be impossible to sever, can you hold one part constitutional and the other part unconstitutional?"

Bradley's point was implicit but clear: the plain language of section 6 seemed to protect both white and black voters from conspiracies to interfere with their rights, whether racially motivated or not. But if the Court felt the post–Civil War amendments only authorized Congress to punish racially motivated violence—which was Bradley's position—how could it salvage any part of the statute? It was an aggressive move by Bradley—a transparent bid to throw the attorney general off his stride and, at the same time, to remind the justices that Williams was asking them to overrule their own colleague.

Williams replied that "the law could be enforced as to those offences which it is admitted are within the power of Congress to provide for." What might those be? Section 6 had to apply at least to elections for Congress, Williams argued, because "the very existence of the government depends upon these elections. If Congress has no power to protect the voters, then the White League of Louisiana, a minority of the people, can stand around the polls and prevent the majority from voting."

Once again, Williams had brought the argument back to contemporary reality. He pressed the point: "The learned counsel on the other side said that the fathers never attempted to exercise these powers. Did the counsel forget the great civil revolution through which we had passed? The fathers had never exercised those powers because there was no necessity to exercise them. Just as it was necessary to exercise certain powers during the rebellion never before exercised, so now it was necessary to exercise powers to maintain the results wrought out of that rebellion. The fifteenth amendment confers upon the colored people the right to vote. Unless Congress has the power to enforce that guarantee it is of no value whatever."

Now Williams was venturing beyond the argument in his brief, invoking the Fifteenth Amendment for the first time. Nathan Clifford, no doubt stirred out of his usual passivity by the presence of so many senators in the audience, noticed the attorney general's improvisation and challenged him on it. He observed that in his home state, Maine, "the colored man always had the right to vote," so there was no need for the Fifteenth Amendment there. Having made the point that, in his view, the Fifteenth Amendment created no new right to vote, even for Negroes, he asked Williams, "If two indictments were found of conspiracy, one to prevent the colored man from voting and the other a white man from voting, would the Circuit Courts of the United States have jurisdiction of both cases?"

"They would in the case of the black man," Williams answered. "I don't contend that they would in the case of the white man."

"Then colored men have more rights in the United States courts than white men," Clifford shot back.

"That does not follow," Williams insisted. "The constitution does not confer upon white people the right to vote, but it does upon colored people and thence the power of Congress arises to protect them in that right." He did not mean to suggest that Negroes have greater rights than whites, Williams added, but surely the purpose of the post–Civil War amendments was to free them from slavery, guarantee them equal rights, and protect them against discrimination. On second thought, Williams said, he might modify his answer to Clifford: to keep it consistent with his answer to Bradley, it would be better to say that the federal government could prosecute a conspiracy to violate a white man's right to vote at a congressional election, but not if the violation was at a state election.

Williams was struggling, but no one on the Court seemed to want to help him. Miller maintained his silence. Finally, Justice William Strong, one of the Grant appointees whose vote Williams had to win, piped up with a friendly question. Could the federal government prosecute a conspiracy to prevent a man from voting because he was the son of an Irishman? "It would certainly be a race discrimination," Strong observed.

Strong was backhandedly, but clearly, countering Clifford's extreme suggestion by offering the attorney general a hypothetical case in which at least some white voters could come under federal protection. But the beleaguered Williams did not at first seem to grasp Strong's point. Congress could provide for such a case, he said, hesitantly, but he was not sure that it had already done so by section 6.

Strong persisted. "Suppose the State of South Carolina, where the majority of the population are colored, should change the constitution of that state and say that no white man should vote, would a remedy against that lie in the United States court?" Now his point was clear. Even under the argument made by Marr, Johnson, and Field, Congress could nullify explicitly discriminatory state *laws*. The example was obvious and showed how silly Clifford's question had been.

Williams got it. Seemingly relieved, he answered that yes, indeed, the federal government could block Strong's hypothetical Negro power grab—and then he tried to focus the Court one last time on the real stakes.

"My idea, in the main, of these amendments was that any and every right guaranteed by them may be protected in the courts of the United States," he declared. "Give that construction to these amendments and they are of some value, give them the other construction and the freedom vouchsafed to the Negro becomes practically a curse. Any doubt as to the validity of this act should be resolved in its favor. Bear in mind that these amendments and the legislation under them were practically made by the same hands. Is it to be supposed that those who drew the amendments did not know their scope? According to the arguments on the other side it must be assumed of the Senators and Representatives"—and Williams had been one of them—"either that they violated their oath or that they did not know the meaning of the language which they used themselves."

Williams begged the Court to reject the racial fear-mongering of his opponents. "Ever since the years of the war," he said, "no matter what was done to preserve the Union, and to protect the rights of the citizens, it has been met with these lugubrious schemes that you are encroaching upon state authority. . . . Millions of people are today waiting with feverish anxiety the verdict of this court, conscious that their lives and liberties are wrapped up in it. If this court decides in favor of this law it will do more to restore peace and quiet to this land than any decision or any legislation since the close of the war."

"I look forward to the day," Williams concluded, "when we can consider ourselves not a nation of inharmonious and warring sovereigns, but a Union whose broad shield shall protect—in all and every right of a freeman and a citizen—her people from one end to the other."

The peroration was Williams at his most eloquent. It was also his final argument as attorney general. Politically damaged and psychologically bruised, Williams resigned a few days after the Supreme Court hearing—undoubtedly feeling that he had sacrificed a once-promising career for the Republican cause.

But when he was done, and the members of the Court had retired behind the velvet curtain that separated the courtroom from their private chambers, it seemed to outside observers that Williams's display of forensic skill and moral conviction had come too late. As the *Philadelphia Inquirer* put it, "The dicta of the judges, the questions which they asked during the arguments . . . indicate a leaning which may prove to be adverse to the authority of Congress to pass a statute of as ultra a character as this particular law presents in its turn."

But it would take months for the country to find out what the Court had decided. There was no time for the justices to vote on the case and draft opinions before their scheduled recess on May 3. After that, the members of the Court would scatter across the country to "ride circuit," followed by their summer recess. They would reassemble in Washington on October 11. Until then, the country would simply have to wait. The federal government's law enforcement program against white terrorism would remain in limbo.

In fact, it all but ceased. Judge William B. Woods decided there could be no more Enforcement Act trials in the Fifth Circuit until the Supreme Court settled the issue. Williams echoed that view, telling U.S. attorneys across the South that he did "not believe any convictions can be obtained under existing circumstances," and that "criminal prosecutions . . . ought to be suspended until it is known whether the Supreme Court will hold them constitutional or otherwise."

And the trouble down South would spread.

NOWHERE WAS THE IMPACT OF BRADLEY'S RULING MORE DEADLY THAN IN Louisiana's next-door neighbor Mississippi. Negroes made up just over 53 percent of that state's 827,000 people. Together with white Republicans, they formed a solid electoral majority. In 1873, they elected members of their race to half of the statewide offices and a Northern-born white Republican, Adelbert Ames, as governor. Protecting colored voters in Mississippi was thus a high priority of the Grant administration. Prior to Bradley's ruling in the Grant Parish case, Mississippi had seen one of the most active federal law-enforcement efforts in the South. But in the twelve-month period following Bradley's ruling, the Justice Department dropped 179 pending Enforcement Act cases in northern Mississippi, while securing only six convictions. During the first half of that period, White League units murdered about three hundred Negroes, until Grant finally sent a company of troops to Vicksburg in January 1875.

Eighteen seventy-five was an election year again in Mississippi, and White League "rifle clubs" set out to crush Negro voting. On September 1, they attacked Yazoo County's Northern-born sheriff and murdered several leading Negro men, including a state legislator. In October, white forces attacked a Coahoma County Republican meeting, leaving six blacks and two whites dead.

Desperate, Governor Ames asked Washington for troops. Grant was well aware of the political risks; his party's leaders had advised him that the Republicans might lose the governor's race in Ohio if he launched another military intervention in the South. "I am somewhat perplexed to know what directions to give in the matter. The whole public are tired out with these annual, autumnal outbreaks in the South," he wrote Attorney General Edwards Pierrepont, who had replaced Williams on April 26, 1875. Grant expressed a wish to avoid sending troops and told Pierrepont that Ames should "exhaust" state efforts before asking for federal aid. But Grant was also clear about the morality of what was happening in Mississippi. He attributed public exhaustion to "unwholesome lying" by the press and told Pierrepont that if Ames could not quell the violence, "the proclamation must be issued; and if it is I shall instruct the commander of the forces to have no child's play."

But Pierrepont, a former Democrat who had been critical of Grant's use of troops in the South, altered Grant's meaning when he replied to Ames. He quoted the "autumnal outbreaks" remark out of context and told Ames, unrealistically, to raise a militia and show "the courage and manhood to *fight* for their rights and to destroy the bloody ruffians." Feeling abandoned, Ames negotiated a peace agreement with white forces that called on him to demobilize what few state troops he had. On Election Day—too late for Washington to intervene—the whites reneged and rampaged through the state. With a four-to-one majority in the resulting state legislature, the Democrats quickly impeached Ames's Negro lieutenant governor and forced Ames to resign lest he be impeached, too. Grant later said Mississippi's new government was "chosen through fraud and violence such as would scarcely be accredited to savages, much less a civilized and Christian people." But he was powerless to reverse it.

IN MID-OCTOBER, AS MISSISSIPPI ENTERED THE FINAL STAGES OF ITS BLOODY election campaign, the Supreme Court reconvened behind closed doors in Washington. In conferences on October 16 and October 30, the justices discussed the *Cruikshank* case, together with *Reese*. On November 6, four days after Mississippi's election, they reached a conclusion: Beckwith's indictments were fatally flawed. The vote was unanimous.

The Court wanted to free Cruikshank, Hadnot, and Irwin. Initially, though, it was not sure precisely why. The Court at first decided to duck the constitutional issues. Waite assigned Nathan Clifford to write an opinion invalidating the indictment on purely technical grounds. All things considered, this was not the worst outcome for the Grant administration: the Enforcement Act would remain on the books, and, depending on what Clifford wrote, federal prosecutors might still have a chance to use it.

But when the justices met again on November 20, there was a change of plans. The Court rejected Clifford's draft opinion. The old Democrat's parsing of the indictment was simply not a satisfactory answer to the momentous questions that Justice Bradley had raised in his circuit court opinion. Chief Justice Waite withdrew the assignment from Clifford and began writing the opinion himself. Waite labored through November, all of December, and into January, when the first rumors of an imminent decision began to surface in the press. Fortunately, he had Bradley's circuit court opinion to guide him, and when Waite finally produced his opinion on March 27, 1876, it followed his friend's reasoning closely.

Waite began with his own restatement of *Slaughterhouse:* "We have in our political system a government of the United States and a government of each of the several States. Each one of these governments is distinct from the others, and each has citizens of its own who owe it allegiance, and whose rights, within its jurisdiction, it must protect. The same person may be at the same time a citizen of the United States and a citizen of a State, but his rights of citizenship under one of these governments will be different from those he has under the other."

The American people, Waite wrote, "required a national government for national purposes." But this was a government of limited, enumerated powers. "No rights can be acquired under the constitution or laws of the United States, except such as the government of the United States has the authority to grant or secure," Waite said. "All that cannot be so granted or secured are left under the protection of the States."

Waite then proceeded to a count-by-count examination of Beckwith's indictment. Waite dismissed count 1, on the grounds that "the right of the people peaceably to assemble for lawful purposes existed long before the adoption of the Constitution of the United States. . . . For their protection in its enjoyment, therefore, the people must look to the States. The power for that purpose was originally placed there, and it has never been surrendered to the United States." It would have been different, Waite conceded, if Beckwith had alleged that the Republicans at Colfax assembled to petition the federal government for a redress of their grievances. Under *Slaughterhouse*, that was one of the "privileges or immunities" of U.S. citizenship. But Beckwith hadn't done so; count 1 must fall.

Count 2, which alleged a conspiracy to violate the men's right to bear arms, was invalid for essentially the same reason, Waite continued. He found count 3, alleging a conspiracy to deprive the Negroes of life and liberty without due process of law, "even more objectionable." Echoing Bradley's opinion almost verbatim, he called it "nothing else than alleging a conspiracy to falsely imprison or murder." Waite agreed with Marr, Field, and Johnson that the federal government lacked the power to punish crimes by private individuals. "The fourteenth amendment," he said, "prohibits a State from depriving any person of life, liberty, or property, without due process of law; but this adds nothing to the rights of one citizen as against another."

Then Waite came to count 4, which alleged that the whites at Colfax conspired to deprive the Negroes of their right generally to be treated equally with whites. To be sure, Waite said, "The fourteenth amendment prohibits a State from denying to any person within its jurisdiction the equal protection of the laws; but this provision does not, any more than the one which precedes it, and which we have just considered, add anything to the rights which one citizen has under the Constitution against another. . . . Every republican government is in duty bound to protect all its citizens in the enjoyment of this principle, if within its power. That duty was originally assumed by the States; and it still remains there." The only thing the federal government can do, Waite said, "is to see that the States do not deny the right." The count might have been valid under the Civil Rights Act, Waite conceded, but it was not, "because . . . it is nowhere alleged in these counts that the wrong contemplated against the rights of these citizens was on account of their race or color." In this, too, Waite closely followed Bradley's opinion.

Now Waite reached count 6, Beckwith's allegation of a conspiracy to violate Nelson's and Tillman's voting rights. *Minor v. Happersett* destroyed any claim that the Fourteenth Amendment gave Congress the power to protect the right to vote, the chief justice said. The Fifteenth Amendment did create "a new constitutional right, which is, exemption from discrimination in the exercise of the elective franchise on account of race, color, or previous condition of servitude." Alas, the indictment did not say that the Grant Parish defendants acted with racist intent. "We may suspect that race was the cause of the hostility," Waite admitted, "but it is not so averred." Count 7 had the same problem.

As for counts 5 and 8, which did allege a racial motive, Waite again echoed what Bradley had said in New Orleans: "They lack the certainty and precision required by the established rules of criminal pleading." If counts 1 through 8 were defective, then so were counts 9 through 16, which were essentially identical. Bradley's ruling must be affirmed, Waite concluded, "and the cause remanded, with instructions to discharge the defendants."

Waite's opinion was almost five thousand words long. Not once did he mention the fact that dozens of freedmen had been killed at Colfax on Easter Sunday, 1873. There was nothing about the burning courthouse; no discussion of Alexander Tillman's desperate flight or the savagery visited upon him as he died; not a word about the way the white men marched their colored prisoners to their deaths, two by two, after dark.

The Court did not quite declare section 6 of the Enforcement Act unconstitutional as Marr, Field, and Johnson had demanded. But as the *Philadelphia Inquirer* noted, the ruling "breaks whatever force the Enforcement Act may have possessed."* Under Waite's opinion, prosecutors would have to prove beyond a reasonable doubt that whites had attacked Negroes because of their race, and with the intent to violate one of their specified rights under the Civil Rights Act. Or they could bring charges where whites, with provably racist intent, violated Negroes' rights to petition the federal government or to vote in a federal election. This was theoretically possible, but very difficult in practice.

Samuel F. Miller's only direct contribution to the *Cruikshank* decision

---

*On the same day, the Court, in an opinion by Waite, struck down the indictment against the state officials in *Reese*, ruling that section 4 of the Enforcement Act was unconstitutional, for the reason, first articulated by Bradley in his Grant Parish opinion, that it did not expressly limit federal authority to cases of overt racial discrimination. See *United States v. Reese*, 92 U.S. 214 (1876).

was to tell Waite that he had forgotten to cite *Slaughterhouse* in his first draft. Thanking Miller for pointing out the error, the chief justice said he was "glad the opinion meets your approbation. It is not easy for a new beginner in such matters to come before such old heads for criticism." For all his Republican loyalty and sympathy for the Negro, Miller was not immune to the general disenchantment with Reconstruction; he still nursed hurt feelings against Grant about being passed over for chief justice; and *Slaughterhouse* had committed him to a narrow view of federal power. Apparently, he and the Grant appointees could accept gutting section 6, as long as the Court did not explicitly strike it down. "I am losing interest in these matters," he confided to a friend in December 1875. "I will do my duty but will *fight* no more."

Judge Hugh Lennox Bond, privately horrified at the ruling, wrote a half-joking note to Waite: "I have been afraid to come and see you since that 'Dred' decision of the enforcement case." But the chief justice, basking in the Northern press's generally favorable reviews of his opinion, brushed off Bond's allusion to *Dred Scott:* "Sorry for the 'Dred,'" Waite replied, "but to my mind there was no escape."

SOUTH CAROLINA WAS THE NEXT STATE TO EXPLODE. NEARLY 60 PERCENT NEGRO, it was still ruled by Republicans in 1876. But an election was coming, and white men, organized as "Red Shirts" led by the Democratic gubernatorial candidate Wade Hampton, rode through the countryside—bent on "redeeming" their state by any means necessary. On the Fourth of July, Red Shirts clashed with outnumbered colored militia in Hamburg, killing five men after they had surrendered and sacking Negro homes and shops. On Election Day, November 7, 1876, Democratic ballot-box stuffing and intimidation produced a victory for Hampton.

Nationally, the Democrats' presidential candidate in 1876, Samuel Tilden of New York, won a majority of the reported popular vote over the Republican, Rutherford B. Hayes of Ohio. Tilden carried every Southern state from which federal troops had been withdrawn, including black-majority Mississippi, where the Republican Party had been smashed in 1875. Violence also plagued Louisiana and Florida, and Democrats declared victory there, too. But in these states, and in South Carolina, there were still detachments of federal troops, as well as Republican governments. The Republican vote-counting boards in South Carolina, Louisiana, and Florida threw out violence-tainted results and declared Hayes and the respective state Republican tickets elected. As it happened, the electoral votes of these three disputed states (plus one disputed vote from Oregon) would be enough to give Hayes a 185–184 Electoral College victory over Tilden. Competing Democratic and Republican slates of electors sent their votes to Congress, but Congress could not decide which ones to count because it was split between a Republican-controlled Senate and a Democratic House.

IN THE RESULTING DEADLOCK, AMERICANS FEARED A NEW CIVIL WAR. IN NEW Orleans, the White League candidate, the former Confederate general Francis T. Nicholls, declared himself governor in January, dispatched White League troops to seize the state supreme court and other key installations, and laid siege to the statehouse, where Stephen B. Packard, the Republican candidate, was holed up.

In Washington, Congress created an electoral commission to decide the winner of the South Carolina, Florida, and Louisiana electoral votes. The commission included five senators and five representatives, evenly divided among Republicans and Democrats. Representing the Supreme Court were Democrats Clifford and Field, Republicans Strong and Miller, and a third Republican whose record gave Democrats confidence in his fairness: Joseph Bradley. On a series of 8–7 party-line votes, with Bradley casting the deciding vote each time, the commission awarded all of the disputed electoral votes to Hayes.

Democrats threatened to use their majority in the House to obstruct a final count. But in a February 26 meeting at Washington's Wormley House hotel, a four-man Democratic delegation, including E. John Ellis of Louisiana, who had been elected to Congress in 1874, worked out a deal with Republicans representing Hayes. Hayes would be permitted to take office, in return for which Hayes would withdraw federal troops protecting Packard in New Orleans and the Republican governor Daniel H. Chamberlain in South Carolina. Nicholls and Hampton would be installed as governors, and the last two black-majority states in the South still ruled by the party of Lincoln would come under white Democratic control.

On March 3, 1877, Rutherford B. Hayes took the oath of office as president, two days ahead of his public inauguration at the Capitol on March 5. Hayes advised Packard to give up. On April 10, after a decent interval, the new president ordered the army out of South Carolina. On April 21, he told federal troops to leave the statehouse in New Orleans. Packard slipped away a few days later. On April 25 the White League occupied the building on behalf of Nicholls. A huge crowd outside roared its approval.

Instead of a new Civil War, there had been a new compromise: a grand bargain between the white Republicans of the North and the white Democrats of the South. The latter had traded the presidency to the former in return for control over their own states. And that meant control of their colored population—because the Supreme Court had decreed that the Negroes must look first to the states for protection against violence and fraud. They must look to the likes of Wade Hampton and Francis Nicholls. The Compromise of 1877 was less formal than the Missouri Compromise or the Compromise of 1850, but its basic logic was similar. The Union was to be preserved at the risk of the rights of four million Americans of African descent. "The Negro," the *Nation* opined, "will disappear from the field of national politics. Henceforth, the nation, as a nation, will have nothing more to do with him."

Reconstruction was over.

EPILOGUE

Reconstruction began with a glorious promise—that America could emerge from the Civil War as the world's first true interracial democracy. But it ended amid bloodshed and crass political bargaining. The Colfax Massacre was a pivotal moment in this tragic saga. Conceivably, Reconstruction might have gone differently if Justice Joseph P. Bradley and his Supreme Court colleagues had upheld James Beckwith's prosecution. Such a show of federal resolve might have shored up William Pitt Kellogg's government and others like it in black-majority states, deterring white terrorists. Greater numbers of Southern blacks and white Republicans might have felt safe voting in 1876. Rutherford B. Hayes might have won clearer victories in states such as Louisiana and South Carolina, and possibly others. There might not have been an election deadlock, or a Compromise of 1877.

Certainly, the unpunished slaughter in Grant Parish and the narrowing of federal law enforcement authority in *United States v. Cruikshank* were milestones on the road to a "solid" Democratic South. The combined impact of mass murder and legal retrenchment made it easier for Southern blacks to be gradually dispossessed of the political power they thought they had won in the Civil War. That step-by-step process would take years to complete, however. For roughly a decade and a half after *Cruikshank*, thousands of men of color in the South continued to deposit their votes in ballot boxes, despite intense white opposition. With white Democrats in control of the state and local vote-counting apparatus, resistance to black voting increasingly took the form of fraud as well as overt violence or intimidation. Men of color who cast Republican votes often found later that they had been counted for the party of white supremacy.

Although *Cruikshank* crippled federal law enforcement at a key moment, it did not actually wipe the Enforcement Act off the books. The Justice Department still had the authority, at least on paper, to protect black voters in federal elections. From 1877 on, Republican prosecutors often tried to use that residual power. "A Free Ballot and a Fair Count" was both a Republican Party slogan and a true expression of Republican Party policy almost until the end of the nineteenth century. For the most part, though, these Republican efforts failed. James Beckwith's successor in New Orleans tried to indict more than a hundred men for violence at the 1878 congressional election. But the case collapsed after two prosecution witnesses were taken from a steamboat on their way to New Orleans and lynched. Democrats in Congress starved the Justice Department of funds; black witnesses feared to testify; white jurors refused to render guilty verdicts. Under Hayes's administration, which lasted until 1881, federal prosecutors brought 282 Enforcement Act cases in the South, but won only 20 convictions. During the next four years, Republican presidents James A. Garfield and Chester A. Arthur improved on Hayes's record, but still won only 147 out of 692 cases.

Cruikshank was no small part of the problem. Even where U.S. attorneys did get cases in front of impartial juries, they bore the heavy burden, imposed by *Cruikshank*, of proving that particular acts of fraud, intimidation, or violence were motivated by racism. As one South Carolina federal prosecutor wrote in 1879: *Cruikshank* "leaves the citizen of the United States nothing to stand on but his race, color, or previous condition and . . . it is absolutely impossible to prove that element of the case. Indeed, there are colored Democrats and white Republicans."

Several Georgia Klansmen who had been found guilty of attacking black Republicans during the 1882 congressional election asked the Supreme Court to overturn their convictions. In March 1884 the Court unanimously rejected the Klansmen's plea. The ruling, *Ex parte Yarbrough*, rested on the argument first limned by Hugh Lennox Bond in the South Carolina Klan trials: Congress has inherent constitutional authority to safeguard elections for its own members, and this power suffices to sustain the Enforcement Act. Justice Samuel F. Miller wrote the opinion; it was one of his finer moments. Miller died in 1890.

Yarbrough mitigated *Cruikshank*. But it did not apply to state elections, which mostly remained under the control of white Democrats. Even in federal elections, *Yarbrough* made little short-term difference, largely because Democrat Grover Cleveland won the 1884 presidential election and put an ex-Confederate officer in charge of the Justice Department. The Republicans retook the White House and Congress in 1889, but brought few successful Enforcement Act cases in the South. Congressional Republicans attempted to enact a tough new federal voting law, but the bill failed due to a Senate filibuster in 1891. And in 1894, a Democratic Congress repealed most of the Enforcement Act. By then, Southern states had begun enacting the poll taxes, literacy tests, and property requirements that would effectively strip blacks of the vote until the 1960s—leaving white state governments free to segregate and oppress them. Louisiana's new white supremacist Constitution, with the full panoply of measures to disenfranchise Negroes, went into effect in 1898.

The Supreme Court had meanwhile interpreted black people's other constitutional rights almost out of existence, *Yarbrough* being the major exception to the trend. In 1883, the Court decided *United States v. Harris*. The case stemmed from a federal indictment of twenty members of a Tennessee lynch mob for violating section 2 of the Enforcement Act, which outlawed conspiracies to deprive anyone of the "equal protection of the laws." Invoking *Slaughterhouse, Cruikshank, Reese*—and Bradley's circuit court opinion in the Grand Parish case—the Court unanimously struck down section 2. The lynching was not a federal matter, the Court said, because the mob consisted only of private individuals.

Justice William B. Woods wrote the opinion. Woods had joined the Supreme Court in January 1881 as an appointee of President Hayes. By this time, the Ohioan-turned-Alabaman was no longer a carpetbagger but a "Southerner," and his elevation was seen as a concession to his adopted region. *Harris* was Woods's best-known Supreme Court case, an ignoble capstone on a career whose highlight might otherwise have been *United States v. Hall* or his courageous performance at the Grant Parish trials. Woods died in 1887 at the age of sixty-three.

In 1883, the Court also considered the last great legislation of Reconstruction: the Civil Rights Act of 1875. Joseph Bradley had never liked this law. After Grant signed it, Bradley wrote privately that "to deprive white people of the right of choosing their own company would be to introduce another kind of slavery. . . . It can never be endured that the white shall be compelled to lodge and eat and sit with the Negro. The latter can have his freedom and all legal and essential privileges without that. The antipathy of race cannot be crushed and annihilated by legal enactment."

In his opinion for the court in *The Civil Rights Cases*, Bradley wrote this notion into law, ruling that the Fourteenth Amendment gave Congress no authority to legislate "social equality." Bradley seemed fed up with the Negro. "When a man has emerged from slavery," he wrote, "and by the aid of beneficent legislation has shaken off the inseparable concomitants of that state, there must be some stage in the progress of his elevation when he takes the rank of a mere citizen and ceases to be the special favorite of the laws, and when his rights as a citizen, or a man, are to be protected in the ordinary modes by which other men's rights are protected." Nine years later, on January 22, 1892, Bradley died, hailed by the *Washington Post* as "a man of profound and varied learning, legal acumen and moral rectitude."

And the Supreme Court upheld Louisiana's 1890 law segregating railroad cars. Opponents of the statute had enlisted Homer Plessy—considered a Negro because one of his grandparents was of African descent—to challenge the law by taking a seat in a white car. He did so in 1892 and was duly arrested and fined. When *Plessy v. Ferguson* reached the Supreme Court in 1896, the justices ruled that Plessy's rights under the Thirteenth and Fourteenth Amendments had not been violated. Separate accommodations for the two races were constitutional as long as they were equal, the Court held.

Surveying the ruins of Reconstruction after he left the White House, Ulysses S. Grant concluded that the South had really needed a benevolent dictatorship. "Military rule would have been just to all," he told an interviewer, "the Negro who wanted freedom, the white man who wanted protection, the Northern man who wanted Union. As state after state showed a willingness to come into the Union, not on their terms but upon ours, I would have admitted them. The trouble about the military rule in the South was that our people did not like it. It was not in accordance with our institutions. I am clear now that it would have been better to have postponed suffrage, reconstruction, State governments, for ten years, and held the South in a territorial condition. But we made our scheme, and must do what we can with it."

Grant's analysis—a characteristic mixture of militarism and idealism—had its attractions. The North might have been within its rights, as the conquering power, to subject the South to an all-out exercise in nation-building. But, as Grant acknowledged, "our people did not like it." The white South was united behind a single agenda: "redemption." The Republican Party was a congeries of industrialists, small farmers, businessmen, freedmen, and Northern-born officeholders in the South. The South pushed on Republican fault lines until they cracked. The Confederate States of America lost the Civil War militarily and economically, but in the ways that mattered most to white Southerners—socially, politically, and ideologically—the South itself did not. Ulysses S. Grant died on July 23, 1885, having tried but failed to secure the new birth of freedom for which he had fought the Civil War.

In the final days of February 1877, Louisiana Democrats made one very specific demand in return for their acceptance of Rutherford B. Hayes as president: James Beckwith must go. Their emissaries in Washington—

including Beckwith's former courtroom adversary, E. John Ellis—told the Republicans that "no peace could exist" in Louisiana as long as the Colfax Massacre prosecutor remained as U.S. attorney.

Beckwith's four-year term was supposed to expire in December 1878, but the Republicans were in no mood to defend him. While George Williams handled the Supreme Court oral argument in *United States v. Cruikshank*, Beckwith had turned to fighting corruption. Throughout 1875 and 1876, he prosecuted two criminal plots: a conspiracy to file false claims for cotton supposedly damaged by Union troops during the Civil War; and the Whiskey Ring, a nationwide scheme to steal federal liquor tax revenues. The latter case implicated prominent federal officials, including men close to President Grant. Beckwith's pursuit of the "Whiskey Thieves" in New Orleans annoyed powerful Republicans in Washington.

Early on March 3, 1877, Beckwith wired the Justice Department: THE COTTON AND WHISKEY THIEVES BELIEVE AND REPORT THAT I HAVE BEEN RE-MOVED. IS IT TRUE? It was; the president had actually nominated his replacement the previous day, as Beckwith found out while reading the New Orleans papers later that morning. Beckwith bowed out gracefully: "I leave this office after six years of service, which has been efficient in so far as my learning and ability permitted," he wrote the Justice Department. "It is a satisfaction to me that I know of nothing in my official conduct that demands either explanation or apology and that my relations with all of the several Attorney Generals, who have succeeded each other during my term of office, have been friendly."

Beckwith could have left the South, as William Pitt Kellogg did. Kellogg held one of Louisiana's two U.S. Senate seats in Washington from 1877 to 1883—his reward for going along with the Compromise—and served in the House until 1885. He died in the nation's capital in 1918. But Beckwith stayed put. "Of course I'll stay in New Orleans. Why should I go away?" he told a *New Orleans Times* reporter who visited him as he was cleaning out his desk at the Custom House. "The climate is salubrious and suits me."

In the late 1870s, Beckwith was part of a movement within the Republican Party to draft Grant for a third term in 1880. Perhaps his Reconstruction experiences had convinced him to get involved in politics for the first time; if so, it was only a brief experiment. In 1882, Beckwith's faction lost a power struggle within the Louisiana party, and from then on, he stuck to the practice of law. He served for many years as chief counsel of the New Orleans Water Works Company, arguing frequently in state and federal courts, including the Supreme Court of the United

States. In the mid-1880s, he represented rivals of the Bell Telephone Company in a quixotic effort to get Alexander Graham Bell's patent revoked.

James and Catherine Beckwith often traveled to New York City and London—sometimes together, and sometimes independently, in keeping with their notions of the proper relationship between husband and wife. They had no children. After Catherine's death in 1895, Beckwith had a lady friend, Cora Roig Lapsley, who lived in Bay St. Louis, Mississippi. Otherwise, he turned for companionship to the Chess, Checkers and Whist Club, founded by New Orleans chess aficionados in 1880. As he aged, he would linger there in an upholstered armchair, sipping lemonade and perusing a book.

IN 1880, THE FEDERAL GOVERNMENT DROPPED ALL THE CHARGES AGAINST Christopher Columbus Nash—and everyone else named in Beckwith's 1874 indictment. The formality removed the last legal cloud over what was, by then, a bright political and economic future for Nash and his erstwhile posse. In 1877, Nash had already served as the Grant Parish tax collector, appointed by Governor Nicholls along with Johnnie Hadnot, who went on the police jury. Bill Cruikshank, who resettled in Pineville, seems to have disappeared into obscurity, as does William R. Rutland, who moved to Mississippi.

In June 1888, Nash, having established a successful commercial firm and married the daughter of a prominent Natchitoches planter, was chosen president of the Grant Parish police jury and mayor of Colfax. A Democratic Party handbill circulated during the 1888 campaign reminded white voters that "the memory of Easter Sunday 1873 is too fresh in the minds of the people of the Parish of Grant for them to rivet anew the shackles they that day struck off."

Willie Calhoun, however, was a spent force, plagued by debt and litigation. In February 1875, he eloped with a white woman from Mississippi. His former mistress, Olivia Williams, did not appreciate this. Her breach-of-promise-to-marry lawsuit against Calhoun had been settled for twenty thousand dollars in May 1873, just two months before the birth of their second son. Upon learning that Calhoun had a new wife, Williams pressed charges against him for allegedly forging Williams's signature on a receipt for the twenty thousand. A New Orleans jury convicted Calhoun in May 1875, but the judge threw out the verdict, finding that "there was a strong and reasonable doubt" as to Calhoun's guilt.

Calhoun served a term on the Colfax town council from 1878 to 1880, but he and his sister Ada let their properties fall into disrepair. The fences tumbled and livestock roamed wild. In late 1882 and early 1883, Calhoun's creditors forced him to sell the Mirabeau and Meredith plantations. At the auction, C. C. Nash bought 150 acres; Nash's nephew and a partner bought 2,700 acres. After Willie Calhoun died on January 14, 1891, his widow sold the last of the land to settle debts she had inherited from her husband. The vast estate that Robert C. Register once described as "an asylum to the oppressed and needy . . . the stronghold of the Republicans of this parish," was no more.

At the time of his death, Willie Calhoun was one of the last three or four white Republicans in Grant Parish. The party's collapse had begun in 1875, when Kellogg appeased the White League by installing a conservative Republican New Orleans lawyer as judge instead of William B. Phillips. The judge promptly fired Sheriff John B. McCoy, the tough Republican Kellogg had appointed when he was still trying to crack down on white terrorists. The new sheriff made Christopher Columbus Nash his deputy. Soon, Grant Parish officials arrested Phillips on trumped-up murder charges, but Phillips made bail and fled to Mississippi.

William Ward had been expelled from the state legislature in February 1875, for coming to the chamber drunk and waving a pistol. White Leaguers threatened Ward's life; he fled the state in January 1876. When Ward returned in late August 1876, he begged the Republican boss Stephen Packard for a job. "This day, sir, I have not one cent to get any dinner. I am in need. I am willing to go any place to help our party to win," he wrote. But Louisiana's Republicans had had their fill of William Ward. Packard refused his plea, and party officials ordered him to keep out of Grant Parish.

Ward was a washed-up politician with nowhere to turn; William B. Phillips was in about the same position. The two men did the only thing they could: they sold out to the Democrats. In early October, they agreed to campaign for the white man's party, in return for "expenses." As part of the deal, they embraced the whites' version of the events in Colfax on April 13, 1873. On October 10, 1876, Ward spoke to the New Orleans Fourth Ward Colored Conservative Democratic Club, blaming the massacre on Kellogg's "hellish plan" to deliberately commission two sets of officers, provoke a battle, "and make political capital out of the dead Negroes for his party." Until now, Ward lied, "[I have] held my peace because the Republicans asked me to do so." But, he assured his audience, "if you vote for Nicholls . . . no more Grant Parish massacres will be deliberately planned to fire the northern heart and the national Congress."

It was a clever ploy by the Democrats, though some in the party did not approve. "Will not Ward's testimony recoil on us far more than it will injure Gov. Kellogg? We think so," the *New Orleans Bulletin* opined. "There is but one style of treatment which Ward deserves at the hands of civilization and that is to be furnished with a hempen necktie and made to dance on nothing."

Whether Ward and Phillips's about-face made any difference or not, the Grant Parish vote in 1876 was again so hotly disputed that no returns were ever agreed upon. But Ward and Phillips were permitted to return to private life. Phillips died in New Orleans in 1881. Ward remained in New Orleans for a few more years, before he and Mary finally relocated to Norfolk, Virginia, where he died in May 1895.

ON APRIL 13, 1921, THE PEOPLE OF COLFAX, LOUISIANA, AWOKE UNDER THREATENing gray skies. But it was a special occasion, and they would not let the weather deter them from the celebration they had been preparing for months.

Shortly before 11:00 a.m., the mayor, local judges, and a brass band assembled at the redbrick LePage Hotel, hard by the bank of the Red River. With them were two dozen old men who had taken part in the storied battle forty-eight years earlier, which had come to be known as the Colfax Riot. These "veterans," in turn, were joined by two women: Mary Hadnot, the daughter of Jim Hadnot, and Mary A. Harris, the widow of Sidney Harris.

At eleven on the dot, the little parade marched to the nearby Colfax Cemetery, where several hundred people, including the entire student body of Colfax High School, waited. In the middle of the crowd stood a tall object, cloaked in white canvas. After the veterans and the widows had taken their seats in chairs set out for them next to the pillar, the students marched in a circle around it, dropping flowers as they passed. Then the youths reassembled, forming a large *L*, and sang a song from Civil War days:

> We've been tenting tonight on the old camp-ground,
> Thinking of days gone by,
> Of the loved ones at home that gave us the hand,
> And the tear that said, "Good-bye!"
>
> Alas for those comrades of days gone by
> Whose forms are missed tonight.
> Alas for the young and true who lie
> Where the battle flag braved the fight.

When the singing ended, Harris's widow and Hadnot's orphan approached the canvas-covered object. They untied the cords that held the veil in place, and slowly revealed a twelve-foot marble obelisk. The one-thousand-dollar monument, paid for with citizen contributions and two hundred dollars in parish funds, was gleaming white and inscribed with these words:

In Loving Remembrance
Erected to the Memory of the Heroes
Stephen Decatur Parish
James West Hadnot
Sidney Harris

Who fell in the Colfax Riot
fighting for White Supremacy
April 13, 1873

Moments later, after Judge Leven L. Hooe—Paul Hooe's son—finished paying tribute to the Colfax Riot veterans, the skies finally opened. The audience hastened to a large pecan tree, which was said to have sheltered the white men during the "riot." Mayor A. G. Buford gave a speech dedicating the "Riot Tree" as a memorial, and the assembly sang "Dixie." Despite the rain, the *Colfax Chronicle* reported, the ceremony "was beauty personified in its simplicity." And when it was done, the veterans retired to the LeSage Hotel for a banquet, accompanied by the local dignitaries and six dozen other guests.

There was only one disappointment: Christopher Columbus Nash could not be there. He was by then an old man living in Natchitoches, and he was suffering from a bad cold. Maybe it augured worse illness, because Nash died just over a year later, on June 29, 1922. He was buried with full military honors at the historic American Cemetery in Natchitoches. A white marble obelisk, almost identical to the monument in the Colfax Cemetery, stands on his grave.

No one raised a monument, official or unofficial, to the victims of the massacre. Not so much as a wooden cross marked the spot where dozens of Negro men lay in a shallow mass grave. Over the years, their resting place was repeatedly disturbed by various construction projects which brought up some of their bones. In October 1927, workers digging a new water main found a skull, "presumably that of a Negro," as the local press put it, about two feet underground near the site of the old courthouse. The project engineer said he would ship it to Louisiana

State University in Baton Rouge for inclusion in a collection of Civil War relics.

During expansion of the modern Grant Parish courthouse in the early 1960s, black workers digging a foundation discovered more bones. A white teenager, W. T. McCain Jr., saw one of them holding what appeared to be a femur. Some of the men walked off the job because they were upset. In 1965, a college student reported in a term paper that the bones had been "piled together in a cardboard box and stuck obscurely in a corner of the *Colfax Chronicle* office."

Disenfranchised, denied equal educational opportunities, and dependent on whites for work, the black generations that grew up in Colfax after Reconstruction were in no position to memorialize their dead or even to challenge the prevailing white myths about the "riot." Still, when no whites were present, the descendants of the victims recounted the horror and the injustice of those bitter years. Inevitably, this oral tradition produced exaggerations of its own, such as the popular legend that carts full of dead white men had been dumped secretly at a place called Rocky Bayou or buried atop a hill called Devil's Backbone.

AFTER WORLD WAR II, THE TALE OF A BRAVE WHITE STAND AGAINST NEGROES, carpetbaggers, and scalawags, already carved in stone at Colfax Cemetery and enshrined in history books, received the imprimatur of the state of Louisiana.

In October 1949, Colfax's mayor, C. Aswell "Hooker" Rhodes, asked the Louisiana Department of Commerce and Industry to put up a historical marker in his town, telling officials that it would "mean a lot" to Colfax. The department agreed, and soon a committee of three local white history buffs was hard at work on the wording. Bureaucracy being what it is, the unveiling did not take place until June 14, 1951. Mary Evelyn Dickerson, executive director of the Department of Commerce and Industry, dedicated the cast-aluminum sign. Seven feet tall and anchored in concrete just outside the courthouse, it read: ON THIS SITE OCCURRED THE COLFAX RIOT IN WHICH THREE WHITE MEN AND 150 NEGROES WERE SLAIN. THIS EVENT ON APRIL 13, 1873 MARKED THE END OF CARPETBAG MISRULE IN THE SOUTH.*

But time was running out on white supremacy in the South, and the myths that had helped sustain it. Like the Civil War, World War II had

---

*In addition to its biased assessment of the massacre's impact, the marker, which still stands in Colfax, gives an inaccurate estimate of the death toll. For a discussion of how many black men died on April 13, 1873, see the appendix.

been a struggle to make men free—and forced Americans to face the contradiction between the ideals they fought for and the denial of human rights to their country's own citizens. A postwar civil rights movement swept the country. As in Reconstruction, federal force played a role, notably in 1957, when President Dwight D. Eisenhower dispatched paratroopers to shield black students from a white mob at Little Rock Central High School. But the revolutionary new ingredient was nonviolence. The dignified resistance of Martin Luther King Jr.'s legions succeeded where William Ward and P. B. S. Pinchback had failed.

The Supreme Court, responding to arguments presented by Thurgood Marshall and other lawyers from the Legal Defense Fund of the National Association for the Advancement of Colored People, catalyzed change in 1954 with its ruling outlawing school segregation in *Brown v. Board of Education*. When Congress, spurred by the civil rights movement, enacted laws protecting African-Americans from discrimination in public accommodations, the workplace, and, most crucially, voting, the Court upheld the new statutes every time.

Though *Brown* overcame *Plessy v. Ferguson*, both Congress and the Supreme Court remained burdened by precedents set in Reconstruction. *Slaughterhouse* eviscerated the "privileges or immunities" clause of the Fourteenth Amendment, so when the Court struck down discriminatory laws it often cited the amendment's guarantee of "equal protection of the laws." Because of *The Civil Rights Cases*, Congress had no power under the Fourteenth Amendment to ban discrimination in public accommodations, so when the Court upheld the 1964 Civil Rights Act, it cited Congress's constitutional power to keep the channels of interstate commerce free of racism.

To this day, the Supreme Court has not overruled its Reconstruction cases, and this has had consequences. In 1994, Congress adopted the Violence Against Women Act. Invoking both its power to regulate interstate commerce and its power to enforce the Fourteenth Amendment, Congress authorized victims of sexual assault to sue their attackers for damages in federal court. Shortly after the law's adoption, Christy Brzonkala alleged that two male students at Virginia Tech raped her, and that the attack left her so distraught that she dropped out of school. She sued. By a vote of 5–4, the Supreme Court struck down the statute upon which her lawsuit was based, in part, the Court said, because the Fourteenth Amendment does not give Congress the authority to punish individual rapists. "The language and purpose of the Fourteenth Amendment place certain limitations on the manner in which Congress may attack discriminatory conduct," Chief Justice William H. Rehnquist wrote for the majority. "These limitations are necessary to prevent the Fourteenth Amendment from obliterating the Framers' carefully crafted balance of power between the States and the National Government. Foremost among these limitations is the time-honored principle that the Fourteenth Amendment, by its very terms, prohibits only state action." As precedent, Rehnquist cited *Harris*, *The Civil Rights Cases*, and *Cruikshank*.

DURING THE CIVIL RIGHTS REVOLUTION, HISTORIANS BEGAN TO REASSESS RE-construction, debunking the tale of carpetbagger corruption and Negro misrule, and treating the Colfax Massacre as an episode in the long and bloody white supremacist resistance to black freedom. Yet James Beckwith's page in history would never be properly written. He died on August 8, 1912—a hundred years after Louisiana's admission to the Union and sixteen years after *Plessy*. By then, Louisiana was a thoroughly segregated one-party state under the control of avowedly white supremacist Democrats. In 1911, eight black men were lynched there, out of a total of sixty-one nationwide.

Beckwith had moved into the Hotel Grunewald, a grand new establishment just off Canal Street in the American sector, not far from the spot where white men had clubbed and shot blacks during the New Orleans Massacre of 1866. The lawyer would return to the Grunewald from his club at six o'clock each evening, padding through the lobby with a worn-out satchel in his hand—and his valet, a colored man named Enos Smith, at his side. On the last morning of Beckwith's life, it was Smith who called for a doctor when Beckwith said he was unable to move his legs. And it was Smith, together with several of Beckwith's white friends, who remained by his bed until the lawyer stopped breathing at 6:20 p.m. Then the valet passed his hands over Beckwith's eyes, squeezing them gently to a close.

The *Daily Picayune* claimed that Beckwith left a personal law library worth eighteen thousand dollars. This was a wild overstatement, seemingly planted by executors to pump up bids at his estate sale. Appraisers did look over not only a huge collection of law books but also such volumes as *John Lubbock on Ants and Wasps* and the memoirs of Grant, Sherman, and Sheridan. They were nearly worthless. Otherwise, Beckwith's estate consisted of a fifty-dollar gold watch, a box of "electrical junk," and a safety razor, among other flotsam and jetsam. His will, written in 1905, declared that he had given away his truly valuable property. The estate sale netted $973.72, all of which went to creditors, lawyers, and notaries, except for fifty dollars paid to Smith "for attendance during last illness."

To be sure, the *Daily Picayune*, the same paper that had execrated his prosecution of the Colfax Massacre, published a long and laudatory obituary. "Judge" Beckwith, as the paper called him, was "eminent," a man of "character" and "genius"—"known throughout the South as one of her foremost lawyers." The paper noted that his name "is associated with the hardest fought and greatest legal battles within the history of New Orleans"—but, avoiding old controversies, the *Daily Picayune* omitted the Grant Parish case.

And that was the last word on James Beckwith until 1989, when Charles Fairman published his history of the Supreme Court during Reconstruction. Fairman, who died in 1991, was a distinguished member of the Harvard and Stanford law faculties, a confidant of Justices Felix Frankfurter and Robert H. Jackson—and a teacher of William Rehnquist. As a scholar, Fairman was best known for his admiring biography of Samuel Freeman Miller, his articles in praise of Joseph P. Bradley, and for arguing—as Reverdy Johnson and Robert H. Marr had argued in the 1870s—that the framers of the Fourteenth Amendment did not intend it to "incorporate" the Bill of Rights. Fairman defended the Supreme Court's reasoning in *Slaughterhouse* and *Cruikshank*, though he conceded their baleful impact.

Fairman was sharply critical of Beckwith's performance in the Colfax Massacre case. He took Beckwith to task for not expressly alleging that the defendants had attacked Levi Nelson and Alexander Tillman because of their race. Fairman derided Beckwith as "not a quick learner," and asserted that "the prosecution in Cruikshank failed because the United States Attorney did not have enough understanding to frame his indictment to charge conspiracy."

Fairman's assessment was unfair to Beckwith, and superficial with respect to Joseph Bradley. Bradley recognized, as he once wrote, that justice was essential to order—that "society can no more subsist with unjust laws than it can without any laws." He declared this in good faith, yet with an implied exception for men and women of African descent. In the Colfax Massacre case, it was James Beckwith who actually practiced what Bradley preached. He insisted that no social order could be founded on the violent subjugation of an entire race of people. It was Beckwith who believed that the United States could not truly call itself a nation of laws as long as the men who spilled a sea of blood in Colfax, Louisiana, on April 13, 1873, went "unwhipped of justice."

He rests forever, alongside Catherine, in their tomb at Metairie Cemetery in New Orleans.

HOW MANY DIED?

The white death toll in Colfax on April 13, 1873—three—is not in any dispute. A precise accounting of the number of blacks killed has proved elusive, however. An 1875 report by U.S. Army lieutenant Edward L. Godfrey claimed "at least" 105 deaths. James Beckwith told a congressional committee in 1875 that the toll was between 60 and 70, or, as he put it, "probably about 70, to a certainty." The state historical marker at Colfax asserts that "150 Negroes" died. Much higher numbers, up to 400, have been bandied about since. Over the years, both races in Louisiana have inflated the death toll: blacks to emphasize their victimization; whites to emphasize their power.

The first body count came from the deputy U.S. marshals, Theodore W. DeKlyne and William Wright, who visited the massacre scene on April 15, 1873. Their written report documents the fact that they buried 54 bodies, left one set of charred remains in the courthouse rubble, and turned over five bodies to friends or family for separate burial. They also saw two men whom they deemed mortally wounded. That would make for a total of sixty-two dead. Their credibility is reinforced by the fact that they supplied a list of the names of all the dead and wounded they saw.

Just two weeks later, on April 29, 1873, Captain Jacob H. Smith of the U.S. Army, after scouring the area for unburied dead, reported in a letter to headquarters that "the number killed or died from wounds of the Negroes proves to be 71." But Smith did not elaborate. Two years after that, on May 29, 1875, Lieutenant Godfrey made his report in response to a request from General Philip H. Sheridan. By this time, the tale was probably growing a bit in the telling. Still, Godfrey listed 81 names of men said by local residents to have been killed on April 13, 1873, most of which also appeared, sometimes under different spellings, on DeKlyne and Wright's list. Godfrey estimated "at least 105" total dead, however, by including 15 to 20 bodies supposedly "thrown in the river." But no witness at either of the two trials testified to anyone's throwing bodies in the river. Godfrey also included 18 unidentified bodies that were secretly buried in Colfax, which seems too vague and insubstantial.

There were probably at most 150 black men defending the courthouse when the whites attacked on April 13, 1873. At least 45 of these men survived, because that is how many testified for the prosecution at one or both of the trials in New Orleans; this fact alone casts great doubt on any claim of 150 killed. Also, the number of prisoners taken by the whites was between 37 and 47, according to witness testimony. But nine prisoners survived and testified. This would mean that between 28 and 38 were killed in this most barbaric phase of the massacre. Even discounting for the effects of bad weather, darkness, and alcohol on the marksmanship of Cruikshank and his men, it is doubtful that the whites could kill many more blacks while they were fleeing the burning courthouse than they later killed at point-blank range.

If we take all these factors into account, the best minimum estimated death toll is 62, the number DeKlyne and Wright confirmed as either buried, dead, or mortally wounded on April 15, 1873. A good maximum estimate would be the 81 dead actually named by Godfrey in his 1875 report. Neither figure includes Jesse McKinney, Edmond Ware, Hamp Henderson, or any of the other men whose murders were related to the Colfax Massacre but were not actually committed on April 13, 1873.

PAGE PROLOGUE

1   *Washington was draped:* Unless otherwise noted, descriptions of Grant's
      second inauguration are from accounts that appeared in the *New York
      Times* (hereafter cited as *NYT*), March 5, 1873; *New York Tribune*, March 5,
      1873; Associated Press, March 5, 1873 (as published in the *Philadelphia In-
      quirer*); Emma Dent Casey, "Tells of the Two Inaugurations of President
      Grant," *Washington Sunday Star*, March 4, 1917.

1   *A blue sky lifted spirits:* "Grant's Re-Inauguration," *New York Tribune*,
      March 5, 1873.

2   *"I don't know why":* Albert D. Richardson, *A Personal History of Ulysses S.
      Grant* (Hartford, CT: American Publishing, 1868), 143.

2   *The legislation required:* Eric Foner, *Reconstruction: America's Unfinished
      Revolution* (New York: Harper and Row, 1988), 271–80; John Hope
      Franklin, *Reconstruction: After the Civil War* (Chicago: University of Chicago
      Press, 1961), 69–83. The Reconstruction Act, 14 Stat. 428 (1867), divided
      "rebel States" into five military districts, under the authority of a U.S.
      general. Each general had authority to protect personal and property
      rights, to suppress insurrection, disorder, and violence, and to punish
      criminals—if necessary through military commissions. States could only
      be restored to representation in Congress—and relieved of military rule—
      after they elected new state constitutional conventions, drafted new con-
      stitutions guaranteeing universal male suffrage, and ratified the
      Fourteenth Amendment.

2   *In 1868, when Johnson:* Jean Edward Smith, *Grant* (New York: Simon and
      Schuster, 2001), 431–57.

3   *He called the amendment:* Ulysses S. Grant, *The Papers of Ulysses S. Grant*,
      vol. 20, ed. John Y. Simon (Carbondale: Southern Illinois University Press,
      1995), 130–33.

3   *Its goals were to:* Kenneth M. Stampp, *The Era of Reconstruction,
      1865–1877* (New York: Vintage, 1965), 200. See also Foner, 412–59;
      Franklin, 150–69. Two book-length studies of the Reconstruction-era Klan
      and related organizations are George C. Rable, *But There Was No Peace: The
      Role of Violence in the Politics of Reconstruction* (Athens: University of
      Georgia Press, 1984) and Allen W. Trelease, *White Terror: The Ku Klux Klan
      Conspiracy and Southern Reconstruction* (Baton Rouge: LSU Press, 1971).

4   *In March 1871, the Klan:* Foner, 342, 427–31.

4   *On May 31, 1870, invoking:* Section 6 of the Enforcement Act, 16 Stat. 140
      (1870), provided that "if two or more persons shall band or conspire to-
      gether, or go in disguise upon the public highway, or upon the premises of
      another, with intent to violate any provision of this act, or to injure,

oppress, threaten, or intimidate any citizen with intent to prevent or hinder his free exercise and enjoyment of any right or privilege granted or secured to him by the Constitution or laws of the United States, or because of his having exercised the same," they would face up to ten years in prison, a five-thousand-dollar fine, and the loss of the right to hold political office.

4   *"These combinations amount to war":* Jean Edward Smith, 545.

4   *In such cases, the president:* Ibid., 546. The Ku Klux Klan Act of 1871 (17 Stat. 13) made it a crime, punishable by up to six years in prison and a five-thousand-dollar fine, for two or more persons to conspire to: levy war against the United States, overthrow or destroy by force the government of the United States, stop the execution of any U.S. law, seize federal property, prevent any person from holding a federal office, force any person to resign from a federal office by injuring him or destroying his property, hinder a U.S. official in the performance of his job, intimidate a witness or a juror, deprive any person or any group of people of the equal protection of the laws, or prevent any eligible citizen from voting in a federal election. The law also empowered the president to call out the state militia or U.S. forces if any state was unable or unwilling to prevent such conspiracies. To prevent the Klan from infiltrating the federal trials contemplated in the statute, no one could be a grand juror or juror without swearing an oath that he was never part of the Klan himself. And anyone who failed to report Klan violence to the authorities would also be liable to civil suit by the victims. But perhaps because it was such a tough statute, Congress would not approve it without a "sunset" provision: the president could no longer ask to suspend habeas corpus "after the end of the next regular session of Congress," i.e., March 4, 1873.

4   *By July 1872, there were:* Trelease, 399–418; Foner, 412–59; William Gillette, *Retreat from Reconstruction: 1869–1879* (Baton Rouge: LSU Press, 1979), 28; Jean Edward Smith, 547.

5   *"The scourging and slaughter of our people":* Frederick Douglass, *U.S. Grant and the Colored People* (Washington, DC: n.p., 1872), 6.

5   *Backed by the Democrats:* Jean Edward Smith, 549; Foner, 503.

5   *In Alabama, Republicans:* Foner, 508; Jean Edward Smith, 551.

6   *Perhaps more important, it betrayed:* Foner, 504–5.

6   *Pale and feeble:* Joint Congressional Committee on Inaugural Ceremonies, "President Ulysses Simpson Grant, 1873," http://inaugural.senate.gov/history/chronology/usgrant1873.htm, U.S. Congress (accessed June 12, 2007).

6   *"And there shall come forth":* This passage of Isaiah is from the actual King James Bible that Grant used at his inauguration—and which is still used by the Supreme Court to administer the oath of office to new justices and new members of the Supreme Court Bar. The Bible was printed in Oxford, England, in 1799 at the Clarendon Press by Dodson, Beasley and Cooke, Printers to the University. I am grateful to William K. Suter, clerk of the Supreme Court of the United States, for permitting me to examine and photocopy this remarkable book.

8   *Yet, "throughout the war":* The text of Grant's second inaugural address is from Ulysses S. Grant, *The Papers of Ulysses S. Grant*, vol. 24, ed. John Y. Simon (Carbondale: Southern Illinois University Press, 2000), 60–64.

8   *Arkansas's Republican Party:* Franklin, 189–210; Foner, 412–25; Charles M. Crook, "The Barbour County Background to the Election of 1872 and Alabama's Dual Legislatures," *Alabama Review* 56, no. 4 (October 2003), 242–77.

CHAPTER ONE: "WHOLESALE MURDER"

9   *The woodpile was about:* Details of the *Southwestern's* voyage and its land-
     ing at Colfax on the evening of April 13, 1873, including direct quotations,
     are from R. G. Hill's account, published in the *New Orleans Times* (hereafter
     cited as *NOT*), April 16, 1873, and Thornton Jacobs's statement, published
     in the *New Orleans Daily Picayune* (hereafter cited as *NODP*), April 16,
     1873.

9   *In the stern, a paddlewheel:* Information concerning the *Southwestern* and
     other Louisiana steamboats is from Frederick Way, *Way's Packet Direc-
     tory, 1848–1939* (Athens, OH: Ohio University Press, 1983), 430; *NODP*,
     March 18, 1874; author interviews with Professor Carl A. Brasseaux, Uni-
     versity of Louisiana, Lafayette, and Professor Paul Paskoff, Louisiana
     State University.

10   *Congress, the president, and:* For descriptions of Colfax in its early days see:
     Testimony of J. R. Beckwith (hereafter cited as Beckwith Testimony I), in
     House Reports, 43rd Cong., 2nd sess., no. 261, "Condition of Affairs in the
     Southern States" (hereafter cited as "Condition of the South"), 409–21;
     Mabel Fletcher Harrison and Lavinia McGuire McNeely, *Grant Parish,
     Louisiana—A History* (Baton Rouge, LA: Claitor's, 1969), 33–34, 103–5;
     Biographical and Historical Memoirs of Northwest Louisiana (Nashville, TN:
     Southern Publishing, 1890), 497–524. On local government meetings, see
     generally Grant Parish Police Jury Minutes, 1869–74, WPA Collection,
     Historical Records Survey, Transcriptions of Louisiana Parish Police Jury
     Minutes—mss. 2984, Grant Parish, reel 216 (microfilm), Louisiana and
     Lower Mississippi Valley Collections, Hill Memorial Library, Louisiana
     State University, Baton Rouge, LA (hereafter cited as Police Jury Min-
     utes).

12   *"You know workmen by":* Beckwith Testimony I, 419.

13   *Beckwith had heard whites say:* Ibid.

13   *He was surprised to learn:* Ibid.

13   *Opposing him on the Republican ticket:* The following account of the
     Louisiana political crisis of 1872–73 is based on Joe Gray Taylor, *Louisiana
     Reconstructed, 1863–1877* (Baton Rouge: LSU Press, 1974), 209–52; Ted
     Tunnell, *Crucible of Reconstruction: War, Radicalism and Race in Louisiana,
     1862–1877* (Baton Rouge: LSU Press, 1984), 151–72; James K. Hogue, *Un-
     civil War: Five New Orleans Street Battles and the Rise and Fall of Radical
     Reconstruction* (Baton Rouge: LSU Press, 2006), 91–109; Rable, *But There
     Was No Peace,* 123–28.

13   *But given the federal court's:* Grant, *Papers,* vol. 24, 51–53.

14   *Kellogg apparently hoped:* NODP, April 15, 1873; Testimony of William Pitt
     Kellogg (hereafter cited as Kellogg Testimony), "Condition of the South,"
     261–64.

15   *"I will report in detail":* James R. Beckwith to George H. Williams, Telegram,
     April 17, 1873, reprinted in *NYT,* April 19, 1873.

15   *In 1854, he joined:* Biographical data for James Roswell Beckwith and
     Sarah Catherine Watrous, including information regarding Cazenovia,
     New York, and the Oneida Conference Seminary (the forerunner of today's
     Cazenovia College), are derived from the following sources: 1850 U.S. Cen-
     sus, Cazenovia, Madison County, NY; 1880 U.S. Census, New Orleans, Or-
     leans Parish, LA; Paul Edmond Beckwith, *Beckwiths* (Albany, NY: n.p.,
     1891), 384; the City of New Orleans, *The Book of the Chamber of Commerce
     and Industry of Louisiana* (New Orleans, LA: Engelhart, 1894), 171–72; *U.S.
     and International Marriage Records, 1560–1900* (database online) (Provo,
     UT: MyFamily.com, 2004); *NOT,* March 4, 1877; William W. Williams, *His-
     tory of Ashtabula County, Ohio* (Philadelphia: Williams Bros., 1878), 33–36;

Mrs. J. R. Beckwith, *The Winthrops* (New York: Carleton, 1864), 53, 236, 296, 298, 318; Mary Kay Ricks, *Escape on the Pearl* (New York: William Morrow, 2007), 217–25; John Robert Greene, *Generations of Excellence: An Illustrated History of Cazenovia Seminary and Cazenovia College, 1824 to the Present* (Syracuse, NY: Syracuse Litho, 2000), 48–49; William Reddy, *First Fifty Years of Cazenovia Seminary, 1825–1875* (New York: Nelson & Phillips, 1877); *NODP*, August 9 and 10, 1912; Beckwith Testimony I, 409; New Orleans Public Library Louisiana Division, "Administrations of the Mayors of New Orleans: Benjamin Franklin Flanders (1816–1896)," http://nutrias.org/info/louinfo/admins/flanders.htm (accessed June 20, 2007); New Orleans City Directories, 1866–74 (hereafter cited as NO Directories) on file at the Microform Reading Room, Library of Congress, Washington, DC; Testimony of James R. Beckwith (hereafter cited as Beckwith Testimony II), in House Reports, 44th Cong., 1st sess., no. 816, "Federal Officers in Louisiana," 168–75; Stephen B. Packard to Amos T. Akerman, October 31, 1870, Personnel Records (hereafter cited as Beckwith Personnel File), records relating to appointments and applications for appointment in the Department of Justice and in federal courts and judicial districts, Records of the Department of Justice, Record Group 60, National Archives, College Park, MD; Packard et al. to Akerman, November 1, 1870, Beckwith Personnel File; Henry Clay Warmoth, Kellogg, et al. to Akerman, November 4, 1870, ibid.; James T. Casey to Ulysses S. Grant, Telegram, November 8, 1870, ibid.; Beckwith to Akerman, January 10, 1871, ibid.

15   *Of the twenty-one men:* Francis X. Clines, "Slave 'Railroad' Buffs Question Museum Site," *NYT*, June 24, 2002.

16   *Because of the foul water:* On public health conditions in nineteenth-century New Orleans, including epidemics, see Ronald M. Labbé and Jonathan Lurie, *The Slaughterhouse Cases: Regulation, Reconstruction and the Fourteenth Amendment* (Lawrence: University of Kansas Press, 2003), 17–37.

16   *A public health expert described:* Ibid., 35.

16   *White men chose "fancy girls":* Ricks, 152–62.

16   *Commerce created work for bankers:* The Louisiana State Museum, "Two Centuries of Louisiana History: The Cabildo—Antebellum Louisiana: Urban Life," http://lsm.crt.state.la.us/cabildo/cab9a.htm (accessed June 20, 2007).

16   *New Orleans was home to:* Ibid.

17   *This was essentially the policy:* Tunnell, *Crucible of Reconstruction*, 26–50.

17   *Once the war was over:* Stampp, 78.

17   *As Carl Schurz observed:* Hogue, 31–52; Tunnell, *Crucible of Reconstruction*, 96; Stampp, 80.

18   *On the morning of July 30:* The following account of the 1866 New Orleans Massacre is derived from Hogue, 31–45, and Tunnell, *Crucible of Reconstruction*, 95–107.

18   *James Beckwith witnessed:* Beckwith Testimony I, 417.

18   *Over three days in September:* Trelease, 129.

19   *The killing lasted through October:* Tunnell, *Crucible of Reconstruction*, 155–56; Trelease, 130.

19   *The terror was so intense:* Trelease, 135.

19   *In her novel:* Mrs. J. R. Beckwith, *The Winthrops*, 296. "Fred Houghton's" imagined biography corresponds to J. R. Beckwith's real one. For example, Beckwith served for a time as a district attorney in Michigan; in the book, he and Frankie Winthrop are described as living "out West," and the narrator refers to Frankie's "husband, Fred Houghton," who was "already District Attorney out there, with *no end* of prospects." Ibid., 292.

20 *At 9:30 a.m. on Monday:* Except as otherwise noted, this account of De-Klyne and Wright's visit to Colfax is based on their report of April 17, 1873, published in *NOR*, April 18, 1873; their testimony at the two trials in the case against the massacre's alleged perpetrators, in ibid., February 26 and May 21, 1874, and in *NODP*, May 22, 1874; Kellogg Testimony, 261–64.

20 *The next morning, the two:* Theodore W. DeKlyne to B. J. Hutchins, November 9, 1868 (National Archives Microfilm Publication M1027, roll 90, vol. 3, p. 8, item 173), Records of the Assistant Commissioner for the State of Louisiana, Bureau of Refugees, Freedmen and Abandoned Lands, 1865–69, Records of the Bureau of Refugees, Freedmen and Abandoned Lands, Record Group 105, National Archives, Washington, DC (hereafter cited as Freedmen's Bureau Records).

20 *Blood saturated the ground:* Alexander Tillman's injuries are described in the trial testimony of Eliza Pearson, *NOR*, March 3, 1874.

22 *The Democrats (white) of Grant Parish:* Beckwith to Williams, Telegram, reprinted in *Boston Daily Globe*, April 19, 1873.

22 *The* Times *demanded:* The editorials from the *Cincinnati Gazette* and *Philadelphia Press* are reprinted in *NOR*, April 27, 1873; *NYT*, April 16, 1873.

22 *Attorney General Williams: NODP*, April 17, 1873.

22 *Brandishing the federal government's:* Williams to Beckwith, Telegram, reprinted in *Boston Daily Globe*, April 19, 1873.

CHAPTER TWO: FROM PLANTATION TO PARISH

23 *In late May:* Hiram C. Whitley to Williams, June 1, 1873 (hereafter cited as Secret Service Report I), Letters Received by the Department of Justice from the Treasury Department, 1871–84, Records of the Department of Justice, Record Group 60, National Archives, College Park, MD. Whitley was chief of the Secret Service Division at the time of the Colfax investigation; he forwarded excerpts from John J. Hoffman's reports to the attorney general.

23 *The information led to hundreds:* Hiram C. Whitley, *In It* (Cambridge, MA: Riverside Press, 1894), 104, 111; Robert J. Kaczorowski, *The Politics of Judicial Interpretation: The Federal Courts, Department of Justice, and Civil Rights, 1866–1876* (New York: Fordham University Press, 2005), 67–68; Trelease, 391, 401.

24 *The Secret Service dispatched:* Beckwith to Williams, Telegram, April 19, 1873, Letters Received by the Department of Justice from the State of Louisiana, 1871–84 (hereafter cited as DOJ Letters from LA), Records of the Department of Justice, Record Group 60, National Archives, College Park, MD; Entry for April 21, 1873, noting receipt of request for detective from Williams, Register of Letters Received by the Chief of the Secret Service Division while in New York, July 27, 1871 to September 1, 1874, Records of the U.S. Secret Service, Record Group 87, National Archives, College Park, MD (hereafter cited as USSS Records); Williams to Beckwith, April 23, 1873, Telegram, Letters Sent by the Department of Justice, General and Miscellaneous, 1818–1904 (National Archives Microfilm Publication M699, reel 14, vol. 1) (hereafter cited as DOJ Letters Sent), Records of the Department of Justice, Record Group 60, National Archives, College Park, MD; Whitley to Hoffman, April 23, 1873, Whitley to James Fitzpatrick, April 24, 1873, Whitley to Beckwith, May 14, 1873, Letters Sent by the Chief of the Secret Service Division while in New York, USSS Records.

24 *Most, in fact:* Secret Service Report I.

24 *But after the Civil War:* Whitley to Williams, July 15, 1873 (hereafter cited as Secret Service Report II), Letters Received by the Department of Justice

from the Treasury Department, 1871–84, Records of the Department of Justice, Record Group 60, National Archives, College Park, MD.

24   *They were on the way:* The following account of events at the polls in the Red River Valley in November 1868, including direct quotations, is derived from the following sources: Testimony of B. C. McKinney and W. S. Calhoun, *Supplemental Report of Joint Committee of the General Assembly of Louisiana on the Conduct of the Late Elections, and the Condition of Peace and Good Order in the State* (New Orleans, LA: A. L. Lee, 1869) (hereafter cited as 1868 Election Report), 295–97; Testimony of William B. Phillips (hereafter cited as Phillips 1868 Election Testimony), House Miscellaneous Documents, 41st Cong., 2nd sess., no. 154, pt. 1 (hereafter cited as "Louisiana Contested Elections"), 376–77; Testimony of W. S. Calhoun (hereafter cited as Calhoun 1868 Election Testimony), ibid., 423–31; Testimony of Lewis Taylor, ibid., 434–36; Testimony of J. G. P. Hooe (hereafter cited as Hooe 1868 Election Testimony), ibid., 594–95; Testimony of Thomas Hickman (hereafter cited as Hickman 1868 Election Testimony), ibid., 627–29; Joel M. Sipress, "The Triumph of Reaction: Political Struggle in a New South Community, 1865–1898" (PhD diss., University of North Carolina, Chapel Hill, 1993), 54–56.

25   *For all his wealth:* Biographical data for William Smith Calhoun are derived from the following sources: 1850 and 1860 U.S. Census Reports for Rapides Parish, LA; 1870 and 1880 U.S. Census Reports for Grant Parish, LA; Nancy M. Rohr, *An Alabama School Girl in Paris, 1842–1844: The Letters of Mary Fenwick Lewis and Her Family* (Huntsville, AL: SilverThreads Publishing, 2001); Calhoun 1868 Election Testimony; Testimony of W. S. Calhoun, House of Representatives, 44th Cong., 2nd sess., ex. doc. no. 30, "Use of the Army in Certain of the Southern States" (hereafter cited as "Use of the Army"), 338; P. A. Dean Jr., *Colfax: Its Place in Louisiana* (Colfax, LA: Dean Art Features, 2003), 7–8, 15; Mary Eleanor Bonnette (Calhoun family historian) to the author, December 14, 2006; *Southern Patriot* (Charleston, SC), August 16, 1842; Sipress, "Triumph of Reaction," 25–26, 38–39, 52, 58–61, 71–74; *M. M. A. Calhoun v. Mechanics' and Traders' Bank*, 30 La. Ann. 772 (1878); *Frederick Calhoun v. United States*, Case No. 10146, Congressional Jurisdiction Case Files, 1884–1943, Records of the United States Court of Claims, Record Group 123, National Archives, Washington, DC.

26   *Leading the whites was the:* Biographical data for Michael Ryan are derived from the following sources: House Miscellaneous Documents, 41st Cong., 2nd sess., no. 32, "Papers in the Contested Election Case of Newsham v. Ryan" (hereafter cited as Newsham v. Ryan I); Calhoun 1868 Election Testimony; Hickman 1868 Election Testimony; Testimony of Samuel B. Shackelford and Alphonse Cazabat (hereafter cited as Cazabat 1868 Election Testimony), "Louisiana Contested Elections," 135–36, 701–3.

26   *In Rapides Parish:* Tunnell, *Crucible of Reconstruction*, 175–76.

26   *Then, having made their point:* "Use of the Army," 333.

27   *The election-season body count:* Death tolls for 1868 in various parishes are reported in Newsham v. Ryan I.

27   *He had openly threatened:* Biographical data for J. G. P. Hooe are from the 1880 U.S. Census for Rapides Parish, LA; Hooe 1868 Election Testimony, Testimony of W. S. Calhoun, "Use of the Army," 338.

28   *When all the votes:* Sipress, "Triumph of Reaction," 56.

28   *In case there was any doubt:* *Louisiana Democrat* (hereafter cited as *LD*), November 9, 1868.

28   *He came by his pugnacity:* Biographical data for William Smith, including his land purchases in Louisiana and family history, are from Rohr, 21–26; Caroline Patricia Smith, "Jacksonian Conservative: The Later Years of

William Smith, 1826–1840" (PhD diss., Auburn University, 1977), 206–332;
John Belton O'Neal, *Biographical Sketches of the Bench and Bar of South
Carolina* (Charleston, SC: Courtenay, 1859), 106–20; *Dictionary of American
Biography* (hereafter cited as *DAB*), s.v. "Smith, William."

29   *Eventually, Smith made:* Caroline Smith, 263–65. William Smith left South
Carolina due to his feud with John C. Calhoun, which peaked during the
Nullification Crisis of 1832. When Congress adopted a tariff on imported
manufactures for which South Carolina traded its cotton, white South Car-
olinians saw it as an effort to impoverish them for the sake of favored
industries in the North. Calhoun, then serving as vice president under President Andrew Jackson, had long propounded a doctrine of nullification, according to which any state could opt out of the Constitution if it considered
the Union too oppressive. The theory was developed over the tariff, but its
true purpose was to preserve slavery in South Carolina at a time of growing
antislavery feeling in the North. Fearing that abolitionists might gain the
upper hand in Congress, thus threatening the prerogatives of South Carolina slaveholders, Calhoun saw nullification as the slave states' ultimate
constitutional weapon. Following Calhoun's theory, on November 24, 1832,
South Carolina whites declared the tariff "null, void and no law" in their
state, and threatened to prosecute any federal official who tried to enforce
it. Calhoun quit Jackson's government and took one of South Carolina's
seats in the U.S. Senate. Jackson ordered the navy to Charleston, warning
that South Carolina stood on "the brink of insurrection and treason."
William Smith sided with Jackson, his friend since boyhood. The Nullification Crisis ended peacefully in March 1833, with a tariff compromise
worked out by Senator Henry Clay of Kentucky. But it cemented Calhoun's
standing as the political boss of South Carolina, and Smith, as his enemy,
felt he had to go. Caroline Smith, 264–65; O'Neal, 109–10; *DAB*, s.v. "Smith,
William," 594. Smith's Red River Valley acquisitions were especially timely.
Would-be planters had dreamed of getting rich there ever since President
Thomas Jefferson bought Louisiana from France in 1803. But a huge log-
jam, the Great Raft, blocked shipping on the Red north of the old French
settlement of Natchitoches. In 1833, the federal government finally hired
Henry Miller Shreve, a New Jersey–born inventor and steamboat operator,
to clear it. Over the next six years, Shreve's steam-powered "snag boats"—a
pair of floating battering rams he called the *Archimedes* and the
Eradicator—hammered away at the Great Raft, until they shoved the last of
it down a Red River tributary on February 15, 1839. Finally, steamboats
could carry people and goods the length of the river. In honor of Shreve's
feat, Louisianans named a port on the Red after him. Removal of the Great
Raft greatly enhanced the value of Smith's acreage. See Edith McCall, "Attack on the Great Raft," *American Heritage of Invention and Technology* 3,
no. 3 (Winter 1988), 10–16.

29   *But it was a massive:* On the Smith slaves' trek, see Donald D. Cameron,
Oral History, n.p., July 19, 1976, on file at the Grant Parish Library, Colfax,
LA (hereafter cited as Cameron Oral History); Harrison and McNeely, 31.

29   *Alligators lazed in the bayous:* Elizabeth Custer, *Tenting on the Plains* (New
York: Charles L. Webster, 1887), 53.

29   *A select handful:* Frederick Law Olmsted, *The Papers of Frederick Law Olmsted*, vol. 2, *Slavery and the South, 1852–1857*, ed. Charles E. Beveridge and
Charles Capen McLaughlin (Baltimore: Johns Hopkins University Press,
1981), 219.

29   *At the time, it was:* Caroline Smith, 325.

30   *It cost him over $100,000:* Harrison and McNeely, 103–4. The original
spelling of Meredith Calhoun's name was "Colhoun." He changed it to

match that of William Smith's political nemesis only after Smith's death. Rohr, 6, 22.

30   *He reigned over fourteen thousand acres:* Ibid.; Olmsted, 222n, 223n.

30   *Everyone in central Louisiana:* Harrison and McNeely, 103–4.

30   *Death frequently visited: Baltimore Sun,* September 4, 1851. Calhoun's plantation managers summoned a doctor from North Carolina, but he, too, contracted the disease. *Floridian and Journal* (Tallahassee, FL), September 13, 1851.

30   *In 1847, Calhoun: NOT,* July 2, 1875.

31   *The slaveholder, unlike:* Olmsted, 229. Meredith Calhoun was a former clerk to the Philadelphia financier Stephen Girard. A collector of fine art, he was fluent in French and traveled widely in Europe, including a period in which he was accompanied by a cook, Victor LaFort, who would later be chef at Delmonico's in New York. "Has Cooked for Kings," *Bismarck (ND) Daily Tribune,* September 4, 1890.

31   *Olmsted fervently believed:* The following account of Olmsted's visit, including direct quotations, is from Olmsted, 216–30.

32   *Sal writhed on the ground:* Ibid., 221. Notwithstanding the cruelty on Meredith Calhoun's plantation, there is little evidence for the oft-made claim that he was the model for Simon Legree of *Uncle Tom's Cabin.* For a particularly elaborate version of that claim, see "Model for Mrs. Stowe," *Washington Post,* July 19, 1896. For a convincing refutation, see J. E. Dunn, "About Uncle Tom's Cabin," *Washington Post,* August 31, 1896. One thing Calhoun did not tolerate from his slaves was unauthorized drinking, in part because it led them to steal from him in order to purchase whiskey from local "vagabond" whites. Olmsted, 218. In 1858, an overseer ordered several Negro men to take a notorious local liquor trader, a white woman, out of her house and deposit her on a raft in the Red River, together with all her belongings. Then they burned her house to the ground. *Boulard v. Calhoun,* 13 La. Ann. 445 (1858). But at the end of each week, the overseers would pour a splash of wine into the men's clay jugs. The exact amount varied according to job performance, as assessed by the bosses. Invisible to anyone but the recipient, the dose of wine forged a secret bond—or confirmed a secret conflict—between master and slave. Cameron Oral History.

32   *Cheney, having concluded that:* Solomon Northup, *Twelve Years a Slave* (New York: Miller, Orton and Mulligan, 1855), 246–48.

32   *In 1860, the killing:* J. Fair Hardin, *Northwestern Louisiana: A History of the Watershed of the Red River, 1714–1937* (Louisville, KY: Historical Record Association, 1939), 442.

33   *"Many of the soldiers":* George G. Smith, *Leaves from a Soldier's Diary* (Putnam, CT: G. G. Smith, 1906), 104.

33   *More than a third of:* Hogue, 25.

33   *They ran along the bank:* William H. Stewart Diary, Entry for April 2, 1864, Southern Historical Collection, University of North Carolina, Chapel Hill.

33   *Elizabeth Custer, whose husband:* Custer, 48.

34   *"If there still be any":* Ibid., 69.

34   *Elizabeth Custer wrote:* Ibid., 51, 68.

34   *He threatened violators with jail:* Sipress, "Triumph of Reaction," 28.

35   *But by the start of 1866:* Ibid., 36.

35   *What little crop they did:* Ibid., 37–38.

35   *A government report from:* Ibid., 38–39; *M. M. A. Calhoun v. Mechanics' and Traders' Bank,* 30 La. Ann. 772; Monthly Report of Lieutenant L. S. Butler, Assistant Inspector of Freedmen for the Parish of Rapides, May 31, 1866, roll 28, National Archives Microfilm Publication M1027, Records of the Assistant Commissioner for the State of Louisiana, Bureau of

Refugees, Freedmen and Abandoned Lands, 1865–69, Freedmen's Bureau Records.

35 *Meanwhile, the freedmen were:* 14 Stat. 27–30.

36 *As a lieutenant in:* Biographical data for Delos W. White are from 1870 U.S. Census for Grant Parish, LA; Testimony of Delos W. White, "Louisiana Contested Elections," 432–34; "Ku-Klux Outlaws," *NOR*, October 8, 1871.

36 *A brother of one fugitive:* Ibid.; "Use of the Army," 333; D. W. White to James Cromie, June 27 and July 10, 1867, roll 28, National Archives Microfilm Publication M752, Registers and Letters Received by the Commissioner of the Bureau of Refugees, Freedmen and Abandoned Lands, 1865–72, Freedmen's Bureau Records.

36 *When a white man attacked:* Sipress, "Triumph of Reaction," 41–42.

37 *And he threw his support:* Ibid., 74n.

37 *Phillips was born and raised:* Biographical data for William B. Phillips are from 1870 U.S. Census for Grant Parish, LA; Phillips 1868 Election Testimony; Confederate military service record for William B. Phillips, National Park Service, Civil War Soldiers and Sailors System, http://www.itd.nps .gov/cwss/ (accessed August 18, 2007).

37 *Then, on the instructions of:* Report of S. G. Willauer, September 20, 1867, roll 27, National Archives Microfilm Publication M1027, Records of the Assistant Commissioner for the State of Louisiana, Bureau of Refugees, Freedmen and Abandoned Lands, 1865–69, Freedmen's Bureau Records.

37 *On May 23, Phillips sent:* "From Rapides Parish" (letter dated May 23, 1867), *NOR*, n.d., n.p. (clipping in microfilmed records of the Freedmen's Bureau).

37 *But he also urged them:* "Speech of William B. Phillips at a Political Meeting at Mr. Layssard's Store in Rapides Parish, La., Delivered Last of June 1867—Some Seven or Eight Hundred Persons Being Present, White and Colored," *New Orleans Semi-Weekly Louisianan*, October 8, 1871.

38 *This reflected his orders:* Tunnell, *Crucible of Reconstruction*, 134.

38 *The document the convention:* Ibid., 111–35.

38 *Among the day's white:* Charles Vincent, *Black Legislators in Louisiana During Reconstruction* (Baton Rouge: LSU Press, 1976), 228, 236.

38 *In all of rural Louisiana:* Tunnell, *Crucible of Reconstruction*, 134.

39 *"Even the pigs were gaunt":* Custer, 76.

39 *"It follows," wrote a journalist:* "Condition of the South," *NYT*, October 24, 1874.

39 *The first "lodge" of Knights:* On the Knights of the White Camellia, see 1868 Election Report; Trelease, 127–36; Testimony of W. F. Howell (hereafter cited as Howell 1868 Election Testimony), "Louisiana Contested Elections," 738–42; Henry E. Chambers, *History of Louisiana*, vol. 1. (Chicago and New York: American Historical Society, 1925), 679; James G. Dauphine, "The Knights of the White Camellia and the Election of 1868: Louisiana's White Terrorists; a Benighting Legacy," *Louisiana History* 30, no. 2 (Spring 1989), 173–90.

39 *A lodge formed near:* Howell 1868 Election Testimony, 739–40.

39 *As one leader put it:* Ibid.

39 *"What does he wish":* 1868 Election Report, 215.

40 *They would have shot him:* "Use of the Army," 334–35.

40 *"The new government is revolutionary":* NODP, April 23, 1868.

40 *Deputy U.S. marshals:* LD, May 13 and July 1, 1868.

41 *Warmoth reluctantly agreed:* Hogue, 67; Joseph G. Dawson III, *Army Generals and Reconstruction: Louisiana, 1862–1877* (Baton Rouge: LSU Press, 1982), 84, appendix 3, n.p.

41 *Statewide, the Democrat Horatio Seymour trounced:* Newsham v. Ryan I, 4.

41 *With the box full of Republican tickets:* LD, November 11, 1868.

41   *Hal Frazier, a man of color:* The following account of Hal Frazier's murder is from Newsham v. Ryan I, 19–20; Testimony of Delos White, "Use of the Army," 334.

42   *Before his resignation, he had:* Delos W. White to James Cromie, October 28, 1867, roll 28, National Archives Microfilm Publication M752, Registers and Letters Received by the Commissioner of the Bureau of Refugees, Freedmen and Abandoned Lands, 1865–72, Freedmen's Bureau Records.

42   *In a letter to Phillips:* W. S. Calhoun to William B. Phillips, December 12, 1868, in Newsham v. Ryan I, 19.

42   *Calhoun was receiving so many:* Testimony of W. S. Calhoun, "Use of the Army," 338.

42   *The statute transferred Michael Ryan's:* Acts Passed by the General Assembly of the State of Louisiana at the Session Begun and Held in the City of New Orleans, January 4, 1869 (New Orleans, LA: A. L. Lee, 1869), 79–81.

42   *Negroes also made up the:* Police Jury Minutes; House Executive Document 91, 42nd Cong., 3rd sess., "Condition of Affairs in Louisiana" (hereafter cited as "Condition of Affairs in Louisiana"), 128.

43   *"The seat of justice will":* LD, March 17, 1869.

43   *At Calhoun's suggestion, Warmoth:* The appointments of Phillips as judge and White as sheriff are recorded in Record of Commissions Issued by the Governor, 1848–1928 (Microfilm reel 2.2, 1868–77), Louisiana State Archives, Baton Rouge, LA (hereafter cited as Record of Commissions).

CHAPTER THREE: POWER STRUGGLE

44   *As spring planting began:* The description of cotton planting is derived from "Scenes on a Cotton Plantation," *Harper's Weekly*, February 2, 1867, 72–73.

44   *One colored man:* The store's owner was Peter Borland, who served as a sergeant in Company H, Second Regiment, U.S. Colored Infantry. Union military service record for Peter Borland, National Park Service, Civil War Soldiers and Sailors System, http://www.itd.nps.gov/cwss/ (accessed July 19, 2007).

44   *Eventually, they hired a teacher:* The schoolteacher was Eli H. Flowers, who served in the U.S. Army during and after the Civil War. See Testimony of Eli H. Flowers, House Miscellaneous Documents, 44th Cong., 2nd sess., no. 34, "Recent Election in Louisiana," 677–78.

45   *"With any kind of favorable chance":* Sipress, "Triumph of Reaction," 65.

45   *With secret passwords and:* NOR, October 8, 1871; The Knights of Pythias, "About the Order," http://www.pythias.org/index_files/About.htm (accessed August 16, 2007).

45   *A white planter's daughter:* Kate Kingston Boyd Grant, "The Battle of Colfax, 1873," unpublished novel, on file in the Reference Section, Colfax Riot Collection, Grant Parish Public Library, Main Branch, Colfax, LA, 6–7. This document, based on the events of April 1873, is an abridged version of the unpublished novel "From Blue to Gray," a complete handwritten text of which is available in the Layssard Family Papers, Louisiana State University, Department of Archives, Hill Memorial Library, Baton Rouge, LA. Though it includes fictional elements and is told with a strong white supremacist bias, the book recounts many actual events using the names of participants.

45   *Negroes even took positions:* Sipress, "Triumph of Reaction," 64n; Record of Commissions. The black officeholders were: Robert Morris, justice of the peace, Abraham Singleton and Lewis Taylor, constables, and O. J. Butler, parish surveyor. Race of the officeholders identified through U.S. Census records and official testimony.

45   *He gave the child:* 1870 U.S. Census for Grant Parish, LA.

45   *The* Louisiana Democrat *called him:* LD, May 13, 1868.

46   *Phillips got similar visits:* Ibid., April 14, 1869.

46   *Some Knights even resumed their:* Chambers, 680.

46   *"We think the majesty of the law":* Article from *NOR* excerpted in the *LD*, April 14, 1869.

46   *Only then, Warmoth said:* Henry Clay Warmoth, *War Politics and Recon-struction: Stormy Days in Louisiana* (New York: Macmillan, 1930), 161.

47   *Warmoth went out of his way:* Tunnell, *Crucible of Reconstruction*, 161–72; Hogue, 58–76.

47   *The new judge was:* Record of Commissions.

47   *Though the cotton crop:* The financial problems of the Calhoun estates are de-scribed in Sipress, "Triumph of Reaction," 70–74, and in the records of two Louisiana Supreme Court cases, docket no. 9137, *M. M. A. Lane v. Robert S. Cameron and Ludlow McNeely,* New Orleans (May 1884), 36 La. Ann. 773, and docket no. 6553, *M. M. A. Calhoun v. Mechanics and Traders Bank,* New Orleans (April 1878), 30 La. Ann., 772 both in Supreme Court of Louisiana Collection of Legal Archives, Archives and Manuscripts/Special Collections Department, mss. 106, University of New Orleans, New Orleans, LA.

48   *The timing suggests as much: Acts Passed by the General Assembly of the State of Louisiana, at the Extra Session, Begun and Held in the City of New Orleans, March 7, 1870* (New Orleans, LA: A. L. Lee, 1870), 70–71; Record of Commissions.

48   *They decided to establish:* LD, September 28, 1870.

48   *But the parish's more conservative:* Biographical data on Alfred Shelby are from 1870 U.S. Census for Grant Parish, LA; *NOR,* November 14, 1871.

48   *During the Union's:* Francis Trevelyan Miller, ed., *The Photographic History of the Civil War, Vol. 3* (New York: The Review of Reviews, 1911–12), 318.

49   *He had the accoutrements:* Trial Testimony of Eli H. Flowers, *NOR,* Febru-ary 26, 1874.

49   *Negroes in Colfax knew:* Beckwith Testimony I, 410.

49   *More likely, Shelby:* Jim Yawn served in a Confederate cavalry unit under Nathan Bedford Forrest. His military record is described in Louisiana Sec-retary of State, Confederate Pension Applications Index Database, reel CP1.150—microdex 4—sequence 37, target card: Yaun, Sarah E. On Yawn's crimes and Shelby's refusal to arrest him, see William B. Phillips, Letter to the Editor, *NOR,* December 2, 1871. On Alfred Shelby's boasted Confeder-ate service, see Milton A. Dunn, "Some Notes About Ex-Sheriff Shelby of Grant Parish," Letter to the Editor, *Alexandria (LA) Town Talk,* December 1903. Shelby, it seems, was a bit of a con man. He told Dunn that he had been on John C. Fremont's early expeditions to California and later became an original "49er," a "filibuster" in William Walker's expedition to Nicaragua, and a soldier in a Louisiana unit attached to Lee's Army of Northern Vir-ginia. His friends in Grant Parish apparently enjoyed and believed his sto-ries, even though there is no evidence to support any of them.

49   *Sheriff Shelby had developed:* "The Courts: United States' Commissioner's Court—Ku Klux Case," *NOR,* November 14, 1871.

49   *As for Phillips, Shelby:* Ibid.

49   *By the second week of:* "The Courts: Before U.S. Commissioner Weller," *NOT,* November 12, 1871.

49   *He did, though:* New Orleans National Republican, November 15, 1871.

49   *In late August, someone fired:* "Ku-Klux Outlaws," *NOR,* October 8, 1871.

49   *Though Phillips helped them escape:* Ibid.; Green D. Brantley, Letter to the Editor, *New Orleans National Republican,* December 7, 1871.

50   *The Yawns were in the mob:* This account of the murder of Delos White is

derived from the following sources: "Ku-Klux Outlaws," *NOR*, October 8, 1871; *NOR*, November 11 and 14, 1871; Green D. Brantley, Letter to the Editor, *New Orleans National Republican*, December 7, 1871; William B. Phillips, Letter to the Editor, *NOR*, reprinted in *New Orleans Semi-Weekly Louisianan*, October 5, 1871; sworn testimony before U.S. commissioner John Weller, New Orleans, as reported in *NOT*, October 29, November 12, 14, 15, 16, 1871; *LD*, November 22, 1871; and *New Orleans National Republican*, November 11, 13, 14, 15, 1871; "Use of the Army," 402–3.

50   *Born in Mississippi on:* Biographical data for Christopher Columbus Nash are from: Confederate Military Service Record for Christopher Columbus Nash; Terry L. Jones, *Lee's Tigers: The Louisiana Infantry in the Army of Northern Virginia* (Baton Rouge: LSU Press, 1991), 78–79, 182–85; "A Ride with Sheriff Nash," *NODP*, May 3, 1873; Milton A. Dunn, "Memorial to Captain Christopher Columbus Nash," n.d. (probably July 1922), n.p., Melrose Collection, scrapbook 69, 129, Cammie G. Henry Research Center, Watson Memorial Library, Northwestern State University of Louisiana, Natchitoches, LA; *Biographical and Historical Memoirs of Northwest Louisiana*, 518; 1860 U.S. Census for Sabine Parish, LA; 1880 Census for Grant Parish, LA; Louisiana Secretary of State, Confederate Pension Applications Index Database, reel CP1.103—microdex 1—sequence 18, target card: Nash, C. C.

52   *In Montgomery the next day:* Jules Lameraux, Letter to the Editor, *NOR*, November 15, 1871.

52   *The fire had consumed:* "Use of the Army," 403.

52   *"I could not get him":* Phillips, Letter to the Editor, *NOR*, reprinted in *New Orleans Semi-Weekly Louisianan*, October 5, 1871.

52   *There was nothing to be done:* Brantley, Letter to the Editor, *New Orleans National Republican*, December 7, 1871.

52   *The rift pitted Warmoth:* Tunnell, *Crucible of Reconstruction*, 149.

52   *He went on to serve:* Hogue, 59–62.

53   *Warmoth was, Grant wrote:* Taylor, 251.

53   *The Custom House Republicans:* On the Custom House faction's plot against Warmoth and the subsequent machinations in New Orleans, see Tunnell, *Crucible of Reconstruction*, 169–70; Hogue, 76–90; Taylor, 209–52; House Reports, 42nd Cong., 2nd sess., no. 92: "Affairs in Louisiana."

54   *William Ward was born:* Biographical data for William Ward are from his Pension File, Records of the Department of Veterans Affairs, Records Relating to Pension and Bounty Claims, Record Group 15, National Archives, Washington, DC (hereafter cited as Ward Pension File). Ward's pension file is remarkably detailed, in part because, after his death, his wife, Mary, continued to argue for increased widow's benefits, and the Pension Bureau subjected her claims to exhaustive scrutiny, including testimony from numbers of witnesses about the entire history of their respective families. The file includes detailed information about not only his military service but also his personal life, including medical records and intimate details attested to under oath by friends and family. See also 1870 U.S. Census for Grant Parish, LA; Testimony of William Ward, House Miscellaneous Documents, 44th Cong., 2nd sess., no. 34: "Recent Election in Louisiana," 115–17.

54   *A fellow slave who met:* Deposition of Joseph Jackson, January 29, 1897, in Ward Pension File.

55   *"In his face he bears":* Committee of 70, "History of the Riot at Colfax, Grant Parish, Louisiana, April 13, 1873," "Condition of the South," 894.

55   *In January, he appointed:* Record of Commissions.

55   *The other spot went to Ward:* Police Jury Minutes. The Grant Parish surveyor, O. J. Butler, had been a friend of Ward's friend, Eli H. Flowers, at Ship Island.

It was this connection that prompted Ward (and Flowers) to move to Grant Parish from New Orleans in early 1870. Sipress, "Triumph of Reaction," 76.

55 *Born in 1826:* Biographical data for William and Andrew Cruikshank are from the 1860 and 1880 U.S. Census for Rapides Parish, LA, and the 1870 U.S. Census for Grant Parish, LA; *Biographical and Historical Memoirs of Northwest Louisiana*, 563.

56 *The remaining three white police:* Police Jury Minutes.

56 *He recruited two lieutenants, eleven noncommissioned officers:* Annual Report of the Adjutant General of the State of Louisiana for the Year Ending December 31, 1871 (New Orleans, 1872), 21, 23.

57 *For now, the only purpose:* Ibid., 4.

57 *Soon, Shelby, Nash, and:* LD, November 1, 1871.

57 *There was also talk of:* Jules Lameraux, Letter to the Editor, *NOR*, November 15, 1871.

58 *He fled to New Orleans:* Ibid.

58 *This secret society, Bullock revealed:* William B. Phillips, Letter to the Editor, *NOR*, December 2, 1871.

58 *On November 2, Warmoth:* Annual Report of the Adjutant General, 47.

58 *"Reports have reached us":* Ibid., 4.

59 *When Ward refused, Longstreet:* Ibid., 48.

59 *Still, it took time to:* LD, December 27, 1871.

59 *The bail hearing began:* NOR, November 14, 1871.

60 *Nowadays, Kearson saw politics as:* Biographical data for Henry Kearson are from the 1880 U.S. Census for Grant Parish, LA; Kearson to Packard, October 6, 1871, in House Miscellaneous Documents, 42nd Cong., 2nd sess., no. 211, 208; Sipress, "Triumph of Reaction," 85n.

60 *To make sure there was no:* NOT, November 15, 1871.

60 *By the same token, Beckwith:* Testimony of J. R. Beckwith, House Miscellaneous Documents, 42nd Cong., 2nd sess., no. 211 (hereafter cited as Beckwith Testimony III), "Testimony Taken by the Select Committee to Investigate Affairs in the State of Louisiana," 470–71.

60 *There was enough evidence:* NOT, November 16, 1871.

60 *This presaged a similar margin:* On the Custom House faction's effort to oust Warmoth in January 1872, see Hogue, 76–85; Tunnell, *Crucible of Reconstruction*, 169–70; Dawson, 114–28; Taylor, 216–27.

61 *The idea was to get:* Beckwith Testimony III, 463.

61 *Sheepishly, the president replied:* Hogue, 82.

61 *Collision with the state government:* Beckwith Testimony III, 468.

62 *Durell instructed the grand jury:* NOR, January 20, 1872.

62 *on February 1, Beckwith:* Docket Book, U.S. District Court for the Eastern District of Louisiana at New Orleans, Entries for *United States v. Alfred Shelby, et al.,* case no. 6624, Record Group 21, National Archives, Southwest District, Fort Worth, TX.

62 *Soon, Shelby and Nash were:* Ibid.

62 *"Armed organizations, secret in their":* Emory to Longstreet, March 15, 1872, in Department of the Gulf, vol. 114, Letters Sent, 1871–1878, Pt. 1, entry 1962, Record Group 393, National Archives, Washington, DC (hereafter cited as Gulf Letters Sent).

62 *Their orders from New Orleans:* Gentry to Commanding Officer, Baton Rouge, Telegram, April 4, 1872, in Department of the Gulf, Telegrams Sent, 1871–1878, entry 1965, Record Group 393, National Archives, Washington, DC.

62 *In fact, Longstreet dissolved:* Annual Report of the Adjutant General of the State of Louisiana for the Year Ending December 31, 1872 (New Orleans, 1873), 27–28.

62   *William B. Phillips resigned:* Record of Commissions; Testimony of William B. Phillips, House Miscellaneous Documents, 44th Cong. 2nd sess., no. 34, "Recent Election in Louisiana," 107.

CHAPTER FOUR: WAR

63   *Warmoth had an office:* This description of the Mechanics' Institute building is derived from Edwin L. Jewell, *Jewell's Crescent City Illustrated* (New Orleans, LA, 1873), n.p.

63   *As proof, he thrust the:* Beckwith Testimony III, 465; *New Orleans Bee* (hereafter cited as *Bee*), January 4, 1872; "That Ignoble Seventy-Six," *NOR*, January 5, 1872.

63   *"He hasn't sense enough":* Taylor, 211.

64   *"Conservative Republican is the new":* LD, December 27, 1871.

64   *Having rid the parish of:* Biographical data for Alphonse Cazabat are from Testimony of Alphonse Cazabat, House Miscellaneous Documents, 41st Cong., 2nd sess., no. 154, pt. 1, 701–3; *New Orleans National Republican*, November 11, 1871.

64   *Ward now asserted himself:* "Mass Meeting," *Rapides Gazette*, February 24, 1872; "Republican Mass Meeting," ibid., July 13, 1872.

65   *And though Phillips and White were gone:* "Republican Mass Meeting."

65   *On the Fourth of July:* Ibid.

65   *The dispute simmered until September:* Testimony of Harry Lott, House Miscellaneous Documents, 44th Cong., 2nd sess., no. 34, pt. 2, 350; Testimony of William Ward, ibid., 483.

65   *All things considered, it was:* NODP, April 16, 1873.

65   *At Warmoth's instructions:* Hogue, 95; Taylor, 240.

65   *In Grant Parish:* "Condition of Affairs in Louisiana," 128.

66   *When the box emerged:* Ibid.

66   *By their count, McEnery:* NODP, April 16, 1873.

66   *Registered colored voters:* "Condition of Affairs in Louisiana," 51, 128.

66   *As part of that bizarre struggle:* LD, January 15, 1873.

66   *On January 2, 1873:* Oath of office of C. C. Nash, in *United States v. C. C. Nash, et al.*, general case no. 12 (hereafter cited as Nash Case File), Records of the U.S. Circuit Court for the Eastern District of Louisiana at New Orleans, Case Files, Record Group 21, National Archives, Southwest District, Fort Worth, TX.

66   *On January 17 and 18:* Record of Commissions.

67   *It was an extraordinary claim:* Trial Testimony of Adolphe LeMay, *NODP*, May 30, 1874; Trial Testimony of Wilson L. Richardson, ibid., May 30, 1874; Closing Argument of James R. Beckwith, *NOR*, March 13, 1874 (hereafter cited as Beckwith Closing Argument).

67   *As collector, Kellogg:* Biographical data for William Pitt Kellogg are from Edmond Gonzales, "William Pitt Kellogg: Reconstruction Governor of Louisiana, 1873–1877," *Louisiana Historical Quarterly* 29 (1946), 394–495; Kellogg Testimony, 256; *National Cyclopedia of Biography*, s.v. "Kellogg, William Pitt."

67   *"I breathe the very air":* Taylor, 215.

67   *By March 1873, Kellogg was:* Kellogg Testimony, 258.

68   *They explained the agitated state:* Ibid., 261; Trial Testimony of William B. Phillips, *NOR*, March 11, 1874; Record of Commissions (showing that officers commissioned by Kellogg in January had not yet submitted their oaths).

68   *"I had it in view":* Kellogg Testimony, 263.

68   *Kellogg even agreed to make:* Record of Commissions; *NOR*, March 27, 1873.

68 *He told Rutland and Richardson:* Record of Commissions.

69 *He asked for another meeting:* "The Riot in Grant Parish," *NOR*, April 10, 1873; Sipress, "Triumph of Reaction," 92; *Shreveport Times*, April 17, 1873.

69 *When the governor repeated:* Trial Testimony of William Ward, William B. Phillips, and H. Conquest Clarke, *NOR*, March 11, 1874; Trial Testimony of William Ward and William B. Phillips, *NODP*, March 11, 1874; Kellogg Testimony, 261–63.

70 *A grassy field lay all around:* Beckwith Testimony I, 412; Harrison and McNeely, 73–74, 105; "Historical," unpublished typescript, Melrose Collection, bound vol. 3.

70 *Nash, who knew about:* Trial Testimony of Daniel W. Shaw, *NOR*, March 5 and June 4, 1874; Beckwith Testimony, 409.

70 *He hopped down to:* Trial Testimony of Robert C. Register, *New Orleans Bulletin* (hereafter cited as *NOB*), May 21, 1874; Beckwith Testimony I, 409.

70 *They promptly sent their oaths:* Record of Commissions.

70 *He took the message to:* Trial Testimony of Wilson L. Richardson, *NOB*, May 29, 1874; Beckwith Testimony I, 409–10; Committee of 70, "History of the Riot," "Condition of the South," 895.

71 *At the top of the list: NOR*, March 27, 1873.

71 *Someone in Kellogg's office:* Kellogg Testimony, 261–62.

71 *"Don't you know you are":* Trial Testimony of William Ward, *NOR*, February 27, 1874; Trial Testimony of Peter Fields, *NOB*, May 27, 1874.

71 *Register instructed Shaw:* Trial Testimony of Eli H. Flowers, *NOR*, February 26 and 28, 1874.

71 *"Get your gun":* Trial Testimony of Kit Smith, *NOB*, May 27, 1974.

72 *But at least the courthouse:* At the Grant Parish trials, several witnesses testified to the poor quality of the Negroes' weaponry and their paucity of ammunition. See, for example, Trial Testimony of Thomas Johnson, *NOR*, May 29, 1874, in which Johnson notes that the blacks "had nothing but birdshot and shotguns [and] four army guns"; Trial Testimony of Eli H. Flowers, ibid., February 27, 1874, in which Flowers states that "four men had old Enfield rifles, of no good"; Trial Testimony of Levi Allen, *NOB*, May 23, 1874, in which Allen says that about two-thirds of the men were carrying "'busted' citizens' rifles and shot-guns tied up with string, [and] no man had more than two rounds of ammunition, and some only one."

72 *Hadn't sat down:* Trial Testimony of Robert C. Register, *NOR*, February 26, 1874; Trial Testimony of Eli H. Flowers, ibid., February 27, 1874; Trial Testimony of Peter Borland, *NODP*, May 30, 1874.

72 *When Calhoun conveyed this:* Olivia Williams to W. R. Rutland, June 30, 1871, in *Louisiana v. W. S. Calhoun*, Case No. 505, Louisiana, Superior Criminal Court for the Parish of Orleans, Case Records, Criminal Courts Collection, City Archives, New Orleans Public Library; Testimony of James Nevins, Docket No. 6553, *M. M. A. Calhoun v. Mechanics and Traders Bank*, New Orleans (April 1878), 30 La. Ann. 1872, Supreme Court of Louisiana Collection of Legal Archives, Archives and Manuscripts/Special Collections Department, Mss. 106, University of New Orleans, New Orleans, LA. Trial Testimony of Robert C. Register, *NOR*, February 26, 1874; Trial Testimony of William Smith Calhoun, ibid., February 27, 1874.

72 *Nervously, they rode:* Notes of John J. McCain, typescript, 1931, Melrose Collection, scrapbook 67, 27.

73 *"I am crazy with fear":* Kate Kingston Boyd Grant, 22.

73 *Fearing that the agitation:* Trial Testimony of Richard Grant, *NOR*, March 8, 1874.

74 *The men left it on:* On the actions of Lewis Meekins and his men, see Arrest

Warrant, "State of Louisiana v. Eli H. Flowers, et al." (hereafter cited as Arrest Warrant), contained in Nash Case File; *LD*, April 9, 1873; R. C. Register et al., "The Troubles in Grant Parish," *NOR*, April 12, 1873; "The Riot in Grant Parish," *NODP*, April 8, 1873; "Fate of the Outlaws of Grant Parish," *NODP*, April 16, 1873; "Statement of Judge Rutland," as reprinted in *NOR*, April 10, 1873. The inflammatory accusation that the black Republicans desecrated the Rutland child's body was wildly, and probably intentionally, exaggerated. Despite the claims of Rutland and other white supremacists, F. W. Howell, a white Republican lawyer who visited Colfax as a peace negotiator prior to the massacre, saw no evidence that the box containing the corpse had been opened or the body disturbed. He made arrangements for it to be shipped to Rutland in Montgomery. Register et al., "The Troubles in Grant Parish"; Beckwith Testimony I, 410.

74   *Once they had left:* "The Prisoners on the Ozark: Their Statements," NOT, November 15, 1873.

74   *Flowers pulled a gun:* Trial Testimony of O. J. Butler, *NODP*, May 30, 1874; Trial Testimony of O. J. Butler and Mrs. O. J. Butler, *NOR*, May 30, 1874.

75   *No one on either side:* Trial Testimony of Eli H. Flowers, *NOR*, February 26, 1874; "Charge of Hon. W. B. Woods, Delivered to the Petit Jury in the Grant Massacre Case" (hereafter cited as Woods Charge), "Condition of the South," 858.

75   *Now the immediate vicinity:* Trial Testimony of Wilson L. Richardson, *NOR*, March 6, 1874, and *NOB*, May 29, 1874.

76   *Apparently, Rutland thought:* Biographical data for W. R. Rutland are from 1870 U.S. Census for Grant Parish, LA; House Miscellaneous Documents, 42nd Cong., 2nd sess., no. 211, 208.

76   *To this lurid yarn:* "Statement of Judge Rutland," *NOR*, April 10, 1873.

76   *It was a legal fig leaf:* Arrest Warrant.

76   *The men spurred:* Affidavit of J. S. Payne, December 28, 1874, attached to petition from Grant Parish defendants and accompanying letter, Beckwith to Williams, February 5, 1875, DOJ Letters from LA.

77   *A tenant farmer and:* Biographical data for Benjamin L. "Levi" or "Levin" Allen are from 1870 U.S. Census for Grant Parish, LA; Trial Testimony of Levi Allen, *NOR*, March 3, 1874, and *NODP*, March 2, 1874.

77   *They left behind two pistols:* Register et al., "The Troubles in Grant Parish."

77   *The only condition was that:* J. S. Payne to the Commanders of the Force at Colfax, transcribed version attached to Petition of the Citizens of Grant Parish, enclosed in letter of U. S. Grant to the Department of Justice, February 28, 1874, DOJ Letters from the President.

78   *"We will not make any":* R. C. Register, William Ward, et al. to the Citizens of Montgomery, Nash Case File.

78   *White men had murdered him:* "The Colfax Riot: Statement of J. M. McCain," *LD*, April 23, 1873; Trial Testimony of Eli H. Flowers, *NOR*, February 26, 1874.

78   *Jesse McKinney had been:* Biographical data for Jesse McKinney are from 1870 U.S. Census for Grant Parish, LA. The account of his last days and his murder is compiled from Trial Testimony of Laurinda McKinney, *NOB*, May 23, 1874; Oscar W. Watson, "An Incident of My Boyhood Days," typescript, 3, Robert DeBlieux Collection, folder 265, Cammie G. Henry Research Center, Watson Memorial Library, Northwestern State University of Louisiana, Natchitoches, LA; Beckwith Testimony I, 410–11.

79   *By nightfall on April 5:* Woods Charge, 859; Trial Testimony of Robert C. Register, *NOR*, February 26, 1874.

80   *He handed it to a:* William Ward to Reverend Jacob Johnson, April 5, 1873, Nash Case File. At some point on April 6, Ward and Register received a visit

from F. W. Howell, a white Republican lawyer from Montgomery who was acquainted with Rutland but sympathetic to Ward's cause and was therefore probably considered a good intermediary by the white men in Montgomery who sent him. Howell desired peace, but his attempt to negotiate came to nothing; he seems to have been surprised, upon reaching Colfax, to learn that things were not quite as his friend Rutland had claimed. Howell was killed by white supremacist terrorists at the Coushatta Massacre in August 1874. Affidavit of J. S. Payne; Trial Testimony of Robert C. Register, *NOR*, February 26, 1874; Trial Testimony of William Ward, ibid., February 27, 1874; Beckwith Testimony I, 410.

80   *Born on the Calhoun:* Biographical data for Alexander Tillman are from U.S. Census for 1870, Grant Parish, LA; Testimony of Harry Lott, House Miscellaneous Documents, 44th Cong., 2nd sess., no. 34, "Recent Election in Louisiana," 350; Testimony of William Ward, ibid., 483; George W. Stafford, "Statement of Colfax Fight," *LD*, May 14, 1873.

81   *Through sheer luck, though:* Watson, "Incident," 2; Kate Kingston Boyd Grant, 29–31.

81   *Heretofore regarded with suspicion:* Trial Testimony of Thomas Railey, *NODP*, March 10, 1874.

81   *What William Ward didn't know:* Trial Testimony of Jacob Johnson, *NOR*, June 2, 1874.

81   *Then Ward handed:* The following account of Willie Calhoun's abortive trip to New Orleans and his treatment at the hands of his captors is drawn from Manie White Johnson, *The Colfax Riot of April, 1873* (Hemphill, TX: Dogwood Press, 1994), 20–21; "The Riot in Grant Parish," *NOR*, April 10, 1873; "Troubles in Grant Parish," ibid., April 11, 1873; Trial Testimony of William Smith Calhoun, ibid., February 27, 1874.

83   *Alphonse Cazabat had told Nash:* Trial Testimony of Wilson L. Richardson, *NOR*, March 6, 1874.

83   *Sleeping in the woods:* Beckwith Testimony I, 410; Kate Kingston Boyd Grant, 28; Trial Testimony of Sam Davis, *NOR*, May 26, 1874.

83   *They were out to found:* "The Grant Parish Trouble," *NOR* April 26, 1873; Watson, "Incident," 1. The white men of the Red River Valley hardly needed much prompting to leap to this frightening conclusion. But in this particular instance the rumor of a Negro conspiracy to commit mass rape appears to have started with a local planter, Adolph Layssard, who claimed to have overheard his field hands discussing the plot. For confirmation that Layssard was the originator of the inflammatory lie, see Kate Kingston Boyd Grant, 21, and Trial Testimony of A. P. Layssard, *NOR*, June 3, 1874.

83   *Nine Winn Parish men arrived:* Information on Jim Bird and his Winn Parish contingent comes from a database documenting the Confederate military service of the whites who took up arms at Colfax, prepared by the military historian James K. Hogue of the University of North Carolina, Charlotte. Professor Hogue's database, in turn, relies on the following authoritative reference work: Janet B. Hewett, *The Roster of Confederate Soldiers, 1861–1865*, 16 vols. (Wilmington, NC: Broadfoot, 1995). I am grateful to Professor Hogue for providing me a copy of this valuable document (hereafter cited as Hogue Database).

83   *Next to arrive were sixteen:* Watson, "Incident," 2.

84   *The cause of the affair:* "The Riot in Grant Parish," *NODP*, April 8, 1873.

84   *"We are not in possession":* *NOR*, April 8, 1873.

84   *He gave a lurid account:* "Statement of Judge Rutland."

85   *Those meetings, too:* Committee of 70, "History of the Riot," "Condition of the South," 896–97; Beckwith Testimony I, 419.

85   *With Wells standing by:* Kellogg to Williams, November 13, 1873, DOJ Letters from LA; Kellogg Testimony, 263; Testimony of Robert P. Hunter, "Condition of the South," 532; Testimony of Thomas C. Manning, ibid., 577–78.

85   *Kellogg told General William H. Emory:* E. M. Hayes to Emory, April 10, 1873, Letters Received, 1873–77, Department of the Gulf, entry 1969, Record Group 393, National Archives, Washington, DC; Hayes to Emory, April 11, 1873, ibid. (hereafter cited as Gulf Letters Received).

86   *"The opinion was entertained":* "The Trouble in Grant Parish," *NOR*, April 10, 1873.

86   *The next day's* Republican *added:* "Troubles in Grant Parish," *NOR*, April 11, 1873.

86   *Longstreet himself inquired:* Kellogg Testimony, 262–64.

86   *He gave them the commissions:* Record of Commissions.

86   *But Ward urged:* Trial Testimony of William Ward, *NODP* and *NOR*, February 27, 1874; Trial Testimony of Eli H. Flowers, *NOR*, June 5, 1874.

87   *"The Republicans of our parish":* "The Sheriff in Peaceful Possession," *NOR*, April 12, 1873.

87   *That gave Ward:* "Ku Klux Kellogg," *NODP*, April 15, 1873; "Grant Parish," *NOR*, April 15, 1873.

87   *Within an hour, another:* "Ride to Colfax," anonymous typescript memoir, 1, John R. Ficklin Papers, Department of Archives, Louisiana State University, Baton Rouge, LA.

88   *On the evening of the:* Ibid., 1–2; Johnson, 20–21.

88   *But the sheriff, a white Republican:* Secret Service Report II.

88   *So the men proceeded:* Ibid.

88   *On Saturday morning:* Ibid.

88   *Now Nash's growing posse:* "Ride to Colfax," 2.

88   *In lawless times:* John Boardman to Milton A. Dunn, May 17, 1920, Melrose Collection, scrapbook 66, 140; Boardman to Dunn, May 31, 1920, Melrose Collection, bound vol. 5.

89   *By evening, the cannon was:* Wes Horn to Dunn, September 10, 1916, Melrose Collection, folder 237; "The Melrose Cannon," unpublished typescript, Francois Mignon Collection, bound vol. 115, Cammie G. Henry Research Center, Watson Memorial Library, Northwestern State University of Louisiana, Natchitoches, LA; Johnson, 23; author's measurement of the cannon, preserved at the home of Ben Littlepage, Colfax, LA.

89   *Nash and his men cheered:* "Ride to Colfax," 2.

89   *The rumor was that Ward's:* "Statement of Colfax Fight," *LD*, May 14, 1873.

89   *He slapped Jim Hadnot:* Johnson, 19.

CHAPTER FIVE: BLOOD ON THE RED

90   No recounting of armed conflict can ever be totally accurate or objective. The following narrative of the fighting and massacre in Colfax on April 13, 1873, represents a best effort based on the widest possible array of documentary evidence. It would be unwieldy to provide individual notes for each fact in the resulting narrative, except for direct quotations. But my principal source for this chapter is the testimony of witnesses in the two federal trials of the Colfax Massacre defendants in New Orleans during the first half of 1874, as reported near-verbatim in four New Orleans daily newspapers: the *Republican, Daily Picayune, Bulletin*, and *Bee*. Testimony in the first trial lasted from February 26 to March 13, 1874; testimony in the second trial lasted from May 21 to June 5, 1874. (An official transcript was made at each trial, but neither document survived.) In addition, I drew on the following sources: 1860, 1870, and 1880 U.S. Census Reports for

Rapides and Grant parishes, LA; Secret Service Reports I and II; Beckwith Testimony I; Beckwith Closing Argument; Woods Charge; Report of T. W. DeKlyne and William Wright, *NOR*, April 18, 1873; Johnson, *The Colfax Riot of April, 1873;* "Ride to Colfax," John R. Ficklin Papers; Stafford, "Statement of Colfax Fight"; Committee of 70, "History of the Riot"; J. E. Dunn, "About Uncle Tom's Cabin," *Washington Post*, August 31, 1896; Watson, "Incident"—and miscellaneous letters, photographs, remembrances, newspaper clippings, and documents contained in the Melrose Collection at Northwestern State University in Natchitoches, LA, which houses probably the most extensive collection of primary source material on the Colfax Massacre, produced, to be sure, by men and women who sympathized with the victors on April 13, 1873.

90   *The result was a reasonable:* Johnson, 23; Wes Horn to Dunn, September 10, 1916, Melrose Collection, folder 237.

90   *Roughly half of the men:* Hogue Database.

91   *At the end of his:* W. L. Tanner to Milton A. Dunn, June 19, 1924, Melrose Collection, scrapbook 67; Johnson, 21.

92   *"You're nothing but a":* Trial Testimony of Sam Cuney, *NODP*, May 30, 1874.

92   *"According to statements most worthy":* "The Strife in Grant Parish," *NOR*, April 12, 1873.

94   *The main thing was to:* Trial Testimony of Daniel W. Shaw, *NOB*, June 4, 1874.

94   *The ex-slave and the:* The dialogue between Allen and Nash is reconstructed from Report of T. W. DeKlyne and William Wright, *NOR*, April 18, 1873; Trial Testimony of Levi Allen, ibid., March 1 and 3, 1874; Trial Testimony of John Miles, ibid., March 10, 1874.

95   *"There is nothing we can do":* Trial Testimony of Benjamin Brim, *NOR*, May 24, 1874.

95   *He asked his friends and:* Steven Kimball's plea is recorded in John I. McCain, unpublished memoir, Melrose Collection, vol. 3, 158–59. According to McCain, Kimball also told the men assembled at the courthouse, "This is our country, but the negro race is not competent to rule." This seems quite unlikely; Kimball could hardly have expected fellow members of his race to respond favorably to such an insulting appeal. McCain claims that Kimball himself told him this. Either McCain is embroidering Kimball's account, or Kimball was telling a white man what he wanted to hear.

95   *Dan Shaw, in short:* "A Victim of the Colfax Massacre—The Late D. W. Shaw," *NOR*, April 30, 1873. This report of Shaw's demise, reprinted from the *Cincinnati Gazette*, was, of course, premature.

96   *"Old man, go away and":* Beckwith Closing Argument.

96   *"Now you women":* Trial Testimony of Fannie Gibbs, *NOR*, March 3, 1874.

97   *He had kept that promise:* The story of Chaney-Powell—the ex-Union soldier who came up with the decisive stratagem, then sold it to Nash's posse based on his "Confederate" credentials—must be one of the strangest subplots of the Colfax Massacre story. His double identity is confirmed by William B. Chaney's Union Civil War pension file, which lists him as "William B. Chaney, Ezekiel B. Powell (alias)." Carded Military Service Record for William B. Chaney, Ezekiel B. Powell (alias), *General Index to Pension Files, 1861–1934* (National Archives Microfilm Publication T288, Roll 80), Records of the Department of Veterans Affairs, Record Group 15, National Archives, Washington, DC. His arrest and subsequent return to the ranks of Nash's posse is described in Johnson, 20. Louisiana land records from the 1890s show "Ezekiel B. Powell" as the owner of a homestead in the Red River Valley.

98   *"This man is an old":* Johnson, 25.

98   *Some buckshot hit Shewman:* Wes Horn to Dunn, September 10, 1916, Mel-
       rose Collection, folder 237; Entry for Sidney Shewman of Montour, NY,
       p. 5, Enumeration District 186, *Special Schedules of the Eleventh Census
       (1890) Enumerating Union Veterans and Widows of Union Veterans of the
       Civil War* (National Archives Microfilm Publication M123, Roll 54), Rec-
       ords of the Department of Veterans Affairs, Record Group 15, National
       Archives, Washington, DC.
99   *Then he pulled the trigger:* Trial Testimony of Wade Ross, *NOB,* May 27,
       1874.
100   *Tanner went off with:* Johnson, 51n.
100   *"We don't know what's in":* Ibid., 25.
101   *Another white man laughed:* Trial Testimony of Pinckney Chambers, *NOR*
       and *NOB,* May 26, 1874.
101   *White cried, holding:* Trial Testimony of Meekin Jones, *NOR,* March 4, 1874;
       Trial Testimony of James Garrett and William Johnson, *NODP,* May 30,
       1874.
102   *Recognizing Shack White's voice:* Trial Testimony of Thomas Johnson, *NOR,*
       May 29, 1874.
102   *"You are shooting our own":* Trial Testimony of Benjamin Brim, *NOR,*
       March 4, 1874.
102   *"I didn't come 400 miles":* Trial Testimony of Levi Nelson, *NOR,* February
       28, 1874.
103   *"I would just as soon":* Trial Testimony of Benjamin Brim, *NOR,* March 4,
       1874.
103   *He took the man:* Johnson, 27–28.
104   *"What are we to do":* Trial Testimony of Benjamin Brim, *NOR,* March 4, 1874.
104   *"Now we have accomplished":* Johnson, 29.
104   *"If we turn you loose":* Trial Testimony of Benjamin Brim, *NOR,* May 24,
       1874.
104   *The* Memphis Daily Appeal *explained:* "Movements of General Forrest: De-
       tails of the Capture of Fort Pillow," *Memphis Daily Appeal,* May 2, 1864.
105   *When told that one of his:* Howard C. Westwood, "Captive Black Union Sol-
       diers in Charleston," in *Black Flag Over Dixie: Racial Atrocities and
       Reprisals in the Civil War,* ed. Gregory J. W. Urwin (Carbondale: Southern
       Illinois University Press, 2004), 41.
105   *"You won't live to see":* Trial Testimony of Levi Nelson, *NOR,* February 28,
       1874; Trial Testimony of Benjamin Brim, ibid., March 4, 1874.
106   *The line of men moved:* Ibid.
106   *Jones cried, and darted over:* Trial Testimony of Meekin Jones, *NOR,* March
       4, 1874.
106   *Brim knew it was:* Beckwith Testimony III, 413.
107   *He fired at Brim's:* Ibid.; Beckwith Closing Argument.
108   *A white man who laughed:* Trial Testimony of Virginia Davis, *NOR,* March 4,
       1874.
108   *"Go and see your husbands":* Trial Testimony of Rebecca Jones, *NOR,* March
       3, 1874.
108   *At the ruined court house:* Trial Testimony of Virginia Davis, *NOR,* March 4,
       1874.
108   *But after Nash was gone:* Trial Testimony of William Kimball, *NOB* and
       NODP, May 26, 1874.

CHAPTER SIX: BLACK-LETTER LAW

110   *It was the logical place:* Photographs of St. James AME are at John and
       Kathleen DeMajo, "Historic New Orleans Churches," http://www.new

orleanschurches.com/stjamesamc/stjamesamc.htm (accessed August 11, 2007); *The African Methodist Episcopal Church: One Hundred Eighty-Eight Years of Progress—Our Beginning*, pamphlet provided to the author by Dr. Dennis C. Dickerson, executive director, Research and Scholarship, African Methodist Episcopal Church, Nashville, TN.

110   *After the war, he found:* The African American Registry, http://www.aaregistry .com/african_american_history/660/Lawyer_and_politician_Thomas_Chester (accessed August 11, 2007); Harrisburg, PA, http://www.harrisburgcitycalendar .org/pressReleases/prArchives/2004/10/chesterBackground.pdf; George F. Nagle, "Chester Tombstone Dedication," *Harrisburg Patriot News*, September 21, 2002.

110   *It was a rhetorical tour de force:* All quotations of Chester's speech are from "The St. James Chapel: The Colored Men in Council," *NOR*, April 23, 1873.

111   *"I know if I had":* Beckwith Testimony I, 420.

111   *"Protection from repetition in":* Beckwith to Williams, June 11, 1873, DOJ Letters from LA.

112   *And Hoffman had identified twenty-three:* Secret Service Report II. Indictment, *United States v. Columbus C. Nash* [sic] *et al.*, Supreme Court of the United States, Transcript, *United States v. Cruikshank*, no. 339 (hereafter cited as Supreme Court Transcript), 5. The grand jury that returned the indictment was impaneled on May 9, 1873; it was actually the second grand jury to look at the case. Beckwith called in an already-existing grand jury immediately after the massacre, and it concluded that what its foreman called "a most unparalleled act of barbarity" had been committed. But it did not return an indictment because its term expired in late April, before it could identify the culprits by name. *Rapides Gazette*, May 10, 1873.

112   *Manning's plea to Governor Kellogg:* Hoffman grand jury testimony, derived from Secret Service Reports I and II.

114   *The Republican-controlled Congress:* Kaczorowski, 38–61.

114   *In two separate counts:* Foner, 427; *United States v. Hall*, 26 F. Cas. 79 (C.C.S.D. Ala., 1871).

114   *Southworth's approach matched:* Richard L. Aynes, "On Misreading John Bingham and the Fourteenth Amendment," *Yale Law Journal* 103 (Fall 1993), 57–104.

115   *And fighting crime:* The defense lawyers' arguments were summarized in Woods's opinion, *United States v. Hall*, 26 F. Cas. 79 (C.C.S.D. Ala., 1871).

115   *U.S. citizenship was:* All quotations of Woods's opinion are from *United States v. Hall*, 26 F. Cas. 79 (C.C.S.D. Ala., 1871).

116   *Finally, they let him run:* Kaczorowski, 99.

116   *They immediately filed:* Lou Falkner Williams, *The Great South Carolina Ku Klux Klan Trials, 1871–1872* (Athens, GA: University of Georgia Press, 1996), 61–75.

116   *Bond was a Methodist:* Richard Paul Fuke, "Hugh Lennox Bond and Radical Republican Ideology," *Journal of Southern History* 45, no. 4 (November 1979), 569–86.

117   *"It is a power necessary":* "Opinion of the Court," December 7, 1871, U.S. Circuit Court, *Proceedings in the Ku Klux Trials at Columbia, S.C., November Term 1871* (Columbia, SC: Republican Printing, 1872), 89–92. Bond privately expressed "disgust" with Bryan; he felt that the judge was siding with the defense in the Klan cases because South Carolina Democrats had promised him the governorship. Kaczorowski, 53–54.

117   *And their rulings had:* Kaczorowski, 106–7.

117   *The Court's decision concerned:* The following account of *The Slaughterhouse Cases* is derived from Labbé and Lurie, *The Slaughterhouse Cases*; Michael A. Ross, "Justice Miller's Reconstruction: The Slaughter-House

Cases, Health Codes, and Civil Rights in New Orleans, 1861–1873," *Journal of Southern History* 64, no. 4 (November 1998), 649–76; Michael A. Ross, *Justice of Shattered Dreams: Samuel Freeman Miller and the Supreme Court during the Civil War Era* (Baton Rouge: LSU Press, 2003), 189–211.

118 *The Louisiana Supreme Court:* Michael A. Ross, "Obstructing Reconstruction: John Archibald Campbell and the Legal Campaign Against Louisiana's Republican Government, 1868–1873," *Civil War History* 49, no. 3 (September 2003), 235–53.

119 *There, he repeated the arguments:* All quotations and paraphrases of Campbell's brief are from *The Slaughterhouse Cases*, 83 U.S. 36, 45–57.

119 *Justice Samuel Freeman Miller:* Miller's biography, especially his early years as a country doctor and lawyer, is explored in Charles Fairman, *Mr. Justice Miller and the Supreme Court, 1862–1890* (Cambridge, MA: Harvard University Press, 1939), 1–17; Ross, *Justice of Shattered Dreams*, 1–64.

120 *Writing their pronunciamientos*: Ross, *Justice of Shattered Dreams*, 200.

120 *And then he proceeded:* All quotations of Miller's opinion are from *The Slaughterhouse Cases*, 83 U.S. 36, 57–83.

122 *The Republican lawyer who:* Because of their restrictive impact on civil rights, *The Slaughterhouse Cases* rank with *Dred Scott* among the Supreme Court's most criticized rulings. See, for example, Charles L. Black Jr., *A New Birth of Freedom* (New Haven, CT: Yale University Press, 1997), 41–85, in which Black mocks Miller for "blow[ing] a kiss at the recently freed slaves." Yet for many years, historians and constitutional lawyers either failed to account for, or ignored, the fact that this "regressive" ruling was written by a staunchly antislavery member of the Court and supported by its most progressive members—while the lawsuit was brought by a deeply racist, ex-Confederate lawyer with an obvious anti-Reconstruction agenda. Scholars such as Michael A. Ross, Jonathan Lurie, and Ronald M. Labbe have found the solution to this riddle: the ruling was, in Miller's mind, a progressive (or at least moderate) pro-Reconstruction, pro–public health decision.

122 *As one of the four dissenting:* The Slaughterhouse Cases, 83 U.S. 36, 96 (dissenting opinion of Justice Stephen J. Field).

122 *But the Enforcement Act:* Robert H. Marr, Letter to the Editor, *NODP*, May 24, 1873.

123 *He was concerned, he wrote:* Beckwith to Williams, Telegram, April 18, 1873, DOJ Letters from LA.

123 *Beckwith's solution was to:* The following description of Beckwith's indictment is based on: Supreme Court Transcript, 5–57; Beckwith to Williams, October 15, 1874, DOJ Letters from LA.

CHAPTER SEVEN: MANHUNT

127 *Lying in the doctor's house:* Hadnot's physician was one A. Cockerille, who is described in Secret Service Report II as an organizer of the Rapides Parish contingent in the massacre. The description of his probable approach to treating Hadnot, and of Hadnot's condition, is based on the author's interviews with George C. Wunderlich, executive director of the National Museum of Civil War Medicine in Frederick, MD, July 2007; Ira Rutkow, medical historian, New York, NY, November 2007; and Alan Hawk, collections manager of the National Museum of Health and Medicine, Washington, DC, October 2007. The powder burns on Hadnot's clothing were first noted by steamboat passenger R. G. Hill. "War at Last!!" *NOT*, April 16, 1873. Deputy U.S. Marshal T. W. DeKlyne verified the position of the two men's wounds. "From Grant Parish," *NOR*, April 18, 1873.

127   "*Persecuted and hunted down*": "Death of James W. Hadnot," *LD*, April 16, 1873.
127   *As the assembled whites: LD*, April 23, 1873.
128   *Register, fifty-six years old:* Biographical data for Robert C. Register are from 1870 U.S. Census for Grant Parish, LA; Robert C. Register Trial Testimony, *NODP*, May 21, 1874.
128   *If so, they were:* "Further From Grant Parish: Outrages Committed After the Massacre," *NOR*, April 30, 1873.
129   "*They entind to kill*": Tunnell, *Crucible of Reconstruction*, 193; "A true frend" to Marshall Harvey Twitchell, April 16, 1873, Marshall Harvey Twitchell Papers, Louisiana Tech University, Ruston, LA.
129   *The attack from Colfax:* Ted Tunnell, ed., *Carpetbagger from Vermont: The Autobiography of Marshall Harvey Twitchell* (Baton Rouge: LSU Press, 1989), 131–36.
130   *Emory promised to send:* Kellogg to William H. Emory, April 15, 1873, Gulf Letters Received.
130   *The attack on Robert C. Register's:* Emory's frantic effort to get a steamboat is detailed in Gulf Letters Sent. See, for example, W. T. Gentry to Commanding Officer, Baton Rouge, April 15, 1873; Gentry to Commanding Officer, Baton Rouge, April 16, 1873; Gentry to Commanding Officer, Baton Rouge, April 17, 1873 (two letters); Gentry to Commanding Officer, Jackson Barracks, April 17, 1873; Emory to Assistant Adjutant General, Division of the South, Louisville, KY, April 17, 1873; Emory to Assistant Adjutant General, Division of the South, April 18, 1873; Gentry to Commanding Officer, Baton Rouge, April 18, 1873.
130   *The village, he wrote:* J. H. Smith to Gentry, April 22, 1873, Gulf Letters Received.
130   *In their absence:* Trial Testimony of Laurinda McKinney and Kit Smith, *NOR*, March 1, 1874.
131   *As a precaution:* Smith to Gentry, April 26, 1873, Gulf Letters Received.
131   *Before he left, however:* "A Ride with Sheriff Nash," *NODP*, May 3, 1873; Smith to Gentry, April 26, 1873.
131   "*The negroes are rapidly*": Smith to Acting Assistant Adjutant General, Department of the Gulf, April 29, 1873, Letters Received by the Office of the Adjutant General (Main Series), 1871–80 (Washington, DC: National Archives Microfilm Publications M666 roll 93), file 4882 of 1872, Records of the Adjutant General's Office, 1780–1917, Record Group 94, National Archives, Washington, DC.
131   "*We shall not pretend*": *Shreveport Times*, n.d. (reprinted in *NOR*, April 27, 1873).
132   *The statement listed three:* "Later From Grant Parish: How the Grant Parish Negro Rioters Treated a United States Colored Postmaster," *NODP*, May 3, 1873.
132   *He recapitulated what he said:* "A Ride with Sheriff Nash."
132   "*While it is to be*": "A True Statement of the Grant Parish Difficulties," *NODP*, May 22, 1873. The newspaper published the letter with the date April 18, 1873, but its contents make clear that this is a misprint.
133   "*According to the laws*": *NODP*, April 22, 1873.
133   "*In regard to the ferocity*": Stafford, "Statement of Colfax Fight."
133   *(Harris, who had not): LD*, April 23 and May 7, 1873.
134   *If anyone deserved:* "Important Testimony Concerning the Colfax Massacre [Special Correspondence of the *Cincinnati Times and Chronicle*]," *LD*, May 21, 1873. These reports were quickly echoed in the *New Orleans Republican*. See *NOR*, April 30, 1873. The historian Joel M. Sipress identified the source of the Cincinnati newspaper's scoop as Robert A. Hunter, a respected

Alexandria lawyer with deep roots in the Rapides Parish Democratic Party but a strong independent streak. His son, Robert P. Hunter, was a leader of the white supremacists in the Red River Valley and a prominent apologist for the Colfax Massacre. Sipress, "Triumph of Reaction," 371. The reports that a "gentleman" of Rapides had blamed Hadnot's death on his own men caused Robert P. Hunter acute embarrassment, and he went to great lengths to deny them publicly, noting that he wanted to avoid an "erroneous impression that would do great injustice to one who is nearly related to" himself. *LD*, May 21, 1873. Notably, too, on April 26—while Robert A. Hunter was in New Orleans meeting with Kellogg, the *New Orleans Republican* published a version of events very similar to that of the Cincinnati paper. "The Grant Parish Trouble: A Short Statement of the Origin," *NOR*, April 26, 1873. Robert A. Hunter never denied being the source. He was called to testify before Beckwith's grand jury in New Orleans but did not comment publicly on what he said. One report said that he "declined to turn informer." *Rapides Gazette*, May 17, 1873.

134   *Federal troops followed:* Taylor, 274–75.

135   *As it was driving away:* "Louisiana: The Recent Troubles in City and State," *NYT*, May 16, 1873; Gonzales, 421–22.

135   *Kellogg echoed that view:* Dawson, 149.

135   *Invoking his constitutional authority:* Grant, *Papers*, vol. 20, 121–23.

135   *On May 31, McEnery yielded:* "Louisiana: The Outstanding Parties at Peace," *NYT*, June 9, 1873.

136   *His testimony could have helped:* Lewis Meekins's death on June 10, 1873, is reported in Record of Commissions, entries for Grant Parish police jurors. The date of the police jury meeting is from Police Jury Minutes.

136   *Shaw appears to have remained:* Shaw trial testimony, *NOR*, March 6, 1874.

136   *He denounced the "riotous" Negroes:* "Statement of D. W. Shaw," *NODP*, May 6, 1873.

136   *On June 1, Hoffman:* Secret Service Reports I and II.

136   *But, as he wrote:* Beckwith to Williams, June 11, 1873, DOJ Letters from LA (letter sent by mail).

137   *Hoffman reported that Paul Hooe:* Secret Service Report II.

137   *The need for mounted troops:* Beckwith to Williams, June 11, 1873, DOJ Letters from LA (letter delivered by John J. Hoffman).

137   *"If this cannot be done":* Beckwith to Williams, June 11, 1873, DOJ Letters from LA (letter sent by mail).

138   *George Henry Williams was born:* Biographical data for George H. Williams are derived from George H. Williams, "Reminiscences of the United States Supreme Court," *Yale Law Journal* 8 (October 1898–June 1899), 300; Homer Cummings and Carl McFarland, *Federal Justice: Chapters in the History of Justice and the Federal Executive* (New York: Macmillan, 1937), 272–93; Charles Henry Carey, *History of Oregon* (Chicago-Portland: Pioneer Historical Publishing, 1922), 527–31; *DAB*, s.v. "Williams, George Henry"; *American National Biography*, s.v. "Williams, George Henry."

139   *Secretary of State Hamilton Fish:* Foner, 458.

139   *Williams, a West Coaster:* Ibid.

139   *Working through the backlog: Annual Report of the Attorney General for the Year 1871* (Washington, DC: Government Printing Office, 1872), 27; *Annual Report of the Attorney General for the Year 1872* (Washington, DC: Government Printing Office, 1873), 3.

140   *In the second half of:* Kaczorowski, 81, 88.

140   *Williams added, somewhat contradictorily:* Williams to James M. Blount, April 15, 1873, DOJ Letters Sent.

141   *"If those persons who were":* Williams to Beckwith, June 16, 1873, DOJ Letters Sent.

141   *In fact, within two weeks:* Dawson, 151.

142   *In January 1873, Kellogg:* "J. Ernest Breda, Attorney," *Biographical and Historical Memoirs*, 325.

142   *He was pleased when:* The following account of J. Ernest Breda's effort to prosecute the Colfax Massacre perpetrators, and the violence that ensued, is derived from his August 11, 1873, letters to Beckwith, Packard, and Williams, all in J. Ernest Breda Letters, Special Collections, Manuscript Department, Howard-Tilton Memorial Library, Tulane University, New Orleans, LA.

143   *More recently, Packard had helped:* Tunnell, 129–30, 237.

144   *All Washington had to do:* Packard to Williams, September 6 and 10, 1873, DOJ Letters from LA; Packard to Emory, September 10 and 12, 1873, Gulf Letters Received.

144   *Attorney General Williams conveyed:* W. W. Belknap to George H. Williams, September 11, 1873, Letters Received by the Department of Justice from the War Department, 1871–84 (hereafter cited as DOJ Letters from War), Records of the Department of Justice, Record Group 60, National Archives, College Park, MD. Belknap's technical objection was that if the army sold its supplies, the proceeds would revert directly to the treasury and would not be available for the army to buy replacement stocks.

144   *His troops would be happy:* Emory to Packard, September 14, 1873, Gulf Letters Sent; Dawson, 152–53.

144   *On October 16, Williams:* Belknap to Williams, October 15, 1873, DOJ Letters from War; Williams to Beckwith, October 16, 1873, DOJ Letters Sent.

145   *It might be too little:* J. H. Smith, Special Order 37, October 23, 1873, Camp Canby LA, entry 6, Special Orders, Department of the Gulf, Record Group 393, National Archives, Washington, DC; J. H. Smith, Special Order 40, October 31, 1873, ibid.

145   *Aware of how desperate:* LD, May 21, 1873.

145   *Kellogg had to pay:* "Affairs in Louisiana: Gov. Kellogg's Check-Book," *NYT*, September 28, 1874.

145   *In the cotton fields:* Dosia Williams Moore, *War, Reconstruction and Redemption on Red River: The Memoirs of Dosia Williams Moore*, ed. Carol Wells (Ruston, LA: McGinty Publications, 1990), 76.

146   *As soon as word reached:* Shreveport Times, November 2, 1873.

146   *The would-be judge:* Ibid.

146   *Oscar Watson, the young man:* Oscar W. Watson to Milton A. Dunn, October 18, 1921, Melrose Collection, folder 309.

146   *Farther north, in Winn Parish:* Johnson, 30.

146   *At the first indication:* Moore, 78.

146   *Having heard a few stray:* DeKlyne to Smith, October 23, 1873, Record Group 393, National Archives, Washington, DC.

147   *DeKlyne left his deputy:* Shreveport Times, November 2, 1873.

147   *Apparently Hule was:* NOT, November 15, 1873. Hule was a Confederate veteran, well known in the community. Joining DeKlyne's posse as an informer earned him the hatred of the entire Red River Valley. LD, April 1, 1874; ibid., November 18, 1874.

147   *When they arrived, DeKlyne:* NOT, November 15, 1873.

147   *They found him calmly sitting:* Shreveport Times, November 2, 1873.

147   *DeKlyne placed all six:* NOT, November 15, 1873.

148   *After ransacking the house:* Kellogg to Williams, November 13, 1873, DOJ

Letters from LA; *LD*, November 26, 1873; G. F. Towle to Assistant Adjutant General (enclosing Vernou's report), November 3, 1873, Camp Canby, LA, Post Letters May 1873–November 1873, part 5, entry 1, vol. 1 of 3, Department of the Gulf, Record Group 393, National Archives, Washington, DC (hereafter cited as Camp Canby Letters).

148   *"We all believe":* "Louisiana: Alleged Outrages by the Metropolitan Police," *Chicago Daily Tribune*, November 3, 1873.

148   *The U.S. House investigated: LD*, November 5, 1873.

148   *The assembly called for:* Ibid.

149   *It would help, Vernou noted:* Towle to Assistant Adjutant General.

149   *But he confirmed that:* Ibid.

149   *In fact, the* New Orleans Republican*:* "The Outrage in Grant Parish," *NOR*, November 6, 1873.

149   *Thomas Montfort Wells believed:* T. M. Wells, Letter to the Editor, *LD*, November 26, 1873.

149   *There, not far from:* Notes accompanying photograph of lynching site, Melrose Collection, scrapbook 67, 53; *Baltimore Sun*, November 14, 1873.

149   *Still, the posse managed: LD*, October 29, 1873; *NOT*, November 15, 1873.

150   *"They are between":* "Bee" to "Darling," n.d., Melrose Collection, folder 356B.

150   *In the coming days:* Johnson, 30.

151   *He left for New Orleans:* "Use of the Army," 168; *NOR*, November 11, 1873.

151   *"We deeply sympathize": LD*, November 5, 1873.

151   *With these angry words:* Moore, 76; "Use of the Army," 342; Testimony of J. Madison Wells, "Condition of the South," 108.

153   *The conflict was:* Testimony of James Forsythe, "Condition of the South," 377–84.

153   *But each time, the suspects:* G. F. Towle to Adjutant General of the Department of the Gulf, November 13, 1873, Camp Canby Letters.

153   *A U.S. Army offficer:* Ibid.

CHAPTER EIGHT: LOUISIANA ON TRIAL

154   *There were two strong:* Description of the Orleans Parish Prison based on text and a line drawing in Jewell, n.p.

154   *They took them to:* "Our Modern Bastille," *NODP*, January 18, 1874.

155   *Clement Penn noted:* "The Prisoners on the Ozark: Their Statements," *NOT*, November 15, 1873.

155   *Nothing came of it:* Taylor, 276–79.

155   *After the war:* Biographical data for Robert Hardin Marr are from J. Curtis Waldo, *Illustrated Visitor's Guide to New Orleans* (New Orleans, LA, 1879), 184–86.

156   *But while Nash wandered:* Biographical data for E. John Ellis are from Luana Henderson, "E. John Ellis Diary, Mss. 2795, Inventory," Louisiana and Lower Mississippi Valley Collections, Special Collections, Hill Memorial Library, Louisiana State University, Baton Rouge, LA.

156   *The* New Orleans Bee *described: Bee*, March 13, 1874.

156   *By 1872, he had gone:* 1880 U.S. Census for Orleans Parish, LA; Testimony of William R. Whitaker, "Condition of the South," 61–62.

157   *A January 18, 1874, story:* "Our Modern Bastille," *NODP*, January 18, 1874.

157   *With newspapers urging readers:* "Report of the Treasurer of the Grant Parish Prisoner Fund," *NOR*, June 28, 1874.

157   *In Alexandria, the town's: LD*, February 18, 1874.

157   *The Shakespeare Club and: NODP*, February 22 and March 13, 1874.

157   *Thanks to the donations:* J. B. Stockton to W. B. Woods, March 23, 1874, in Nash Case File.

157   *The defense team was not: LD*, February 18, 1874.

158   *The name of Jesse McKinney:* Petition delivered by John D. McEnery to President Ulysses S. Grant, February 25, 1874, and forwarded to the Attorney General, Letters from the President, 1871–84, Records of the Department of Justice, Record Group 60, National Archives, College Park, MD.

158   *But the menace must:* Beckwith Testimony I, 418.

158   *Beckwith had to supply:* Beckwith to Williams, January 28 and June 19, 1874, DOJ Letters from LA.

158   *The episode probably:* On Williams's nomination as chief justice, see Jean Edward Smith, 560–61; Ross, *Justice of Shattered Dreams*, 214–15; *American National Biography,"* s.v. "Williams, George Henry."

159   *Hers was the role of:* Mrs. J. R. Beckwith, 242, 296.

159   *But their presence might deter:* E. R. Platt to Commanding Officer, Alexandria, LA, November 14, 1873, Gulf Letters Sent.

159   *They arrested sixty-two-year-old: NODP*, January 18, 1874.

160   *Early in his investigation:* Secret Service Report II.

160   *But Shaw was a weak: NOR*, March 6, 1874.

160   *On February 23, 1874: Bee*, February 23, 1874.

161   *For the Negroes from:* For a contemporary description of the Custom House, see *NOR*, May 30, 1875. On the history of the building, see Stanley C. Arthur, *A History of the United States Custom House, New Orleans* (New Orleans: Survey of Federal Archives in Louisiana, 1940).

161   *To the left of:* Photographs of the Custom House courtroom's interior are in *NODP*, July 9, 1916. A sketch of the exterior as it appeared in 1872 is in *Jewell's Crescent City Illustrated.*

162   *"Much popular interest": NODP*, February 22, 1874.

162   *Woods's ruling in:* Biographical data for William B. Woods are derived from *Dictionary of National Biography*, s.v. "Woods, William Burnham"; *National Cyclopedia of Biography*, s.v. "Woods, William Burnham"; Thomas E. Baynes Jr., "Yankee from Georgia: A Search for Justice Woods," *Supreme Court Historical Society Yearbook, 1978* (Washington, DC: Supreme Court Historical Society, 1978), 31–42; *Proceedings of the Bench and Bar of the Supreme Court of the United States: In Memoriam William B. Woods* (Washington, DC: Government Printing Office, 1887); *The Supreme Court Justices: Illustrated Biographies, 1789–1993* (Washington, DC: Congressional Quarterly, 1993), 221–25.

162   *The trial had been:* Beckwith to Williams, January 28, 1874, DOJ Letters from LA.

162   *Beckwith had insisted:* Ibid.; Beckwith to Williams, June 19,1874, DOJ Letters from LA.

163   *And that would be: NODP*, February 24, 1874.

164   *Yet under Woods's direction:* Ibid., February 25, 1874.

165   *He worked for the federal:* Jurors' names, with various spellings, are in accounts of the New Orleans newspapers and Supreme Court Transcript, 59. Biographical data on the jurors are derived from the U.S. Census for the period, Civil War military service records, and Committee of 70, "History of the Riot," 900.

166   *They may even have: NOR*, February 26, 1874; *NODP*, February 26, 1874.

167   *But when he returned: NOR*, February 26, 1874.

167   *He emphatically identified:* Ibid., February 27, 1874.

167   *William Ward, who had been:* Ibid.

167   *He said that his: NOR*, March 1 and 2, 1874.

168   *Cruikshank. Irwin. Penn:* Ibid., February 28, 1874.
168   *"As he did so":* "Jottings in the Grant Parish Trial," *NOR*, March 1, 1874.
168   *Alabama Mitchell testified: NOR*, February 28, 1874.
168   *She unhesitantly pointed:* "Jottings in the Grant Parish Trial," *NOR*, March 1, 1874.
169   *It was only fair: NODP*, February 27, 1874.
169   *He also denied that the Negroes:* Ibid.
170   *"Questions as to distance": NOR*, February 28, 1874.
170   *"Nothing," Elzie responded:* Ibid.
170   *When Whitaker shoved a piece: NOR*, March 3, 1874.
171   *But that was as far:* Ibid., March 4, 1874.
171   *And then, after seven long:* Ibid.
171   *Charles Smith, the white Republican: NOR*, March 6, 1874.
171   *O. J. Butler and Sam Cuney: NODP*, March 10, 1874; *NOR*, March 10, 1874.
172   *Penn watched the battle: NOR*, March 7 and 8, 1874; *NODP*, March 7 and 8, 1874.
172   *After this, he saw: NODP*, March 10, 1874; *NOR*, March 10, 1874.
172   *There was abundant evidence: NODP*, March 7, 1874.
173   *Beckwith believed in the old:* Beckwith Closing Argument.
173   *Richard Grant, for example: NOR*, March 8, 1874.
174   *"I do, sir":* Verbatim excerpt of J. C. Morantini's trial testimony, "Condition of the South," 854–56.
174   *"The colored men were not":* This account of Shaw's direct testimony and cross examination is from *NODP*, March 6, 1874, and *NOR*, March 6, 1874.
175   *But whatever the letter's origins: NOR*, September 10, 1873.
176   *But it might have helped: NODP*, March 11, 1874.
177   *Woods ruled the newspaper out: NOR*, March 11, 1874.
177   *Sensing its potential: NODP*, March 11, 1874.
177   *"Flowers did all my writing":* Ibid.; *NOR*, March 11, 1874.
178   *The* Daily Picayune *told its: NODP*, March 13, 1874.
178   *When Woods gaveled court to order: NOR*, March 12, 1874.
178   *The U.S. marshal rented:* Ibid., March 15, 1874.
178   *The prisoners, by contrast:* Ibid., March 12, 1874.
179   *Probably Beckwith was conserving:* Ibid.
179   *But a guilty verdict: Bee*, March 12, 1874.
180   *The pro-defense* New Orleans Bee: Ibid.; *Bee*, March 13, 1874; *NOR*, March 13, 1874.
180   *"You don't need the brilliance": Bee*, March 13, 1874.
180   *"If that's true, then what":* Ibid.
180   *"His words produced a profound":* Ibid.
181   *Every seat was still occupied: NOR*, March 13, 1874.
182   *Though the jurors had not: Bee*, March 12, 1874.
183   *And at 10:40 p.m.:* Beckwith Closing Argument.
185   *"And I pray God":* Woods Charge, 856–65.
185   *It was just after noon: NOR*, March 14, 1874.

CHAPTER NINE: A JUSTICE'S JUDGMENT

186   *The jury stayed mute: NOR*, March 15, 1874.
186   *"Am exhausted and sick":* Beckwith to Williams, Telegram, March 14, 1874, DOJ Letters from LA.
186   *But Williams, still pinching:* Beckwith to Williams, n.d., March 1874, DOJ Letters from LA.
186   *At the same time: NOR*, March 17, 1874.
187   *There had been "but little":* Ibid.; "Condition of the South," 900.

187   William Ward, a "full-blooded": Committee of 70, "History of the Riot," 891, 894.
187   Beyond that the judge: NODP, March 28, 1874.
188   The show netted $1,073.95: "Report of the Treasurer of the Grant Parish Prisoner Fund," NOR, June 28, 1874.
188   This, "Civis" argued: NODP, April 18, 1874.
188   A Republican reported the attack: "A Republican" to Packard, April 6, 1874, in "Use of the Army," 338.
188   The Daily Picayune noted: NODP, May 19, 1874.
188   "On its very face": NOB, May 19, 1874.
189   He was sure to get: H. T. Lawler to President Ulysses S. Grant, n.d., forwarded to the Attorney General, Letters from the President, 1871–84, Records of the Department of Justice, Record Group 60, National Archives at College Park, College Park, MD.
189   Arriving in New Orleans: Diary of Joseph P. Bradley (hereafter cited as Bradley Diary), Entries for May 14–18, 1874, Joseph P. Bradley Papers, Manuscript Collection, New Jersey Historical Society, Newark, NJ.
189   The oldest of twelve children: Biographical material on Joseph P. Bradley is derived from Leon Friedman and Fred L. Israel, eds., The Justices of the United States Supreme Court: Their Lives and Major Opinions, vol. 2 (New York: Chelsea House, 1979), 580–99; Charles Fairman, "The Education of a Justice: Justice Bradley and Some of His Colleagues," Stanford Law Review 1, no. 2 (January 1949), 217–55; Jonathan Lurie, "Mr. Justice Bradley: A Reassessment," Seton Hall Law Review 16 (1986), 343–75; Clare Cushman, ed., The Supreme Court Justices: Illustrated Biographies, 1789–1993 (Washington, DC: Congressional Quarterly, 1993), 201–5; Ruth Ann Whiteside, "Joseph Bradley and the Reconstruction Amendments" (PhD diss., Rice University, 1981).
191   "Calculating the transit of": George Williams, 303.
191   And New Jersey, Bradley's adopted home state: Daniel R. Ernst, "Legal Positivism, Abolitionist Legislation, and the New Jersey Slave Case of 1845," Law and History Review 4, no. 2 (Autumn 1986), 340.
191   The only dissent came: Ibid., 353–56.
192   Bradley, who regarded abolitionists: Charles Bradley, ed. Miscellaneous Writings of the Late Hon. Joseph P. Bradley (Newark: Hardham, 1901), 98–102.
192   "I do not care": Ibid., 134, 137.
192   "This is the great question": Bradley to "My dear daughter," April 30, 1867, MG 26, box 3, correspondence 1867, Bradley Papers.
192   Bradley granted Campbell a: Live-Stock Dealers' & Butchers' Ass'n v. Crescent City Live-Stock Landing & Slaughter-House Co. et al., 15 F. Cas. 649 (C.C.D.La., 1870). Bradley's involvement in Slaughterhouse began in May 1870, less than two months after his confirmation by the Senate, when he was riding circuit for the first time. Just a few weeks earlier, the Supreme Court of Louisiana had upheld the slaughterhouse law. Now the lawyers for the butchers wanted to appeal to the U.S. Supreme Court. That required a "writ of error" from their circuit judge or, if he happened to be there, the circuit justice. Providentially for them, Bradley was in Galveston, Texas, so, on May 13, the butchers' legal team brought him the necessary paperwork—and the justice signed it. Bradley took a steamer to New Orleans, which he reached on May 27. Both sides in the case asked him whether the state would have to suspend enforcement of the slaughterhouse law until the Supreme Court ruled. Bradley wasn't sure; he urged the parties to take that question to the full Court, too. In the resulting confusion, the state militia launched a crackdown on unauthorized butchers, and soon police and butchers were fighting in the streets, surrounded by rotting cartloads of confiscated meat. Campbell returned to Bradley, de-

manding an injunction to prevent Louisiana from enforcing its law until the Supreme Court ruled on his clients' appeal. Bradley scheduled oral arguments on the motion for June 9. He would conduct the hearing in tandem with Fifth Circuit Judge William B. Woods. On the night before the scheduled hearing, the Butchers' Association held a noisy rally on Canal Street, and the courtroom was crowded for the hearing. Campbell argued that the Civil Rights Act and the Fourteenth Amendment were not intended exclusively for the benefit of Negroes but protected all men's "right to labor" and "right to equality." At first, Bradley did not quite know what to do. In an oral ruling, he agreed with Campbell that the slaughterhouse law was unconstitutional, but said that he could not prevent its enforcement because of a "technical objection." Possibly, Bradley was trying to offer something for everyone on his first trip to his new circuit, but it just didn't add up. Surely the New Orleanians who had thronged the streets and the courtroom expected more. The very next day, Bradley changed his mind. "This portion of the opinion," he announced, "had not been put in writing at the time and was somewhat hastily expressed." "On a more careful examination," he continued, the butchers were entitled to an injunction after all. Bradley's overnight switch made him a hero among the whites of New Orleans. The *Bee* called his revised decision "luminous." The *Daily Picayune* said it was "one of the ablest that has ever been delivered from the bench." Labbé and Lurie, 148.

192   *Bradley admired the white supremacist:* Labbé and Lurie, 108.
192   *His opinion echoed not only: The Slaughterhouse Cases*, 83 U.S. 36, 120 (dissenting opinion of Justice Joseph P. Bradley).
193   *The* Daily Picayune *mockingly reported:* NODP, May 19, 1874.
193   *"The facts that you have":* NOB, May 19, 1874.
193   *Beckwith occasionally consulted:* Ibid., May 20, 1874.
194   *The defense rejected a police:* Names of dismissed jurors are from *NOR*, May 20, 1874. Their biographical data are from ibid.; NO Directories; U.S. Census Records for 1850–80.
194   *Only three jurors:* Names of jurors are from *NOR*, May 21, 1874. Biographical information is derived from *NOR*, May 20, 1874; NO Directories; U.S. Census for Orleans Parish, LA, 1850–80.
194   *In 1870 he told the:* Florville Foy's biographical data are derived from: U.S. Census for Orleans Parish, LA, 1850 and 1870; Patricia Brady, "Florville Foy, F.M.C.: Master Marble Cutter and Tomb Builder," *Southern Quarterly* 31, no. 2 (Winter 1993), 8–19.
195   *"We ask that Judge Bradley":* NOB, May 22, 1874.
195   *It was not until the morning:* Ibid.
196   *The defense lawyer could proceed:* Ibid.
196   *In some states, Marr noted:* Ibid.; NODP, May 22, 1874.
197   *For Beckwith, the justice's presence:* Beckwith to Williams, June 25, 1874, DOJ Letters from LA.
197   *Unwilling to decide such: United States v. Avery*, 80 U.S. 251 (1871).
197   *"I will hold myself ready":* NOB, May 23, 1874.
197   *With that, the justice rose and:* Bradley Diary, Entries for May 23, 1874.
197   *Beckwith was angry:* Beckwith to Williams, June 25, 1874, DOJ Letters from LA.
198   *Their lives, Marr told the:* "Letter from New Orleans," LD, May 27, 1874.
198   *"Apparently bringing forward these":* NODP, May 29, 1874.
198   *Some thirty-two prosecution witnesses:* Ibid.
198   *One of his new witnesses: NOR*, May 26, 1874.
198   *The defense team countered:* Defense witness count derived from reports of testimony at both trials in the New Orleans newspapers.

198   *"A man who could not": NOR*, May 31, 1874.
198   *Yes, Levi Allen had: NOB*, June 4, 1874.
199   *In the infernal heat:* Ibid., June 3, 1874.
199   *Beckwith's outburst was a gift:* Ibid., May 27, 1874.
200   *Without hesitation, Johnson fingered: NOR*, June 5, 1874.
200   *With this ingenious model: NOB*, June 5, 1874; *NOR*, June 5, 1874.
200   *They stood there: NOB*, June 7, 1874.
200   *Of course, he told the:* Ibid., June 6, 1874.
200   *Earlier in the case: Bee*, May 21, 1874.
200   *Now, though, even the: NODP*, June 6, 1874.
200   *The* Bulletin *conceded that he: NOB*, June 6, 1874.
201   *A flutter of applause: NODP*, June 6, 1874.
201   *In effect, Whitaker was asking: NOB*, June 7, 1874; *NOR*, June 7, 1874.
202   *"He inspired fury and indignation": Bee*, June 9, 1874.
202   *At 6:00 p.m. on June 9: NODP*, June 9, 1874; *NOR*, June 9, 1874.
202   *"The lives of eight white men": NOB*, June 10, 1874.
203   *They had a verdict: Bee*, June 11, 1874; *NODP*, June 11, 1874; *NOR*, June 11, 1874.
203   *He wrote to Attorney General:* Beckwith to Williams, June 25, 1874, DOJ Letters from LA.
204   *The verdict, said the: NODP*, June 14, 1874.
204   *The outcome of the trial: NOB*, July 11, 1874.
204   *The only real question was:* Ibid., July 12, 1874.
204   *When Marr reminded him:* Ibid.
204   *"There will doubtless be":* Beckwith to Williams, June 11, 1874, DOJ Letters from LA.
204   *But it was notoriously easy:* Ibid.; Beckwith to Williams, June 24, 1874, DOJ Letters from LA.
205   *On the morning of June:* Temperatures for the period of the second trial are reported in the *Bee*, various dates, May–June 1874.
205   *Beckwith cabled Bradley:* Beckwith to Williams, June 25, 1874, DOJ Letters from LA.
205   *On he went, through Atlanta:* Bradley Diary, Entries for June 24–26, 1874.
205   *Court would adjourn until: NOB*, June 28, 1874.
206   *Yet, in court, he read:* "Judge Bradley's Manner on the Bench," *NOB*, July 1, 1874.
206   *"The main ground of objection":* All quotations of Bradley's opinion are from *United States v. Cruikshank*, 25 F. Cas. 707 (C.C.D.La., 1874).
206   *The justice dipped the pen:* "Judge Bradley's Manner on the Bench."
207   *And the victim was dead: Blyew v. United States*, 80 U.S. 581, 594.
207   *In his strongest statement:* Ibid., 599.
210   *"A Daniel come to judgment":* "Justice Bradley's Decision," *NOB*, June 28, 1874.
210   *Yes, Bradley answered:* Joseph P. Bradley to William B. Woods, January 3, 1871, MG 26, box 3, Correspondence, 1870–74, Bradley Papers.
211   *"Federal rights," Bradley wrote:* Bradley to Woods, March 12, 1871, MG 26, box 3, Correspondence, 1870–74, Bradley Papers.
211   *"But my opinion on": NOR*, June 28, 1874.
212   *"I am not through":* "Judge Bradley's Manner on the Bench."
212   *Hundreds of people rushed: NOB*, June 28, 1874; *Bee*, June 28, 1874.
212   *The steamer piped a cheery:* "The Grant Parish Prisoners," *Caucasian* (Alexandria, LA), July 4, 1874.
212   *But now, the paper continued:* "The Effect of Judge Bradley's Decision," *NOB*, June 30, 1874.
212   *The* Bulletin *later published: NOB*, July 12, 1874.

212 *Joseph Bradley probably didn't:* Bradley Diary, Entry for June 27, 1874.
213 *He mailed one each:* Ibid., Entries for July 1 and 3, 1874.
213 *He breezily conceded that:* Joseph P. Bradley to Frederick Frelinghuysen, July 19, 1874, Bradley Papers.
213 *"Hard times and heavy taxes":* Jean Edward Smith, 568.
213 *Northern papers that had:* "Justice at Last in Louisiana," *Chicago Daily Tribune*, June 29, 1874.
213 *The would-be governor John McEnery:* Kellogg to Williams, August 26, 1874, DOJ Letters from LA.
214 *The rampage was intended to:* Gillette, 100–3, 139–45; Foner, 528, 558; Frank J. Scaturro, *President Grant Reconsidered* (Lanham, MD: Madison Books, 1999), 80–87.
214 *He grumbled in a letter:* Beckwith to Williams, July 9, 1874, DOJ Letters from LA.
214 *As he probably expected:* Williams to Beckwith, July 14, 1874, DOJ Letters Sent.
214 *Yet unless and until:* Beckwith to Williams, June 25, 1874, DOJ Letters from LA.

CHAPTER TEN: "IF LOUISIANA GOES . . ."
215 *The* Louisiana Democrat *billed the: LD*, July 8, 1874.
215 *"de debil when he gets":* "Wake Up Jake," by George Holman, sheet music, Library of Congress, Performing Arts Reading Room, http://lcweb2.loc.gov/diglib/ihas/loc.music.sm1848.450800/enlarge.html?page=2&size=640&from pageturner&section= (accessed August 11, 2007).
215 *But a new newspaper in: Caucasian*, July 11, 1874.
215 *The anger in them all:* The following account of violence in Grant Parish in the weeks after Bradley's ruling is based on Captain Arthur W. Allyn to Major E. R. Platt, July 27, 1874, DOJ Letters from War; Testimony of Arthur W. Allyn (hereafter cited as Allyn Testimony), "Condition of the South," 155–57.
216 *McCoy had served in a:* Sipress, "Triumph of Reaction," 113–14; Record of Commissions.
216 *Register had no choice but:* Allyn Testimony, 156.
216 *For the rest of the:* Ibid., 157.
216 *And down in St. Martin:* Hogue, 126–27; Rable, *But There Was No Peace*, 132–33.
217 *"If Louisiana goes":* Kellogg to Williams, August 26, 1874, DOJ Letters from LA.
217 *Its first manifesto, published:* Hogue, 125.
217 *The article concluded with:* J. Smith, "Sheriff Nash," *Caucasian*, May 16, 1874.
218 *All six of the murdered:* For a detailed account of the Coushatta Massacre, see Tunnell, *Crucible of Reconstruction*, 173–209.
218 *"Unless protected by military force":* A. P. Field to Williams, Telegram, September 1, 1874, DOJ Letters from LA.
218 *Word of the crisis reached:* Beckwith to Williams, July 18, 1874, DOJ Letters from LA; Williams to Beckwith, July 24, 1874, DOJ Letters Sent.
218 *Beckwith cabled Kellogg that he:* "The Troubles in the South," *Baltimore Sun*, September 7, 1874.
219 *On September 5, Beckwith:* Beckwith to Williams, September 5, 1874, DOJ Letters from LA.
219 *It was up to Attorney:* Beckwith to Williams, Telegram, September 13, 1874, DOJ Letters from LA.
219 *Meanwhile, the attorney general instructed:* Kaczorowski, 156.

219 *On September 13, Kellogg's men:* This account of the White League coup attempt, sometimes known as the Battle of Liberty Place, is based on Hogue, 116–43; Taylor, 291–96; "Condition of the South," 798–844.

219 *"Call out the troops!":* Ibid., 802.

220 *"This is the happiest city":* Jean Edward Smith, 564.

220 *Bill Irwin, out on bail:* "Condition of the South," 779.

220 *The mob gathered weapons:* Ibid.

221 *Allyn ordered his drummer:* Allyn Testimony, 156; Allyn to E. R. Platt, October 2, 1874, House Reports, 43rd Cong., 2nd sess., no. 101, 63–64.

221 *On September 19, the White:* Wheeling (WV) *Daily Register,* September 17, 1874; Hogue, 144–45; Taylor, 295–96.

221 *Compton got the hint:* Allyn to John J. Compton, September 21, 1874; Compton to Allyn, September 21, 1874; Allyn to Platt, October 2, 1874, House Reports, 43rd Cong., 2nd sess., no. 101, 62–64.

221 *Wilson L. Richardson would:* "Condition of the South," 779.

221 *He wrote Williams that the:* Beckwith to Williams, October 17, 1874, DOJ Letters from LA.

222 *The White League, Beckwith explained:* Beckwith to Williams, October 7, 1874, DOJ Letters from LA.

222 *A belief so general that:* Beckwith to Williams, October 17, 1874, DOJ Letters from LA.

222 *He explained that there was:* Williams to Beckwith, October 20, 1874, DOJ Letters Sent.

222 *The officials, represented by the:* For background on this case (*United States v. Reese*), see Robert M. Goldman, *Reconstruction and Black Suffrage: Losing the Vote in Reese and Cruikshank* (Lawrence: University Press of Kansas, 2001), 60–70.

223 *"Any trial in the present":* Beckwith to Williams, October 27, 1874, DOJ Letters from LA.

223 *"Persons hereafter arrested for":* Williams to Beckwith, November 7, 1874, DOJ Letters Sent.

223 *The state registrar of voters:* "Louisiana Affairs," *NYT,* October 12, 1874.

223 *None of them voted:* Allyn Testimony, 157.

224 *From a normal level:* "Use of the Army," 400.

224 *Ultimately, Calhoun only got:* Testimony of James E. Zunts, "Condition of the South," 127–28; Testimony of F. C. Zacharie, "Condition of the South," 41.

224 *They set the place on:* LD, November 18, 1874; S. Van Dusen to Packard, "Use of the Army," 402; E. S. Godfrey to Platt, November 16, 1874, in Senate Executive Documents, 43rd Cong., 2nd sess., no. 17, 21–22; Testimony of William Ward, House Miscellaneous Documents, 44th Cong., 2nd sess., no. 34, 120.

224 *William Ward, indicted for his:* Godfrey to Platt; Sipress, "Triumph of Reaction," 131–32.

224 *"And the same remark applies":* Godfrey to Platt.

225 *Angry whites threatened to kill:* Affidavit of William B. Phillips, "Use of the Army," 402.

225 *Those would have to be:* Taylor, 304.

225 *Among the colored students forced:* Hogue, 146.

225 *The situation was "volcanic":* Beckwith to Williams, December 11, 1874, DOJ Letters from LA.

226 *"Treat the negro as a":* Jean Edward Smith, 565.

226 *At 2:00 p.m., soldiers escorted:* Taylor, 304–5; Hogue, 148–50.

227 *"I think that the terrorism":* Hogue, 150.

227 *Grant's reaction was favorable:* Jean Edward Smith, 566.

227   *Senator Carl Schurz:* Ibid.

228   *Best of all:* Beckwith to Williams, January 9, 1875, DOJ Letters from LA.

228   *"Fierce denunciations ring through":* Grant, *Papers*, vol. 26, 7.

228   *But the pact held:* Foner, 555; Hogue, 154–57.

CHAPTER ELEVEN: THE COURT SPEAKS

229   *The project had bankrupted:* Michael Farquhar, "The City's Pretty New Face: 'Boss' Shepherd Got the Job Done—at a Steep Price," *Washington Post*, November 28, 2000.

230   *"The constitutional right of Congress":* Congressional Record, vol. 2, pt. 5, 43rd Cong., 1st sess. (Washington, DC: Government Printing Office, 1876), 4782–86.

230   *It was the same hallowed:* Descriptions of the Supreme Court chamber in 1875 are derived from: U.S. Senate, "Old Senate Chamber, 1810–1859," online version of brochure, http://www.senate.gov/artandhistory/art/resources/pdf/Old_Senate_Chamber.pdf (accessed July 30, 2007); http://www.latrobesamerica.org/members/capitol.htm (accessed July 30, 2007); Office of Senate Curator, *United States Senate Catalogue of Graphic Art* (Washington, DC: Government Printing Office, 2006), 10, 60, 75, 79, 86, 97, 101.

231   *At the bench was:* W. H. Smith, "Supreme Court and Its Justices in Days Following the Civil War," *Sunday Star* (Washington, DC), April 22, 1923 (hereafter cited as Smith Memoir).

231   *Yet, of the first four:* On the nomination of Morrison R. Waite as chief justice, and related politics, see Jean Edward Smith, 559–62; C. Peter Magrath, *Morrison R. Waite, The Triumph of Character* (New York: Macmillan, 1963), 8, 12.

231   *The* Nation *said that Waite:* Nation, January 22, 1874.

231   *Ebenezer Rockwood Hoar:* Magrath, 97.

231   *Miller wrote privately that he:* Ibid., 107.

231   *In letters home, Waite:* Ibid., 106.

231   *This was the start:* Ibid., 95, 100; Bruce R. Trimble, *Chief Justice Waite: Defender of the Public Interest* (Princeton, NJ: Princeton University Press, 1938), 262–63. In 1878, Waite wrote, half in jest, to Bradley, regarding an opinion Waite was then writing, "I will take the credit and you shall do the work, as usual." In 1883, apparently in a more serious vein, Waite wrote to Bradley, "There is no one whose help in such matters I value more than yours." Trimble, 263.

232   *Waite's slogan, "Union for":* Magrath, 68.

232   *At Waite's immediate right:* On Justice Nathan Clifford's personality, see Magrath, 103; George Williams, 297; and Smith Memoir.

232   *He had presided over:* Magrath, 104.

232   *Then he would make a:* Smith Memoir.

232   *Of all the justices:* Ibid.

233   *They had met in Iowa:* George Williams, 297.

233   *"He had the shuffling":* Ross, *Justice of Shattered Dreams*, 214.

233   *Citing unspecified "difficulties" with:* United States v. William J. Cruikshank, William D. Irwin, and John P. Hadnot, Brief for the United States, February 11, 1875, 3.

234   *This claim was hardly far-fetched:* Ibid., 7.

234   *And* that *was a valid:* Ibid.

234   *Minor's argument was similar:* Minor v. Happersett, 88 U.S. 162 (1875). Waite wrote in *Happersett* that the post–Civil War amendments had "not added the right of suffrage to the privileges and immunities of citizenship as they existed at the time it was adopted." *Nor* was "suffrage . . . one of the

rights which belonged to citizenship" at the time of the Constitution's adoption, for the very obvious reason that women were citizens, but not allowed to vote. "For nearly ninety years the people have acted upon the idea that the Constitution, when it conferred citizenship, did not necessarily confer the right of suffrage," Waite wrote. Ibid., 171–72.

234   *Late into the night on: Chicago Daily Tribune,* March 31, 1875.

235   *That was all the delay:* Going into the oral argument, the lawyers representing Cruikshank, Hadnot, and Irwin were confident that the full Court would sustain Bradley's circuit court opinion. Philip Phillips, another of the celebrated outside counsel who aided Marr, wrote a friend on March 13, 1875, that he had "little doubt" his side would win. Magrath, 125. In fact, Marr had been agitating for an expedited hearing since the day after the Democratic victory in the November election. On November 4, Marr filed a motion—cosigned by John Archibald Campbell—asking the Supreme Court to schedule argument "on the 5th day of January or some early day in the term." Marr and Campbell cited the "large number of prosecutions [which] are pending in which the same questions arise against other persons," and the fact that his clients "are still subject to the jurisdiction of the circuit court and pray for a speedy determination." R. H. Marr and John A. Campbell, "Motion to Advance Cause," November 4, 1874, in Case File, *United States v. Cruikshank,* no. 339, October Term 1874, Appellate Case Files, Records of the Supreme Court of the United States, Record Group 267, National Archives, Washington, DC. For Marr, the chance to appear before the Supreme Court was about much more than defending his clients. This was Marr's opportunity to shine, to stand up for his region, and to make himself a hero. In contrast to Williams, he had been eagerly awaiting it. "The case is so important to us, I mean the Southern people, that we must make every effort to be heard when the hearing is fixed," he had written to the Supreme Court clerk D. W. Middleton. R. H. Marr to D. W. Middleton, October 23, 1874, in Case File, *United States v. Cruikshank,* no. 339, October Term 1874, Records of the Supreme Court of the United States.

235   *None of the justices bothered: Baltimore Sun,* April 1, 1875.

235   *"All the serious, far-reaching":* "Argument for Defendants of R. H. Marr," *United States v. Cruikshanks* [*sic*], *Irwin, and Hadnot,* February 23, 1875, 30–31.

235   *"The shackles will have fallen":* Ibid., 32.

235   *"The continuance of the state": Baltimore Sun,* April 1, 1875.

236   *Field now lent his awesome:* Field's biography is from U.S. Congress, Biographical Directory of the U.S. Congress, entry for David Dudley Field, http://bioguide.congress.gov/scripts/biodisplay.pl?index=F000104 (accessed August 10, 2007). Field, like Johnson, regularly argued against Reconstruction measures in the courts, usually for free or for a reduced fee. Ross, *Justice of Shattered Dreams,* 124.

236   *But the country had so:* Quotations of Field's argument, unless otherwise noted, are from *The United States against William Cruikshank and Two Others: Argument of Mr. David Dudley Field on Behalf of the Defendants* (New York: John Polhemus, 1875), 1–35.

236   *"If Congress had no right":* The exchange among Miller, Bradley, and Field is from the *Baltimore Sun,* April 1, 1875.

237   *When he addressed the justices:* Smith Memoir.

237   *Each amendment was a modest:* All quotations of Reverdy Johnson's oral argument are from the *Baltimore Sun,* April 2, 1875.

238   *This couldn't be:* All quotations of George H. Williams's oral argument are from the *Baltimore Sun,* April 2, 1875.

242   *As the* Philadelphia Inquirer *put it:* "The Arguments on the Enforcement Law," *Philadelphia Inquirer,* April 5, 1875.

242   *Judge William B. Woods:* Woods to Bradley, December 28, 1874, Bradley Papers, MG26, box 3, Correspondence, 1870–74.

242   *Williams echoed that view:* Everette Swinney, "Enforcing the Fifteenth Amendment, 1870–1877," *Journal of Southern History* 28, no. 2 (May 1962), 208.

243   *But in the twelve-month period: Annual Report of the Attorney General,* December 6, 1875, 22–23.

243   *During the first half of:* Foner, 558.

243   *In October, white forces attacked:* Ibid., 559–60.

243   *He attributed public exhaustion:* Ibid., 560–61.

243   *With a four-to-one:* Ibid., 561–62. For a discussion of the Mississippi election of 1875 and the overthrow of the Adelbert Ames administration, see Nicholas Lemann, *Redemption* (New York: Farrar, Straus and Giroux, 2006), 100–164.

244   *Grant later said Mississippi's new:* Scaturro, 90.

244   *The vote was unanimous:* Morrison R. Waite, Docket Book, October Term 1875, Entry for *United States v. Cruikshank,* Morrison R. Waite Papers, Manuscripts Collection, Library of Congress, Washington, DC (hereafter cited as Waite Papers).

244   *Chief Justice Waite withdrew:* Ibid.; Magrath, 125–26.

244   *"The same person may be":* All quotations of Waite's opinion are from *United States v. Cruikshank,* 92 U.S. 542 (1876).

246   *But, as the* Philadelphia Inquirer: *Philadelphia Inquirer,* March 29, 1876.

247   *Thanking Miller for pointing out:* Magrath, 126.

247   *"I will do my duty":* Fairman, *Mr. Justice Miller,* 374.

247   *But the chief justice:* Hugh L. Bond to Morrison R. Waite, April 4, 1876, Waite Papers; Magrath, 129.

247   *On Election Day:* On the election of 1876 in South Carolina, see Foner, 570–75.

248   *In the resulting deadlock:* On the end of the 1876–77 election standoff in Louisiana, see Tunnell, *Crucible of Reconstruction,* 210; Hogue, 160–79.

248   *Nicholls and Hampton would:* Foner, 580–82.

249   *"The Negro," the* Nation *opined: Nation,* April 5, 1877.

EPILOGUE

251   *Certainly, the unpunished slaughter:* On black voting in the South after Reconstruction, and Republican attempts to protect Negro suffrage, see Robert M. Goldman, *"A Free Ballot and a Fair Count": The Department of Justice and the Enforcement of Voting Rights in the South, 1877–1893* (New York: Fordham University Press, 2001); J. Morgan Kousser, *The Shaping of Southern Politics: Suffrage Restriction and the Establishment of the One-Party South, 1880–1910* (New Haven, CT: Yale University Press, 1974); Michael Perman, *Struggle for Mastery: Disfranchisement in the South, 1888–1908* (Chapel Hill: University of North Carolina Press, 2001); Xi Wang, *The Trial of Democracy; Black Suffrage and Northern Republicans, 1860–1910* (Athens, GA: University of Georgia Press, 1997).

252   *During the next four years:* Wang, 300–301.

252   *As one South Carolina:* Goldman, *"A Free Ballot,"* 81.

252   *In 1884, the Supreme Court: Ex Parte Yarbrough,* 110 U.S. 651.

253   *The Court unanimously struck down: United States v. Harris,* 106 U.S. 629 (1883).

253   *By this time, the Ohioan:* Among the strongest supporters of Woods's nomination was John Archibald Campbell. Baynes, 31–42.

253   *After Grant signed it:* Whiteside, 203.

253 *"When a man has emerged": Civil Rights Cases*, 109 U.S. 3 (1883).

254 *Nine years later, on January 22:* "Quietly Passed Away: Death of Justice Joseph P. Bradley of the Supreme Court," *Washington Post*, January 23, 1892.

254 *Separate accommodations for the two: Plessy v. Ferguson*, 163 U.S. 537 (1896).

254 *"But we made our scheme":* John Russell Young, *Around the World with General Grant*, ed. Michael Fellman (Baltimore: Johns Hopkins University Press, 2002), 336–37.

254 *Their emissaries in Washington:* "The Official Axe: Grant Has Swung It Over Louisiana," *NOT*, March 3, 1877.

255 *The latter case implicated prominent:* On Beckwith's career as a corruption fighter in 1875 and 1876, see "The Retired District Attorney," *NOT*, March 4, 1877; "The New Orleans Whiskey Ring," *NOT*, May 22, 1878; "Fraud's Last Stand," *Washington Post*, August 1, 1878. In his 1877 interview with the *New Orleans Times*, Beckwith suggested that he was fired due to administration unhappiness with his pursuit of the Whiskey Ring cases. Washington also interfered with his attempts to prosecute fraudulent cotton claims. In 1876, Beckwith had secured an indictment against a lawyer named George Taylor for conspiring to cheat the government out of forty thousand dollars by falsely suing over the purported confiscation of one hundred bales of cotton during the Civil War. Edwards Pierrepont, while attorney general, urged Beckwith to back off, but Beckwith refused, even after Pierrepont sent Beckwith a letter of recommendation on Taylor's behalf from a Republican federal judge. "I did all I could to caution the district attorney against rash acts against you," Pierrepoint wrote Taylor in June 1876. Beckwith to Edwards Pierrepoint, February 26, 1876; Beckwith to Pierrepoint, February 29, 1876; Beckwith to Alphonso Taft, June 13, 1876, DOJ Letters From LA; Pierrepoint to George Taylor, June 21, 1876, DOJ Letters Sent.

255 *Early on March 3, 1877:* Beckwith to Taft, Telegram, March 3, 1877, DOJ Letters from LA.

255 *"It is a satisfaction":* Beckwith to Taft, March 3, 1877, DOJ Letters from LA.

255 *"The climate is salubrious":* "The Retired District Attorney," *NOT*, March 4, 1877.

255 *In the late 1870s:* "Louisiana: The Rumored Break," *Chicago Daily Tribune*, June 1, 1880.

255 *In 1882, Beckwith's faction:* "Louisiana: The Congressional Contests," *Chicago Daily Tribune*, September 22, 1882.

256 *In the mid-1880s, he represented:* On Beckwith's representation of the New Orleans water company in the Supreme Court, see, for example, *New Orleans Water Works Co. v. New Orleans*, 164 U.S. 471 (1896). On the telephone case, see Watts van Benthuysen, Letter to the Editor, *NYT*, September 11, 1885; "The Telephone Monopoly," ibid., September 28, 1885; "Crumbs of Comfort for Bell," ibid., June 1, 1886.

256 *James and Catherine Beckwith:* "Departures for Europe," *NYT*, June 9, 1880; "Americans in London," ibid., September 25, 1881.

256 *After Catherine's death in 1895:* In his last weeks, Beckwith left instructions that Mrs. Lapsley be notified in case of his death. "Judge J. R. Beckwith, Who Won Fame As Soldier, Lawyer and Prosecutor, And Was Prominent Despite His Disinclination, Dies in Lonely Old Age," *NODP*, August 9, 1912 (hereafter cited as Beckwith Obituary). The *Daily Picayune* article incorrectly claimed that Beckwith had seen service in "a New York Regiment" and was wounded during the Civil War.

256 *As he aged, he:* Ibid.

256 *In 1880, the federal government:* Motion and Order for Nolle Prosequi, Circuit Court Criminal Docket, no. 11, et al., November 1, 1880, Records of the

U.S. Circuit Court for the Eastern District of Louisiana at New Orleans, Record Group 21, National Archives, Southwest District, Fort Worth, TX.

256 *Bill Cruikshank, who:* 1880 U.S. Census, Rapides Parish, LA; 1880 U.S. Census, Covington County, MS.

256 *A Democratic Party handbill:* "An Address to the Voters of Grant Parish on the Political Issues Involved in the Present Campaign," Melrose Collection, scrapbook 67, 1b.

256 *Willie Calhoun, however, was a spent:* Georgia Weekly Telegraph, May 18, 1875; "Opinion on Motion for New Trial," in *Louisiana v. W. S. Calhoun,* Case No. 505, Louisiana Superior Criminal Court for the Parish of Orleans, Case Records, Criminal Courts Collection, City Archives, New Orleans Public Library. Olivia Williams died in 1881. Family legend—probably apocryphal—holds that she contracted yellow fever, and was buried alive by Willie's sister Ada, who hated her. Author interview with Tybring Hemphill, September 2007.

256 *Calhoun served a term: Biographical and Historical Memoirs of Northwest Louisiana,* 504.

257 *He and his sister Ada:* Certified Copy of Mortgages, docket no. 9137, *M. M. A. Lane v. Robert S. Cameron and Ludlow McNeely,* New Orleans (May 1884), 36 La. Ann. 773, Supreme Court of Louisiana Collection of Legal Archives, Archives and Manuscripts/Special Collections Department, Mss. 106, University of New Orleans, New Orleans, LA.

257 *At the auction, C. C. Nash:* Sipress, "Triumph of Reaction," 151–52.

257 *After Willie Calhoun died:* Ibid., 209–10.

257 *The vast estate that:* Robert C. Register to Kellogg, July 6, 1875, William Pitt Kellogg Papers, Louisiana State University, Department of Archives, Hill Memorial Library, Baton Rouge, LA.

257 *The new sheriff made:* Sipress, "Triumph of Reaction," 135–36.

257 *Soon, Grant Parish officials:* Testimony of William B. Phillips, House Miscellaneous Documents, 44th Cong., 2nd sess., no. 34, pt. 1, 106; Testimony of Harry Lott, House Miscellaneous Documents, 44th Cong., 2nd sess., no. 34, "Recent Election in Louisiana," 349; William B. Phillips, "A Little History of Affairs in Grant Parish," *NOR,* January 3, 1875; *NOT,* July 25, 1875. It appears that the charges against Phillips were intended to silence him because he had accused several legislators of accepting bribes to override Kellogg's veto of a levee bill. Ironically, Alfred Shelby and William Ward were accused, also falsely, of abetting Phillips's purported crime.

257 *William Ward had been expelled:* Testimony of Eli H. Flowers, House Miscellaneous Documents, 44th Cong., 2nd sess., no. 34, "Recent Election in Louisiana," 677–78; Sipress, "Triumph of Reaction," 133.

257 *Packard refused his plea:* Sipress, "Triumph of Reaction," 134; Testimony of William Ward, House Miscellaneous Documents, 44th Cong., 2nd sess., no. 34, "Recent Election in Louisiana," 115–21; Testimony of Eli H. Flowers, ibid., 144; Testimony of Harry Lott, ibid., 349.

257 *In early October, they agreed:* Testimony of William Ward, House Miscellaneous Documents, 44th Cong., 2nd sess., no. 34, "Recent Election in Louisiana," 118; Testimony of Eli H. Flowers, ibid., 144; Testimony of William B. Phillips, ibid., 108.

257 *But, he assured his audience:* "Bloody Colfax," *Colfax Chronicle,* October 14, 1876.

258 *"There is but one style":* "Ward of Grant," *NOB,* October 12, 1876.

258 *But Ward and Phillips were:* State of Louisiana, Secretary of State, Division of Archives, Records Management, and History, *Vital Records Indices* (Baton Rouge, LA), vol. 78, 197.

258 *Phillips died in New Orleans:* "Condition of the South," 89.

258   *Ward remained in New Orleans:* Pension File for William Ward, Records of the Veterans Administration, Records Relating to Pension and Bounty Claims, Record Group 15, National Archives, Washington, DC. Ward and Mary, having formally married in a New Orleans church, relocated to Norfolk, Virginia, in 1880. There, he made a living for a while as a "pension attorney," helping fellow veterans negotiate with the federal government for their benefits. The erstwhile cavalry sergeant also pursued increases in his own pension, which averaged about ten dollars a month, claiming service-related illnesses and injuries based on creative affidavits from his close friends—and one or two that he forged himself. The Pension Bureau in Washington considered Ward a crooked nuisance and disbarred him in 1885. In 1894, Ward spent nine months in jail for pension fraud.

By that time, Ward's past had caught up with him. In 1881, his daughter, Emma, a teenager, had come to Norfolk and confronted Mary, saying that she was Ward's child. Ward denied everything; Mary didn't believe him. She went to see Sarah Pierce in Hampton. Sarah, too, denied that the young woman was Ward's child. But as Ward spiraled deeper and deeper into poverty and his health worsened, he embraced Christianity, and with it, his daughter. She was his only child, since he and Mary had none of their own.

"I know you is my child," he wrote Emma on February 28, 1895, "and I love you as my self and my dear if it weren't for one thing, I would have you living with me or somewhere near where I could see you, and . . . you ain't with me but my child you is my own baby and I love you as I do myself." On April 2, 1895, Ward wrote Emma of his worsening illnesses and of his fear that soon he would be dead. "I do not feel that my soul will be lost," he wrote, "I trust in the lord Jesus Christ. . . . Send your old father your pantagraph so I can have it to look at. Dear Baby, our days are fast winding up. From your father, William Ward."

258   *But it was a special:* The description of the ceremony at Colfax is derived from "Colfax Riot Monument Unveiled," *Colfax Chronicle*, April 14, 1921, and "Monument at Colfax Unveiled," newspaper clipping (possibly from *Alexandria Town Talk*), April 14, 1921, Melrose Collection, scrapbook 67, 29.

259   *The one-thousand-dollar monument, paid for:* "Shaft for Colfax Riot Heroes Will Be Erected," newspaper clipping, n.d., n.p., Melrose Collection, scrapbook 66, 140.

259   *He was by then an:* Newspaper clipping reporting on the absence of C. C. Nash due to "grip," n.p., n.d., Melrose Collection, scrapbook 67, 26.

259   *The project engineer said:* "Skull of Human is Excavated at Colfax," newspaper dated October 1927, n.p., Melrose Collection, scrapbook 67, 12.

260   *Some of the men walked:* Author interview, W. T. McCain Jr., 2007.

260   *In 1965, a college student:* Catherine Wall, "Destruction During Reconstruction: The Colfax Riot, 1873," unpublished term paper, July 29, 1965, on file in Reference Section, Colfax Riot Collection, Grant Parish Public Library, Main Branch, Colfax, LA.

260   *Inevitably, this oral tradition:* "Tragedy at Colfax," *Angolite*, November–December 1989, 50, on file in Reference Section, Colfax Riot Collection, Grant Parish Public Library, Main Branch, Colfax, LA.

260   *In October 1949, Colfax's mayor:* C. Aswell Rhodes to C. E. Frampton, October 19, 1949, Records of the Department of Culture, Recreation and Tourism, Louisiana State Archives, Baton Rouge, LA.

260   *The department agreed, and soon:* Rhodes to Frampton, February 13, 1950, Records of the Department of Culture, Recreation and Tourism, Louisiana State Archives.

260   *"This event on April 13":* "Colfax Riot Marker to be Dedicated June 14," *Colfax Chronicle*, June 8, 1951.

261   *Because of* The Civil Rights Cases: *Heart of Atlanta Motel v. United States*, 379 U.S. 241 (1964).
262   *As precedent, Rehnquist cited: United States v. Morrison*, 529 U.S. 598 (2000), 620–21.
262   *In 1911, eight black men:* "Louisiana Lynchings, 1878–1946": http:// academic.evergreen.edu/p/pfeifer/Louisiana.html (accessed August 27, 2007; "Time Line of African American History, 1901–1925," http://memory .loc.gov/ammem/aap/timelin3.html (accessed August 27, 2007).
262   *Then the valet passed his:* Beckwith Obituary.
262   *This was a wild overstatement:* Ibid.
262   *The estate sale netted $973.72:* James R. Beckwith, will dated January 2, 1905, proved August 15, 1912, Orleans Parish Court of Probates, will book 36, 84, on file in the City Archives, New Orleans Public Library, New Orleans, LA; Succession of James R. Beckwith, Civil District Court, Division "C," case no. 101475, Orleans Parish (New Orleans), LA, filed August 30, 1912, on file in the City Archives, New Orleans Public Library, New Orleans, LA.
263   *The paper noted that his:* Beckwith Obituary; see also "Judge Beckwith Will Be Interred in Metairie Cemetery To-Day," *NODP*, August 10, 1912.
263   *As a scholar, Fairman was:* Charles Fairman, "Does the Fourteenth Amendment Incorporate the Bill of Rights?" *Stanford Law Review* 2, no. 1 (1949), 5–139.
263   *Fairman defended the Supreme Court's:* Charles Fairman, *The Oliver Wendell Holmes Devise History of the Supreme Court of the United States*, vol. 6, *Reconstruction and Reunion, 1864–1888*, part 1 (New York: Macmillan, 1989), 282.
263   *Fairman derided Beckwith as:* Ibid., 276–87; Bradley, 247.

APPENDIX

265   *An 1875 report by:* "Use of the Army," 436–38.
265   *James Beckwith told a:* Beckwith Testimony I, 416.
265   *Over the years, both races:* Milton A. Dunn, a physician and amateur historian, was responsible for much of the exaggeration. The obelisk in the cemetery was Dunn's idea. He arranged for it to be made in a Vicksburg marble yard, and for the "veterans" and the surviving family members to be present at the ceremony in their honor on April 13, 1921. Dunn worshipped Nash, whom he considered "a true type of the Southerner, brave and courageous to a fault." When Nash died, Dunn published a memorial pamphlet that claimed that "after three and a half hours of fighting, 185 white men defeated 800 negroes, killing 168 of them." Dunn, the son of C. C. Dunn, who procured the cannon for Nash's force, was himself a participant in the massacre. See Milton A. Dunn, *Christopher Columbus Nash: A Tribute*, pamphlet printed by the *Colfax Chronicle*, Melrose Collection, scrapbook 69, 129. Dunn kept the little cannon at his plantation home in Melrose, just across the river from Colfax in Natchitoches Parish. It was sold at auction in the 1970s and now stands on the front lawn of Ben Littlepage's farm in Colfax, which formerly made up part of the Calhoun estate. Author interview with Ben Littlepage, Colfax, LA, November 13, 2006.
265   *But Smith did not elaborate:* Smith to Acting Assistant Adjutant General, Department of the Gulf, April 29, 1873. Letters Received by the Office of the Adjutant General (Main Series), 1871–80 (Washington, DC: National Archives Microfilm Publications, M666, Roll 93), file 4882 of 1872, Records of the Adjutant General's Office, 1780–1917, Record Group 94, National Archives, Washington, DC.
265   *But no witness at either:* "Use of the Army," 438.

· SELECTED BIBLIOGRAPHY ·

MANUSCRIPT COLLECTIONS

Grant Parish Public Library, Main Branch, Colfax, LA
    Reference Section, Colfax Riot Collection

Library of Congress, Manuscripts Division, Washington, DC
    Morrison R. Waite Papers

Louisiana State Archives, Baton Rouge, LA
    Parish Maps of Louisiana Captured from Confederates, 1864
    Records of Commissions Issued by the Governor, 1848–1928 (Microfilm)
    Records of the Department of Culture, Recreation and Tourism

Louisiana State University, Department of Archives, Hill Memorial Library, Baton
    Rouge, LA
    John R. Ficklin Papers
    Henry Hyams Papers
    William P. Kellogg Papers
    Layssard Family Papers
    WPA Collection of Parish Police Jury Minutes

Louisiana Tech University, Ruston, LA
    Harvey Marshall Twitchell Papers

National Archives, College Park, MD
    Records of the Department of Justice, Record Group 60
    Records of the U.S. Secret Service, Record Group 87

National Archives, Washington, DC
    Records of the Department of Veterans Affairs, Record Group 15
    Records of the Adjutant General's Office, Record Group 94
    Records of the Bureau of Refugees, Freedmen and Abandoned Lands, Record
        Group 105
    Records of the U.S. Court of Claims, Record Group 123
    Records of the Supreme Court of the United States, Record Group 267
    Records of the U.S. Army, Department of the Gulf, Record Group 393

National Archives, Southwest Region, Fort Worth, TX
    Records of the U.S. Circuit Court for the Eastern District of Louisiana,
        Record Group 21

New Jersey Historical Society, Newark, NJ
  Joseph P. Bradley Papers

New Orleans Public Library
  Records of the Orleans Parish Civil Courts
  Records of the Orleans Parish Criminal Courts

New York Historical Society, New York, NY
  E. H. Durell Papers

Northwestern State University of Louisiana, Cammie G. Henry Research Center,
  Natchitoches, LA
    Melrose Collection

Tulane University, Special Collections, New Orleans, LA
  J. Ernest Breda Letters

University of New Orleans, Special Collections Department
  Supreme Court of Louisiana Collection of Legal Archives, Archives and Man-
    uscripts

University of North Carolina, Southern Historical Collection, Chapel Hill, NC
  William H. Stewart Diary

GOVERNMENT DOCUMENTS: FEDERAL

U.S. Congress. House Miscellaneous Documents, 41st Cong., 1st sess., no. 32: "Pa-
  pers in the Contested Election Case of Newsham v. Ryan."
———. House Reports, 41st Cong., 2nd sess., no. 61, "Newsham v. Ryan."
———. House Reports, 42nd Cong., 2nd sess., no. 92, "Affairs in Louisiana."
———. House Miscellaneous Documents, 42nd Cong., 2nd sess., no. 211, "Testi-
  mony Taken by the Selection Committee to Investigate Affairs in the State of
  Louisiana."
———. House Reports, 43rd Cong., 2nd sess., no. 261, "Condition of the South."
———. House Executive Documents, 44th Cong., 2nd sess., no. 30, "Use of the
  Army in Certain of the Southern States."
———. House Miscellaneous Documents, 44th Cong., 2nd sess., no. 34, "Recent
  Election in Louisiana."
*Proceedings of the Bench and Bar of the Supreme Court of the United States: In Memo-
  riam William B. Woods.* Washington, DC: Government Printing Office, 1887.
Annual Report of the Attorney General of the United States, 1870–1874.

GOVERNMENT DOCUMENTS: STATE

Annual Report of the Adjutant General of the State of Louisiana, 1870–1873.
General Assembly of Louisiana. *Supplemental Report of Joint Committee on the
  Conduct of the Late Elections, and the Condition of Peace and Good Order in the
  State.* New Orleans: A. L. Lee, 1869.

BOOKS

Anderson, Eric, and Alfred A. Moss Jr., eds. *The Facts of Reconstruction: Essays in
  Honor of John Hope Franklin.* Baton Rouge: Louisiana State University Press,
  1991.
Arthur, Stanley C. *A History of the United States Custom House, New Orleans.* New
  Orleans: Survey of Federal Archives in Louisiana, 1940.

Beckwith, Mrs. J. R. *The Winthrops*. New York: Carleton, 1864.

Biographical and Historical Memoirs of Northwest Louisiana. Nashville, TN: Southern Publishing, 1890.

Black, Charles L., Jr. *A New Birth of Freedom*. New Haven, CT: Yale University Press, 1997.

Bradley, Charles, ed. *Miscellaneous Writings of the Late Hon. Joseph P. Bradley*. Newark, NJ: Hardham, 1901.

Carey, Charles Henry. *History of Oregon*. Chicago-Portland: Pioneer Historical Publishing, 1922.

Chambers, Henry E. *History of Louisiana*, Vol. 1. Chicago and New York: American Historical Society, 1925.

City of New Orleans. *The Book of the Chamber of Commerce and Industry of Louisiana*. New Orleans, LA: Engelhardt, 1894.

Cummings, Homer, and Carl McFarland. *Federal Justice: Chapters in the History of Justice and the Federal Executive*. New York: Macmillan, 1937.

Cushman, Clare, ed. *The Supreme Court Justices: Illustrated Biographies, 1789–1993*. Washington, DC: Congressional Quarterly, 1993.

Custer, Elizabeth. *Tenting on the Plains*. New York: Charles L. Webster, 1887.

Davis, William Watson. "The Federal Enforcement Acts." In *Studies in Southern History and Politics*. Port Washington, NY: Kennikat Press, 1964.

Dawson, Joseph G., III. *Army Generals and Reconstruction: Louisiana, 1862–1877*. Baton Rouge: LSU Press, 1982.

Dean, P. A., Jr. *Colfax: Its Place in Louisiana*. Colfax, LA: Dean Art Features, 2003.

DuBois, W. E. B. *Black Reconstruction in America*. New York: Harcourt, Brace, 1935.

Fairman, Charles. *Mr. Justice Miller and the Supreme Court, 1862–1890*. Cambridge, MA: Harvard University Press, 1939.

———. *The Oliver Wendell Holmes Devise History of the Supreme Court of the United States*, Vol. 6, *Reconstruction and Reunion, 1864–1888*, part 1. New York: Macmillan, 1989.

Foner, Eric. *Reconstruction: America's Unfinished Revolution*. New York: Harper and Row, 1988.

Franklin, John Hope. *Reconstruction: After the Civil War*. Chicago: University of Chicago Press, 1961.

Fuchs, Richard L. *An Unerring Fire: The Massacre at Fort Pillow*. Rutherford, NJ: Fairleigh Dickinson University Press, 1994.

Gillette, William. *Retreat from Reconstruction: 1869–1879*. Baton Rouge: LSU Press, 1979.

Goldman, Robert M. *"A Free Ballot and a Fair Count": The Department of Justice and the Enforcement of Voting Rights in the South, 1877–1893*. New York: Fordham University Press, 2001.

———. *Reconstruction and Black Suffrage: Losing the Vote in Reese and Cruikshank*. Lawrence: University Press of Kansas, 2001.

Grant, Ulysses S. *The Papers of Ulysses S. Grant*. Edited by John Y. Simon. 28 vols. Carbondale: Southern Illinois University Press, 1967–2007.

Greene, John Robert. *Generations of Excellence: An Illustrated History of Cazenovia Seminary and Cazenovia College, 1824 to the Present*. Syracuse, NY: Syracuse Litho, 2000.

Hardin, James Fair. *Northwestern Louisiana: A History of the Watershed of the Red River, 1714–1937*. Louisville, KY: Historical Record Association, 1939.

Harrison, Mabel Fletcher, and Lavinia McGuire McNeely. *Grant Parish, Louisiana: A History*. Baton Rouge, LA: Claitor's, 1969.

Hogue, James K. *Uncivil War: Five New Orleans Street Battles and the Rise and Fall of Radical Reconstruction*. Baton Rouge: LSU Press, 2006.

Jewell, Edwin L. *Jewell's Crescent City Illustrated*. New Orleans, LA, 1873.

Johnson, Manie White. *The Colfax Riot of April, 1873*. Hemphill, TX: Dogwood Press, 1994.

Jones, Terry L. *Lee's Tigers: The Louisiana Infantry in the Army of Northern Virginia*. Baton Rouge: LSU Press, 1991.

Kaczorowski, Robert J. *The Politics of Judicial Interpretation: The Federal Courts, Department of Justice, and Civil Rights, 1866–1876*. New York: Fordham University Press, 2005.

Kousser, J. Morgan. *The Shaping of Southern Politics: Suffrage Restriction and the Establishment of the One-Party South, 1880–1910*. New Haven, CT: Yale University Press, 1974.

Kousser, J. Morgan, and James M. McPherson, eds. *Region, Race and Reconstruction: Essays in Honor of C. Vann Woodward*. New York: Oxford University Press, 1982.

Labbe, Ronald M., and Jonathan Lurie. *The Slaughterhouse Cases: Regulation, Reconstruction and the Fourteenth Amendment*. Lawrence: University Press of Kansas, 2003.

Lemann, Nicholas. *Redemption*. New York: Farrar, Straus and Giroux, 2006.

Lonn, Ella. *Reconstruction in Louisiana after 1868*. New York: Knickerbocker Press, 1918.

Magrath, C. Peter. *Morrison R. Waite, The Triumph of Character*. New York: Macmillan, 1963.

McGinty, Garnie W. *Louisiana Redeemed: The Overthrow of Carpet-bag Rule, 1876–1880*. New Orleans: Pelican Publishing, 1941.

Moore, Dosia Williams. *War, Reconstruction and Redemption on Red River: The Memoirs of Dosia Williams Moore*. Edited by Carol Wells. Ruston, LA: McGinty Publications, 1990.

Northup, Solomon. *Twelve Years a Slave*. New York: Miller, Orton and Mulligan, 1855.

Office of Senate Curator. *United States Senate Catalogue of Graphic Art*. Washington, DC: Government Printing Office, 2006.

Olmsted, Frederick Law. *Papers of Frederick Law Olmsted*. Vol. 2, *Slavery and the South, 1852–1857*. Edited by Charles E. Beveridge and Charles Capen McLaughlin. Baltimore: Johns Hopkins University Press, 1981.

O'Neal, John Belton. *Biographical Sketches of the Bench and Bar of South Carolina*. Charleston: Courtenay, 1859.

Perman, Michael, *Struggle for Mastery: Disfranchisement in the South, 1888–1908*. Chapel Hill: University of North Carolina Press, 2001.

Rable, George C. *But There Was No Peace: The Role of Violence in the Politics of Reconstruction*. Athens, GA.: University of Georgia Press, 1984.

Ricks, Mary Kay. *Escape on the Pearl*. New York: William Morrow, 2007.

Ross, Michael A. *Justice of Shattered Dreams: Samuel Freeman Miller and the Supreme Court during the Civil War Era*. Baton Rouge: LSU Press, 2003.

Scaturro, Frank J. *President Grant Reconsidered*. Lanham, MD: Madison Books, 1999.

Smith, George G. *Leaves from a Soldier's Diary*. Putnam, CT: G. G. Smith, 1906.

Smith, Jean Edward. *Grant*. New York: Simon and Schuster, 2001.

Stampp, Kenneth M. The *Era of Reconstruction, 1865–1877*. New York: Vintage, 1965.

Taylor, Joe Gray. *Louisiana Reconstructed, 1863–1877*. Baton Rouge: LSU Press, 1974.

Tompkins, F. H. *North Louisiana*. Cincinnati, OH: A. H. Pugh, 1886.

Trelease, Allen W. *White Terror: The Ku Klux Klan Conspiracy and Southern Reconstruction*. Baton Rouge: LSU Press, 1971.

Trimble, Bruce R. *Chief Justice Waite: Defender of the Public Interest*. Princeton, NJ: Princeton University Press, 1938.

Tunnell, Ted, ed. *Carpetbagger from Vermont: The Autobiography of Marshall Harvey Twitchell*. Baton Rouge: LSU Press, 1989.

————. *Crucible of Reconstruction: War, Radicalism and Race in Louisiana, 1862–1877.* Baton Rouge: LSU Press, 1984.
Urwin, Gregory J. W., ed. *Black Flag Over Dixie: Racial Atrocities and Reprisals in the Civil War.* Carbondale: Southern Illinois University Press, 2004.
Vincent, Charles. *Black Legislators in Louisiana During Reconstruction.* Baton Rouge: LSU Press, 1976.
Wang, Xi. *The Trial of Democracy: Black Suffrage and Northern Republicans, 1860–1910.* Athens: University of Georgia Press, 1997.
Warmoth, Henry Clay. *War, Politics and Reconstruction: Stormy Days in Louisiana.* New York: MacMillan, 1930.
Warren, Charles. *The Supreme Court in United States History.* Vol. 3. Boston: Little, Brown, 1922.
Way, Frederick. *Way's Packet Directory, 1848–1939.* Athens, OH: Ohio University Press, 1983.
White, Howard A. *The Freedmen's Bureau in Louisiana.* Baton Rouge: LSU Press, 1970.
Whitley, Hiram C. *In It.* Cambridge, MA: Riverside Press, 1894.
Williams, Lou Falkner. *The Great South Carolina Ku Klux Klan Trials, 1871–1872.* Athens, GA: University of Georgia Press, 1996.

ARTICLES

Ayres, Richard L. "On Misreading John Bingham and the Fourteenth Amendment." *Yale Law Journal* 103 (Fall 1993), 57–104.
Baynes, Thomas E., Jr. "Yankee from Georgia: A Search for Justice Woods." *Supreme Court Historical Society Yearbook, 1978* (Washington, DC: Supreme Court Historical Society, 1978), 31–42.
Crook, Charles M. "The Barbour County Background to the Election of 1872 and Alabama's Dual Legislatures." *Alabama Review* 56, no. 4 (October 2003), 242–77.
Dauphine, James G. "The Knights of the White Camellia and the Election of 1868: Louisiana's White Terrorists: a Benighting Legacy." *Louisiana History* 30, no. 2 (Spring 1989), 173–90.
Ernst, Daniel R. "Legal Positivism, Abolitionist Legislation, and the New Jersey Slave Case of 1845." *Law and History Review* 4, no. 2 (Autumn 1986), 337–65.
Fairman, Charles. "Does the Fourteenth Amendment Incorporate the Bill of Rights?" *Stanford Law Review* 2, no. 1 (December 1949), 5–139.
————. "The Education of a Justice: Joseph Bradley and Some of His Colleagues." *Stanford Law Review* 1, no. 2 (January 1949), 217–55.
Fuke, Richard Paul. "Hugh Lennox Bond and Radical Republican Ideology." *Journal of Southern History* 45, no. 4 (November 1979), 569–86.
Gonzales, John Edmond. "William Pitt Kellogg: Reconstruction Governor of Louisiana, 1873–1877." *Louisiana Historical Quarterly* 29 (1946), 394–495.
Lurie, Jonathan. "Mr. Justice Bradley: A Reassessment." *Seton Hall Law Review* 16 (1986), 343–75.
McCall, Edith. "Attack on the Great Raft." *American Heritage of Invention and Technology* 3, no. 3 (Winter 1988), 10–16.
Rable, George C. "Republican Albatross: The Louisiana Question, National Politics and the Failure of Reconstruction." *Louisiana History* 9 (Summer 1982), 109–30.
Roche, John P. "Civil Liberty in the Age of Enterprise." *University of Chicago Law Review* 31, no. 1 (Autumn 1963), 103–35.
Ross, Michael A. "Justice Miller's Reconstruction: *The Slaughter-House Cases*, Health Codes, and Civil Rights in New Orleans, 1861–1873." *Journal of Southern History* 64, no. 4 (November 1998), 649–76.

————. "Obstructing Reconstruction: John Archibald Campbell and the Legal Campaign Against Louisiana's Republican Government, 1868–1873." *Civil War History* 49, no. 3 (September 2003), 235–53.

Sipress, Joel M. "From the Barrel of a Gun: The Politics of Murder in Grant Parish." *Louisiana History* 42, no. 3 (Summer 2001), 303–21.

Swinney, Everette. "Enforcing the Fifteenth Amendment, 1870–1877." *Journal of Southern History* 28, no. 2 (May 1962), 202–18.

Williams, George H. "Reminiscences of the United States Supreme Court." *Yale Law Journal* 8 (October 1898–June 1899), 296–305.

NEWSPAPERS

Alexandria (LA) Caucasian
Alexandria (LA) Louisiana Democrat
Alexandria (LA) Rapides Gazette
Baltimore Sun
Boston Globe
Chicago Daily Tribune
Colfax (LA) Chronicle
Grant Parish (LA) Enterprise
Natchitoches (LA) People's Vindicator
New Orleans Bee
New Orleans Bulletin
New Orleans Daily Picayune
New Orleans National Republican
New Orleans Republican
New Orleans Semi-Weekly Louisianian
New Orleans Times
New York Herald
New York Times
Philadelphia Inquirer
Shreveport Times
Washington Evening Star
Washington Post

THESES AND DISSERTATIONS

Sipress, Joel M. "The Triumph of Reaction: Political Struggle in a New South Community, 1865–1898." PhD diss., University of North Carolina, Chapel Hill, 1993.

Smith, Caroline Patricia. "Jacksonian Conservative: The Later Years of William Smith, 1826–1840." PhD diss., Auburn University, 1977.

Whiteside, Ruth Ann. "Joseph Bradley and the Reconstruction Amendments." PhD diss., Rice University, 1981.

· ACKNOWLEDGMENTS ·

I had never heard of the bloody events of April 13, 1873, in Colfax, Louisiana, until 2003, when I read a remarkable travelogue in the *Atlantic* by the journalist Richard Rubin. Rubin had visited Colfax while doing some research and stumbled upon the historical marker commemorating the "riot." His article, based on readings in the local library and conversations with residents, intriguingly sketched the story but left me intensely curious: I wondered how I could be ignorant of such a horrible clash in my own country more than a century ago. I soon learned that the Colfax Massacre was not only a dramatic spasm of local violence but a pivotal event in the political and constitutional history of post–Civil War America.

I could not have written this book without a lot of help. I would first like to thank my college classmate, Jonathan G. Cedarbaum, for insisting that I should do "that book about *Cruikshank*"—even at a time when I wasn't 100 percent serious about it myself. The next crucial booster was my literary agent, Scott Waxman, whose confidence got the project off the ground and whose enthusiasm helped sustain it through the inevitable tribulations. I consider Scott a full partner in the effort, along with my editor at Henry Holt, George Hodgman, whose skill and wisdom are, I hope, reflected on every page. George worked very hard to make me a better writer (no small task), and I'll always be grateful to him. Editors David Patterson and Kenn Russell, also of Henry Holt, shepherded the book through the final production process with skill and care. Patrick Clark lent much-needed assistance with the footnotes and many other things. Vicki Haire copy-edited brilliantly.

Thanks are due to my then boss at the *Washington Post*, Assistant Managing Editor Liz Spayd, for granting me a six-month book-writing leave in November 2006. (Thanks also to her predecessor, Jackson Diehl, who hired me to cover the Supreme Court, one of the best breaks I ever got.) Others at the *Post*, including Executive Editor Leonard Downie, Editorial Page Editor Fred Hiatt, Michael J. Abramowitz, Lynda Robinson, David Von Drehle, Marc Fisher, Laura Blumenfeld, Kevin Merida, Michael Fletcher, Keith Alexander, and Benjamin Wittes, offered counsel and encouragement. A former *Post* colleague, Glenn Frankel, now at Stanford University, pitched in with some well-taken writing advice early on.

I did most of my work in a quiet, comfortable scholar's study at the Edward Bennett Williams Law Library of the Georgetown University Law Center. For this marvelous little sanctuary I am indebted to Dean Alex Aleinikoff and Professor Randy Barnett, who spontaneously offered it to me for no reason other than their generous desire to support my project. Matt Ciszek graciously made sure that I had all the books and equipment I needed while working at the library. Erin Rahne Kidwell helped me find what I was looking for in the library's rare book collection.

I am deeply grateful to Professor James K. Hogue of the University of North

Carolina–Charlotte, an innovative scholar who has been, for me, a font of knowledge and analysis on nineteenth-century politics and political violence in Louisiana. His detailed comments on several drafts of the book were worth gold. I also wish to thank Professor Jonathan Lurie of Rutgers University for reviewing several draft chapters. Other helpful advice came from John Donvan, Jason Zengerle, Ross Davies, Baruch Weiss, Graham Hodges, J. Morgan Kousser, Gary Gerstle, John Barrett, Michael Ross, Robert J. Kaczorowski, Ted Tunnell, and R. Thomas Howell.

When I had specific legal questions, I turned to Walter Dellinger, Miguel A. Estrada, Paul A. Engelmayer, Akhil Amar, and Erwin Chemerinsky. Stephen Halbrook provided me with invaluable copies of the New Orleans press coverage of the Grant Parish cases. Professor Michael J. Glennon of the Fletcher School of Law and Diplomacy at Tufts University, my uncommonly wise mentor on constitutional law, took the time to read a draft of the book and gave freely of his expertise.

Willie Calhoun's descendant, Tybring Hemphill of Victoria, B.C., was a marvelous source of information about his family's illustrious history, and I am deeply indebted to him. Dr. David G. Borenstein of Arthritis and Rheumatism Associates of Washington, D.C., Philip M. Teigen of The National Library of Medicine in Bethesda, Maryland, and George Wunderlich, executive director of the National Museum of Civil War Medicine in Frederick, Maryland, provided answers to my questions about the diagnosis and treatment of disease and injuries in the nineteenth century. Professor Eliot A. Cohen of the Johns Hopkins School of Advanced International Studies chipped in with some key Civil War facts. Clark "Doc" Hawley of New Orleans was generous with his knowledge of Louisiana's glorious steamboat history, as were Professors Carl A. Brasseaux of the University of Louisiana–Lafayette and Paul Paskoff of Louisiana State University. On the history of Cazenovia, New York, I called on Russell Grills and Judge Hugh Humphreys. Kater Hake of Cotton Incorporated helped with agricultural history.

Not even Hurricane Katrina was powerful enough to diminish the energy and good humor of my New Orleans–based researcher, Melissa Smith, who was resourceful and efficient as she hunted down obscure documents in the Crescent City's storm-ravaged archives and libraries. Judy Riffel did the same with equal aplomb in Baton Rouge. Professors Michael Gerhardt of the University of North Carolina–Chapel Hill Law School and Douglas A. Berman of the Moritz College of Law at Ohio State University rummaged through the libraries of their respective universities and found much-needed texts I could not have gotten otherwise.

In researching this book, I spent many hours in archives and libraries, coming away not only with information but also with a new appreciation for the work that these institutions do. Without exception, I found staffers at the National Archives in Washington, D.C., and College Park, Maryland, the Library of Congress, the Louisiana State Archives, and Louisiana State University's library system to be informed, helpful, and polite—even if in many cases I never learned their names. Special mention is due Fred Romanski and Trevor Plante of the National Archives, Barbara Gusky and Bill Stafford of the Louisiana State Archives, Phyllis Kinnison of LSU, and Mariam Touba of the New York Historical Society.

A deep bow also to those librarians and archivists whom I never met in person, but who took the time to communicate with me by phone and e-mail, and then to send me the documents I requested: Mary Linn Wernet of Northwestern State University, Natchitoches, Louisiana; Barbara Rust of the National Archives in Fort Worth, Texas; Maureen O'Rourke of the New Jersey Historical Society in Newark; Lou-Anne Williams of Louisiana Tech University in Ruston, Louisiana; Kathryn Page and Kacy Godso of the Louisiana State Museum in Baton Rouge; Irene Wainwright of the New Orleans Public Library; Pamela D. Arceneaux of the Historic New Orleans Collection; Sally Reeve of the Louisiana Historical Society; and Bob Greene of Cazenovia College.

Officials of the Supreme Court of the United States were very helpful to me in preparing this book, as they always were in my reporting for the *Post*. I would like to thank William K. Suter, the clerk of the Court; Kathleen L. Arberg, the Court's public information officer; research librarian Linda C. Corbelli; as well as Jennifer Carpenter, Patricia McCabe, Edward Turner Jr., and Ella Hunter. Thanks also to Dick Carelli of the Administrative Office of the U.S. Courts, Bruce Ragsdale of the Federal Judicial History Office at the Federal Judicial Center, and Mary Baumann of the U.S. Senate Historical Office.

During my visit to Grant Parish in November 2006, I enjoyed the hospitality (and homemade pecan candies) of Tom and Judy Vogel at their Fairmount Plantation B & B. Mayor Gerald Hamilton welcomed me at his office in Colfax. Doris Lively of the Grant Parish Public Library guided me through the Colfax Riot collection at the main branch in Colfax. With abundant good humor, the Colfax based researcher Avery Hamilton, a direct descendant of Jesse McKinney, opened doors for me around town—and opened my eyes to the history of Central Louisiana's African-American community. Glynn Maxwell showed me the historical sites of Colfax and was an eager correspondent. Thanks also to Gladys Morris and Ben Littlepage for receiving me at their homes and sharing their memories. Willie Calhoun's descendant, Mary Eleanor Bonnette, provided photos and documents and helped me learn more about her family's remarkable history. Wilbur T. McCain Jr. informed me about events during the 1960s in Colfax.

Let's say you're traveling in Louisiana and you find out in the middle of the night that some water leaked into your basement back home, soaking the research materials you unwisely stashed downstairs. Who ya gonna call? I called Catarina Bannier, my wife of thirteen years, who proceeded to dry out the documents one by one. Thanks, Honey, for that and much more. Everyone else in my family— Bruce and Ann Lane, Gloria Bannier and Hans-Joachim Genzmehr, Richard and Jill Lane, Sue Ellen and Steve Silber—has been supportive, as always. But no one has suffered longer than my children, David, Nina, and Johanna, who have been asking for some time now when I would be finished writing, so that they could regain access to me and—perhaps more important—my computer. OK, kids, I'm done.

Charles Lane
Washington, D.C.
November 2007

INDEX

Entries in *italics* refer to maps.

· ABOUT THE AUTHOR ·

CHARLES LANE first learned of the Colfax Massacre case while covering the Supreme Court for the *Washington Post*. His journalism career has taken him from Washington to Tokyo, Berlin to Bosnia, Havana to Johannesburg. A former editor of the *New Republic*, Lane has written for *Foreign Affairs*, the *New York Review of Books*, and the *Atlantic*. He graduated Phi Beta Kappa from Harvard and studied law at Yale. He lives in the Washington, D.C., area.